Escaping the Labyrinth

Cretan Neolithic in Context

Sheffield Studies in Aegean Archaeology, 8

SHEFFIELD STUDIES IN AEGEAN ARCHAEOLOGY

ADVISORY EDITORIAL PANEL

SHEFFIELD STUDIES IN
AEGEAN ARCHAEOLOGY

Escaping the Labyrinth
——————— The ———————
Cretan Neolithic in Context

Edited by

Valasia Isaakidou and Peter D. Tomkins

Oxbow Books

Published by
Oxbow Books, Oxford, UK

ISBN 978 1 84217 291 9

A CIP record for this book is available from the British Library

This book is available direct from
Oxbow Books, Oxford, UK
(Phone: 01865-241249; Fax: 01865-794449)

and

The David Brown Book Company
PO Box 511, Oakville, CT 06779, USA
(Phone: 860-945-9329; Fax: 860-945-9468)

or from our website

www.oxbowbooks.com

Cover design: Above, view to N from Mt. Juktas over Herakleion valley
and bay (photo: V. Isaakidou). Below, Neolithic Knossos 1959, House C
under excavation (photo: J. D. Evans) and finds from J. D. Evans' excavations
(photos: V. Tzevelekidi and V. Isaakidou)

Printed in Great Britain by
Short Run Press, Exeter

To John D. Evans and Andrew Sherratt

Contents

Abbreviations

AAA	*Athens Annals of Archaeology*
ADelt	*Arkhaiologiko Deltio*
AE	*Arkhaiologiki Efimeris*
AEMTh	*To Arkhaiologiko Ergo sti Makedonia kai Thraki*
AJA	*American Journal of Archaeology*
AM	*Mitteilungen des Deutschen Archäologischen Instituts, Athenische Abteilung*
AR	*Archaeological Reports*
ASA	*Annuario della Scuola Archeologica di Atene*
BAM	Beiträge zur Ur- und Frühgeschichtlichen Archäologie des Mittelmeer-Kulturraumes
BAR	*British Archaeological Reports*
BCH	*Bulletin de Correspondance Hellénique*
BICS	*Bulletin of the Institute of Classical Studies of the University of London*
BSA	*Annual of the British School at Athens*
CAJ	*Cambridge Archaeological Journal*
CMS	Corpus der minoischen und mykenischen Siegeln
CP	*Classical Philology*
Ergon	*To Ergon tis Arkhaiologikis Etairias*
G&R	*Greece and Rome*
JAS	*Journal of Archaeological Science*
JHS	*Journal of Hellenic Studies*
JMA	*Journal of Mediterranean Archaeology*
Kr Chron	*Kritika Chronika*
OJA	*Oxford Journal of Archaeology*
PAE	*Praktika tis en Athinais Arkhaiologikis Etairias*
PBA	*Proceedings of the British Academy*
PPS	*Proceedings of the Prehistoric Society*
PCPS	*Proceedings of the Cambridge Philological Society*
SIMA	Studies in Mediterranean Archaeology
SMEA	*Studi Micenei ed Egeo-Anatolici*

Contributors

CESARE D'ANNIBALE
Parks Canada, 111 Water St East, Cornwall, Ontario K6H 6S3.

CYPRIAN BROODBANK
Institute of Archaeology, University College London, 31–34 Gordon Square, London WC1H 0PY, UK.

JAMES CONOLLY
Trent University Archaeological Research Centre, Peterborough, Ontario, K9J 7B8, Canada.

SERENA DI TONTO
Via Elio Vittorini, 10 80129 Napoli, Italy.

JOHN D. EVANS
Melbury Cottage, 5 Love Lane, Shaftesbury, Dorset SP7 8BG, UK.

NENA GALANIDOU
Department of History and Archaeology, University of Crete, 74 100 Rethymnon, Greece.

PAUL HALSTEAD
Department of Archaeology, University of Sheffield, Northgate House, West St., Sheffield S1 4ET, UK.

VALASIA ISAAKIDOU
Department of Archaeology, University of Sheffield, Northgate House, West St., Sheffield S1 4ET, UK.

KOSTAS KOTSAKIS
Department of Archaeology, Aristotle University of Thessaloniki, 54124 Thessaloniki, Greece.

KATYA MANTELI
3rd EPKA, Makedonias 25, Filothei, Athens 152 37, Greece.

MARIA MINA
Kapodistriou 82, Rhodes 85100, Greece.

KRZYSZTOF NOWICKI
Institute of Archaeology and Ethnology, Polish Academy of Sciences, Al. Solidarnosci 105, 00-140 Warszawa, Poland.

YIANNIS PAPADATOS
Hellenic Open University, Giannakou 23, 72200 Ierapetra, Greece.

SUSAN SHERRATT
Department of Archaeology, University of Sheffield, Northgate House, West St., Sheffield S1 4ET, UK.

THOMAS F. STRASSER
Art and Art History Department, Providence College, 549 River Avenue, Providence RI 02918-0001, USA.

SIMONA TODARO
Mediterranean Centre for Arts and Science, Via Roma 124, 96100 Siracusa, Italy.

PETER D. TOMKINS
Département d'Archéologie et d'Histoire de l'Art, Université Catholique de Louvain, Place B. Pascal 1, B-1348 Louvain-la-Neuve, Belgium.

SEVI TRIANTAPHYLLOU
Department of Archaeology, University of Sheffield, Northgate House, West St., Sheffield S1 4ET, UK.

1

Introduction: Escaping the Labyrinth

Valasia Isaakidou and Peter D. Tomkins

A Brief History of Cretan Neolithic Studies

In 1900, Arthur Evans and Duncan Mackenzie first encountered Neolithic levels in deep soundings at Knossos. Study of pottery from these soundings resulted in publication of a tripartite phasing of the Knossos Neolithic sequence (Mackenzie 1903) and reports soon followed on excavations at Phaistos (Mosso 1908) and at the small upland site of Magasa (Dawkins 1905). The Cretan Neolithic was thus discovered only a few months after its Thessalian counterpart and initially aroused considerable scholarly interest (Evans 1901; 1928), but was thereafter overshadowed by research in northern Greece.

One reason for this neglect of the Neolithic of Crete was undoubtedly the extraordinary wealth of the Minoan Bronze Age that still dominates archaeological research on the island today. Prehistorians working in Thessaly have largely been free of such distractions and Tsountas was able to expose the Neolithic settlements of Sesklo and Dimini (Tsountas 1908) on a scale that was (and remains) impossible beneath the Cretan palaces. On the other hand, Neolithic pottery with distinctive styles of painted and incised decoration made Thessaly an attractive target for culture historians seeking to build intra- and inter-regional relative chronologies (*e.g.*, Tsountas 1908; Wace and Thompson 1912; Grundmann 1934; Milojcic 1960). The abundance of highly visible tells in Thessaly also encouraged a long tradition of research on a regional scale (*e.g.*, Tsountas 1908; Wace and Thompson 1912; Grundmann 1937; Theocharis 1973). By contrast, the Neolithic of Crete received little further attention – in the field or in print – until the 1950s, when Furness reworked the ceramic chronology of Mackenzie and Evans (Furness 1953), Levi resumed investigation of the Neolithic levels at Phaistos (Vagnetti 1973; Vagnetti and Belli 1978), and John Evans was invited to do the same at Knossos, as he describes below (Evans this volume).

John Evans' two campaigns at Knossos (1957–60, 1969–70) set new standards in stratigraphical and contextual excavation, in the application of radiocarbon dating and in the recovery of bioarchaeological as well as artefactual remains (Evans 1964; 1968; 1971; Jarman and Jarman 1968). Perhaps the most dramatic result of renewed excavation was the exposure of an initial aceramic layer at the base of the Knossos mound. The radiocarbon dates had two principal consequences. First, they demonstrated that the established tripartite periodisation of the Cretan Neolithic was considerably out of step with that for mainland Greece (Tomkins this volume, table 3.1). This reinforced the impression, created by the relative paucity of distinctively decorated ceramics and of systematic research, that the Neolithic culture of the island had developed in isolation from the rest of the Aegean. Secondly, as elsewhere, radiocarbon dating and subsequent calibration stretched the chronology of the Cretan Neolithic so that it began as early as the beginning of the seventh millennium BC. Bioarchaeological research, in collaboration with the British Academy-funded 'Early History of Agriculture' project, involved pioneering attempts at systematic retrieval (using dry-sieving and flotation) of faunal and botanical remains and showed that domestic animals and crops were present from the earliest aceramic phase of occupation. The early date of this Initial Neolithic phase, coupled with the bioarchaeological results and the insular location of Knossos, earned the site a prominent place in discussions of the origins of agriculture and neolithisation of Europe (*e.g.*, Higgs and Jarman 1969). Also influential on subsequent research was John Evans' model (based on a series of sondages cut for this purpose in his second excavation campaign) of the steady expansion of the Knossos settlement through the Neolithic (Evans 1971; 1994).

From the 1970s onwards, Neolithic studies in mainland Greece, and especially Thessaly, increasingly shifted away from chronological and culture historical problems to explore settlement patterns, demography, subsistence practices, social change and the dynamics of production and consumption of material culture (*e.g.*, Theocharis 1973; Hourmouziadis 1979; Halstead 1981; 1989; Kotsakis 1983; 1992; Washburn 1983; Cullen 1984; Vitelli 1989; Perlès 1992). In a similar vein, Broodbank and Strasser (1991) interpreted the initial Neolithic colonisation of Crete in terms of a planned transfer of people and domesticates, Lax and Strasser (1992) proposed that early colonists played a role in the extinction of the island's endemic fauna, and Broodbank (1992) related the growth of Neolithic Knossos to changes in material culture and to a suggested increase in the proportion of cattle. These studies were based on preliminary reports from John Evans' excavations and the empirical basis of Broodbank's paper was rapidly questioned (Whitelaw 1992).

From the late 1990s, a series of independent projects tackled re-analysis and publication of Neolithic material from Crete, principally from Knossos with encouragement from John Evans, but also from Phaistos and other sites. Some new excavation also took place at Knossos (Efstratiou *et al.* 2004), but the focus of fieldwork in recent years has shifted away from Knossos to recognition in surface surveys (and in some cases excavations) of numerous short-lived sites from the last stages of the Neolithic in other parts of the island (*e.g.*, Vasilakis 1987; 1989/ 90; Vagnetti *et al.* 1989; Manteli 1992; 1993; Vagnetti 1996; Branigan 1999; Nowicki 2002). This new fieldwork finally offered the opportunity to place the long occupation sequence at Knossos in a regional context, although excavation of short-lived FN sites had by and large failed to provide the stratigraphic evidence needed to resolve significant outstanding problems of relative and absolute dating.

The Round Table

With post-excavation study at Knossos well advanced and with increasing fieldwork and study projects in other parts of the island, it seemed that research into the Neolithic of Crete had finally achieved the critical mass that might enable significant advances in the field to be made. To this end it was decided to devote one of the informal annual Round Tables of the Sheffield Centre for Aegean Archaeology to the theme of 'Rethinking the Cretan Neolithic'. The aims of the meeting were to present some of the diversity of current research into the Cretan Neolithic, to explore ways of reconnecting it with Neolithic scholarship in the rest of the Aegean and to re-examine how the Cretan Neolithic is conceptualised. The Round Table, held on 27–29 January 2006, brought together the group of scholars engaged in post-excavation work on Neolithic Knossos (Evans, Conolly, Isaakidou, Mina, Strasser, Tomkins, Triantaphyllou and White-law) and colleagues engaged in similar study and fieldwork elsewhere in the island (D'Annibale, Di Tonto and Todaro, Galanidou and Manteli, Nowicki, Papadatos). To counter the isolation of Cretan Neolithic studies, we also invited papers from colleagues active in Neolithic research elsewhere in the Aegean or Mediterranean (Broodbank, Halstead, Kotsakis, A. and S. Sherratt). In addition, Adonis Vasilakis presented a poster on his own important excavations (published elsewhere) and, together with Keith Branigan and Peter Warren, helped to guide discussion. The result was a series of diverse and highly stimulating papers and a lively and enriching exchange of views that bodes well for the future health of Neolithic research in Crete. Of those who presented papers to the Round Table, only Todd Whitelaw was unfortunately unable to contribute to this resulting volume.

The volume begins with a series of papers whose point of departure is Neolithic material from Knossos. That so much that is new can be done with this material is testimony to the excellence of the excavations directed by John Evans. In the first of the Knossos papers, he recounts the journey that brought him to Crete and recalls the environment within which the excavations took place. Peter Tomkins then explores the temporal and spatial frameworks within which the Cretan Neolithic has been conceptualised and argues that recent improvements in chronological resolution transform our understanding of developments both at Knossos and in the wider Cretan Neolithic landscape. At Knossos, refinement in the phasing of deposits underpins a radically different picture of the changing extent of the settlement, in which long periods of minimal growth (IN–MN and FN) are punctuated by short periods of rapid expansion coupled with significant social and material transformation (LN and EM I–II). The modest size and slow expansion of the early settlement underlines the demographic dependence of Knossos on connections with other communities within or beyond Crete and challenges previous notions of isolation and uniqueness. At a regional level, sharper definition of ceramic phases within the Final Neolithic makes clear that most of the expansion in the number of known settlements across Crete took place very rapidly towards the end of this period. Finally, a revised chronological nomenclature is proposed that realigns the Cretan Neolithic with other regions of Greece, bringing to an end the intellectual isolation of Cretan Neolithic studies and highlighting the existence of interaction (and potentially of analogous patterns of regional development) between Crete and other parts of the Aegean. Most contributors to this volume have adopted this revised chronology (Tomkins 2007) and, where they do not, the correspondence between traditional and new terms (Tomkins this volume, table 3.1) is indicated.

Issues of scale are also taken up by Kostas Kotsakis, with reference to the neolithisation of Crete and the Aegean. While arguing that the Aegean Sea is as much a connecting as isolating medium for its island populations, he stresses the empirical and theoretical problems that attend current attempts to recognise human migration in the archaeological record. He concludes that appeals to diffusionist/migrationist and indigenist models alike obscure rather than illuminate complex and fluid processes of neolithisation that are ultimately shaped by human agency and practice. Material evidence for connections with or parallels to other parts of Crete and the Aegean are a recurring theme in the 'Knossian' papers. James Conolly, examining knapped stone (mainly obsidian) technology in the earliest Neolithic levels at Knossos, draws attention to intensive use of raw material suggestive of 'resource stress' and so perhaps of limited contact with off-island sources of obsidian. On the other hand, technological similarities (as well as contrasts) with the Initial Neolithic assemblage from mainland Franchthi Cave and continued use of obsidian at Knossos during the EN argue against isolation. Maria Mina and Sevi Triantaphyllou discuss the role of anthropomorphic figurines and human remains respectively in the construction of social identity during the Neolithic on Crete. Figurines from Knossos and elsewhere on Crete are differentiated – as elsewhere in the Aegean – by a range of (mostly female) anatomical features, posture and decoration, although they lack decoration suggestive of distinctions in clothing or jewellery such as is seen in LN northern Greece. Scattered bones of adult humans, suggestive of secondary burial rites, can now be added to the inhumations of children previously reported from Neolithic Knossos by John Evans. The evidence from Knossos thus matches a broadly consistent picture of Neolithic burial practice emerging on the mainland of Greece. The anthropomorphic figurines and human skeletal remains point to important parallels between Crete and the rest of the Aegean both in the central role of gender and age in constructing Neolithic social identity and in the broadly shared symbolic expression of these distinctions. Tom

Strasser addresses another aspect of prevailing ideas of isolation in his demonstration that stone axes, like ceramic fabrics (Tomkins and Day 2001), provide tangible evidence, in this case LN–FN in date, of interaction between Knossos and other parts of Crete where there is little or no known trace of settlement. Valasia Isaakidou's re-study of the faunal material from Knossos broadly confirms the increase through time in cattle, previously discussed by Broodbank and questioned by Whitelaw, but also cites a wealth of bone pathological evidence that cows were used for draught. On present evidence, such use is not well documented elsewhere in Europe from such an early date (EN, late seventh millennium BC), raising the possibility that the plough was adopted at Knossos as a response to highly seasonal rainfall and a consequently narrow window for sowing crops. Discussion of the social implications of draught cattle provides a perspective on settlement growth and household competition that complements those of Broodbank (1992) and Tomkins (2004) based on the analysis of material culture.

A second group of papers examines the Neolithic archaeological record of Crete outside Knossos. Nena Galanidou and Katya Manteli report on the relocation and study of material from Alexiou's excavation of a LN I house at Katsambas, a site of considerable importance both for its relatively early date and for its close proximity to Knossos. Serena Di Tonto and Simona Todaro explore the ceramic and contextual evidence of FN III–IV date for what may be ceremonial consumption beneath the Bronze Age palace at Phaistos. This study is particularly significant, given that excavated levels of this date at Knossos appear to have been deposited under different conditions and are insufficiently preserved to allow a similar analysis. Yiannis Papadatos presents an admirably prompt account of recent excavations at FN–EM I Petras Kephala in eastern Crete. In addition to early (probably FN IV) evidence for metallurgy, the site affords important insights into the transformation of material culture between FN IV and EM I. Although the EM I ceramics exhibit a significant increase in stylistic diversity over FN IV, study of fabrics indicates continuity. On the thorny issue of the origin (see below) of the inhabitants of Petras Kephala, Papadatos retains an open mind, noting the presence of 'cheese-pots', which point to contact in FN IV with other regions of the Aegean, but also of earlier FN material, which indicates that the site was not a new foundation. The obsidian from Petras Kephala, in marked contrast with that from IN Knossos studied by Conolly, includes a high proportion of blades, but is again used intensively and analysis of debitage suggests that raw material may have arrived only sporadically. Cesare D' Annibale focuses primarily, however, on changing chipped stone technology at Petras Kephala, arguing that the increasingly standardised production of prismatic blades between the FN IV and EM I phases is attributable partly to greater specialisation but also partly to the adoption of a metal punch, made possible by developments in metallurgy. Two papers consider the evidence for FN settlement expansion from rather different perspectives. Krzysztof Nowicki looks in detail at late FN site locations (often coastal and/or defensive) and the off-island affinities of associated material culture to argue that the observed expansion of settlement was partly due to immigration from outside Crete, resulting in conflict with the indigenous population. Paul Halstead evaluates this expansion in terms of 'marginal colonisation', a phenomenon reported from many parts of the Aegean, dating towards the end of the Neolithic and often linked to suggested subsistence innovations such as adoption of the plough, exploitation of milk and/or wool, and seasonally mobile management of large herds. Drawing partly on Isaakidou's faunal work at Knossos and partly on studies of recent herders, he concludes that dispersed habitation and a shift in emphasis from intra- to inter-settlement exchange are more likely enabling factors than are subsistence innovations.

The two papers that conclude the volume shift focus outwards to look at the Neolithic of Crete from a broader geographical and temporal perspective. Reflecting on the current evidence for human colonisation of Mediterranean islands (and its implications for the development of sea-faring), Cyprian Broodbank assesses the likelihood that a pre-Neolithic human presence on Crete may yet (with appropriate research strategies) be discovered, and argues that the early farming settlement at Knossos should no longer occasion surprise. In contrast to Kotsakis, he regards the origin of the earliest settlers as a viable and worthwhile research question and provocatively plays down the growing evidence that Neolithic Crete was not isolated from the rest of the Aegean: 'it may have been no Easter Island, but it was equally no Lipari'. He ends with the suggestion that the contrasting approaches of Halstead and Nowicki to FN settlement expansion should take account of growing evidence for a shift to more arid and seasonal climate in this period. Andrew and Susan Sherratt explore the insights that can be gained by examining the Aegean from further east. Undeterred by the warnings of Kotsakis, they see the Neolithic of Crete and of Thessaly as arriving from different oriental sources and by different mechanisms (littoral conversion and deliberate plantation, respectively), possibly stimulated by an episode of extreme climate ca. 6200 BC. At the later end of our period, the dispersed settlement pattern and hints of metallurgy that characterise the FN of Crete should be situated in similar and inter-related changes in settlement and the use of material culture to construct social identity across Europe. To a significant extent, these changes had their origins in the economies of scale and capital accumulation of urban societies in the Near East. Such world systems thinking is much easier on the back of a common chronological currency and, to this end, the Sherratts argue (seconded by Broodbank) that Tomkins' revised chronology represents a lost opportunity to bring Aegean terminology for the late fifth and fourth millennia BC in line with those of Anatolia and the Balkans. Perhaps unsurprisingly, debate on this issue was lively and inconclusive, with many Aegeanist participants reluctant to trade in their familiar Final Neolithic for an exotic Chalcolithic.

Retrospect and Prospect

Looking back on the Round Table, there is much to be pleased about. Cretan Neolithic research has plainly achieved the critical mass that it has long lacked and the papers in this volume do indeed demonstrate the breadth and depth of valuable work that we had hoped to bring together. And, although Cyprian Broodbank, Andrew and Susan Sherratt, and (in a rather different way) Kostas Kotsakis have urged us to broaden further our frames of reference, the Cretan Neolithic is no longer intellectually or empirically isolated. On the contrary, the contributors to this volume tackle similar issues to those pursued in neighbouring regions and are already beginning to identify some respects in which culture change on Crete was broadly in step with other parts of the Aegean and other respects in which it followed a distinctive pathway or rhythm. Looking to the future, there is a pressing need to complete publication of post-excavation work at Knossos, but also to initiate further targeted fieldwork both at Knossos and elsewhere. Understanding of the Neolithic of Crete, and also of Knossos, will be greatly enhanced when the wealth of artefacts and ecofacts from the mound on the Kephala hill can be compared with assemblages of a reasonable size from sites in other parts of the island.

As usual, the Round Table was a symposium in all senses and we are grateful to Nong Branigan, Debi Harlan, Sevi Triantaphyllou, Maria Mina, Angeliki Karagianni and Christina Tsoraki (with unskilled assistance, as ever, from Keith Branigan and Nancy Krahtopoulou) for food and hospitality, and to INSTAP for the funding which made it possible to bring participants from North America and from five European countries other than Britain. Last, but not least, we thank Paul Halstead and John Bennet whose support and advice made it all possible. The Round Table was a lively and invigorating forum and moved Andrew and Susan Sherratt to spend the evening of the closing day writing the response that is the last paper in this volume. Sadly, this was one of the last texts produced by Andrew. We dedicate this volume to John Evans, who has been a constant source of generous encouragement to the new generation of Neolithic researchers at Knossos, and to the memory of Andrew Sherratt, whose ideas and enthusiasm inspired us all.

Bibliography

Branigan, K.
    1999   Late Neolithic colonization of the uplands of eastern Crete. In P. Halstead (ed.), *Neolithic Society in Greece* (SSAA 2): 57–65. Sheffield: Sheffield Academic Press.
Broodbank, C.
    1992   The Neolithic labyrinth: social change at Knossos before the Bronze Age. *JMA* 5: 39–75.
Broodbank, C. and T. F. Strasser
    1991   Migrant farmers and the Neolithic colonization of Crete. *Antiquity* 65: 233–45.

Cullen, T
    1984   Social implications of ceramic style in the Neolithic Peloponnese. In W. D. Kingery (ed.), *Ancient Technology to Modern Science, volume 1*: 77–100. Columbus: American Ceramic Society.
Dawkins, R. M.
    1905   Excavations at Palaikastro IV. 2. Neolithic settlement at Magasa. *BSA* 11: 260–68.
Efstratiou, N., A. Karetsou, E. S. Banou and D. Margomenou
    2004   The Neolithic settlement of Knossos: new light on an old picture. In G. Cadogan, E. Hatzaki and A. Vasilakis (eds.), *Knossos: Palace, City, State*: 39–49. London: British School at Athens.
Evans, A. J.
    1901   The Neolithic settlement at Knossos and its place in the history of early Aegean culture. *Man* 1: 184–86.
    1928   Chapter 33: discovery of Late Neolithic houses beneath Central Court: traditional affinities with mainland east. In A. J. Evans, *The Palace of Minos* (Volume II:I): 1–21. London: Macmillan.
Evans, J. D.
    1964   Excavations in the Neolithic settlement at Knossos, 1957–60. *BSA* 59: 132–240.
    1968   Knossos Neolithic, Part II, summary and conclusions. *BSA* 63: 267–76.
    1971   Neolithic Knossos: the growth of a settlement. *PPS* 37: 95–117.
    1994   The early millennia: continuity and change in a farming settlement. In D. Evely, H. Hughes-Brock and N. Momigliano (eds.), *Knossos, a Labyrinth of History, Papers Presented in Honour of Sinclair Hood*: 1–20. London: British School at Athens.
Furness, A.
    1953   The Neolithic pottery of Knossos. *BSA* 48: 94–134.
Grundmann, K.
    1934   Donaulandischer Import im steinzeitlichen Thessalien. *AM* 59: 123–36.
    1937   Magula Hadzimissiotiki. *AM* 62: 56–69.
Halstead, P.
    1981   Counting sheep in Neolithic and Bronze Age Greece. In I. Hodder, G. Isaac and N. Hammond (eds.), *Pattern of the Past*: 307–39. Cambridge: Cambridge University Press.
    1989   The economy has a normal surplus: economic stability and social change among early farming communities of Thessaly Greece. In P. Halstead and J. O'Shea (eds.), *Bad Year Economics*: 68–80. Cambridge: Cambridge University Press.
Higgs, E. S. and M. R. Jarman
    1969   The origins of agriculture: a reconsideration. *Antiquity* 43: 31–41.
Hourmouziadis, G.
    1979   *To Neolithiko Dimini*. Volos: Etairia Thessalikon Erevnon.
Jarman, M. R. and H. N. Jarman
    1968   The fauna and economy of Neolithic Knossos. *BSA* 63: 241–64.
Kotsakis, K.
    1983   *Keramiki Tekhnologia kai Keramiki Diaforopoiisi: Provlimata tis Graptis Keramikis tis Mesis Neolithikis Epokhis tou Sesklou*. PhD dissertation, University of Thessaloniki.
    1992   O neolithikos tropos paragogis: ithagenis i apoikos. In *Praktika Diethnous Sinedriou gia tin Arkhaia Thessalia*: 120–135. Athens: Ministry of Culture.
Lax, E. and T. F. Strasser
    1992   Early Holocene extinctions on Crete: the search for the cause. *JMA* 5: 203–24.
Mackenzie, D.
    1903   The pottery of Knossos. *JHS* 23: 157–205.

Manteli, K.
  1992   The Neolithic well at Kastelli Phournis in Eastern Crete. *BSA* 87: 103–20.
  1993   *The Transition from the Neolithic to the Early Bronze Age in Crete, with Special Reference to Pottery*. PhD dissertation, University of London.
Milojcic, V.
  1960   *Hauptergebnisse der Deutschen Ausgrabungen in Thessalien 1953–58*. Bonn: Rudolf Habelt.
Mosso, A.
  1908   Ceramica neolitica di Phaestos e vasi dell'Epoca Minoica Primitiva. *Monumenti Antichi* 19: 142–228.
Nowicki, K.
  2002   The end of the Neolithic in Crete. *Aegean Archaeology* 6: 7–72.
Perlès, C.
  1992   Systems of exchange and organisation of production in neolithic Greece. *JMA* 5: 115–64.
Theocharis, D. R.
  1973   *Neolithic Greece*. Athens: National Bank of Greece.
Tomkins, P.
  2004   Filling in the 'Neolithic background': social life and social transformation in the Aegean before the Bronze Age. In J. C. Barrett and P. Halstead (eds.), *The Emergence of Civilisation Revisited* (SSAA 6): 38–63. Oxford: Oxbow Books.
  2007   Neolithic: Strata IX–VIII, VII–VIB, VIA–V, IV, IIIB, IIIA, IIB, IIA and IC Groups. In N. Momigliano (ed.), *Knossos Pottery Handbook: Neolithic and Bronze Age (Minoan)*: 9–48. London: British School at Athens.
Tomkins, P. and P. M. Day
  2001   Production and exchange of the earliest ceramic vessels in the Aegean: a view from Early Neolithic Knossos, Crete. *Antiquity* 75: 259–60.
Tsountas, Ch.
  1908   *Ai Proïstorikai Akropoleis Dhiminiou ke Sesklou*. Athens: I en Athenais Archaiologiki Etaireia.
Vagnetti, L.
  1973   L'insediamento neolitico di Festòs. *ASA* 50–51: 7–138.
  1996   The Final Neolithic: Crete enters the wider world. *Cretan Studies* 5: 29–39.
Vagnetti, L. and P. Belli
  1978   Characters and problems of the final Neolithic in Crete. *SMEA* 19: 125–63.
Vagnetti, L., A. Christopoulou and I. Tzedakis
  1989   Saggi ne gli stati Neolitici. In I. Tzedakis and A. Sacconi (eds.), *Scavi a Nerokourou, Kydonias* (Recherche Greco-Italiane in Creta Occidentale I): 9–97. Roma: Edizioni Dell'Ateneo.
Vasilakis, A.
  1987   Anaskaphi neolithikou spitiou stous Kalous Limenes tis notias Kritis. *Eilapini: Studies in Honour of Professor N. Platon*: 45–53. Herakleion: Dimos Irakleiou.
  1989/90   Proistorikes theseis sti Moni Odhigitrias, Kaloi Limenes. *Kritiki Estia* 3: 11–80.
Vitelli, K. D.
  1989   Were pots first made for food? Doubts from Franchthi. *World Archaeology* 21: 17–29.
Wace, A. J. B. and M. S. Thompson
  1912   *Prehistoric Thessaly*. Cambridge: Cambridge University Press.
Washburn, D. K.
  1983   Symmetry analysis of ceramic design: two tests of the method on neolithic material from Greece and the Aegean. In D. K. Washburn (ed.), *Structure and Cognition in Art*: 138–64. Cambridge: Cambridge University Press.

Watrous, V.

1994   Review of Aegean Prehistory III: Crete from earliest Prehistory through the Proto-
palatial period. *AJA* 98: 695–753.

Whitelaw, T. M.

1992   Lost in the Labyrinth? Comments on Broodbank's 'Social change at Knossos before
the Bronze Age'. *JMA* 5: 225–38.

2

Approaching the Labyrinth

John D. Evans

Introduction

To be invited out of the blue, as I was, to excavate a key site as obviously important as that of Neolithic Knossos, especially when you have not previously worked in the area, is an unexpected piece of good fortune. I have been asked to introduce this volume by explaining how I came by it. What immediately comes to mind is the phrase 'time and chance', the words from Ecclesiastes which were taken by Joan Evans as the title for her family history. I hasten to add, though, that, although I share that common Welsh surname, there is no connection with the family of Sir Arthur. Nevertheless, I certainly found archaeology fascinating from very early years, though it seemed highly unlikely as a career when I was a boy in Liverpool in the 1930s. In fact it was another interest, in English literature, that gave me the chance to go to University. I won a scholarship in English to Pembroke College, Cambridge in December 1942, and it being wartime, was allowed to take it up in the following January for the six months before I was due for call-up. Oddly enough, though, one of the first books I bought during this time in Cambridge was Pendlebury's *Archaeology of Crete*, which I found on a shelf at Heffers' bookshop. I had at that time no idea that he had also been an undergraduate at Pembroke in the 1920s! It was not until 1947 that I returned to finish Part 1 of the English Tripos. During that year I discovered that you could do Part 2 of the Archaeology and Anthropology Tripos without having previously done Part 1, so I applied to make the change, was accepted by the then Disney Professor Dorothy Garrod, and at the end of the year did well enough to be offered the opportunity to go on to postgraduate work.

Both Ends of the Mediterranean

My supervisor, Glyn Daniel, knowing my interest in the Mediterranean and that I had opted for Spanish rather than German at school, suggested a subject based on a conjecture by Gordon Childe, in the then latest edition of his *Dawn of European Civilization*, that the origin of some features of the Early Bronze Age El Argar culture of southeast Spain might lie in contacts with western Anatolia. I was happy to accept this highly speculative notion, not simply because the idea of such long distance contacts was rather fashionable at that time, but also because it would take me to both ends of the Mediterranean, the area in which I knew I wanted to specialise. Also, in those grey, post-war years the prospect of travel, this time thankfully not 'at his Majesty's expense', seemed very alluring.

The result was two fascinating years, during which I gained a great deal of archaeological and general experience, but ended up with the conviction that Childe's suggested links were illusory and that I had no prospect of producing a Ph.D. thesis on that basis. One experience during this time proved to be particularly valuable, however, in the light of later developments. This was my participation, during the Ankara Institute's winter closure, in the first season of Kathleen Kenyon's excavations at Jericho. It was the first time I had taken part in the excavation of a site with really deep stratification and been practically introduced to 'the Wheeler method'. The Pre-pottery Neolithic levels were already exposed at various points, due to Garstang's earlier work there, although they had not been recognised by him for what they really were. This made it possible to start work on this period right away and gave some indication of the discoveries to come in the later seasons. Another significant experience a few months later was taking part in Seton Lloyd's excavation at the massive tell known as Sultantepe, near Harran in southeast Turkey. Then during the summer, back in England, I also had the luck to be able to join Grahame Clark's team for his last season at Starr Carr, which was a complete contrast, but equally formative.

Malta

Apart from a much broadened experience, however, I returned pretty empty-handed from these travels. A thesis could not be built on a mere negative. My salvation came when, on my return to Cambridge, Glyn told me that Stuart Piggott, Childe's successor in the Edinburgh chair, was looking for someone to carry out a project in Malta. The Inter-University Council for Higher Education in the Colonies, (as it was then called) had been persuaded to make a grant to the University of Malta to carry out a detailed survey of the prehistoric monuments and museum collections on the islands. He had been appointed as one of the Commissioners to oversee this (Bryan Ward-Perkins, the Director of the British School at Rome, being the other), and was looking for someone to undertake the work in the field. This seemed at last to be a real opportunity to get to grips with a body of fascinating archaeological material, as well as providing much needed subsistence for a period, and so I found myself in Malta in October of 1952 ready to begin.

The situation was slightly anomalous in that I was employed by the University, but actually based in the National Museum, which not only held the collections, but was also in effect the antiquities service for the islands, charged with the custody of all monuments and the oversight of all fieldwork. Its then Director, J. G. Baldacchino was, not unnaturally, somewhat prickly about this and the situation might have been difficult for me but for the great kindness and understanding of the man most immediately affected, the Curator of Archaeology, Charles Zammit, the son of the great Sir Themistocles Zammit. He not only exerted himself greatly to smooth my path with the Director, but gave me every other possible help and encouragement in my task.

The job was to compile a complete record of all the monuments and material available for the study of the prehistory of the Maltese islands. It was not a research project in itself but was intended to provide a sound basis for future research. It involved preparing new plans of all the monuments, with the assistance of architecture students of the University, and compiling the first catalogue of the Museum collections. During the war the collections had been packed up and put in the basement of the building which had housed the Museum, the old Auberge d'Italie of the Knights of Malta, and had remained there afterwards because most of the building was serving as the Law Courts. For some reason the collection of stuffed birds had remained above ground and it was among these cases that my desk was placed! Some of the complete or restored archaeological objects, mostly pottery or figurines, had also been replaced in display cases, but to get at the bulk of the material it was necessary to descend to the basement and investigate the contents of the many big packing-cases. For several months I divided my time between studying and cataloguing the Museum collections and visiting the monuments to check and add detail to the outline plans drawn up by the architecture students. This was the bread-and-butter of the job, but at the same time the unsolved problem of the origin and development of the mysterious 'temple'-builders was naturally very much in my mind.

Up to then there had been no satisfactory answer to these questions, though many ideas, including quite a lot that were downright lunatic, had been put forward at various times. The one definite link with the wider world which was then known lay in the occurrence of pottery decorated with impressed patterns very similar to the Early Neolithic Stentinello pottery of Sicily at the cave site of Ghar Dalam in Malta (Bernabò Brea 1950: 13). I found that a few sherds of this type also occurred on one or two of the 'temple' sites, which gave a possible starting point. I then noted that some of the 'temples' which appeared to be more roughly built and less elaborate in plan than the major monuments, notably the two conjoined ones at Ta' Hagrat, Mgarr, excavated in the 1920s by Sir Themistocles Zammit, had yielded a great deal of pottery with less refined shapes and decoration than that which predominated at the larger and more elaborate sites. There was, of course, no stratigraphic evidence of how this pottery was related chronologically to the latter. Zammit had thought that it was later and represented a degeneration, but some similarities with Sicilian Neolithic types suggested to me that it might in fact represent earlier phases. Following this line of thought, I went on to construct a hypothetical five-phase development from the Ghar Dalam impressed ware to the elaborate styles which characterized the largest and most complex 'temples'. The occurrence of certain types of raw material in both 'temples' and tombs (*e.g.*, flint, obsidian, igneous rock) that do not occur in Malta confirmed the existence of contacts with Sicily (and places further afield) during the whole of this period. Furthermore, in what I was now thinking of as the latest phase of the 'temple'-culture, I felt, as others had before me, that there was also evidence which pointed to possible contacts with the Aegean. At that time I thought, like some earlier students, that these could have been with the Mycenaean or Minoan civilizations. However, the radiocarbon chronology resulting from more recent work means that, if real, they must rather have been with Early Cycladic.

The background of the post-'temple' phases was also a puzzle. The people who immediately succeeded the 'temple' builders were so different that they had always been assumed to be incomers, though no one had any idea of where they originated. However, the then recent excavations of Bernabò Brea in Lipari suggested to me that the first phase, known as the Tarxien Cemetery culture, had links with the recently discovered Early Bronze Age culture of the Aeolian (or Lipari) islands, which he had called Capo Graziano. The second Bronze Age phase in Malta, best represented at Borg in-Nadur, had quite a different material culture. With the aid of some of the pre-First World War volumes of the *Bullettino di Paletnologia Italiana* in the Museum Library I was able to point to almost identical pottery in the cemeteries of the Thapsos culture of Sicily, excavated long ago by Paolo Orsi. These tombs had also contained Mycenaean imports, so I was delighted when I was able to identify a small fragment of undoubtedly Mycenaean pottery in one of the Borg in-Nadur crates. The third and final phase seemed to belong to the Iron Age, and appeared to be basically a development of the Borg in-Nadur culture, but perhaps with some Italian mainland influences.

As I stressed in the paper outlining these ideas, published in *Proceedings of the Prehistoric Society* for 1953, this scheme was essentially a museum class-ification, especially the suggested phases of the Neolithic, which relied basically on typology. It is not surprising therefore that it has been subject to considerable modification as a result of subsequent work, particularly that of David Trump, who was Curator of Archaeology at the National Museum for several years after my departure. The most dramatic of these, which came as a result of his meticulous excavation of the 'temples' at Skorba, was the intercalation of two hitherto quite unsuspected phases into my framework and the chronological reversal of two others. The two new phases were characterised by pottery entirely unlike those of the other phases; the few fragments of this found in older excavations had been thought to be imports because of their striking unlikeness to all the other Maltese Neolithic wares and their close resemblance to a type of Neolithic pottery found in both Sicily and Lipari. These two phases followed the initial Ghar Dalam phase, and do, in fact, seem to have developed from it. The two succeeding ones appeared in the Skorba stratigraphy in the reverse order to what, following what appeared to be a plausible development of the decorative styles, I had postulated, which illustrates quite plainly the limitations of the typological method. Nevertheless, my scheme provided a hypothetical framework which could later be refined and modified as necessary.

The other main problem was the origin of the 'temples' themselves. The presence of a few Ghar Dalam sherds on some of the 'temple' sites, and the quantities of sherds of what appeared to be less sophisticated types at some of the smaller, less elaborate temples, indicated a long period of use for these sites and a gradual elaboration of the plans of the monuments themselves. In 1955 I excavated a series of early rock-cut chamber tombs on the Xemxija heights, which flank the northwest side of St. Paul's Bay on the north coast of Malta. Noting the similarity of the 'lobed' plan of one of these (produced by leaving part of the rock in position to prevent the collapse of the roof) to that of the smaller 'temple' at Mgarr, and the tendency of some of the tombs to link into small groups, I constructed a developmental sequence for the 'temples' and rock-tombs, arguing for a very close link between them, with the form of the earliest 'temples' imitating that of rock-tombs, such as some of the Xemxija ones. In at least one instance the gradual agglomeration of tombs led to the development of an elaborate 'catacomb' (the Hal Saflieni Hypogeum), complete with rock-cut imitations of the 'temple' architecture. Although there is no evidence that burials were ever made in the 'temples', the link is supported by similarities in objects and in the installations and decorative features. Thus there was no need to seek an external origin for these developments; they were entirely a local process. Although the initial premise remains almost inevitably hypothetical, and the chronological priority of the simplest temple-plans remains unproven, I still believe that my conjecture provides the most likely explanation of the evidence.

Into the Labyrinth

In 1953 I was elected to a Research Fellowship at my college in Cambridge, and eventually completed a Ph.D. In 1956 my Fellowship was about to run out and I had to look for a job. As it happened, Gordon Childe was due to retire from the combined Directorship and Chair of Prehistoric European Archaeology at the Institute of Archaeology in London that year and it was decided that these should become two separate posts. William Grimes, then Director of the London Museum, was appointed to the Directorship and the Chair was subsequently advertised. Never having held any teaching post, however junior, I did not dream of applying until it was suggested to me by Glyn Daniel that I should. When I demurred on the grounds of my inexperience, he suggested that I should also consult Grahame Clark. When he also indicated that he thought it would be reasonable for me to apply I felt that I must take their advice and, though still rather embarrassed about it, I finally delivered my application at the last possible moment. I was short-listed, and eventually, to my great surprise, offered the appointment. Looking back, I can see that I had one great advantage. The others people on the short list were all considerably senior to me and had already a great deal of teaching as well as excavation experience, but they had all specialised exclusively in British prehistory, which was also Grimes' field. To appoint me would introduce a new dimension and avoid duplication.

Taking on Childe's extensive lecture programme at a few months notice kept me fully occupied during that first year and the early part of the following one saw our move from the original home of the Institute in Regent's Park to the new purpose-built accommodation that is still its home on the north side of Gordon Square. Shortly after the move had been completed Sinclair Hood invited me to lunch at his house and offered me the opportunity to take charge of the new soundings into the Neolithic levels at Knossos which he had started in the 1957, as part of his re-examination of the whole Palace site. As the fieldwork in Malta had more or less come to an end (though the writing up of the Survey still remained), I was looking for a new project and this one attracted me a great deal. On a personal level, I had always wanted to work in Greece, but circumstances had so far taken me to other parts of the Mediterranean. I naturally remembered Pendlebury's reference to the Neolithic site in his *Archaeology of Crete* as 'one of the largest Neolithic settlements in Europe and the Near East'. Even if more recent work had made its size a bit less unusual, it was still a very impressive accumulation of Neolithic deposits, apparently unique in Crete and virtually unexplored. Such an opportunity to delve once more into the origins and early development of an island community was too tempting to be refused – though perhaps I ought to have done so, if I had considered the work still to be done on writing up the results of the Malta Survey!

Arrival at the British School in Athens was, I have to admit, a bit of a culture shock. While the Bronze Age was generally viewed as a legitimate field of scholarship, we had the distinct impression that earlier periods were less so, and those concerned with them a rather lower form of scholarly life. Considering the School's pre-World War I activities in particular, this seemed somewhat surprising and of course changed very considerably in following years, with the arrival of more of our breed.

The soundings below the Central Court at Knossos had actually been started during the 1957 season, under the care of P. M. Fraser, but the results from the uppermost levels had not been very encouraging – a few detached stretches of walling and a great deal of abraded and comminuted pottery were all that had been found. The hope was that the quality of the remains would improve below these superficial levels, a hope that was soon realized. The first, small-scale season in 1958 produced in the two northern trenches the foundations of a substantial square room with annexe (very similar to the so-called 'but-and-ben' building at Magasa), located in Square D to the northeast, and part of what seemed to be a smaller, trapezoidal room in Square B to the northwest (Houses A and B). These could be dated to different stages of the Middle Neolithic.

It was felt that these remains merited preservation, so in the next two seasons

(1959–60) work was confined to the two southern squares (Squares A and C). In 1959 we continued to a considerable depth, finding clearly stratified deposits, comprising patches of flooring, sometimes with traces of the activities which had taken place on them, and large amounts of potsherds and other material. Relatively little in the way of architectural remains was encountered until, at a depth of a little over five metres, the foundations of two adjoining rectangular rooms were found, evidently part of a larger building. The pottery was by this time in the style which had long been known as EN I.

The final season in 1960 was devoted chiefly to clearing the remaining deposits in these two squares (now joined into one 11 m × 5 m area) and produced exciting results. Beneath the house found at the end of the previous season were the foundations of parts of two superimposed rooms, the walls of the lower one being composed of mud bricks, burnt to a variety of colours (Houses D and E). The deposit in these two levels was also colourful, consisting as it did mainly of broken fragments of burnt mud-brick. This was quite unexpected as the previous buildings were all of pisé on stone foundations. An even greater surprise was the thin level between House E and the bedrock. It was dark in colour, and finds of potsherds, which had been becoming less frequent in the preceding levels, now ceased entirely. It contained, however, plentiful evidence of activity, including threshing and grain grinding, together with a small cemetery of child burials. The radiocarbon date, when it became available, of 8050 ± 180 bp was a surprise in view of the scepticism about the antiquity of the Knossos Neolithic which then prevailed. It also upset Dr Hans Helbaek, who had undertaken to study the grain, particularly the large find from the lowest Aceramic level, because the bread wheat from Knossos was more advanced than the somewhat later finds he had been studying from Çatalhöyük. Though obliged to accept the evidence of a second date, obtained on some of the grain itself (7740 ± 140 bp), he sadly decided not to allow his full report to be published.

The other activity of the 1960 season was the opening of a small sounding (Trench X/Y) intended to test the nature of the Neolithic deposits as far away from the Central Court as possible. The area chosen was the beyond the Palace to the north near the northern edge of the mound. Although this was a somewhat narrow trench, constricted by the remains of Minoan houses, remains of three superimposed buildings were found, all dating from the EN II period. Clearly the settlement had not expanded so far before then and if there were originally any later levels, they had been removed.

That was the end of the matter, for the present. Further study of the material and the writing up of the report took up most of the time I could spare from other duties in the next couple of years. But I was not happy to leave the matter there. I felt that at least another sounding of comparable size in a different part of the site was needed to put the findings in some sort of perspective. In view of the constraints imposed by the need to safeguard the Palace remains, it seemed that this would have to be in the West Court.

A Forgotten Cycladic Islet

However, while preparing the report on the 1957–60 excavations at Knossos, I was invited to join Colin Renfrew, then a research student preparing a thesis on the Early Cycladic period, in excavating an apparently Neolithic site on a tiny islet just off the coast of Antiparos, which he had visited in the course of his research and regarded as highly promising. We worked together at Saliagos for two seasons, 1964 and 1965, and were able to demonstrate that it was it was indeed earlier than any other excavated site in the Cyclades and of great interest from many points of view. As well as its very striking pottery and the rich lithic industry, the site was of great interest because of its peculiar position. The results of an underwater survey, carried out as part of the investigations, together with calculations of the probable changes in sea level since the occupation of the site, suggested that it was originally situated on a slightly elevated projection on an isthmus linking together Paros and Antiparos. At the very least it must once have been well over twice its present size. Not surprisingly, fishing loomed large in the economy, and included an unexpectedly large amount of tunny. However, no fish-hooks were found, but objects which may have been net-sinkers were present, and the very numerous finely-worked tanged points may have been used to shoot or spear fish, since it seemed unlikely that so many would be needed for hunting, and there was no evidence of warfare.

Return to Knossos

With the Saliagos excavations concluded and the report in progress, I could again think about further work at Knossos. I had in mind an area in the northeast corner of the West Court near the western facade of the Palace, which would, of course, necessitate the removal of quite a large number of the Minoan paving stones. In addition I thought that a series of small soundings round the edges of the Palace site might throw some new light on the extent of the Neolithic settlement and perhaps also the nature of activity there. Organising the funding and obtaining the permit took some time, but in 1969 I was able to start the work. After my earlier work at Knossos I had obtained a permit to ship the animal bones to London for study. As the specialists at the Institute were all engaged on other projects I approached Eric Higgs in Cambridge, who assigned two members of his Early Agriculture Project to the job. This time we had the services of a team of specialists, again provided by Eric Higgs, to work with us and study the plant and animal remains on the spot, which seemed an ideal arrangement. Unfortunately, Eric's need to continually move on to new projects, fuelled not only by his own restless mind, but also by the practical necessity of obtaining continued funding for his unit, meant that afterwards the study of the material recorded on the spot was never completed. It is only in recent years that it has been possible for work to be resumed and carried to a conclusion.

We began in the West Court by planning, marking and removing the relevant paving slabs so that they could eventually be put back in their original positions. Excavations here (Area AABB) first encountered the substantial remains of a small part of what must have been an important EM II building. Below this the latest Neolithic levels were absent, no doubt removed in levelling the ground for the later building. Such LN levels as survived produced only fragmentary architectural remains, and the MN ones, though somewhat better preserved, were not particularly informative. Fortunately, the EN II levels were more enlightening, containing remains of three successive building levels, like those found in Trench X/Y of 1960, but this time exposing more of the ground plan of each. They all appeared to be divided into quite small rooms, like the later ones in the Central Court, which appeared to confirm that this was the norm for houses from at least EN II to LN and made the square one-roomed building of 1958 seem exceptional. We still have no complete plan of any of them, but many of the rooms seem too cramped for living spaces and often have blocked doorways or none at all, which suggests that they must be storage areas, perhaps under-floor ones. The lowest levels of the West Court excavation, EN I, produced only some scrappy evidence of buildings, but these show the same construction techniques as in the levels above. I have suggested, based on both the building techniques and the quantity of pottery found, that these remains may be equated with Stratum VII in the AC area in the Central Court (Evans, J. D. 1994: 4). The lowest of all seemed to consist entirely of midden material, presumably emanating from the occupied area to the East. So it seemed that the settlement had taken a while to expand westwards as far as this.

In addition to this West Court sounding, however, I was anxious to investigate a larger area of the Middle Neolithic settlement in the Central Court, encouraged by the fact that we had located part of a very substantial wall of that period in the southern section of Square C in 1960. This was begun right away, and soon uncovered a considerable part of a large, multi-roomed building, apparently very similar to those found just below the surface of the Central Court by Sir Arthur Evans in 1923–4 (Evans, A. J. 1928), along with a portion of a similar one partly overlying it in the southeast corner of this area (Area KLMN).

The peripheral soundings were intended to throw further light on the expansion of the settlement, but one of them (Trench ZE), on the southern side of the site, produced startling new evidence about the Aceramic stage. Just below a Minoan mud brick wall was an Aceramic deposit containing the remains of two walls, both constructed of unfired mud bricks, entirely different in shape and size from the Minoan ones above. This completely overturned the idea that the 'Aceramic' stage might have been just a short preliminary phase of site organization. This was reinforced by a small, follow-up sounding in the southern part of the Central Court (Square X), which indicated that at that point there was an Aceramic deposit nearly two metres thick, containing traces of constructions incorporating a variety of materials, including old querns and unfired mud bricks, much like the walls found in Stratum IX to the north in 1960. It now appeared that the Aceramic phase had lasted for a considerable time and incorporated solid structures, which were periodically renewed.

At the other end of the time spectrum, a square opened in the northern part of the West Court (Square FF) produced a large amount of LN pottery, which included some very distinctive types characteristic of the Phaistos Neolithic deposits. I was disappointed at the time that, despite these finds, the gap between the Neolithic and earliest Minoan pottery had apparently not been fully bridged, so it is gratifying that more recent studies of the ceramic remains from this and other areas, have in fact enabled the gap to be credibly spanned.

The question of the area occupied by the Neolithic settlement was also addressed while the excavations were still in progress. Based on the depth at which natural was reached in various soundings, both old Evans-Mackenzie ones and our own, our surveyor, Col. De Quincy, was able to make to make a contour plan showing the approximate shape of Kephala before any habitation began. Using our own data and Mackenzie's records it was then possible to plot the occurrence of remains of each phase and get a rough idea of the area that had been covered by occupation. When the hypothetical boundary line of the Aceramic settlement was laid over the contour map it turned out to be centred on a small eminence in the southern part of the site, which seemed to be a very reasonable position for the earliest settlers to have chosen. Subsequent expansion to the south, southeast and southwest was somewhat limited by the contours of the hill, so it was mostly to the north and west. The EN I expansion was pretty convincingly attested, but the EN II boundary, though established to the north, was more speculative to the west and northwest. I did not attempt to plot the limits of the MN and LN settlements.

More recent advances in this, as in many other aspects of the study of Neolithic Knossos, of the Neolithic of Crete and of the southern Aegean more generally, are presented in this volume. It is good to see the real importance of this apparently earliest period of the Cretan story being given due attention at last.

Bibliography

Bernabò-Brea, L.
  1950   *The Prehistoric Culture Sequence in Sicily. Sixth Annual Report of the University of London, Institute of Archaeology.* London: Institute of Archaeology.
Evans, A. J.
  1928   *The Palace of Minos* (Volume II: I). London: Macmillan.
Evans, J. D.
  1994   The early millennia: continuity and change in a farming settlement. In D. Evely, H. Hughes-Brock and N. Momigliano (eds.), *Knossos, a Labyrinth of History. Papers Presented in Honour of Sinclair Hood*: 1–20. London: British School at Athens.

3

Time, Space and the Reinvention of the Cretan Neolithic

Peter D. Tomkins

The twentieth century saw the birth of four separate traditions of research into the Neolithic of the regions of the Aegean, a first on the island of Crete (Evans 1901; Tomkins 2000b), a second on the Greek mainland (Tsountas 1909; Andreou *et al.* 1996), a third in the Aegean regions of modern Turkey (Esin 1999), while the medley of cultures defined in the Balkan regions of the north Aegean might be loosely termed a fourth (Bailey 2000: 11–12). These research traditions have followed different trajectories of development, guided equally by archaeological circumstance and modern political and cultural affiliations, employing different chronological schemata, building datasets of varying quality and quantity and developing a range of explanatory theories and models. All four deal with the same period of human existence within an area that we conventionally term the Aegean (Renfrew 2005: 154 for a definition), presenting prehistorians with a range of challenges in identifying and exploring the higher level patterns of interaction, development and divergence that define the Aegean Neolithic world system.

No region exemplifies this situation better than Crete. Its existing chronology originates in a tri-partite division (Early, Middle, Late) of the continuous Neolithic sequence at Knossos made by its early excavators (Mackenzie 1903; Evans 1904; Tomkins 2000b: 77), subsequently formalised and refined by later scholarship, and bracketed by additional earlier (Aceramic or Initial Neolithic) and later (Final Neolithic) phases (Table 3.1; Furness 1953; J. D. Evans 1964; Vagnetti and Belli 1978). When the tripartite ordering of the Greek Neolithic sequence was first formulated, it was directly equated with the Knossos sequence (Weinberg 1947: 181 table). Such an optimistic and favourable ordering would not, however, survive the radiocarbon revolution, which demonstrated *inter alia* that Crete's traditional tripartite scheme was considerably out of step with the rest of Greece (Table 3.1).[1] From then on the island was treated at arms-length, as something intrinsically different from the rest of the Aegean in the structure and form of its material and social development (*e.g.*, Weinberg 1965: 287). Chronological work has generally ignored Crete (*e.g.*, Eslick 1992), treated it as an isolated case (*e.g.*, Weinberg 1970: 608–18) or else failed to appreciate the full extent of the chronological mismatch (*e.g.*, Branigan 1970: 10–11; Warren and Hankey 1989:

Neolithic Phases	Revised Knossos Sequence	Traditional Cretan Neolithic Phases	Greece	W/SW Anatolian and East Aegean	Syria	Approx. Dates (cal. BC)
Initial Neolithic	Stratum X	Aceramic	Aceramic/Initial	Aceramic/ Early Neolithic	Final PPNB or PPNC/ Early Neolithic	c.7000– c.6500/6400
Early Neolithic	Stratum IX–VIII	Early Neolithic I (Furness 1953)	Early Neolithic Franchthi FCP1	Late Neolithic Hacilar IX–VI Ulucak IV–V Kuruçay 13–11	Late Neolithic (Pre-Halaf and 'Transitional' Samarra)	c.6500/6400– c.5900
Middle Neolithic	Strata VII–VIB; Stratum P		Middle Neolithic Franchthi FCP2–3	Early Chalcolithic Hacilar V–I Kuruçay 10–7	Early Chalcolithic (Halaf)	c.5900–c.5300
Late Neolithic I	Strata VIB–V; Strata N, M, L		Late Neolithic I Saliagos Franchthi FCP4	Middle Chalcolithic Emporio X–VIII Kum Tepe IA Beşiktepe	(Late Ubaid)	c.5300–c.4900
Late Neolithic II	Stratum IV; Strata K, H, G	Early Neolithic II (Furness 1953; Evans 1964)	Late Neolithic II Saliagos	Kizilbel/ Lower Bagbasi	(Late Ubaid)	c.4900– c.4500/4400
Final Neolithic IA	Stratum IIIB; Strata F, E, D	Middle Neolithic (Furness 1953; Evans 1964)	Final Neolithic	? Middle Chalcolithic ?	Late Chalcolithic 1	c.4500/4400– c.4200
Final Neolithic IB	Stratum IIIA; Strata C, B	Middle-Late Neolithic 'Transition' (Evans 1964)	Franchthi FCP5	Late Chalcolithic 1 Beycesultan XL–XXXV Kum Tepe IB1	Late Chalcolithic 2	c.4200–c.3900
Final Neolithic II	Stratum IIB	Late Neolithic I (Evans 1964; Manteli 1993)		Late Chalcolithic 2 Beycesultan XXXIV–XXIX Kum Tepe IB2 Tigani I	Late Chalcolithic 3	c.3900–c.3600
Final Neolithic III	Stratum IIA	Final Neolithic (Vagnetti 1973; Vagnetti and Belli 1978)	Kephala	Late Chalcolithic 3 Beycesultan XXVIII–XXV Kuruçay 6 Kum Tepe IB3 Emporio VII Tigani II	Late Chalcolithic 4	c.3600–c.3300
Final Neolithic IV	Stratum IC	Final Neolithic (Vagnetti 1973; Vagnetti and Belli 1978)	Ayia Irini I	Late Chalcolithic 4 Beycesultan XXIV–XX Kum Tepe IB4 Emporio VI Tigani III	Late Chalcolithic 5	c.3300–c.3000

Table 3.1. The relationship between traditional and new Cretan chronological schemata and other Aegean and East Mediterranean regional chronologies (after Tomkins 2007b: 12, table 1.1).

12–13; Manning 1995: 169). Incorporation, when attempted, has relied on radiocarbon dates, but changes and errors in calculation and calibration have caused the Cretan sequence to 'float' in relationship to other Aegean sequences (Tomkins 2007b: 19, table 1.5). This has made it impossible to relate Cretan Neolithic development to that of other Aegean regions, severely restricting the extent to which ideas, explanations and models developed elsewhere over the last thirty years have influenced Cretan Neolithic studies (Tomkins 2004: 39–41).

This chronological incompatibility reflects long-standing difficulties in identifying secure links between Knossos and other sequences in Crete and elsewhere, exemplified by interpretations of ceramic development that, until recently, emphasised homogeneity, idiosyncrasy and local production (Furness 1953: 95, 103, n.16; J. D. Evans 1964: 194; Tomkins *et al.* 2004: 51–52 for a discussion). The perceived absence of external linkages, whether in the form of imports, exports or stylistic emulation, seemed to find correlation beyond Knossos in an apparent absence of earlier Neolithic (IN–MN) sites, with the Cretan landscape generally considered empty or sparsely settled until the FN period (Cherry 1990: 161; Watrous 1994: 700; Manning 1999: 469–70). Even during FN, when the number of known sites substantially increases (see below; Nowicki this volume), major problems of correlation remain. Originally defined, alongside the rest of the Aegean, as a long phase, comprising Knossos Strata I–II, Neolithic Phaistos and the 'Sub-Neolithic' Group (Renfrew 1972: 71–72), the Cretan 'FN' phase has come to denote a much shorter period of time, partly of necessity because the end of Cretan 'LN' is much later than that of Greek LN (Table 3.1), partly as a response to problems correlating the two main excavated sequences at Knossos and Phaistos (J. D. Evans 1968: 276; Vagnetti and Belli 1978; Hood 1990; Manteli 1993a; 1993b; Wilson and Day 2000: 54; Nowicki 2002: 11–15; Tomkins 2007b: 14–17 for a discussion). The recent identification at Knossos of stratified 'FN' material of Phaistian type, in deposits which hitherto had been dated to the 'LN' period, exemplifies current confusion regarding the definition of these two phases (*e.g.*, Vagnetti 1996; cf. Branigan 1998).

Perhaps unsurprisingly, a framework for Neolithic Crete has developed that emphasises, first, Knossos' isolation and, second, its unique importance, whether as the primary population centre for the whole island during the earlier Neolithic or as an exceptionally (by Aegean standards) large (*i.e.*, 4–5 ha) and populous (ca. 500–1500) Neolithic 'super-site', transcending demographic thresholds for social organization not crossed elsewhere in the Aegean until the Early Bronze Age and prefiguring its later position of dominance in the Bronze Age (Pendlebury 1939: 36–37; Renfrew 1964: 111–12; J. D. Evans 1968: 273–76; 1971: 114; 1994: 14; Vagnetti and Belli 1978: 126; Cherry 1985: 24, 27; Broodbank 1992: 40–49, 64–69; Whitelaw 1992: 227; 2004: 147; Manning 1994: 232, 239–40; 1995: 42; 1999: 469–72; Vagnetti 1996: 30; Manteli 1996: 132). Equally unusual is the apparent slow-down or stalling in growth at Knossos that occurs during EM I–II (Broodbank 1992: 68; Wilson and Day 2000: 59; Whitelaw 2000b: 225, table 1), at a time when elsewhere in Crete and the Aegean settlements go through a phase of expansion (Halstead 1981b: 196–200).

This paper challenges the present orthodoxy of chronological and cultural uniqueness over similarity and of isolation over interaction. Following a recently-completed review of stratigraphy and phasing at Knossos, it has proved possible to increase the number of recognisable phases and to integrate them with those of neighbouring Aegean regions, allowing them to be re-labelled so as to reflect chronological usage in the rest of Greece (Tomkins 2007b for a full phase-by-phase discussion). This new chronology has been employed throughout this paper,[2] allowing spatial (and demographic) development at Knossos and in the wider Cretan landscape to be explored with new precision. The result is a radically different picture of Knossos and the Cretan Neolithic landscape, characterised by interaction and a pattern of development broadly analogous to other Aegean regions.

A World Apart? Cretan Neolithic Chronology in Review

Making Time

Restudy of the Knossian Neolithic sequence began as a combined macroscopic (fabric, form, finish, firing, frequency, use-wear) and microscopic (petrology, Scanning Electron Microscopy) study of EN–LN II ceramics from the well-stratified deposits excavated in Area ABCD between 1957 and 1960 (Strata IX–IV; J. D. Evans 1964; 1968; Tomkins 2001; Tomkins *et al.* 2004), which was subsequently extended to include also the FN sequence (Strata IIIB–IC; Tomkins 2007b). All assemblages were sorted first by fabric and then, within these fabric groups, by form and finish. This revealed a greater degree of variation in form and finish subsumed within existing ware and form categories – the building blocks of the traditional chronology – thus bringing new dimension and detail to the study of ceramic development at Knossos. Exploration of the full range of this ceramic variation, specifically the inter-relations between fabric, form, finish and frequency, allowed Neolithic ceramic assemblages at Knossos to be sub-divided into three main groups, the frequency of which varies (within certain limits) between contexts and phases (Tomkins *et al.* 2004: 54, 56; Tomkins 2004: 48, 53):

> *Group 1*: A broadly 'local' group (ca. 50–85% of any context) of related fabrics, compatible with a local provenance and well-represented typologically. Stylistic variation is generally minor, but often of chronological significance.
> *Group 2*: A broadly 'Cretan' group (ca. 15–50% of any context) of fabrics, exhibiting a range of mineralogies. Stylistic variation is greater but the main features find good parallels with Group 1. The chronological significance of this variation is not always clear in cases when sample size is small.
> *Group 3*: A broadly 'off-island' (≤2.5% of any context) and mineralogically and technologically varied group of fabrics. Stylistic variation is high, but the closest parallels are not with Groups 1 or 2, but in assemblages from neighbouring regions of the Aegean. The correspondence between rare/unique types of form and finish and rare/unique fabrics is a striking feature.

The identification of a range of imported material allowed the Knossos sequence for the first time to be linked securely to other assemblages and sequences within and beyond Crete (Tomkins 2007b for a detailed discussion). Further external links were provided by a review of published assemblages from neighbouring Aegean regions, which identified a small group of ceramic material stylistically similar to material of Groups 1 and 2 at Knossos and considered unique or unusual at its site of deposition. The series of radiocarbon dates from Knossos (J. D. Evans 1994: 20, table II; Efstratiou *et al.* 2004: 44, table 1.1) served as a useful control and provided important additional information about the absolute date range of phases and phase-transitions.

Stratigraphy

The stratigraphy for Area ABCD, originally presented by John Evans (1964), was reviewed and linked to that recorded in adjacent areas excavated in 1923–4 (Evans 1928) and 1969–70 (Areas KLMN, RST; Trenches P and Q; J. D. Evans 1971). Modifications were relatively minor, the most serious occurring in the final part of the sequence (Strata III–I) spanning the full length of the Aegean FN period (Table 3.1; J. D. Evans 1964: 172–92; see Tomkins 2007b: 16–18, 32–44). The original sub-division of Stratum III into early (IIIB) and late (IIIA) sub-strata was confirmed, with some minor modifications and on the basis of this, two pottery groups were defined corresponding to successive ceramic phases (FN IA and FN IB). Stratum II also proved divisible into early (IIB) and late (IIA) sub-strata, comprising two pottery groups that form the basis for the definition of successive sub-phases of FN (FN II and FN III), the latter contemporary with the earlier stratum at Phaistos (Tomkins 2007b: 38–41, fig. 1.12; Todaro and Di Tonto this volume). In previous work, Stratum I has been treated as a single-phase deposit, variously thought to be earlier than (Manteli 1993a: 26–29, 59; 1993b: 32–59) or contemporary with the Neolithic strata at Phaistos (Renfrew 1972: 71; Vagnetti and Belli 1978: 132, 157; Warren and Hankey 1989: 12). Restudy has revealed a more complex internal stratigraphy divisible into three sub-units (IA–C). Pure, single-phase deposits are rare, but sufficient to demonstrate clearly that Stratum IC corresponds to the latest phase of FN (FN IV), as represented at Nerokourou, Petras Kephala and Phaistos (later stratum) (Vagnetti 1973; Vagnetti *et al.* 1989; Tomkins 2007b: 41–44, fig. 1.15; Papadatos this volume; Todaro and Di Tonto this volume). The bulk of the material from Stratum I is fill material from external areas and its mixed nature (FN II and later), together with the poor preservation of Stratum IIA within Area ABCD, accounts for previous difficulties in locating pure deposits of Phaistian-type material (*i.e.*, FN III–IV) at Knossos (J. D. Evans 1968: 276). Stratum IB is a much denuded deposit that had been almost entirely removed by levelling activity that took place prior to the deposition of Stratum IA. Although scanty traces of architecture and external surfaces could be traced, only a handful of material, the latest dating to EM I, could be tentatively associated with their construction or use. More definitive support for a direct stratigraphical relationship between FN IV and EM I is provided by the recent identification of stratified FN IV–EM I sequences elsewhere at Knossos (D.VII.21; Trench FF, Levels 4 and 10; Tomkins 2007b: 44–48), in the recent excavations at Phaistos (Todaro and Di Tonto this volume) and Petras Kephala (Papadatos this volume).

Phasing

In common with recent work on Bronze Age ceramic phasing at Knossos

(Cadogan *et al.* 1993), issues of labelling and terminology were set aside and priority given to the task of identifying a series of pottery groups that might be considered stylistically and stratigraphically coherent and thus representative of the sequence of ceramic development at Neolithic Knossos. A total of nine groups are now recognised and these have been named after the stratigraphical units in which they occur and as these units appear in a revised version of John Evans' sequence of strata (Strata IX–IC, Table 3.1; Tomkins 2007b: 16–17). Each pottery group has been related on the basis of imports, stylistic parallels and, wherever possible, radiocarbon dates to other Neolithic assemblages from elsewhere in Crete and from neighbouring regions beyond the island. This has allowed a more secure alignment of Cretan ceramic phasing with other Aegean regional chronologies (Table 3.1).

Sticky Labels

This greater level of integration opens up a range of alternative solutions to the question of labelling. Ideally, chronological terminology should be sufficiently neutral as to convey no more than a relative position within a sequence. This condition is admirably fulfilled by the 'Initial', 'Early', 'Middle', 'Late' and 'Final' labels, currently in use in the Greek-speaking Aegean, but markedly less well by the 'Early', 'Middle' and 'Late Chalcolithic' labels used to describe the mid-late part of the west/southwest Anatolia sequence. 'Chalcolithic' will always be a laden term, enshrining metal as the dominant material commodity and raising an expectation that metal objects or evidence for metallurgy will be found, either of which for Crete appear appropriate only for the very latest phase of FN (FN IV), at least on present evidence (Papadatos this volume; Todaro and Di Tonto this volume). Equally inappropriate is the alignment of the west/southwest Anatolian sequence with regions further east, creating, somewhat artificially, an earliest ceramic phase (Anatolian Early Neolithic; ca. 7300–6500 BC; Esin 1999: 17–19), which is yet to be properly documented in the Aegean regions of Anatolia and is contemporary with an aceramic phase in Greece and Crete. Arguably, greater clarity could be gained from an alignment of the Aegean regions of Anatolia with their Aegean neighbours, evidence for which is particularly strong from the later Neolithic (Eslick 1992: 83–87).

Reapplication of the traditional Cretan schema would be least disruptive for current researchers working on Crete, but would do nothing to resolve long-standing problems of chronological incompatibility and intellectual isolation and would obscure any parallels in development. Thus the decision was made to abandon the traditional chronological schema (*i.e.*, 'EN I', 'EN II', 'MN', *etc.*) and to reassign the labels 'Early', 'Middle', 'Late' and 'Final' to those pottery groups at Knossos that can now be shown to be equivalent to those same phases on the Greek mainland. Disruption caused by this change is mediated by the fact that almost all Cretan sites currently known outside Knossos are classifiable as FN under either system, the only new change being the addition of a more precise sub-phase number (*i.e.*, FN IA–IV), which has the double advantage of eliminating internal semantic and existential difficulties regarding 'LN' and 'FN', whilst making clear the relationship with Late Chalcolithic I–IV Anatolia with which the final four Cretan FN phases (FN IB–IV) are broadly compatible. Most importantly, Phaistos (and other contemporary sites) can now be fully correlated with Knossos (Tomkins 2007b: 35–44; Todaro and Di Tonto this volume). A very small number of Cretan sites can now be dated to phases earlier than FN (see below), but, since their chronology had previously been unclear, the changes fill an existing vacuum. The only site to be seriously affected is thus Knossos and it is hoped that current and future work on a range of unpublished material (chipped stone, ground stone, faunal remains) will adopt the new chronology.

Death of a Neolithic 'Super-site': Knossos and the Settled Landscapes of Neolithic Crete

In the absence of more direct evidence, at least in the phases preceding FN, our vision of the Cretan Neolithic landscape has always reflected what we think we know about spatial and demographic development at Knossos. The idea of a large, isolated and demographically self-sustaining Knossian community lies at the core of a narrative of the pre-FN Cretan landscape that emphasises the emptiness of some regions, sparse, probably temporary cave occupation in others and direct procurement of non-local materials consumed at Knossos (Branigan 1970: 36–37; Broodbank 1992: 41, 47–49; Manning 1994: 239–40; Watrous 1994: 700). During FN, when considerably more sites are known for Crete, the exceptionally large estimated size of Knossos perpetuates the picture of a Neolithic *primus inter pares* and helps sustain the notion that the increase in known sites in different regions of the island reflects a process of internal colonization originating from the mother community of Knossos (Broodbank 1992: 50, 68–69; Manning 1994: 232, 239–40). This in turn has encouraged narratives of its subsequent emergence as an urban centre that see Neolithic origins for the cultural and cosmological significance it may have enjoyed during the Bronze Age (Soles 1995; Manning 1999: 471–72; Wilson and Day 2000: 61).

Making Space

In the following section this picture of Neolithic Knossos and its relationship with the Cretan landscape will be challenged drawing both on a recently completed re-evaluation of spatial (and thus demographic) development at Knossos (Tomkins in prep.) and on a comprehensive chronological review of all reported Neolithic assemblages (Tomkins 2007b), not only well-stratified deposits, but also those with poor stratigraphical associations (*i.e.*, caves, funerary and survey sites) previously dated in only the vaguest terms. The approach taken to demographic reconstruction at Knossos relies on the established practice of applying a population density multiplier to an estimate of the inhabited area (usually 100–200 persons/hectare; *e.g.*, Halstead 1989: 70; Broodbank 1992: 43). Previous estimates of inhabited area at Neolithic sites around the Aegean have produced varying readings, with estimates based on mound size (Halstead 1981a; 1981b) notably lower than those based on sherd scatters (Perlès 2001: 176–80). While mound size has poor chronological resolution, sherd scatters are particularly susceptible to taphonomic bias, especially at intensively over-built and reworked sites like Knossos. While extreme biases can be factored out by the measurement of sherd densities (*e.g.*, Whitelaw 1992: 227–28 for Neolithic Knossos), sherd scatters remain poor indicators of the nature and structure of buried deposits and cannot easily distinguish between inhabited area, contemporary edge-of-site activity areas and areas where large quantities of Neolithic material might have been re-deposited at a later date. All three can be identified at Knossos, but only the former offers an appropriate basis for estimating population size. Thus, for all excavated deposits at Knossos where the stratigraphy and context can be accurately reconstructed, a distinction has been drawn between those that preserve direct or indirect evidence for inhabitation (*i.e.*, walls, building material; thick deposits of material) and those that correspond to edge-of-site activity areas (*i.e.*, thin strata, ash, pits) that do not.

The approach taken to Neolithic settlement beyond Knossos represents a departure from previous work in treating the dataset, not at face-value, but as one that is fragmented and incomplete. It has been inspired by the recognition of a fundamental and irreconcilable incompatibility between the distribution of *known* Neolithic settlement on Crete, especially in its earlier phases when Knossos is apparently the only site and the suspected distribution of Neolithic ceramic producing groups, as identified by combined macroscopic and microscopic (petrology) study of the EN–FN ceramic assemblage from Knossos (Tomkins 2001; Tomkins *et al.* 2004). Although consistency in the selection and processing of a specific set of raw materials (*i.e.*, fabric) is the most obvious defining feature of each of these groups, such consistency often also extends to other aspects of technology, such as methods of surface treatment and specific features of vessel form and finish (Tomkins 2001). A number of these producing groups can be shown to be exploiting clay and temper sources that are non-local (>5–7 km) to Knossos, some located in distant regions, such as the Mirabello Bay in east Crete (70 km from Knossos) (Tomkins and Day 2001; Tomkins *et al.* 2004: 56). The likelihood that these fabric groupings represent ceramic production at other unknown settlement locations is high and finds further support in declining frequency of these fabrics at Knossos, with distance from raw material source (where identifiable) increasing. This picture of multiple producing groups situated in regions of Crete where known settlement is sparse or absent, finds a parallel in provenance work on Cretan LN–FN stone axes (Strasser 2004; this volume; Strasser and Fassoulas 2004). Furthermore, additional indirect evidence for an undiscovered earlier Neolithic settlement in the Malia Plain ('la marée')

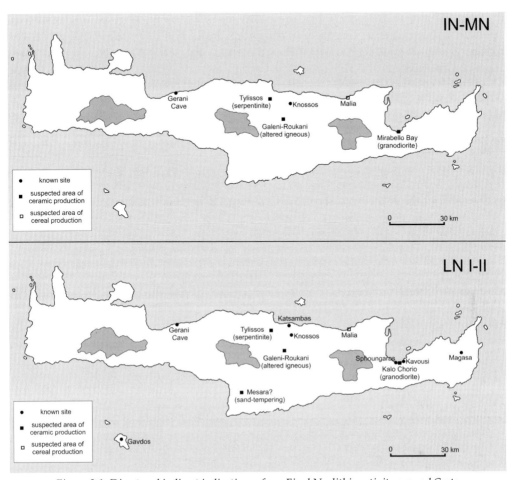

Figure 3.1. Direct and indirect indications of pre-Final Neolithic activity around Crete.

may be provided by the identification, in the base of a core, of cereal pollen, the date of which can be no later than the latter half of the seventh millennium BC ('Carotte VI'; Ly-7122: 7440 ± 80 bp; Dalongeville *et al.* 2001; Müller pers. comm.).

Such strong hints as to the existence of undiscovered sites (Figure 3.1) should encourage us to think more creatively about what form the Cretan landscape might have taken during the Neolithic. More can be made of the settlement data, if known sites are treated not as unique cases, as has been the case with Knossos, but *pars pro toto* as fragments of an originally much larger and now highly partial dataset. Comparison with better documented regions of the Aegean and a full exploitation of the possibilities of predictive modelling can, if cautiously applied, produce further insights. For example, the Gerani Cave, at present seemingly the earliest known site outside Knossos (?MN; Tomkins 2007b: 25), not only seems to reflect a preference for caves in marine locations that is observable elsewhere in the earlier Neolithic Aegean, but may also hint at the existence of undiscovered open-air settlements in the Rethymnon area, if, as has been argued, such caves served as ritual sites for communities permanently settled in open-air locations (Tomkins in press). The reasons why certain aspects of the Neolithic landscape have so thoroughly escaped our attention are varied, but major factors are likely to be the small size of these sites, especially those of the earlier Neolithic (<1 ha), and a preference for low-land, riverine locations, where a range of concealing processes may have been active (*e.g.*, alluviation, erosion, over-building) and where intensive archaeological exploration has often not yet been undertaken (*e.g.*, Herakleion Basin). Ultimately, it is only by exploring and explaining the presences *and* the absences in the data that we might glimpse underlying patterns in the settlement record of Neolithic Crete and place each phase of occupation at Knossos in a more meaningful context.

The Earlier Neolithic (IN–MN; >7000–5300 BC)

With the greater resolution brought by the new system of ceramic phasing and after comprehensive study of early (by Arthur Evans and Duncan Mackenzie, 1900–1924) and recent (by John Evans, 1957–60; 1969–70) excavated material, it has proved possible to refine the picture of settlement development considerably, particularly during the first two millennia of its existence (Figures 3.3–4; J. D. Evans 1971; Tomkins in prep.). Evidence for IN habitation is confined to the southeastern part of the mound, where a sequence of up to four levels of mudbrick and stone architecture was revealed in Trenches X and ZE (Figure 3.2; J. D. Evans 1971: 99–103). Early in EN the area of habitation, comprising two to three building horizons (Area AC, Strata IX–VIII; J. D. Evans 1964: 144–50, figs. 8–10; Tomkins 2007b: 21–23), shifts northwards and westwards, probably as far as the west and north wings of the later Palace (Figure 3.2). During MN, habitation characterised by up to two building levels and a new pisé construction technique (Area AC, Strata VII–VIB; J. D. Evans 1994: 8, 10; Tomkins 2007b: 23–27), spreads further to the north and west, reaching the eastern half of the later West Court towards the end of this phase (Area AABB).

Three important conclusions can be drawn from the earlier Neolithic data. First, from IN onwards habitation at Knossos seems to have been continuous and permanent. Evidence for frequent episodes of occupation and abandonment noted for the 1997 test (Efstratiou *et al.* 2004: 47) come from what appears to be an edge-of-site area (thin levels, no architecture) situated just beyond the area of habitation. Trenches within the inhabited area indicate some movement of its spatial limits over time (Tomkins 2000a: 228–29), but, when taken together, show no obvious breaks in the stratigraphical and cultural sequence. Secondly, growth appears to have remained more-or-less static during IN and EN, with expansion only beginning at some point during the MN period (Table 3.2; Figure 3.2). This contradicts the belief held since Arthur Evans (Tomkins 2000b: 77, 79) that the site expanded continuously, albeit at varying rates (Broodbank 1992: 44–45, fig.

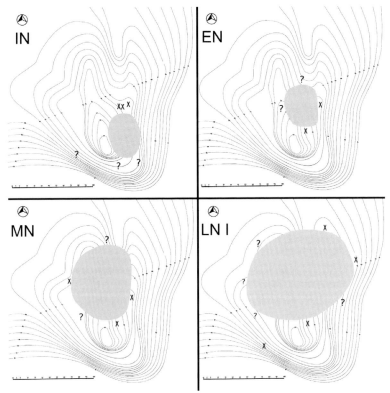

Figure 3.2. Estimated extent of inhabited area at Knossos (IN–LN I). NB X = edge-of-site activity area.

2), from its inception until the end of the Neolithic (J. D. Evans 1971; Whitelaw 1992; 2000b). Thirdly, it is now clear that at no point during the earlier Neolithic did the community at Knossos reach what is usually regarded as a demo-graphically self-sustaining figure (ca. 300–500 people: Broodbank and Strasser 1991: 236, 239–240), instead remaining small (<100 people) for at least the first millennium of its existence. In order to have sustained itself this community must have regularly interacted with a larger, external demographic group, a conclusion that strengthens the case for a horizon of undiscovered earlier Neolithic settlement and pushes back their existence to the inception of farming on the island in IN. Far from being exceptional, earlier Neolithic Knossos seems to be broadly typical of earlier Neolithic open-air settlements in the Aegean in size (ca. 0.5–1 ha: Renfrew 1972: 238; Halstead 1994: 200), subsistence economy (Halstead 1981b: 194–95; Isaakidou this volume), preferred location (Sherratt 1981: 315) and social organization (Tomkins 2004: 42–50; 2007a).

Recognition of our failure to identify other earlier Neolithic settlements forces us to reflect on how little we know about the Cretan landscape before the fourth millennium BC and how much there is that awaits discovery. There is at present no adequate explanation for why Crete should be the only one of the largest

Phase	Estimated Maximum Extent (ha)
Initial Neolithic	*c.* 0.25–0.35
Early Neolithic	*c.* 0.25–0.35
Middle Neolithic	*c.* 0.7–0.8
Late Neolithic I	*c.* 1.4–1.75
Late Neolithic II	*c.* 1.75–2.5
Final Neolithic I-IV	*c.* 1.75–2.5

Table 3.2. Estimated extent of inhabited area at Knossos per Neolithic phase.

Mediterranean islands to lack clear evidence of a pre-Neolithic presence (Broodbank 2006; this volume) nor has a systematic search for such evidence, driven by predictive modelling and comprehensive sampling strategies (*e.g.*, Runnels *et al.* 2005), yet been initiated. Once we start looking properly, we may find that the present picture of pre- and earlier Neolithic human activity on Crete changes radically and rapidly.

Ultimately, it may well prove that the Neolithization of Crete – conventionally accepted to have been a single migratory episode by a small, off-island group that specifically targeted the Knossos valley (Broodbank and Strasser 1991: 236, 239–40) – develops into a more complex and contentious discussion of the role of indigenous and exogenous agencies (Kotsakis this volume). At the very least, it would appear that the presently-favoured migration model needs further nuancing to reflect the strong likelihood that the peopling of Knossos was but an episode in a more widespread process of initial agricultural expansion in Crete. Any externally-sourced migratory movement would have been guided by the constraints of maritime technology and the configuration of maritime pathways through the extreme eastern and western ends of the island (Cherry 1985: 21–22; Broodbank and Strasser 1991: 241). Occupation of available favourable niches is likely to have begun from these areas and, under the terms of the early farmer model (EFM), are likely have proceeded too rapidly for anything other than broad regional stages in expansion to be detectable archaeologically (Sherratt 1981; 2004). In the case of Greece early farming communities are most dense in the east, probably reflecting a westward trend and maritime focus in the initial spread of farming (Perlès 2001: 113–20). On this basis and in view of indirect hints of early activity beyond Knossos (see Figure 3.1), we might predict for Crete an east-west and/or west-east chain of demographic expansion focused on favourable niches in riverine locations on or within easy reach of the north coast (*e.g.*, Mirabello Bay [east], Malia Plain [east-central], Knossos [north-central], Rethymnon [west]). Viewed in such terms Knossos' position, in an attractive but by no means unique niche some way down this pathway of expansion, coupled with its early foundation date (ca. 7000 BC), suggests that it was not the earliest such foundation and that the time-scale of initial expansion was short. Following establishment, the EFM would predict static demographic growth within individual communities, as indeed is the case at IN–EN Knossos, limited by technical and ecological constraints and controlled by a variety of social

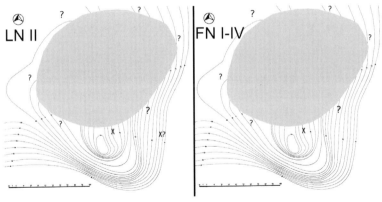

Figure 3.3. Estimated extent of inhabited area at Knossos (LN II–FN IV). NB X = edge-of-site activity area.

mechanisms (Sherratt 1981). During EN and MN the consumption and deposition of non-local ceramic vessels at Knossos testifies to the connectedness of these communities long after initial Neolithization (Tomkins *et al.* 2004), confirming the important role played by exchange, over short and long distances, in maintaining their social and economic viability (Halstead 1981a; 1989; 1999) and revealing, through further contextual study, the principal mechanism through which status was negotiated and reproduced (Tomkins 2004: 45–50; 2007a: 192–93). A similar picture of movement and interaction within and beyond the island could, on the basis of the chipped stone, be suggested for the preceding IN period (Conolly this volume). Stepping back, it becomes apparent that the initial phase of demographic and agricultural expansion in Crete was an intense episode in a long-term process of movement and interaction that may have extended back into pre-Neolithic periods and certainly continued long after 'colonization'.

Late Neolithic (ca. 5300–4500 BC)

During LN I the settlement at Knossos expands significantly to the north, west and east, perhaps in continuation of the phase of growth detected in late MN levels (*e.g.*, Area AABB; Table 3.2; Figure 3.2). LN II habitation can be detected in all areas occupied in LN I and there is evidence for additional, sustained expansion to the north (Area XY; three building levels) the limits of which probably lie just beyond the Palace site (Whitelaw pers. comm.; Figure 3.3). Thanks, on the one hand, to a combination of Minoan levelling and terracing activity and, on the other, to a lack of modern tests to bedrock in the areas that border the Kephala Hill (Whitelaw 1992: 227), the western and eastern limits of LN II and FN habitation are at present imprecisely defined (Table 3.2).

A small number of assemblages from sites beyond Knossos may be assigned to the Late Neolithic period (Figure 3.1; Tomkins 2007b: 29). Small quantities of material, apparently of LN type, have been illustrated from the Gerani Cave

(Manteli 1998b), from below the modern village of Kavousi (Haggis 1996: 309–400, 391, fig. 5: nos. 338–41) and, most recently, from surface collections made on the island of Gavdos (Kopaka and Papadaki 2006: 77, pls. 1, 1–2 [knobbed wishbone handles]). The Gavdos material is of special interest, not only because it is the earliest direct evidence for activity along the south coast/Mesara, but also because its insular location suggests a LN phase of activity on Crete's offshore islets to match that known from elsewhere in the insular Aegean at this time (*e.g.*, Broodbank 2000: 117–26, 145–49). An indirect hint of activity in the Mesara is provided by the rare presence in LN and later levels at Knossos of sand-tempered fabrics (Tomkins 2001), some of which may link to EM tempering traditions that have been located in south-central Crete (Wilson and Day 1994; Day *et al.* 2006: 41–44).

Published assemblages from Magasa (Siteia), Sphoungaras (Mirabello Bay) and Katsambas (north-central Crete; Galanidou and Manteli this volume) may with some confidence be dated to LN I (Knossos Strata VIA–V Group: Tomkins 2007b: 27–30), making them the earliest open-air sites currently known outside Knossos. All of these seem on present evidence to represent a new category of small site, consisting of one or a small group of dwellings. Demographically and most probably also socially and economically such sites are likely to have been dependent on larger village-type settlements that must also have existed in their vicinity. The greater archaeological visibility of satellite sites over villages may not be serendipitous but could relate to differences in function and topographical signature. In the case of Magasa, its upland location and large assemblage of stones axes and rubbing/polishing tools may indicate a specialised production site (Dawkins 1905) dependent on an, as yet, undiscovered, lowland village. A similar relation of dependence may have existed between the house at Katsambas and Knossos (Galanidou and Manteli this volume).

These changes in the settled landscape find a corollary in a series of material and social changes at LN Knossos that have been interpreted as representing the emergence of the household as a self-conscious and independent socio-economic unit (Tomkins 2004). A broadly similar and contemporary phenomenon may be identified at LN villages elsewhere in the Aegean (Halstead 1995; 1999; Tomkins 2004). During LN I Thessaly sees a realignment of settlement with abandonment in some areas coinciding, in others, with infill and expansion, such as the colonization of the arid southern Larisa plain by small, short-lived 'hamlets' (<0.5 ha) (Halstead 1994: 200; Johnson and Perlès 2004: 71–75). By the end of LN, settlement size seems to have increased notably, with large villages (>1.0 ha) being the norm (Halstead 1981b: 197). On Crete, there is also evidence for a simultaneous emergence of large villages (*e.g.*, LN I Knossos) and smaller hamlets (*e.g.*, LN I Kastambas) during LN. This may reflect the development of a two-tier site hierarchy that facilitated demographic expansion by extending the areas of landscape exploited by a single settled community and thus its overall pro-ductivity (see also Isaakidou this volume). This development might plausibly be understood as arising from a desire to increase the quantity and/or quality of household productive output, itself driven by status competition between households (Tomkins 2004).

The Final Neolithic (ca. 4500–3100/3000 BC)

Previous reconstructions of FN spatial development at Knossos have assumed that expansion continued at or just below the rate documented during LN, producing estimates of site size in the region of 4 to 5 ha by the end of FN (J. D. Evans 1971; Broodbank 1992: 43, table 1; Whitelaw 2000b: 225, table 1; 2004: 156, fig. 10.7). Once cautiously expressed, relying on a conjectural reading of unstratified sherd scatters beyond the Kephala Hill (J. D. Evans 1971: 114; Whitelaw 1992: 226–27), these figures have in time come to be treated as facts upon which to base further interpretation (*e.g.*, Broodbank 1992; Manning 1999; Mee 2001). If, however, one focuses purely on stratified deposits of FN material, then a rather different trajectory of development emerges between the relatively certain estimates for the end of LN I (ca. 1.4–1.75 ha) and EM II (ca. 5 ha). While FN I habitation can be documented over much the same area as that occupied by the LN II settlement, evidence for habitation in subsequent phases of FN is confined to areas, such as the summit slopes, that escaped later disturbance. Since no evidence for FN habitation has yet been found beyond the area occupied during LN, it is surely far safer to conclude at present that the community at Knossos did *not* continue to expand during FN (see also Hood 1981: 6) but rather stayed broadly within the limits reached in LN II (*i.e.*, ca. 1.75–2.5 ha; Table 3.2). This brings Knossos back into line with other large FN open-air villages (*e.g.*, Phaistos, ca. 2.0 ha; Watrous and Hadzi-Vallianou 2004: 221). Similarly long periods of stability, with zero or minimal net site growth seem to be the norm at earlier Neolithic sites on the Greek mainland (Halstead 1981a: 312–13; Perlès 2001: 173–99), as indeed they are at Knossos (see above). During the later Neolithic, Thessalian sites go through cycles of rapid growth, regression and even abandonment, resulting in discontinuous stratigraphical sequences and, as a consequence, poorly-defined local relative ceramic sequences (Andreou *et al.* 1996: 558 *et passim*; Johnson and Perlès 2004: 75).

Under this new reading, Knossos has an unexceptional pattern of later Neolithic-EB II demographic development, comprising two discrete phases of expansion that previous studies had conflated into one (Figure 3.4). Demographic expansion usually reflects broader socio-economic changes and it is perhaps significant that the first rapid phase of expansion (late MN–LN I) at Knossos coincides with a series of profound social and material changes in production, exchange, consumption, spatial organization, architecture, ideology and social organization (Tomkins 2004; for LN II see also Broodbank 1992 and Whitelaw 1992). This is followed by the long FN period, which, aside from a slightly quicker turnover of ceramic styles (Table 3.1), has not yet provided evidence for

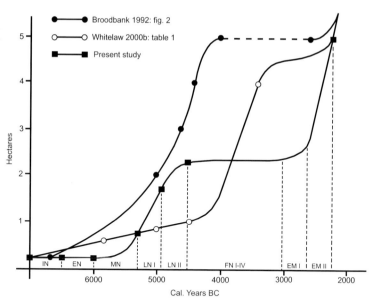

Figure 3.4. Reconstructions of demographic development at Knossos (Neolithic-EM II).

socio-economic changes of a scale and nature comparable to LN. The second discrete phase of expansion (EM I–II), taking Knossos beyond the village threshold (ca. 5 ha, Whitelaw 1983: 339), coincides with the next period of major socio-economic change at the site (*e.g.*, technology, production and distribution of ceramics: Wilson and Day 1994; 2000) and, more generally, with a phase of settlement expansion in the Aegean (Halstead 1981b: 196–200; Whitelaw 2000a: 136–40, 151–52) that probably marks the beginnings of urbanism (Konsola 1986).

The FN period in the Aegean is thought to mark an expansion in settlement, characterised in many areas, including Crete, by the occupation of defensible locations (hills, ridges, promontories, rock ledges) and the colonization of agriculturally more marginal landscapes, such as upland regions and smaller islands (Warren and Tzedakis 1974; Watrous 1982; Halstead 1994: 200; this volume; Branigan 1998; Broodbank 2000: 153–56; Nowicki this volume). For Crete this has been characterised as a 'flight to the hills' in the face of one or more waves of off-island immigrants, bringing with them what was or would eventually become the EM I culture (Hood *et al.* 1964: 51; Nowicki this volume). With the greater chronological resolution now available for FN Crete it is possible to break-up what had previously been treated as a single horizon of activity and glimpse stages and regionality in a long-term process of development (Figure 3.5; Tomkins 2007b: 32–44 for details of dating).

From FN I, there is direct or indirect evidence for open-air village settlement in most areas of high agricultural productive potential (Figure 3.5). Although major gaps in known settlement remain (*e.g.*, Malia, Isthmus of Ierapetra, Rethymnon, Chania), indirect hints of activity, in the form of pollen cores (*e.g.*, Akrotiri peninsula: Moody *et al.* 1996; Malia: Dalongeville *et al.* 2001; Müller

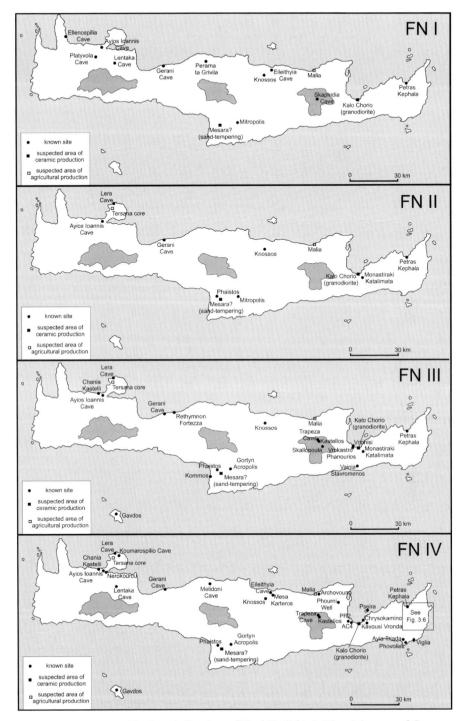

Figure 3.5. Direct and indirect indications of Final Neolithic I–IV activity around Crete.

pers. comm.), ceramic provenance (*e.g.*, Mirabello Bay) and cave usage (*e.g.*, Gerani, Platyvola), suggest that these absences reflect taphonomic and research biases. Evidence for FN I occupation in what previously may have been peripheral areas, such as the fertile upland Lasithi plateau, increases the likelihood that all areas of high agricultural productivity had been colonised by the end of the fifth millennium BC.

The occupation of 'defensible' locations in Crete now appears to have a relatively deep history, beginning at least as early as FN I with the occupation of steep-sided, coastal promontories, such as Petras Kephala. During FN II–III (Figure 3.5), however, movement to defensible locations becomes a particular feature of inland settlement, at least within *some* of the main zones of high agricultural productivity, notably the Isthmus of Ierapetra (*e.g.*, Katalimata, Vainia Stavromenos, Vrionisi VN2) and the Mesara (*e.g.*, Phaistos, Gortyn Acropolis, Kamilari). There is, however, little, if any, support for the idea that this was a response to an exogenous and/or hostile influx of population at this time: not only did occupation in lower-lying locations continue in other areas, such as the Herakleion Basin (*e.g.*, Knossos), but also there is no obvious surge in off-island styles, cultural traits or technologies during FN II–III. Rather the greater concern for security seen in some areas may reflect intensifying local competition within and/or between sites, manifest in a developing sense of territoriality and resource circumscription, perhaps caused or exacerbated by a major shift towards greater climatic uncertainty that may occur around this time (mid fourth millennium BC, Broodbank this volume).

It is against this model of increased competition, resource stress and uncertainty during FN II–III that one should probably understand the subsequent expansion into marginal areas with lower and less reliable agricultural productivity (Figure 3.6). Well-attested, but poorly dated in most regions of the Aegean, on Crete the main phase of marginal colonization in some areas seems to be FN IV (*e.g.*, Siteian uplands; Figure 3.6), in others probably EM I (*e.g.*, south coast). In the Peloponnese there are hints that the colonization of marginal areas was also a late FN–EB I phenomenon (Vitelli 1999: 98–99), suggesting parallels in timing and perhaps nature. There has been a tendency to view this major increase in the numbers of known sites as reflecting significant demographic expansion (Vagnetti and Belli 1978: 161; Cherry 1990: 161; Broodbank 1992: 69; J. D. Evans 1994: 19; Watrous 1994: 700). Although some form of population growth does indeed seem likely, it is important to note that most of these new sites are small, possibly short-lived and possessing a high archaeological visibility (*i.e.*, defensible places; areas of thin soil cover), that distracts attention away from lowland, riverine settings, where agricultural and demographic productivity could (and should) have been higher than it at present appears but where the sites are, arguably, less visible. In the case of Crete at least, the likelihood that a large proportion of IN–LN lowland settlement is yet to be discovered surely entitles us to be suspicious about a pattern of known FN settlement that still leaves lowland

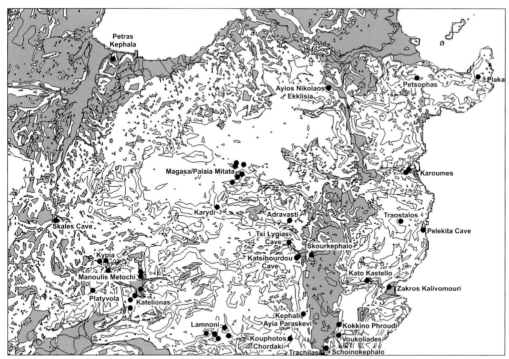

Figure 3.6. FN IV settlement in the Siteia region of East Crete. NB principal areas of agricultural land are shaded.

areas empty or markedly under-populated (Figure 3.6). Until we can satisfy ourselves that we have a comprehensive view of the size, nature and density of FN settlement in all topographical locations, meaningful estimates of the scale and nature of FN demographic development will be impossible.

The rationale behind marginal colonization is likely to reflect a variety of push and pull factors. In the face of more aggressive acquisitive strategies by more successful households, some households in large lowland villages may have become less able to survive short-term productive failures and may, eventually, have chosen to take their chances with migration and economic diversification. It may be more than simple irony that marginal colonization in Crete appears to coincide with a shift towards increased aridity and interannual variation in precipitation (Broodbank this volume), a change which may have made farming such landscapes more unpredictable than at any point in the previous three millennia. Factors enabling this process must have included a drastically different assessment and management of risk coupled perhaps with changes in technology and the development of a series of related subsistence strategies. In the absence of positive evidence for specialised subsistence modes, such as pastoralism (Halstead 1989; 2000; this volume) such strategies are likely to have retained a diversified approach to subsistence (*i.e.*, a mixed farming core) but, perhaps, now with specific emphasis on or specialization in a specific activity particularly suited to the prevailing environment, such as herding (Halstead this volume), wool/textile production, olive cultivation (approximately mid fourth millennium BC [*i.e.*, late FN] on the marginal Akrotiri peninsula: Moody *et al.* 1996: 282, fig. 8; 285–86, 289) or perhaps, in the case of coastal communities like Petras Kephala, the maintenance of off-island trading links. The presence of an FN IV well, the earliest so far identified in Crete, in an upland basin near the modern village of Phourni (Manteli 1992; Tomkins 2007b: 44), may reflect the application of new technologies of water management.

Clarification of the precise relationship between these new dispersed FN IV communities in marginal landscapes and the older, more concentrated population foci in lowland locations remains an urgent priority. Current thinking sees these two forms as co-existing as separate interaction zones (Halstead 1994: 203), managing risk primarily by constructing links with other similar communities. However, in the case of FN IV Crete, there is evidence for interaction between these two formations that tends to demonstrate differential access to what would be, and perhaps already were, the resources of power (agricultural surplus and high-value/exotic ideas, practices, products and materials). The consumption of fineware pouring vessels, used for a high-value beverage, seems to have been confined to lowland villages (*e.g.*, Knossos, Phaistos, Petras Kephala) (Tomkins 2004: 55; Todaro and Di Tonto this volume). In the Siteia region, preliminary comparison of the FN IV assemblage from the coastal site of Petras Kephala with contemporary upland sites (Figure 3.6; *e.g.*, Lamnoni and Katelionas: Branigan 1998) suggests the former enjoyed preferential access to valued categories of ceramic vessel (*e.g.*, fineware and off-island vessels) as well as off-island practices (*e.g.*, 'cheese-pots'), materials (*e.g.*, obsidian; Carter 1998; D'Annibale 2006; this volume) and technologies (*e.g.*, metallurgy; Papadatos this volume). That said, however, the rare presence of obsidian and, on one occasion a copper axe, at certain upland locations cautions against a simplistic reading of the relationship between lowland and marginal sites as one-sided and exploitative. Clearly, valued products were travelling in both directions, underlining how little we currently know about the economies of marginal colonization.

Reinventing the Cretan Neolithic

Improvements in the definition of the temporal and spatial parameters of the Cretan Neolithic, inevitably impact on how we understand its nature and frame its development. It is clear now that previous notions of Knossos and Crete developing in isolation and along unique or exceptional lines can no longer be sustained. The results from ceramic analyses and demographic reconstruction at Knossos can only be explained if we accept that the community on the Kephala Hill was always embedded within a wider social environment, consistently connected with other communities within the island, in ways that clearly developed during the course of the Neolithic (Tomkins 2004: 48–50, 53–55). Acceptance of this necessitates a new approach to the evidence for settlement beyond Knossos, one that recognises its fragmentary state and adopts the principal that absence of evidence is not necessarily evidence of absence. The greatest gap in our present picture of the pre-Bronze Age Cretan landscape, it is suggested here, concerns occupation in the most agriculturally productive habitats, here glossed as 'lowlands', such as valley bottoms and fluvial zones. Those Neolithic sites that have come to our attention over a century of exploration are generally located – Knossos being a notable and serendipitous exception – in other topographical settings, such as valley slopes, 'defensible' locations (peaks, promontories, ridges), caves or upland areas, that have been less prone to taphonomic concealment and/or more comprehensively explored by archaeologists. Until we know more about this poorly represented category of site, the precise nature and configuration of the Cretan world beyond Knossos before FN IV will be unclear.

For the present, therefore, Knossos remains a 'touchstone' for the Cretan Neolithic, but a rather different one from before. Its significance now lies, not in the exceptional trajectory of development that once seemed its defining characteristic, but in its very normality, specifically in the way it illustrates what life may have been like and how it may have changed over the course of the Neolithic at other, as yet undiscovered, villages in lowland fluvial zones. Detailed studies of ceramic and lithic material culture are beginning to reveal something about the nature and extent of interaction between Knossos and other communities (*e.g.*, Tomkins 2001; Tomkins *et al.* 2004; Conolly this volume; Strasser this volume). Unsurprisingly, this seems to have been most intense at the local level, with mobility over relatively short distances accounting for the unique and distinctively regional aspects of Cretan Neolithic material development. More notable is the evidence that throughout the Neolithic regular, if infrequent, journeys were being made beyond the island to the east and west, as demonstrated variously by the presence at Knossos of obsidian and imported lithics (*e.g.*, IN: Conolly this volume), off-island ceramic vessels (*e.g.*, EN–MN: Tomkins 2007b: 23, 25, 27) and off-island ceramic motifs and forms (*e.g.*, LN–FN: Tomkins 2007b: 29–44). At the end of FN, this interaction with the Aegean reaches a new level of intensity, only exceeded by that reached in subsequent phases of the Bronze Age (Vagnetti 1996; Tomkins 2007b: 44; D'Annibale this volume; Papadatos this volume). All of which suggests a Cretan Neolithic simultaneously connected to, but separate from, the rest of the Aegean, insular and continental, Aegean 'megalonisos' but also southern Aegean 'mainland', enclosing the southern insular Aegean and bridging southern Greece and southwest Anatolia.

Such inter-regional connections, however infrequent, represent a conduit along which ideas, innovations and individuals could move and their influence on the Cretan Neolithic can perhaps be glimpsed in seemingly analogous developmental features shared with other Aegean regions, such as the appearance of ceramic

containers in the mid-seventh millennium BC or the socio-economic transformations that accompany the Middle to Late Neolithic transition (ca. 5500/5300 BC;
Halstead 1995; 1999; Tomkins 2004). Recognition of inter-regional connectivity
and its significance should encourage us to break free of our regional special-
izations and the tendency to view the Aegean, whether before, during or after the
initial spread of agriculture, in terms of separate, largely isolated enclaves, in
order to achieve a more global view of the nature and agencies of early Holocene
culture change, from the impact of climatic shifts (Broodbank this volume) to the
ripples cast across the Aegean pond by socio-economic transformation in
neighbouring regions of the Mediterranean (Sherratt and Sherratt this volume).

Chronological integration with other Aegean regions effectively means the
end of Cretan Neolithic studies as a separate, intellectually-isolated research
tradition and its beginning as a regional branch of the Greek Neolithic, a move
which will hopefully be welcomed for the benefits in understanding it will bring
to both sides. Researchers on Crete are finally in a position to draw fully upon the
rich body of theory and data that has been generated in Greece over the last
century. Although there are naturally risks involved in comparing datasets of
differing quantity and quality from different regions, the cautious exploration of
such analogies may, for example, help us better understand absences and presences
in the fragmented picture of pre-FN settlement, opening up new possibilities for
predictive modelling and targeted, comprehensive sampling techniques (*e.g.*,
geophysical survey, coring, deep trenching of rock-shelters and caves). Positive
impacts in the opposite direction should also be expected with Greek Neolithic
studies likely to gain most from Cretan insights into the Initial and Final Neolithic
phases, both of which are more comprehensively attested and defined at Knossos
than at any other site in the modern Greek-speaking Aegean. In the case of Cretan
FN in particular, its five well-defined ceramic sub-phases bring a level of
chronological precision and opportunity to the study of FN socio-economic
development, previously only available in regions further east (Table 3.1; Lloyd
and Mellaart 1962; Akkermans and Schwartz 2003: 186–97, fig. 6.3; Schoop 2005).
Elsewhere in Greece the absence of a similarly complete FN settlement sequence
means that, at best, only two sub-phases of this long period of Aegean prehistory
can currently be defined (*i.e.*, LN IIA and LN IIB, Sampson 1992).

Although the inspiring vision of Knossos as a later Neolithic 'super-site'
should now be laid to rest, there remains the question that has so long
preoccupied Cretan prehistorians, namely of when, why and how Knossos rose
to a position of regional dominance. Under the present reading of the data, the
material and social conditions for its emergence as a regional centre, namely
demographic growth beyond the village threshold and influence over a wider
hinterland (effectively a form of urbanization), are unlikely to have been met
before the EBA (perhaps EM I–II), when there is evidence for a major restructuring of production and distribution and Knossos itself develops from a
large village into a small town, transcending its immediate locality and entering

into a symbiotic developmental relationship with the newly-founded (EM I) harbour settlement of Poros (Wilson and Day 2000; Wilson *et al.* 2004) that would last throughout the Bronze Age.

Acknowledgements

The data upon which this paper is based were gathered as part of a three-year doctoral research project on the EN–LN II ceramics from Knossos, supervised by Dr. P. M. Day and funded by grants from the Natural Environment Research Council and the GEOPRO TMR Research Network (European Commission contract no. ERBFMRX-CT980165). Subsequent research has been funded by a two-year European Commission Marie Curie Research Fellowship (contract no. HPMF-CT-2001-01385), a one-year INSTAP fellowship and grants from the Knossos Donated Fund and the White-Levy Programme. I would especially like to thank John Evans for his advice and encouragement and for allowing me unfettered access to excavated material and unpublished information from his excavations at Knossos. For permission to study and sample Neolithic ceramic material from Knossos I would also like to thank the Council of the British School at Athens, Herakleion Ephoreia and the Conservation Directorate of the Hellenic Ministry of Culture. Whilst grappling with the Knossos Neolithic sequence I have benefited from advice, help and insight from Peter Day, David Wilson, Tim Campbell-Green, Valasia Isaakidou, Yiannis Papadatos, Peter Warren and Todd Whitelaw, as well as successive Knossos Curators Colin Macdonald, Eleni Hatzaki and Don Evely. Paul Halstead and Valasia Isaakidou provided valuable comments on an earlier version of this paper.

Notes

1   All dates are calibrated calendrical BC.
2   References to phases in the traditional Cretan chronology are indicated by the use of inverted commas (*e.g.*, 'EN I'; see Table 3.1).

Bibliography

Akkermans P. and G. M. Schwartz
   2003   *The Archaeology of Syria – From Complex Hunter-Gatherers to Early Urban Societies, ca. 16,000–3000 BC*. Cambridge: Cambridge University Press.
Andreou, S., M. Fotiadis and K. Kotsakis
   1996   Review of Aegean Prehistory V: The Neolithic and Bronze Age of northern Greece. *AJA* 100: 537–97.
Bailey, D. W.
   2000   *Balkan Prehistory. Exclusion, Incorporation and Identity*. London: Routledge.
Branigan, K.
   1970   *The Foundations of Palatial Crete*. London: Routledge.
   1998   Prehistoric and early historic settlement in the Ziros region, eastern Crete. *BSA* 93: 23–90.

Broodbank, C.
  1992   The Neolithic labyrinth: social change at Knossos before the Bronze Age. *JMA* 5: 39–75.
  2000   *An Island Archaeology of the Early Cyclades*. Cambridge: Cambridge University Press.
  2006   The origins and early development of Mediterranean maritime activity. *JMA* 19: 199–230.
Broodbank, C. and T. F. Strasser
  1991   Migrant farmers and the Neolithic colonization of Crete. *Antiquity* 65: 233–45.
Cadogan, G., P. M. Day, C. F. Macdonald, J. A. MacGillivray, N. Momigliano, T. M. Whitelaw and
      D. E. Wilson
  1993   Early Minoan and Middle Minoan pottery groups at Knossos. *BSA* 88: 21–28.
Carter, T.
  1998   The chipped stone. *BSA* 93: 47–50.
Cherry, J. F.
  1985   Islands out of the stream: isolation and interaction in early East Mediterranean insular
         prehistory. In A. B. Knapp and T. Stech (eds.), *Prehistoric Production and Exchange: the
         Aegean and Eastern Mediterranean*: 12–29. Los Angeles: UCLA.
  1990   The first colonisation of the Mediterranean islands: a review of recent research. *JMA* 3:
         145–221.
Dalongeville, R., L. Lespez, G. Poursoulis, J.-F. Pastre, B. Keraudren, R. Mathieu, A. Prieur, J.
      Renault-Miskovsky, F. Darmon, S. Kunesh, P. Bernier, V. Caron, V. Pelc, T. Le Campion,
      A. Pantazidou, J. Evin, C. Oberlin, C. Noirel-Schutz, P. Sibella, M. Vallat and J. Viret.
  2001   Malia: un marais parle. *BCH* 125: 67–88.
D'Annibale, C.
  2006   Production and consumption of obsidian in the Siteia bay area: Final Neolithic through
         Late Minoan. *Pepragmena tou TH' Diethnous Kritologikou Synedriou*: 333–45.
Dawkins, R. M.
  1905   Excavations at Palaikastro IV. 2. Neolithic settlement at Magasa. *BSA* 11: 260–68.
Day, P., M. Relaki and E. W. Faber
  2006   Pottery making and social reproduction in the Bronze Age Mesara. In M. H. Wiener
         (ed.), *Pottery and Society: The Impact of Recent Studies in Minoan Pottery. Gold Medal
         Colloquium in Honor of Philip P. Betancourt*: 22–72. Boston: Archaeological Institute of
         America.
Efstratiou, N., A. Karetsou and E. S. Banou and D. Margomenou
  2004   The Neolithic settlement of Knossos: new light on an old picture. In G. Cadogan, E.
         Hatzaki and A. Vasilakis (eds.), *Knossos: Palace, City, State*: 39–49. London: British
         School at Athens.
Esin, U.
  1999   Introduction. The Neolithic in Turkey: a general review. In M. Özdoğan and N.
         Başgelen (eds.), *Neolithic in Turkey, the Cradle of Civilization. New Discoveries*: 13–23.
         Istanbul: Arkeoloji ve Sanat Yayınları.
Eslick, C.
  1992   *Elmali-Karatas I. The Neolithic and Chalcolithic: Bagbasi and Other Sites*. Bryn Mawr: Bryn
         Mawr College.
Evans, A. J.
  1901   The Neolithic settlement at Knossos and its place in the history of early Aegean
         culture. *Man* 1: 184–86.
  1904   The palace of Knossos. *BSA* 10: 1–62.
  1928   Chapter 33: discovery of Late Neolithic houses beneath Central Court: traditional
         affinities with mainland east. In A. J. Evans, *The Palace of Minos* (Volume II:I): 1–21.
         London: Macmillan.

Evans, J. D.
  1964   Excavations in the Neolithic settlement at Knossos, 1957–60. *BSA* 59: 132–240.
  1968   Knossos Neolithic, Part II, summary and conclusions. *BSA* 63: 267–76.
  1971   Neolithic Knossos: the growth of a settlement. *PPS* 37: 95–117.
  1994   The early millennia: continuity and change in a farming settlement. In D. Evely, H.
          Hughes-Brock and N. Momigliano (eds.), *Knossos, a Labyrinth of History, Papers Presented
          in Honour of Sinclair Hood*: 1–20. London: British School at Athens.
Furness, A.
  1953   The Neolithic pottery of Knossos. *BSA* 48: 94–134.
Haggis, D. C.
  1996   Archaeological survey at Kavousi, East Crete. Preliminary report. *Hesperia* 65: 373–431.
Halstead, P.
  1981a   Counting sheep in Neolithic and Bronze Age Greece. In I. Hodder, G. Isaac and N.
          Hammond (eds.), *Pattern of the Past*: 307–39. Cambridge: Cambridge University Press.
  1981b   From determinism to uncertainty: social storage and the rise of the Minoan palace. In
          A. Sheridan and G. Bailey (eds.), *Economic Archaeology* (BAR International Series 96):
          187–213. Oxford: British Archaeological Reports.
  1989   The economy has a normal surplus: economic stability and social change among early
          farming communities of Thessaly Greece. In P. Halstead and J. O'Shea (eds.), *Bad Year
          Economics*: 68–80. Cambridge: Cambridge University Press.
  1994   The north-south divide: regional paths to complexity in prehistoric Greece. In C.
          Mathers and S. Stoddart (eds.), *Development and Decline in the Mediterranean Bronze Age*:
          195–219. Sheffield: J. R. Collis.
  1995   From sharing to hoarding: the Neolithic foundations of Aegean Bronze Age Society. In
          R. Laffineur and W.-D. Niemeier (eds.), *POLITEIA. Society and State in the Aegean Bronze
          Age* (Aegaeum 12): 11–21. Liège: Université de Liège and P.A.S.P.
  1999   Neighbours from hell? The household in Neolithic Greece. In P. Halstead (ed.), *Neolithic
          Society in Greece* (SSAA 2): 77–95. Sheffield: Sheffield Academic Press.
  2000   Land use in postglacial Greece: cultural causes and environmental effects. In P.
          Halstead and C. Frederick (eds.), *Landscape and Land Use in Postglacial Greece* (SSAA 3):
          110–28. Sheffield: Sheffield Academic Press.
Hood, M. S. F.
  1981   Neolithic Knossos (ca. 6000–3000 B.C.). In S. Hood and D. Smyth, *Archaeological Survey
          of the Knossos Area*. London: British School at Athens/Thames and Hudson.
  1990   Autochthons or settlers? Evidence for immigration at the beginning of the Early Bronze
          Age in Crete. *Pepragmena tou ST' Diethnous Kritologikou Synedriou*: 367–75.
Hood, M. S. F., P. M. Warren, and G. Cadogan
  1964   Travels in Crete. *BSA* 59: 50–99.
Johnson, M. and C. Perlès
  2004   An overview of Neolithic settlement patterns in eastern Thessaly. In J. Cherry, C.
          Scarre and S. Shennan (eds.), *Explaining Social Change: Studies in Honour of Colin Renfrew*:
          65–79. Cambridge: McDonald Institute for Archaeological Research.
Konsola, D.
  1986   Stages of urban transformation in the Early Helladic period. In R. Hägg and D. Konsola
          (eds.), *Early Helladic Architecture and Urbanization* (SIMA 76): 9–19. Göteborg: Paul Åström.
Kopaka, K. and Ch. Papadaki
  2006   Proistoriki keramiki apo tin Epiphaneiaki erevna sti Gavdo. To paradeigma mias
          mikronisiotikis viotechnikis paragogis. *Pepragmena tou TH' Diethnous Kritologikou
          Synedriou*: 63–78.

Lloyd, S. and J. Mellaart
  1962   *Beycesultan I: The Chalcolithic and Early Bronze Age Levels*. London: British Institute of Archaeology at Ankara.
Mackenzie, D.
  1903   The pottery of Knossos. *JHS* 23: 157–205.
Manning, S. W.
  1994   The emergence of divergence: development and decline on Bronze Age Crete and the Cyclades. In C. Mathers and S. Stoddart (eds.), *Development and Decline in the Mediterranean Bronze Age*: 221–70. Sheffield: J. R. Collis.
  1995   *The Absolute Chronology of the Aegean Early Bronze Age*. Sheffield: Sheffield Academic Press.
  1999   Knossos and the limits of settlement growth. In P. Betancourt, V. Karageorghis, R. Laffineur and W.-D. Niemeier (eds.), *MELETEMATA: Studies in Aegean Archaeology Presented to Malcolm H. Weiner* (Aegaeum 20): 469–82. Liège: Université de Liège.
Manteli, K.
  1992   The Neolithic well at Kastelli Phournis in Eastern Crete. *BSA* 87: 103–20.
  1993a   *The Transition from the Neolithic to the Early Bronze Age in Crete, with Special Reference to Pottery, Volume I*. PhD dissertation, University of London.
  1993b   *The Transition from the Neolithic to the Early Bronze Age in Crete, with Special Reference to Pottery, Volume II*. PhD dissertation, University of London.
  1996   Crete (Pottery). In G. A. Papathanassopoulos (ed.), *Neolithic Culture in Greece*: 132–34. Athens: Goulandris Foundation.
Mee, C.
  2001   Nucleation and dispersal in Neolithic and Early Helladic Laconia. In K. Branigan (ed.), *Urbanism in the Aegean Bronze Age* (SSAA 4): 1–14. Sheffield: Sheffield Academic Press.
Moody, J., O. Rackham and G. Rapp
  1996   Environmental archaeology of prehistoric NW Crete. *Journal of Field Archaeology* 23: 273–97.
Nowicki, K.
  2002   The end of the Neolithic in Crete. *Aegean Archaeology* 6: 7–72.
Pendlebury, J. D. S.
  1939   *The Archaeology of Crete*. London: Methuen.
Perlès, C.
  2001   *The Early Neolithic in Greece*. Cambridge: Cambridge University Press.
Renfrew, A. C.
  1964   Crete and the Cyclades before Rhadamanthus. *Kritika Chronika* 18: 107–41.
  1972   *The Emergence of Civilisation: The Cyclades and the Aegean in the Third Millennium BC*. London: Methuen.
  2005   Round a bigger pond. In J. F. Cherry, D. Margomenou and L. E. Talalay (eds.), *Prehistorians Round the Pond. Reflections on Aegean Prehistory as a Discipline*: 153–59. Ann Arbor: Kelsey Museum of Archaeology.
Runnels, C., E. Panagopoulou, P. Murray, G. Tsartsidou, S. Allen, K. Mullen and E. Tourloukis
  2005   A Mesolithic landscape in Greece: testing a site-location model in the Argolid at Kandia. *JMA* 18: 259–85.
Sampson, A.
  1992   Late Neolithic remains at Tharrounia, Euboea: a model for the seasonal use of settlements and caves. *BSA* 87: 61–101.
Schoop, U. D.
  2005   *Das Anatolische Chalkolithikum. Eine Chronologische Untersuchung zur Vorbronzezeitlichen*

Kultursequenz im Nördlichen Zentralanatolien und den Angrenzenden Gebieten. Remshalden: Bernhard. A. Greiner.

Sherratt, A.
1981   Water, soil and seasonality in early cereal cultivation. *World Archaeology* 11: 313–30.
2004   Fractal farmers: patterns of Neolithic origin and dispersal. In J. Cherry, C. Scarre and S. Shennan (eds.), *Explaining Social Change: Studies in Honour of Colin Renfrew*: 53–63. Cambridge: McDonald Institute for Archaeological Research.

Soles, J. S.
1995   The functions of a cosmological center: Knossos in palatial Crete. In R. Laffineur and W.-D. Niemeier (eds.), *POLITEIA. Society and State in the Aegean Bronze Age* (Aegaeum 12): 405–14. Liège: Université de Liège.

Strasser, T. F.
2004   Three axe groups from Neolithic Knossos. In G. Cadogan, E. Hatzaki and A. Vasilakis (eds.), *Knossos: Palace, City, State*: 61–65. London: British School in Athens.

Strasser, T. F. and C. Fassoulas
2003–4   Granodiorite axes from Knossos and their implications for Neolithic trade on Crete. *Aegean Archaeology* 7: 9–12.

Tomkins, P.
2000a   Isolation or interaction? Putting the Early Neolithic community at Knossos in context. *BICS* 44: 228–29.
2000b   The Neolithic period. In D. Huxley (ed.), *Cretan Quests. British Explorers, Excavators and Historians*: 76–85. London: British School at Athens.
2001   *The Production, Circulation and Consumption of Ceramic Vessels at Early Neolithic Knossos, Crete.* PhD dissertation, University of Sheffield.
2004   Filling in the 'Neolithic background': social life and social transformation in the Aegean before the Bronze Age. In J. C. Barrett and P. Halstead (eds.), *The Emergence of Civilisation Revisited* (SSAA 6): 38–63. Oxford: Oxbow Books.
2007a   Communality and competition. The social life of food and containers at Aceramic and Early Neolithic Knossos, Crete. In C. Mee and J. Renard (eds.), *Cooking Up the Past. Food and Culinary Practices in the Neolithic and Bronze Age Aegean*: 174–99. Oxford: Oxbow Books.
2007b   Neolithic: Strata IX–VIII, VII–VIB, VIA–V, IV, IIIB, IIIA, IIB, IIA and IC Groups. In N. Momigliano (ed.), *Knossos Pottery Handbook: Neolithic and Bronze Age (Minoan)*: 9–48. London: British School at Athens.
in press Domesticity by default. Rethinking Neolithic cave use in the Aegean. In H. Moyes (ed.), *Journeys into the Dark Zone: Cross Cultural Perspectives on the Ritual Use of Caves*. Colorado: University Press of Colorado.

Tomkins, P. and P. M. Day
2001   Production and exchange of the earliest ceramic vessels in the Aegean: a view from Early Neolithic Knossos, Crete. *Antiquity* 75: 259–60.

Tomkins, P., P. M. Day and V. Kilikoglou
2004   Knossos and the early Neolithic landscape of the Herakleion Basin. In G. Cadogan, E. Hatzaki and A. Vasilakis (eds.), *Knossos: Palace, City, State*: 51–59. London: British School at Athens.

Tsountas, Ch.
1908   *Ai Proïstorikai Akropoleis Dhiminiou ke Sesklou.* Athens: I en Athenais Archaiologiki Etaireia.

Vagnetti, L.
1973   L'insediamento neolitico di Festòs. *ASA* 50–51: 7–138.
1996   The Final Neolithic: Crete enters the wider world. *Cretan Studies* 5: 29–39.

Vagnetti, L. and P. Belli
   1978   Characters and problems of the final Neolithic in Crete. *SMEA* 19: 125–63.
Vagnetti, L., A. Christopoulou and I. Tzedakis
   1989   Saggi negli stati Neolitici. In I. Tzedakis and A. Sacconi (eds.), *Scavi a Nerokourou, Kydonias* (Recherche Greco-Italiane in Creta Occidentale I): 9–97. Roma: Edizioni Dell'Ateneo.
Vitelli, K. D.
   1999   *Franchthi Neolithic Pottery: Volume 2. The Later Neolithic Ceramic Phases 3 to 5.* Bloomington and Indianapolis: Indiana University Press.
Warren, P. M. and Y. Tzedakis
   1974   Debla, an Early Minoan settlement in western Crete. *BSA* 69: 299–342.
Warren, P. M. and V. Hankey
   1989   *Aegean Bronze Age Chronology.* Bristol: Bristol Classical Press.
Watrous, L. V.
   1982   *Lasithi, a History of Settlement on a Highland Plain in Crete.* Princeton: American School of Classical Studies at Athens.
   1994   Review of Aegean Prehistory III: Crete from earliest Prehistory through the Proto-palatial period. *AJA* 98: 695–753.
Watrous, L. V. and D. Hadzi-Vallianou
   2004   Initial growth in social complexity (Late Neolithic-Early Minoan I). In L. V. Watrous, D. Hadzi-Vallianou and H. Blitzer (eds.) *The Plain of Phaistos. Cycles of Social Complexity in the Mesara Region of Crete*: 221–31. Los Angeles: Cotsen Institute of Archaeology, UCLA.
Weinberg, S. S.
   1947   Aegean Chronology: Neolithic period and Early Bronze Age. *AJA* 46: 119–25.
   1965   The relative chronology of the Aegean in the Stone and Early Bronze Ages. In R. W. Ehrich (ed.) *Chronologies in Old World Archaeology*: 285–320. Chicago: University of Chicago Press.
   1970   The Stone Age in the Aegean. In I. E. S. Edwards, C. J. Gadd and N. G. L. Hammond (eds.), *Cambridge Ancient History. Volume I. Part 1. Prolegomena and Prehistory*: 557–618. Cambridge: Cambridge University Press.
Whitelaw, T. M.
   1983   The settlement at Fournou Korifi, Myrtos, and aspects of Early Minoan social organisation. In O. Kryzszkowska and L. Nixon (eds.), *Minoan Society*: 323–45. Bristol: Bristol Classical Press.
   1992   Lost in the Labyrinth? Comments on Broodbank's 'Social change at Knossos before the Bronze Age'. *JMA* 5: 225–38.
   2000a Settlement instability and landscape degradation in the southern Aegean in the third millennium BC. In P. Halstead and C. Frederick (eds.), *Landscape and Land Use in Postglacial Greece* (SSAA 3): 135–61. Sheffield: Sheffield Academic Press.
   2000b Beyond the palace: a century of investigation in Europe's oldest city. *BICS* 44: 223–26.
   2004   Estimating the population of Neopalatial Knossos. In G. Cadogan, E. Hatzaki and A. Vasilakis (eds.), *Knossos: Palace, City, State*: 147–58. London: British School at Athens.
Wilson, D. E. and P. M. Day
   1994   Ceramic regionalism in Prepalatial central Crete: the Mesara imports from EM IB to EM IIA Knossos. *BSA* 89:1–87.
   2000   EM I chronology and social practice: pottery from the early palace tests at Knossos. *BSA* 95: 21–63.
Wilson, D. E., P. M. Day and N. Dimopoulou-Rethemiotaki
   2004   The pottery from Early Minoan I–IIB Knossos and its relations with the harbour site of Poros-Katsambas. In G. Cadogan, E. Hatzaki and A. Vasilakis (eds.), *Knossos: Palace, City, State*: 67–74. London: British School at Athens.

4

A Sea of Agency: Crete in the Context of the Earliest Neolithic in Greece

Kostas Kotsakis

Introduction: Some Theoretical Concepts

A few decades ago, islands were considered ideal biogeographical units, neatly self-defined and isolated (Renfrew and Wagstaff 1982). Common sense dictated that whatever was not originally present on an island had come from somewhere else. This obviously applied to humans and to biological resources alike, and hence to material culture in its broadest sense. Recently, however, Broodbank (2000) identified the need to move beyond the simple insularity concept, a view not dissimilar to ideas in contemporary Greek historiography on the insularity of the Aegean. Asdrahas, discussing the Greek Archipelago during the Ottoman period, long ago proposed that the Aegean formed a unity, a single 'far-flung city' of criss-crossing islands and settlements within networks of communication and of economic and political interdependence (Asdrahas 1985). The idea was repeated by Romano (1994), who saw the continuous space of the Aegean as forming a 'dispersed liquid city'. The implication is that human agency, active in historical contexts, can overcome the physical barriers imposed by natural features that are usually perceived as determining factors.

In abstract terms, the barrier concept introduces the simplicity of the presence/absence dichotomy to what has been described as the dense space of history where 'there are countless human actions and social processes' (Little 2007). It is this dense historical space which forms the deeper object of study of any historical transformation. Paying less attention to situated human actions and processes might be a convenient strategy for producing broad unifying narratives of the spread of the Neolithic or for accommodating particular instances to general schemes with wide-ranging application, such as universal models of colonization (*e.g.*, Anthony 1990; Fiedel and Anthony 2003), but it is restricted to the production of causal explanations of history only, leaving the interpretation of actions and intentions outside its focus. Such simplified versions of culture change, as we will see below, are particularly popular in culture historical reconstructions current in Near Eastern and Anatolian archaeology, and by extension in Greece (and Crete in particular). The deeper argument informing this paper is that to deal with the process of Neolithization as a historical reality and a cultural outcome, and to reach a hermeneutical under-standing of any human actions that current research is in a position to identify, these simplified narratives are inadequate.

Of course, no one is so naïve anymore as to perceive the Neolithic as a checklist of traits transferred through space and time, as culture history used to do, but overemphasis on familiar and recognizable Neolithic diagnostics, such as lithic techniques and subsistence resources, implicitly singles out particular aspects of the Neolithic experience and takes their explanatory significance for granted. Once we move away from the culture historical paradigm to a contextualized perspective, processes and actions behind the phenomena emerge in their complexity and their continuous and mutual interaction. A diversity of explan-atory structures is needed that is able to accommodate this inherent multiplicity, since the formalized reconstructions of culture history are clearly not adequate. Interpretation and understanding demands the recognition of the complexity of contingent processes and of the reassembly of their significances. The directionality of causality latent in narratives of emergence and origins is clearly inappropriate.

Undoubtedly, as we are primarily dealing with the materiality of all things archaeological, these webs of significance can only be reconstructed through the definition of empirical facts and this highlights the need for archaeology to develop appropriate tools for such empirical investigation. As a discipline, archaeology is still far from acquiring the dense evidence that is needed to touch the multiplicity of human action; the formality of conventional analytical categories certainly does not help here. On the other hand, emphasizing the importance of thorough investigation of the evidence should not be taken as advocating the essential primacy of the empirical. As we know from the hermeneutic tradition of historical thinking (Warnke 1988; Hodder 1991; Johnsen and Olsen 1992), the engagement of analytical categories with historically situated meanings is so deep that verification and correspondence to facts remain characteristically underdetermined by existing evidence.

Notwithstanding these ontological reservations, we should turn our attention to the set of analytical categories that shapes empirical understanding of the beginning of the Neolithic in the island of Crete. This by no means implies that the value of empirical investigation is questioned. On the contrary, as I hope will become apparent, the dearth of good quality archaeological evidence restricts productive discussion of this issue. Crete, perhaps more than any other part of Greece, is a clear case of Neolithic colonization, at least on the available evidence. This does not mean that we understand clearly what happened in the island around the end of the 8th millennium BC. We will try therefore to define the concepts involved in dealing with empirical evidence, especially concerning the delicate process of settling down in this 'unfamiliar landscape' (Rockman and Steele 2003). It is the interpretative content given by research to empirical evidence which is under consideration here, as arguments for the inception of agriculture in Crete rely primarily on concepts of insularity and on the confirmation of human absence prior to it (Reese 1996). They vividly illustrate the circularity of the argument of absence as an interpretative device: there would not be much to explain if agriculture was not a phenomenon introducing a marked discontinuity in the record of human activity.

The 'Neolithic Package'

Research on the beginning of agriculture in SE Europe exhibits a distinct fixation with the 'Neolithic package', usually defined as a set of key domesticates. Since Childe's time, the spread of this 'Neolithic package' has been reaffirmed countless times (*e.g.*, Colledge *et al.* 2004, for the Eastern Mediterranean). The essentialism of the 'package' concept is so pervasive that, in some cases, it has even taken in what is perceived as the mode of Neolithic living (Özdoğan 2005: 23–26), becoming thus yet more essentialized and reductionist. Yet, even if the spread of the 'package', so familiar in maps and diagrams in the literature, were accepted as a straightforward process of movement in time and place, a set of critical questions would still remain to be answered. Usually such questions are sidestepped, or at best, deferred for 'future research'. Among these, probably the most central, but also the least addressed, concern the contents of this 'package'. Are practices also transferred? Obviously yes, but what sort of practices were they? Did they include cognitive modes and norms, like symbolic negotiations of the everyday (Hodder 1990; Cauvin 2000) or particular perceptions of the landscape, together with the more easily definable technological or subsistence routines, like flint knapping and husbandry regimes? Even so, we know since the work of Lemonnier (1993) that we cannot regard technological choices simplistically as devoid of significance for the reconstruction of identities. In migratory contexts, elements of material culture are known to have been deliberately and actively employed to achieve specific social ends of particular agents (Burmeister 2000: 541). The reference to identity (and to the agency related to it), therefore, points to these practices as being closely intertwined and, in the process, changing drastically in significance if not in form.

We thus touch upon the question of correspondence of form and content of cultural expressions, a perennial interpretative problem of anthropological analysis (*e.g.*, Lévi-Strauss 1963) and one evidently of fundamental significance here, but beyond the scope of this paper. More to the point, the correspondence between material culture and movement is a recurring cul-de-sac for archaeo-logical discussion, as Chapman and his collaborators have argued (Chapman and Dolukhanov 1992; Chapman and Hamerow 1997). Fiedel and Anthony have recently suggested that constructed beliefs coming from the marginal frontier were central to Neolithic movement episodes, and that the 'architecture of the flow of that information' defined the size, composition or destination of the migrant group (2003: 145–46). Burmeister (2000: 552–53), using North American colonization as an example, had already proposed a distinction between 'public' and 'private' material culture brought by settlers. Despite the huge problems of distinguishing between 'public' and 'private' spheres in the largely unknown social context of the final 8th millennium BC, the remarks by Burmeister and by Fiedel and Anthony suggest that the settler's package did not contain only things, *i.e.*, expressions of material culture. On the contrary, the 'package' contained objects and practices, but also relations and levels of significance, eventually much more than the artefacts, techniques, plants and animals, that it is conventionally thought to contain (*e.g.*, Perlès 2005, esp. table 1).

These practices, relations and levels of significance would compensate for what Andrew Sherratt had called 'the lack of three-dimensionality' in our archaeological understandings of things so remote from modern experience (Sherratt 1989). These are precisely the elements that contextualize the process, and therefore challenge the limits of our colonisation paradigms. From this perspective, regardless of origins and colonizing movements, the founding communities of Neolithic Crete would still be autonomous entities, with their own particular conditions of farming, living and reproducing – or reorganizing – their social fabric, materially and symbolically. Similarly, despite claims to the contrary (*e.g.*, Özdoğan 1995; 2005), it is difficult to foresee the ultimate answer to the question of the place of origin of those migrant populations, an origin that will offer a fossilized picture of their cultural identities; nor can there be any certainty whether we are dealing with a single place of origin or with multiple, overlapping locations. Contrary to historical colonization, where the link to the metropolis was retained at least to some extent, there is here no materially traceable lineage that connects the colony with the metropolis (*e.g.*, Kopytoff 1987: 12–14; Turner 1994; Carter 2006: 13–15). Symbolic or imaginary ties to a genealogy of descent are obviously far more difficult to define archaeologically, certainly within the present theoretical and analytical paradigm. And, as analogies with historically documented migrations indicate, often practices and techniques, well established in the place of origin, are abandoned on purpose to ensure economic viability (Burmeister 2000: 541). One can only imagine what this does to the rest of the 'package'.

Furthermore, within this theoretical paradigm, the meagre archaeological evidence available does not permit a clear decision on whether the arrival of immigrants represents a single well planned and organized wave, as Broodbank and Strasser have suggested (Broodbank and Strasser 1991; Broodbank 1999; 2006) or numerous small episodes, distinct in time, and resulting in a gradual infiltration spread over several generations, as Cherry has proposed (1981: 60). Similar problems are presented by the possibility, which Broodbank and Strasser do not preclude (1991: 236), of accidental visitors (or 'scouts', as proposed for Cyprus – Peltenburg *et al.* 2001: 56) before the advent of the Neolithic. Serious questions of temporal scales are involved here, highlighting the limits of our reconstructions. In the case of mobile early agriculturalists in Greece and the Aegean, therefore, issues of theoretical resolution and empirical evidence hamper any attempt to canonize what was predominantly a contingent and fluid process, cross-cutting any place and time systematics. This contingent and fluid process still remains largely unaccounted for in contemporary research.

Evidently the 'package' is not a clear and simple ideal entity that was 'wrapped up' in Anatolia (or anywhere else for that matter) and then sent abroad in different directions (*e.g.*, Özdoğan 1997, esp. fig. 4). But even if the 'Neolithic package' is not what culture history makes of it, there is still cultural displacement to be accounted for. New archaeological evidence from southwest Anatolia (Duru 1999, summarized in Özdoğan and Başgelen 1999; Duru 2002; 2004) seems to confirm the east-west chronological cline, which was traditionally associated with the *Drang nach Westen* movement of agriculturalists.

The Movement

Movement has been a conceptual category integral to culture historical argu-ments, and the movement of people has been assumed, or claimed, on many different occasions in the 'Neolithization' process throughout the southeast Mediterranean, as summarized recently by Asouti (2006). Examples range from the 'expansionist ethos' of the PPNB perceived by Cauvin (2000: 204–6) as a 'messianic' – if arguably ill-defined (Hodder 2001; Rollefson 2001) – expression of cultural dynamics, through movement between 'interaction spheres' (*e.g.*, Bar-Yosef 2001), to the broad demic diffusion of Ammerman and Cavalli-Sforza (1984) or the subtler model of van Andel and Runnels (1995) with its targeted diffusion towards advantageous niches. And, to return to the topic of this paper, there is the suggested Cyprus-Crete connection (Efstratiou and Matzourani 1997; Efstratiou 2005: 150). In all these cases, migratory movements of some sort are present.

From a certain perspective, movement is a trivial aspect of the whole Neolithization phenomenon. Being precisely geographical, *i.e.*, taking place within a particular spatial framework, the movement of the Neolithic is but another expression of its spatiality. In relevant literature, early Neolithic communities often appear like an endless series of Russian dolls, in which every site 'contains' the other (*e.g.*, Kozlowski and Aurenche 2005). A range of cultural products and forms actively 'move', and archaeological scrutiny can end up, in A. Sherratt's words (Sherratt 2006), in 'noting what is widespread and what is localized…what begins locally and spreads widely' within the various entities and their cultural manifestations postulated for southwest Asia. Taking together all other contrasting views on the southwest Asian Neolithic expansion (Asouti 2006), we conclude that all entities are interconnected by a continuous criss-crossing pattern of diffusion and movement.

Of more interest are the reasons behind these migratory movements, of whatever scale and denomination. Before accepting migration, perhaps too hastily, as part of the *Homo sapiens* evolutionary inheritance, together with mutation, selection and genetic drift (Cavalli-Sforza 2000: 198), we should look more closely at the reasons why Neolithic mobility may have a particular character. Is the ubiquity of movement and migration, even within the so-called core area, a diagnostic and inherent element of the Neolithic? This is definitely a possibility, but if this is the case, the degree of mobility of hunter-gatherers, the mobile communities *par excellence*, needs to be reconsidered. We may concur with Ingold (1995; 2000) that 'dwelling' was the predominant condition of mobile hunter-gatherers in their interaction with the landscape, and suggest that 'dwelling' shaped the nature, if not the scale, of mobility. Hunter/gatherer mobility was inscribed in the landscape as an embodied and 'reciprocal practical engagement' (Mazzarella 2002: 151), while farmers can be conceived as constructing their 'dwelling' by standing apart, in a mode of engagement that privileged possession of the landscape in an uninterrupted process of appropriation within space. After all, is sedentism not ultimately a form of possession of the landscape?

'Dwelling' is the crucial term here. This is precisely the concept lacking from Cauvin's perception of an 'expansionist culture' of the PPNB. An 'expansionist culture' displaces the Neolithic phenomenon from the reciprocal practical engagement with the landscape to the realm of an anti-materialist 'psycho-cultural' mental transformation. According to Cauvin, this pivotal transformation appeals to the collective Neolithic psyche, preferably to the masculine one (Cauvin 2000: 132–34, 210), but he does not give any clues to the archaeological signature of this collective psyche. Too many assumptions are concealed behind this idea, and the argument can become an easy target for criticism. But that is not my concern here. To understand the ubiquity of mobility in the Neolithic, Ingold's insight of the 'dwelling perspective' is far more incisive than the psycho-cultural mental transformation: the domestication of animals was made possible by controlling humans' own animality, hence urging them to set themselves apart from the rest of their 'being in the world' and measure their own humanity, creating 'nature' (Ingold 1994; 2000). Domestication thus set the pace for the very long history of self-alienation that eventually formed an unmistakable part of western modernity (Mazzarella 2002). Extending control to all 'nature' created in this way, with everything that such a mode entails, would be the next predictable step.

Movement, therefore, is anything but the unexpected outcome of the Neolithic condition, and colonizing movements of various scales and ranges can be assumed to be deeply embedded in the Neolithic 'being in the world'. In this respect, contrary to various hypotheses offered for the spread of the Neolithic, demographic, environmental, *etc.*, special causal circumstances are not required to initiate that process. Movement is a recurrent feature in the Mediterranean: mobility of people, organized or non-organized, was a documented historical constant, and the absence of overpopulation or environmental collapse apparently did not impair mobility in the least (Horden and Purcell 2000: 338–41, 383–88;

but see also Owen 2005: 6–8, for the perils of interpretation of textual evidence). Rather, it is the periodical immobility that demands closer scrutiny. We know now that Neolithic movement seems to be punctuated and to build up in enclaves where local transformative processes were in play (Bogucki 2000; Zilhão 2000), rather than following the continuous radial expansion that was predicted by the wave-of-advance model of the 1980s (Ammerman and Cavalli-Sforza 1984). It is only, as discussed above, in the framework of culture history that migratory movements have an explanatory significance in themselves.

The special significance attached to mobility could well be the result of our own cultural bias. We tend to assume that 'village societies' are immobile, in contrast to 'urban dwellers' who engage in trade, commerce, and other forms of mobility. This is similar to the 'hybrid' amalgam of cities, as opposed to the 'purity' and 'stillness' (and of course the occasional 'backwardness') of the countryside, one of the core ideologies of modernity (Fotiadis 1995). Neolithic here is equated with 'rural' and therefore placed within the zone of immobility, despite the fact there were no urban centres, and consequently the other pole of that dialectical antithesis had not yet materialized. The old concept of sedentism, traditionally considered an essential trait of the Neolithic, undoubtedly made this mix-up easier (Shewan 2004, for a recent examination of Levantine sedentism). Sedentism, however, as recent research in Central Anatolia shows, can have many different aspects, not necessarily related to new relationships with plants and animals, or the Neolithic in the strict sense (Baird in press). It can be a far more fluid condition, therefore, than we normally assume.

There is a marked tendency in contemporary discussion on migration to lay more emphasis on the conditions and the active transformational quality of the phenomenon than on questions of origins and causes of migration (*e.g.*, Burmeister 2000; Rockman and Steele 2003). This results partly from the difficulty of recognizing origins in the archaeological record, but also, on a more profound level, from dissatisfaction with the culture historical theoretical postulates of the origins concept, which do not resonate well with broader contemporary discourse (Kotsakis 2002). Regardless of the way various schools of thought have interpreted this shift in emphasis (processual/functionalist, post-processualist, *etc.*) the main issue here is that the transformational processes intervening between the point of origin of an entity and its final formation in an archaeologically recognizable form introduce a strong element of fluidity in established social entities. This fluidity affects both the identities of the migratory groups and the material culture with which these identities are expressed and makes the identification of a fixed origin an impossible and perhaps somewhat redundant task. This is the theoretical approach adopted here.

In fact, migrating groups were exposed to changing contextual realities, in which issues of agency were central. Immigrant groups are not likely to create clones of the parent culture. If nothing else, culture is something to participate in, rather than belong to. Social knowledge of the community is not co-extensive with every separate member of that community. Every such member commands a part of the social knowledge, the totality of which exists only abstractly on the level of the community as a whole. Thus, colonizers do not have to recruit, as visualized by Fiedel and Anthony, from 'specific places and social segments' (2003: 150). Immigrant groups are not ideal communities in transit. They are de-contextualized transformative mechanisms that re-arrange the whole fabric of social life on the fragmented pieces of social knowledge that survive the expedition. Historically documented colonizations (with the exception of Robinson Crusoe and his little island settlement) produced similarly fractured versions of the original culture (Graham 1983; Hurst and Owen 2005), occasionally to press consciously particular political statements or identities (van Dommelen 1997; Tronchetti and van Dommelen 2005). This might explain better the regional variability of the Neolithic in Greece, which remains unaccounted for, either in brief epitomes (Fiedel and Anthony 2003: 151–54) or in analytical presentations of the Greek Early Neolithic (Perlès 2001). We will return to this issue at the end of this paper.

The Evidence

The fact that these, or similar, questions are not often asked by researchers is partly the result of the lack of enough supportive archaeological evidence. Clearing up theoretical aspects is vital to evaluation of existing evidence, as well as to future production of new evidence. Nonetheless, it is becoming progressively clearer that Greece was not an empty place at the beginning of the Holocene (Kotsakis 2003). Since the last systematic review of the Mesolithic in Greece (Runnels 2001), the number of sites belonging to the 8th millennium has risen steadily. Already in 2003, the volume edited by Galanidou and Perlès (2003) revealed a wealth of ongoing research and even a cursory glance at maps of Mesolithic sites in Greece published during the last five years reveals a steady increase in numbers (compare, for instance, Perlès 2001: map 2.1, with Runnels *et al.* 2005: fig. 1. Big voids in the relevant maps, such as Central Greece or Macedonia, are areas where specialized surveys have not been carried out yet). Unavoidably, of course, the rate of increase reflects the number and extent of field projects targeting this particular period, which are still very small.

It has only recently been realized that diachronic, intensive survey methods are inadequate to detect the small, lithic scatters of the Mesolithic. Such projects have become more productive with the recognition that, rather than distributions of artefacts in space, the target of specialized surveys should be the Mesolithic landscape itself (Runnels *et al.* 2005: 281). Failure to consider the broader landscape is a direct result of the pronounced quantitative rather than qualitative methodology of surface surveys (Andreou and Kotsakis 1999: 42) and of the well-known reluctance to make any prior assumptions. Moreover, the small regions covered, an inherent characteristic of the method that has been criticized as 'Mediterranean myopia' (Blanton 2001), are probably significantly smaller than the nodes of Mesolithic networks of movement. A recent specially designed survey by Runnels and associates in Kandia, in the Argolid, produced the staggering number of 15 verified Mesolithic sites in an area covering 30 sq km (Runnels *et al.* 2005). This is almost twice the number of the Neolithic sites located in the Langadas basin, an area twice the size of the Kandia survey (Andreou and Kotsakis 1999). Analogous results were produced further north, in Albania, another region where the Mesolithic was considered underrepresented (Runnels *et al.* 2004). On the basis of this experience, the same scholar predicts similar results in the 'Bay of Volos, the Navarino Bay, the Chalkidiki and the island of Crete' (Runnels *et al.* 2005: 281). Although obviously Holocene hunter-gatherers were not thriving all over mainland Greece, they seem to be significantly present, occasionally in quite dense numbers.

The full sequence of sixty radiocarbon dates available now from Theopetra Cave definitively proves, despite problems with stratigraphic integrity, that the site was occupied throughout the Mesolithic and into the Neolithic (Facorellis *et al.* 2001). The significance of Theopetra is not solely to prove the presence of a Mesolithic population in western Thessaly – by itself this does not change significantly the overall image of the Mesolithic in Greece (Runnels 2001: 257–58). Obviously, however, the cave was but one node in a wider network of sites, part of a larger demographically viable group. Theopetra, with evidence of burials, hearths and exploitation of local raw material resources (Adam 2000: 166; Kyparissi-Apostolika 2003), probably occupied a more permanent position in this presumed network, acting as a residential base camp or aggregation site. More significantly, Theopetra and its associated network arguably lays the foundation for a zone of active interaction between the earliest Neolithic sites of eastern Thessaly, where Runnels argues that no Mesolithic substratum existed (Runnels 1988), and the hilly west of Thessaly, where Mesolithic hunter-gatherers were already well established. This is strongly reminiscent of the 'PPNB interaction sphere' proposed by Bar-Yosef for the Levantine Neolithic (Bar-Yosef 2001, esp. figs. 6, 7) and, of course, of Zvelebil's availability zone (Zvelebil 2000). Some indications of continuity of practice, related to the procurement of raw materials and tool making (Adam 2000; Skourtopoulou 2000; Kyparissi-Apostolika 2003), can be better interpreted as aspects of this interactive negotiation.

Another important finding is that of obsidian in the Cave of Cyclope on the island of Youra. Obsidian artefacts are well dated by a series of radiocarbon measurements to the Upper Mesolithic, although the excavator initially expressed some reservations concerning their stratigraphical integrity (Sampson *et al.* 1998: 128; Sampson *et al.* 2003: 128), which he later abandoned (Sampson 2005: 132–33). Nonetheless, regardless of the line of procurement, the absence of obsidian from Mesolithic Theopetra, further inland, offers some indication of this interaction zone, where coastal farmers had to deal with indigenous populations.

It gives a tangible example of the transformational challenges to which immigrant groups were exposed. Nor was this the case only for immigrant groups. Mesolithic settlements on the nearby island of Alonnesos were also outside the obsidian network (Panagopoulou *et al.* 2001).

Taking these observations together, despite reservations about interpretation and gaps in evidence and dates (Thissen 2005), it is clear that Greece and the Aegean were far from uninhabited during this critical period (Katsarou-Tzeveleki 2001; Erdoğu 2003; Sampson 2005). The Mesolithic presence in the Aegean and on the mainland, and their interconnections, clearly had constructed a well-embedded social reality in which settling farmers were one way or another enmeshed. Migrant farmers would have had somehow to negotiate their own relationship with that reality, not only to procure obsidian or other raw materials and resources, but conceivably also to reorganize their identities and to construct their new social domains, by symbolic (and perhaps not only symbolic) confront-ation with existing groups. Evidently, this involved much more than simple adaptation to a new natural and social environment. The presence of obsidian even in the basal Aceramic levels in Knossos indicates that this connection was already established when these people arrived in Crete.

The insularity, on the other hand, of Crete has been stressed by many researchers. A consequence of this insularity is the absence of any population resident on the island prior to its colonization (Reese 1996). Indeed, despite claims of anthropogenic animal extinction in Crete (Lax and Strasser 1992), comparable to that recently identified at Aetokremnos in Cyprus (Simmons 1999), there does not seem to be any solid evidence for human habitation on the island prior to the onset of the Neolithic (Hamilakis 1996; Jarman 1996). For the time being, we have no evidence of any Mesolithic people living on the island, with whom settlers would have had to negotiate their identities. Does that mean, however, that the first colonizers were pure Neolithic populations living in isolation? We need here to remember Asdrahas and consider again the Aegean as a single entity. This entity, needless to say, always included the coasts of Anatolia.

We have already noted that the material corollary of these settlers, the 'Neolithic package', appears far from simple and uniform. There is no doubt that the picture of the settling farmers with their seeds and animals is an idealization (the Noah's ark view, see Davis 1984), since we have no way of detecting the gear of those settlers, except from their developed farming practices that found their way into our bioarchaeological samples. These practices, however, were the cumulative result of trial and error, rather than of rational decisions and forward planning. It is more likely that things would have happened piecemeal, in many ensuing attempts and passages (Halstead 1996). Once again, this is directly negotiated by agency and, similarly to the versatility of material culture, agency produces variability. Farming practices were the result of choice, but also, expectedly, the result of contingency – the combined outcome of the various life histories and experiences that each settler or group of settlers carried with them.

The choice of 'founder crops' in the first agricultural settlements in Greece varied considerably. We are still far from understanding the causes of that variability. In early Neolithic archaeobotanical assemblages from mainland Greece, for example, there is a marked preference for einkorn as opposed to emmer, and varieties of wheat, recently recognized as part of some of the introduced 'packages', possibly indicate a wider diversity of routes of incoming cultivation practices and foodstuffs (Valamoti and Kotsakis 2007: 84–86). The 'intriguing' presence of *T. aestivum* in Knossos, with its domestication centre placed in the southwest Caspian belt, is perhaps the most interesting case (Colledge and Conolly 2007: 65). Similarly, animals included in the 'package' could vary widely, probably related to perceptions of food, and to different husbandry practices. This can be particularly significant for island regimes. Bovines, for instance, are not clearly represented in Cypriot assemblages and most probably disappear a few centuries following their introduction (Vigne *et al.* 1999; Vigne 2001), but are common in Knossos (Isaakidou 2006). Some wild animals are thought to have been introduced to the Cretan fauna (Jarman 1996), as *Dama dama mesopotamica* was introduced to Cyprus (Peltenburg *et al.* 2001: 46). Further variability is introduced, of course, when the relative frequencies of different species, preferences in age of slaughter, use of secondary products, *etc.*, are examined. Their assessment is a more complicated issue, becoming even more complicated when questions of sampling are also taken into consideration. The same applies, of course, to the archaeobotanical samples, the validity of which is greatly affected by retrieval techniques and the practice or otherwise of context-based excavation (Colledge *et al.* 2004: 44–46).

Dissimilarities of this kind could be accounted for by cultural descent and origin, but the problem with this bio-cultural version of culture history is that it assumes a cultural identity that consists not of actions and practices vis à vis reality, but of ideal concepts. As we know from anthropology, ideal concepts are there just to be negotiated by reality (Herzfeld 1987: 49). Or, alternatively, they can represent an adaptation to specific environments and micro-environments. But there must be another aspect to this variability as well, one that stresses more clearly the additive and practical aspect of any activity happening within the cultural web. In this respect, dissimilarities represent life contexts, the cross-cutting of habitus and cultural norms with contingency and changing reality, of which the settlers themselves formed an integral part (Frankel 2000; Broodbank and Kiriatzi 2007). If that was the case, the settlers arriving in Crete had already incorporated in their cumulative, mediated habitus, their contact with the seafaring hunter/fisher-gatherers of the Aegean. The key concept and the driving force in the theory of practice (Bourdieu 1977), which bridges the objective aspects of habitus – those potentially observable archaeologically – to its subjective parts – the ones remaining largely archaeologically invisible – is precisely practice, and practices are shaped, transformed, accepted or rejected inexorably in dealing with the transformations of the outside world.

This is how colonization acquires a new meaning in the context of the emergence of the Neolithic. Anthony has made the important point that colonization is primarily a social strategy (Anthony 1997). This substantive outlook transfers the centre of interest from an observable and measurable factor such as demography or environment to the internal structure of social groups. In a heterogeneous migrant group, consisting, as we have already discussed, of fluid social identities and agendas, the final resolution can be highly unpredictable. For example, Cherry has drawn a distinction between the exploitation of an island and its eventual colonization (Cherry 1981) and Fiedel and Anthony, on a more general level, have discussed the central role of exploring pathfinders visiting far away places (Fiedel and Anthony 2003). Likewise, van Andel and Runnels (1995) assume the presence of 'wandering seafarers' exploring Thessaly prior to the settlement of agriculturalists, an idea that can readily be extended to Crete. The point is that all these differing groups with their embedded perceptions of the landscape had a major impact on the formation of the variable immigrant identities and their social networks, and in consequence on their archaeological signature.

To highlight the significance of this final remark, but also to stress the huge difficulties involved in identifying these processes archaeologically, one final point can be made. Despite the fact that this discussion has been around for some time now, no evidence has yet been seriously sought in the earliest Neolithic of Greece for such short-term, temporary sites created by these 'wandering seafarers', 'scouts' or earliest transient agriculturalists, in locations distinct from the basal layers of the long-lived, successful Neolithic settlements (Kotsakis 2003: 218–19). This possibility was underlined recently by Reingruber on the occasion of her re-examination of the earliest Neolithic of Argissa Magoula (Reingruber 2005).

The same possibility probably applies to Crete, where the consensus, based on the lack of other early sites located on the island, is for an island uninhabited outside Knossos. Similar voids in the archaeological record have been habitually questioned as a mere result of post-depositional factors, skewing the earliest evidence. Tomkins and Day examined the earliest pottery from the site of Knossos and concluded that it was already part of an extensive exchange network, which reached as far east as the Bay of Mirabello (Tomkins and Day 2001). No early Neolithic sites have been located there, despite systematic exploration of the landscape by a number of surface surveys. The earliest pottery from Knossos thus serves as another useful warning against lightly inferring an absence of population from gaps in the archaeological record.

One way or another, these earliest populations of Crete were not as isolated as research usually portrays them. They, too, belonged to the core-periphery system of the final 8th millennium, whichever that core and periphery were. As we have argued, we can anticipate a network of interactions with other islands, some of which preserve traces of earlier settlement, and we can imagine them as harbouring small groups of colonizing seafarers, either as permanent inhabitants or as occasional visitors. This regional interaction, built up earlier on, continues in later periods: some of the early sherds in the Tomkins and Day analysis possibly came from outside the island (Tomkins and Day 2001: 259).

Throughout that formative period, the population of the mainland, particularly that of the relatively close Argolid, was easily accessible to seaborne travellers. The knapped-stone industries of Knossos, as examined by Conolly (this volume), exhibit technological similarities with the relevant industries of Franchthi Cave in the Argolid. According to the same scholar, cultural transmission between the two groups cannot be excluded, although Knossos retained its own particular character. Many 'Mesolithic' traits surviving in the Franchthi lithic industries represent, according to the prevailing opinion, indigenous inhabitants of the Argolid maintaining older technological traditions of hunter-gatherers but adopting selected components of the new practices (Perlès 1990: 130). The 'Mesolithic' traits of Knossos can well be the result of the participation of that group in this wider network of communication and exchange, active in the Aegean. Concerning this last point, however, it is perhaps significant that, at both Franchthi and Knossos, the most intensive crushing and reduction is observed on obsidian, a material representing the active interaction of populations, and signifying the transfer of knowledge, information and technological skills.

These remarks underline the argument that the people of Knossos were actively engaged in cultural interaction with the surrounding world. To make things more complicated, however, it is interesting to note that, in other technological respects, such as the introduction of small blades or the presence of microliths, Knossos lay on the periphery of Aegean developments (Conolly n.d.: 46). Cultural transmission, therefore, does not appear uniform and does not involve all expressions of social life. Pottery, for instance, when it appeared at Knossos, looked distinctively dissimilar from that of the mainland, continuing the skeuomorphism of the non-ceramic containers related to food consumption (Tomkins 2007). Despite its subsequent incorporation into the inter-regional pattern of the Aegean, it retained distinctive characteristics throughout the Neolithic (Evans 1964; Efstratiou *et al.* 2004; Thissen 2005). This hint of structural complexity in the archaeological record, where every trait incorporates a specific, situated cultural significance that may not be immediately apparent to archaeologists, is a serious limitation on cultural re-creations.

Discussion and Conclusions

This presentation ends with the unsurprising conclusion that the little evidence available for the initial Neolithic in Greece limits the kind of arguments that can be decisively put forward for the case of Crete. To a certain degree this is the outcome of the nature of evidence and the condition of its preservation. But to an equal degree, the conceptual tools we are applying are just as ineffective. The virtual resurrection of the culture historical approach that largely dominates the relevant literature of the wider southwestern Asian Neolithic (Asouti 2006), despite claims to the contrary, leaves little space for the development of analytical subtleties, driven as it is by its inherent tendency to handle evidence as part of wide, normative regularities. It directly affects the discussion for the earliest Neolithic of Greece, too.

What has been argued here primarily follows a line of reasoning that drives the process of Neolithization back to its social context. I defend an approach that will treat Neolithization not as a cultural blueprint of an abstract prototype, but as a distinct, unique social process. In such a process, any divergence from the prototype represents much more than an index of cultural influence or affiliation revealing a direction of movement. Divergences are primarily active, situated negotiations of identities that engage and rearrange all aspects of practical life in a profound way. In fact, the actual divergences from the 'prototype' are so many and variable, that they seriously question its usefulness as such. For any of these points, however, to have some validity, we need to lay down an appropriate archaeological strategy. Small-scale excavations that do not bring out the fine grain of the variability of Neolithic lives, cannot take us beyond the abstractions of cultural norms. Nonetheless, this is all we have, when it comes to the earliest Neolithic of Greece.

I have presented also various aspects of the models invoking migration and movement as an explanatory device for the emergence of the Neolithic in Crete and Greece, and more widely, in the southeastern Mediterranean. A clear conclusion of this discussion is that, with notable exceptions, these models are seriously under-theorized. As a result, there exist only vague descriptions of the constitutive parts of migratory movements, while rarely is the complexity involved seriously addressed. Specific parameters that define, for instance, the scale, the social networks, or the cultural variability of any migratory movement, still remain undefined and unrecognized as patterned human behaviour (Anthony 1992; Burmeister 2000; Rockman and Steele 2003). On the other hand, there is a growing literature on colonization and colonies, some of which has successfully grasped the multiple facets of this bilateral bond within the broader framework of post-colonialist discussion. Perceptions of Neolithization would certainly gain significantly by tapping into this discussion, not guided by a spirit of false analogy, but in order to engage with the subtle interconnections perceived between shifting identities, changing contexts, and their expressions in material culture that colonization entails (*e.g.*, Lyons and Papadopoulos 2002; Hurst and Owen 2005; Malkin 2005; Owen 2005). So, instead of Neolithic archaeology *invoking* migration and movement as an explanation of transformation, it might as well start *studying* migration. We are unfortunately still very far from this.

Movement has been approached here as a trivial aspect of the Neolithic. To a great extent it is inherent in the Neolithic way of life, and the propagation of Neolithic landscapes is a notion that most archaeologists feel very comfortable with. The one-way direction, nevertheless, implicit in migration, often takes a privileged position in discussions of the Neolithization of the southeastern Mediterranean. I take this persistence to reveal a covert return to the 'ex oriente lux' postulates. In fact, it is far more likely that movement occurred in many different directions, including reverse or two-way movements, across and within the Aegean, and indeed into and from Crete from the earliest arrival of humans on the island. Despite the ubiquity of movement, archaeological scrutiny is time and again exhausted in fingerprinting migratory episodes. This is not to say that this task is inevitably pointless, although sometimes it may not be particularly rewarding, especially when dealing with movement into a previously unexploited area, like Crete or Greek Central Macedonia. But it should be the start of the analysis, not the end. In this respect, restricting discussion to questions of origin, direction and cultural affiliation reveals a disappointingly poor research design. On the other hand, denying the movement of population during that period, as in any other for that matter, would be totally unacceptable, on archaeological and theoretical grounds. This last comment applies, of course, to pure indigenist approaches, which are equally misconstrued.

A central incongruity in migration as an explanatory concept is that it needs to deny agency to the moving population. It has a similar attitude to the colonized also (see Given 2004), but in the case of Crete, this is not yet a concern. Colonizers are considered quasi-automata, 'uninhabited bodies' to use Meskell's expression for the disciplinary eclipse of agency (1998), fulfilling the Neolithic process. The question today, however, is not whether people have moved within the wider eastern Mediterranean region, but whether these people were anything more than merely convenient research abstractions. In other words, contemporary perceptions of Neolithic agents tend to perceive them as social subjects with real lives and identities inscribed in time and space, and expressed through distinctive material cultures. Agency, the active interaction of people with contexts, shifting in the immediate vicinity or in the surrounding world, is a central preoccupation of current approaches and, as discussed in this paper, there are many elements of the 'package' that would interact in a relevant way. The re-empowerment of Neolithic agents thus leads directly to the practical concerns of the everyday.

A clear expression of agency and of interaction with shifting contexts is hybridization. Colonies, interaction zones, borders in general, are nurseries of hybridity, places of active cultural production (Kotsakis 2005). A vast literature originating from the experience of the postcolonial world discusses hybridity as the outcome of the continuous re-contextualization of all cultural forms in the contact zones (Bhabha 1994). The crucial point here is that hybridization excludes any fixed, binary identities, and rejects in effect any cultural rootedness (Falck 2003). Consequently, it makes all diffusionist arguments obsolete, to the degree that their deeper essence is the recognition of a 'pure' cultural form with a recognizable 'root'. Needless to say, in this respect, this ideal prelapsarian rootedness is equally problematic for the 'indigenous' Neolithic of the Levant and Anatolia. Indeed, an active interaction even in the presumed stable 'core' areas can be inferred from the high degree of morphological variability in the Levantine and Anatolian Neolithic populations (Pinhasi and Pluciennik 2004: 73).

No discussion of hybridity can be usefully transferred to archaeology without close integration with the materiality of cultural forms. We can trace hybridity in the new cultural forms that emerge in the earliest Neolithic of Crete, but perhaps more so in the pronounced regional diversity that characterizes the earliest Neolithic in Greece. Despite the insufficient evidence available from these formative periods, we can still maintain that the Early Neolithic communities of Crete and mainland Greece had developed novel and unique ways in every aspect of social practice. All identified differences and idiosyncrasies, such as the thin material expression of ritual in the Greek Neolithic, rather than being considered as traits discarded from some original essence, should rather be perceived as novelties, participating actively in social construction.

Gosden, in his overview of colonialism in archaeology makes an excellent point about the connection of colonial events with material culture. According to Gosden, 'colonialism is a particular grip that material culture gets on the bodies and minds of people, moving them across space' (Gosden 2004: 3). Relevant literature abounds with examples of the reshaping of identities and meanings through the active manipulation of material culture in conditions of contact and negotiation (*e.g.*, Thomas 1991; Dietler 1995). In all these cases, people and things form an entangled mesh of power relations with agency of individual persons (Strathern 1988) and of things (Gell 1998) in the centre. Power emanating from things during practice – any practice – makes this negotiation possible. Consequently, any attempt to engage material culture and social practice needs to start, as Toulmin would say, from the particular and not the universal, the local and not the general, the timely and not the timeless (Toulmin 1990). Fortunately, this is precisely what the primary archaeological record represents.

So, to bring this discussion to a conclusion, there are four main points that are at the centre of the argument presented here. First, the recognition that archaeological migration models are fundamentally under-theorized sets the aim of future research as definition and elucidation of migratory processes and their constitutive parts, tapping the vast discussion already present in other disciplinary contexts. Secondly, the disassociation of movement *per se* from explanatory arguments inevitably turns the focus towards the conditions of movement and away from generic perceptions of 'origins', 'roots', etc., that mimic explanatory arguments. Thirdly, the recognition that Neolithic farmers were active agents, transforming their social contexts through their daily practices, places high demands on the quality and density of archaeological evidence. Fourthly, on theoretical grounds, and not only from pure archaeological necessity, this discussion places the material expressions of cultural forms in the centre. We are still very far from reconstructing the dense historical space of the Neolithic, where, as said in the introduction to this paper, countless human actions and processes took place, but these four points potentially set a new agenda for the archaeological study of the Neolithic transformation that is radically different from mainstream approaches and from any metaphysics of diffusion.

Ultimately, this is all about the definition of human culture. We accept the deeper connection of the long term with the short term as two sides of human experience. Similarly, an indigenist and a diffusionist view describe culture in a framework which, on a more abstract analysis, is far more similar than proponents of the two positions are willing to accept. Both understand culture as consisting of stable, immobile entities, created in platonic perfection, and which materialize in a place only by translocation or because they were always there in the first place. The profound question, however, is whether culture is best described as that ideally conceived entity, or rather as the multiple and fluid outcome of agency and practice. The answer, as usual, is not as simple as it looks.

Acknowledgements

Part of this paper was researched and written while I was an INSTAP fellow on a Tytus Visiting Scholar Program at the Department of Classics, University of Cincinnati. I wish to thank INSTAP and Prof Getzel Cohen, Director of the Tytus program, for giving me this opportunity. I also wish to thank Prof. Jack Davis and Shari Stocker at UC, for being such fantastic hosts, and to Dr Y. A. Lolos, for sharing ideas and pasta. Finally, many thanks go to the editors of this volume, for being so wonderfully patient. Last, but not least, Paul Halstead, to whom my lasting debt goes a long way back.

Bibliography

Adam, E.
    2000   Oi anoteres Palaiolithikes kai Mesolithikes lithotechnies tou spilaiou Theopetras kai i symvoli tous stin ektimisi tis xrisis tou spilaiou kata to teliko Pleistokaino kai proimo Holokeno. In N. Kyparissi-Apostolika (ed.), *Theopetra Cave. Twelve Years of Excavation and Research 1987–1998*: 163–71. Athens: Ministry of Culture.
Ammerman, A. J., and L. L. Cavalli-Sforza
    1984   *The Neolithic Transition and the Genetics of Populations in Europe*. Princeton, New Jersey: Princeton University Press.
van Andel, T. H. and C. N. Runnels
    1995   The earliest farmers in Europe. *Antiquity* 69: 481–500.
Andreou, S., and K. Kotsakis
    1999   Counting people in an artefact-poor landscape: the Langadas case, Macedonia, Greece. In J. Bintliff and K. Sbonias (eds.), *Reconstructing Past Population Trends in Mediterranean Europe (3000 BC–AD 1800)*: 35–43. Oxford: Oxbow Books.
Anthony, D. W.
    1990   Migration in archaeology: The baby and the bathwater. *American Anthropologist* 92: 895–914.
    1992   The bath refilled: migration in archaeology again. *American Anthropologist* 94: 174–76.

1997   Prehistoric migration as social process. In J. C. Chapman and H. Hamerow (eds.), *Migrations and Invasions in Archaeological Explanation* (BAR International Series 666): 21–32. Oxford: Archaeopress.

Asdrahas, S.
1985   The Greek archipelago. A far-flung city. In V. Sphyroeras, A. Avramea and S. Asdrahas (eds.), *Maps and Map-Makers of the Aegean*: 235–48. Athens: Olkos.

Asouti, E.
2006   Beyond the Pre-Pottery Neolithic B interaction sphere. *Journal of World Prehistory* 20: 87–126.

Baird, D.
in press Pınarbası; from Epipalaeolithic camp site to sedentarising village in central Anatolia. In M. Özdoğan and N. Başgelen (eds.), *Neolithic in Turkey, the Cradle of Civilization: New Discoveries*. (2nd edition). Istanbul: Arkeoloji ve Sanat Yayınları.

Bar-Yosef, O.
2001   The world around Cyprus: From Epi-Palaeolithic foragers to the collapse of the PPNB civilization. In S. Swiny (ed.), *The Earliest Prehistory of Cyprus*: 129–64, Vol. 2. Boston: American School of Oriental Research.

Bhabha, H. K.
1994   *The Location of Culture*. London: Routledge.

Blanton, R. E.
2001   Mediterranean myopia. *Antiquity* 75: 627–29.

Bogucki, P.
2000   How agriculture came to North-Central Europe. In D. T. Price (ed.), *Europe's First Farmers*: 197–218. Cambridge: Cambridge University Press.

Bourdieu, P.
1977   *Outline of a Theory of Practice*. Cambridge: Cambridge University Press.

Broodbank, C.
1999   Colonization and configuration in the insular Neolithic of the Aegean. In P. Halstead (ed.), *Neolithic Society in Greece* (SSAA 2): 15–41. Sheffield: Sheffield Academic Press.
2000   *An Island Archaeology of the Early Cyclades*. Cambridge: Cambridge University Press.
2006   The origins and early development of Mediterranean maritime activity. *JMA* 19: 199–230.

Broodbank, C. and E. Kiriatzi
2007   The first 'Minoans' of Kythera revisited: technology, demography, and landscape in the Prepalatial Aegean. *AJA* 111: 241–74.

Broodbank, C. and T. F. Strasser
1991   Migrant farmers and the Neolithic colonization of Crete. *Antiquity* 65: 233–45.

Burmeister, S.
2000   Archaeology and migration: approaches to an archaeological proof of migration. *Current Anthropology* 41: 539–67.

Carter, J. C.
2006   *Discovering the Greek Countryside at Metaponto*. Ann Arbor: University of Michigan.

Cauvin, J.
2000   *The Birth of the Gods and the Origins of Agriculture*. Cambridge: Cambridge University Press.

Cavalli-Sforza, L.
2000   *Genes, Peoples, and Languages*. New York: North Point Press.

Chapman, J. and P. M. Dolukhanov
1992   The baby and the bathwater: pulling the plug on migrations. *American Anthropologist* 94: 169–74.

Chapman, J. and H. Hamerow
  1997   On the move again – Migrations and invasions in archaeological explanation. In J. C. Chapman and H. Hamerow (eds.), *Migrations and Invasions in Archaeological Explanation:* 1–20. Oxford: Archaeopress.
Cherry, J. F.
  1981   Pattern and process in the earliest colonization of the Mediterranean. *PPS* 47: 41–68.
Colledge, S. and J. Conolly
  2007   A review and synthesis for the origins of farming on Cyprus and Greece. In S. Colledge and J. Conolly (eds.), *The Origins and Spread of Domestic Plants in Southwest Asia and Europe:* 54–75. Walnut Creek, CA: Left Coast Press.
Colledge, S., J. Conolly and S. Shennan
  2004   Archaeobotanical evidence for the spread of farming in the Eastern Mediterranean. *Current Anthropology* 45: 35–58.
Conolly, J.
  n.d.   The knapped-stone industry of initial and early Neolithic Knossos. Unpublished report.
Davis, S. J. M.
  1984   Khirokitia and its mammal remains. A neolithic Noah's ark. In A. Le Brun (ed.), *Fouilles récentes à Khirokitia (Chypre)1977–1981*: 147–62. Paris: Editions Recherche sur les Civilisations.
Dietler, M.
  1995   The Cup of Gyptis: rethinking the colonial encounter in Early Iron-Age Western Europe and the relevance of world-systems models. *Journal of European Archaeology* 3: 89–111.
Duru, R.
  1999   The Neolithic of the Lake District. In M. Özdoğan and N. Başgelen (eds.), *Neolithic in Turkey. The Craddle of Civilization. New Discoveries*: 165–91. Istanbul: Arkeoloji ve Sanat Yayınları.
  2002   Bademağacı Höyük excavations. *Beleten* 66: 576–94.
  2004   Excavations at Bademağacı. Preliminary report 2002 and 2003. *Belleten* 68: 540–60.
Efstratiou, N.
  2005   Tracing the story of the first farmers in Greece – a long and winding road. In C. Lichter (ed.), *How Did Darming Reach Europe?*: 143–53. Istanbul: Ege Yayınları.
Efstratiou, N. and E. Matzourani
  1997   The beginning of the Neolithic period in Greece and Cyprus: Common research and interpretation problems. *Cyprus and the Aegean in Antiquity. From the Prehistoric Period to 7th c. B.C.*: 7–20. Nicosia.
Efstratiou, N., A. Karetsou, E. S. Banou and D. Margomenou.
  2004   The Neolithic settlement of Knossos: new light on an old picture. In G. Cadogan, E. Hatzaki, and A. Vasilakis (eds.), *Knossos: Palace, City, State*: 39–48. London: British School at Athens.
Erdogu, B.
  2003   Visualizing Neolithic landscape: the early settled communities in western Anatolia and eastern Aegean islands. *European Journal of Archaeology* 6: 7–23.
Evans, J. D.
  1964   Excavations in the Neolithic settlement of Knossos, 1957–60. Part I. *BSA* 59: 132–240.
Facorellis, Y., N. Kyparissi-Apostolika and Y. Maniatis
  2001   The cave of Theopetra, Kalambaka: radiocarbon evidence for 50,000 years of human presence. *Radiocarbon* 43: 1029–48.

Fuluk, T.
  2003   Polluted places: harbours and hybridity in archaeology. *Norwegian Archaeological Review* 36: 105–18.
Fiedel, S. and D. W. Anthony
  2003   Deerslayers, pathfinders, and icemen. Origins of the European Neolithic as seen from the frontier. In M. Rockman and J. Steele (eds.), *Colonization of Unfamiliar Landscapes*: 144–68. London: Routledge.
Fotiadis, M.
  1995   Modernity and the past-still-present: politics of time in the birth of regional archaeological projects in Greece. *AJA* 99: 59–78.
Frankel, D.
  2000   Migration and ethnicity in prehistoric Cyprus: technology as habitus. *European Journal of Archaeology* 3: 167–87.
Galanidou, N. and C. Perlès (eds.)
  2003   *The Greek Mesolithic: Problems and Perspectives.* London: British School at Athens.
Gell, A.
  1998   *Art and Agency.* Oxford: Clarendon Press.
Given, M.
  2004   *The Archaeology of the Colonized.* London: Routledge.
Gosden, C.
  2004   *Archaeology and Colonialism.* Cambridge: Cambridge University Press.
Graham, A. J.
  1983   *Colony and Mother City in Ancient Greece.* Chicago: Ares.
Halstead, P.
  1996   The development of agriculture and pastoralism in Greece: when, how, who, and what? In D. R. Harris (ed.), *The Origins and Spread of Agriculture and Pastoralism in Eurasia*: 296–309. London: University College London Press.
Hamilakis, Y.
  1996   Cretan Pleistocene fauna and archaeological remains: the evidence from Sentoni Cave (Zoniana, Rethymnon). In D. S. Reese (ed.), *Pleistocene and Holocene Fauna of Crete and its First Settlers*: 231–39. Madison: Prehistory Press.
Herzfeld, M.
  1987   *Anthropology Through the Looking Glass.* Cambridge: Cambridge University Press.
Hodder, I.
  1990   *The Domestication of Europe.* London: Routledge.
  1991   Interpretive archaeology and its role. *American Antiquity* 56: 7–18.
  2001   Symbolism and the origin of agriculture in the Near East. *Cambridge Archaeological Journal* 11: 107–12.
Horden, P. and N. Purcell
  2000   *The Corrupting Sea: a Study of Mediterranean History.* Oxford: Blackwell.
Hurst, H. and S. Owen (eds.)
  2005   *Ancient Colonizations: Analogy, Similarity and Difference.* London: Duckworth.
Ingold, T.
  1994   Humanity and animality. In T. Ingold (ed.), *Companion Encyclopaedia of Anthropology*: 14–32. London: Routledge.
  1995   Building, dwelling, living. How animals and people make themselves at home in the world. In M. Strathern (ed.), *Shifting Contexts*, 59–80. London: Routledge.
  2000   *The Perception of the Environment.* London: Routledge.

Isaakidou, V.
    2006   Ploughing with cows: Knossos and the 'secondary products revolution'. In D.
            Serjeantson and D. Field (eds.), *Animals in the Neolithic of Britain and Europe*: 95–112.
            Oxford: Oxbow Books.
Jarman, M. R.
    1996   Human influence in the development of the Cretan mammalian fauna. In D. S. Reese
            (ed.), *Pleistocene and Holocene Fauna of Crete and its First Settlers*: 211–30. Madison:
            Prehistory Press.
Johnsen, H. and B. Olsen
    1992   Hermeneutics and archaeology: on the philosophy of contextual archaeology. *American
            Antiquity* 57: 419–36.
Katsarou-Tzeveleki, S.
    2001   Aegean and Cyprus in the Early Holocene: brothers or distant relatives? *Mediterranean
            Archaeology and Archaeometry* 1: 43–55.
Kopytoff, I.
    1987   The internal African frontier: the making of African political culture. In I. Kopytoff
            (ed.), *The African Frontier. The Reproduction of Traditional African Societies*: 3–84. Indiana:
            Indiana University Press.
Kotsakis, K.
    2002   Book review: The Early Neolithic in Greece. *European Journal of Archaeology* 5: 373–77.
    2003   From the Neolithic side: the Mesolithic/Neolithic interface. In N. Galanidou and C.
            Perlès (eds.), *The Greek Mesolithic: Problems and Perspectives*: 217–21. London: British
            School at Athens.
    2005   Across the border: unstable dwellings and fluid landscapes in the earliest Neolithic of
            Greece. In D. Bailey, A. Whittle and V. Cummings (eds.), *(un)settling the Neolithic*: 8–15.
            Oxford: Oxbow Books.
Kozlowski, S. K. and O. Aurenche
    2005   *Territories, Boundaries and Cultures in the Neolithic Near East*. Oxford: Archaeopress.
Kyparissi-Apostolika, N.
    2003   The Mesolithic in Theopetra cave: new data on a debated period in Greek prehistory.
            In N. Galanidou and C. Perlès (eds.), *The Greek Mesolithic: Problems and Perspectives*:
            189–205. London: British School at Athens.
Lax, E. and T. F. Strasser
    1992   'Early Holocene extinctions on Crete; the search for the cause'. *JMA*: 203–24.
Lemonnier, P.
    1993   Introduction. In P. Lemonnier (ed.), *Technological Choices. Transformation in Material
            Cultures Since the Neolithic*: 1–35. London: Routledge.
Lévi-Strauss, C.
    1963   *Structural Anthropology*. (translated by B.G. Schoepf). New York: Basic Books.
Little, D.
    2007   Philosophy of history. In E. N. Zalta (ed.), *The Stanford Encyclopedia of Philosophy*. URL:
            http://plato.stanford.edu/entries/history.
Lyons, C. L. and J. K. Papadopoulos (eds.)
    2002   *The Archaeology of Colonialism*. Los Angeles: Getty Research Institute.
Malkin, I.
    2005   *Mediterranean Paradigms and Classical Antiquity*. London: Routledge.
Mazzarella, W. T. S.
    2002   Book review: The perception of the environment: essays in livelihood, dwelling and
            skill. *Mind, Culture & Activity* 9: 150–57.

Meskell, L.
  1998   The irresistible body and the seduction of archaeology. In D. Montserat (ed.), *Changing Bodies, Changing Meanings: Studies of the Human Body in Antiquity*: 139–61. London: Routledge.
Owen, S.
  2005   Analogy, archaeology and Archaic Greek colonization. In H. Hurst and S. Owen (eds.), *Ancient Colonizations. Analogy, Similarity and Difference*: 5–22. London: Duckworth.
Özdoğan, M.
  1995   Neolithization of Europe: A view from Anatolia. Part 1: the problem and the evidence of East Anatolia. *Porocilo o raziskovanju paleolitika, neolitika in eneolitika v Sloveniji* XXII: 25–46.
  1997   The beginning of Neolithic economies in southeastern Europe: an Anatolian perspective. *Journal of European Archaeology* 5: 1–33.
  2005   The expansion of the neolithic way of life: What we know and what we do not know. In C. Lichter (ed.), *How Did Farming Reach Europe?*: 14–27. Istanbul: Ege Yayınları.
Özdoğan, M. and N. Başgelen
  1999   *Neolithic in Turkey, the Cradle of Civilization: New Discoveries*. Istanbul: Arkeoloji ve Sanat Yayınları.
Panagopoulou, E., E. Kotzampopoulou and P. Karkanas
  2001   Geoarxaiologiki ereuna stin Alonneso: nea stoixeia gia tin Palaeolithiki kai Mesolithiki ston aigiako choro. In A. Sampson (ed.), *Archaeology in the Northern Sporades, Greece*: 121–44. Alonnesos: Municipality of Alonnesos.
Peltenburg, E. J., S. Colledge, P. Croft, A. Jackson, C. McCartney and M. Murray
  2001   Neolithic dispersals from the Levantine Corridor: a Mediterranean perspective *Levant* 33: 35–64.
Perlès, C.
  1990   *Les industries lithiques taillées de Franchthi (Argolide, Grèce). Les industries du Mésolithique et du Néolithique. Volume 5.* Bloomington & Indianapolis: Indiana University Press.
  2001   *The Early Neolithic in Greece: The First Farming Communities in Europe.* Cambridge: Cambridge University Press.
  2005   From the Near East to Greece: Let's reverse the focus. Cultural elements that didn't transfer. In C. Lichter (ed.), *How Did Farming Reach Europe?*: 275–90. Istanbul: Ege Yayınları.
Pinhasi, R. and M. Pluciennik
  2004   A regional biological approach to the spread of farming in Europe: Anatolia, the Levant, South-Eastern Europe, and the Mediterranean. *Current Anthropology* 45: S59–S82.
Reese, D. S. (ed.)
  1996   *Pleistocene and Holocene Fauna of Crete and its First Settlers*. Madison: Prehistory Press.
Reingruber, A.
  2005   The Argissa Magoula and the beginning of the Neolithic in Thessaly. In C. Lichter (ed.), *How Did Farming Reach Europe?*: 155–171. Istanbul: Ege. Yayınları.
Renfrew, C. and M. Wagstaff
  1982   *An Island Polity.* Cambridge: Cambridge University Press.
Rockman, M. and J. Steele (eds.)
  2003   *Colonization of Unfamiliar Landscapes.* London: Routledge.
Rollefson, G. O.
  2001   An archaeological Odyssey. *CAJ* 11: 112–14.
Romano, R.
  1994   *Paese Italia. Venti Secoli di Identità.* Rome: Donzelli.

Runnels, C.
  1988   A prehistoric survey of Thessaly: new light on the Greek Middle Paleolithic. *Journal of Field Archaeology* 15: 277–90.
  2001   The Stone Age in the Aegean. In T. Cullen (ed.), *Aegean Prehistory: A Review*: 225–58. Boston: Archaeological Institute of America.
Runnels, C., M. Korkuti, M. L. Galaty, M. E. Timpson, J. C. Whittacker, S. R. Stocker, J. L. Davis, L. Bejko and S. Muçaj
  2004   The Palaeolithic and Mesolithic of Albania: survey and excavation at the site of Kryegjata B (Fier District). *JMA* 17: 3–29.
Runnels, C., E. Panagopoulou, P. Murray, G. Tsartsidou, K. Mullen and E. Tourloukis
  2005   A Mesolithic landscape in Greece: testing a site-location model in the Argolid at Kandia. *JMA* 18: 259–85.
Sampson, A.
  2005   New evidence from the early productive stages in the Aegean basin from the 9th to the 7th millennium BC. In C. Lichter (ed.), *How Did Farming Reach Europe?*: 131–41. Istanbul: Ege Yayınları.
Sampson, A., J. Kozlowski and M. Kaczanowska
  1998   Entre l' Anatolie et les Balkans: Une séquence Mésolithique-Neolithique de l' île de Gioura (Sporades du Nord). In M. Otte (ed.), *Préhistoire d' Anatolie. Genèse de deux mondes*: 125–40. Liège: University of Liège.
  2003   Mesolithic chipped stone industries from the Cave of Cyclope on the island of Youra (northern Sporades). In N. Galanidou and C. Perlès (eds.), *The Greek Mesolithic: Problems and Perspectives*: 123–30. London: British School at Athens.
Sherratt, A.
  1989   Review of S. Gregg 'Foragers and Farmers: Population Interaction and Agricultural Expansion in Prehistoric Europe'. *Journal of Field Archaeology* 16: 348–50.
  2006   Review of S. K. Kozlowski and O. Aurenche 'Territories, Boundaries and Cultures in the Neolithic Near East'. *The Prehistoric Society*. URL: http://www.ucl.ac.uk/prehistoric/reviews/06_01_kozlowski.htm.
Shewan, L.
  2004   Natufian settlement systems and adaptive strategies: the issue of sedentism and the potential of strontium isotope analysis. In C. Delage (ed.), *The Last Hunter-Gatherers in the Near East* (BAR International Series 1320): 55–94. Oxford: Archaeopress.
Simmons, A. H. and associates
  1999   *Faunal Extinction in an Island Society. Pygmy Hippopotamus Hunters of Cyprus.* New York: Kluwer Academic/Plenum Press.
Skourtopoulou, K.
  2000   I epexergasia apolepismenou lithou sto spilaio Theopetras kata ti diarkeia tis Neolithikis epochis. In N. Kyparissi-Apostolika (ed.), *Theopetra Cave. Twelve Years of Excavation and Research 1987–1998*. Athens: Ministry of Culture.
Strathern, M.
  1988   *The Gender of the Gift: Problems with Women and Problems with Society in Melanesia.* Berkeley: University of California Press.
Thissen, L.
  2005   Coming to grips with the Aegean prehistory: an outline of the temporal framework 10000–5500 cal BC. In C. Lichter (ed.), *How Did Farming Reach Europe?*: 29–40. Istanbul: Ege Yayınları.

Thomas, N.
  1991   *Entangled Objects: Exchange, Material Culture, and Colonialism in the Pacific*. Cambridge, MA: Harvard University Press.
Tomkins, P.
  2007   Communality and competition: the social life of food and containers at Aceramic and Early Neolithic Knossos, Crete. In C. Mee and J. Renard (eds.) *Cooking Up the Past: Food and Culinary Practices in the Neolithic and Bronze Age Aegean*: 174–99. Oxford: Oxbow Books.
Tomkins, P. and P. M. Day
  2001   Production and exchange of the earliest ceramic vessels in the Aegean: a view from Early Neolithic Knossos, Crete. *Antiquity* 75: 259–60.
Toulmin, S. E.
  1990   *Cosmopolis. The Hidden Agenda of Modernity*. New York: Free Press.
Tronchetti, C. and P. van Dommelen
  2005   Entangled objects and hybrid practices: colonial contacts and elite connections at Monte Prama, Sardinia. *JMA* 18: 183–208.
Turner, F. J.
  1994   *Rereading Frederick Jackson Turner. 'The significance of the frontier in American history' and other essays. With commentary by John Mack Faragher.* New Haven & London: Yale University Press.
Valamoti, S. M. and K. Kotsakis
  2007   Transitions to agriculture in the Aegean: the archaeobotanical evidence. In S. Colledge and J. Conolly (eds.), *The Origin and Spread of Domestic Plants in SW Asia and Europe*, 76–92. Walnut Creek, CA: Left Coast Press.
van Dommelen, P.
  1997   Colonial constructs: colonialism and archaeology in the Mediterranean. *World Archaeology* 28: 305–23.
Vigne, J.-D.
  2001   Large mammals of Early Aceramic Neolithic Cyprus: preliminary results from Parekklisia Shillourokambos. In S. Swiny (ed.), *The Earliest Prehistory of Cyprus. From Colonization to Exploitation*: 55–60. Boston, MA: American School of Oriental Research.
Vigne, J.-D., H. Buitenhuis and S. J. Davis
  1999   Les premiers pas de la domestication animale à l' Ouest de l' Euphrate: Chypre et l' Anatolie centrale. *Paléorient* 25: 49–62.
Warnke, G.
  1988   *Gadamer, Hermeneutics, Tradition, and Reason*. Cambridge: Polity Press.
Zilhão, J.
  2000   From the Mesolithic to the Neolithic in the Iberian peninsula. In D. T. Price (ed.), *Europe's First Farmers*, 144–82. Cambridge: Cambridge University Press.
Zvelebil, M.
  2000   The social context of the agricultural transition in Europe. In C. Renfrew and K. Boyle (eds.), *Archaeogenetics: DNA and the Population Prehistory of Europe*: 57–79. Cambridge: McDonald Institute of Archaeological Research.

5

The Knapped Stone Technology of the First Occupants at Knossos

James Conolly

Introduction

Recent research on Neolithic chronology, material culture, subsistence practices and palaeoclimate independently suggests that there was some degree of population movement from southwest Asia to southeast Europe during the seventh millennium BC (van Andel and Runnels 1995; Colledge *et al.* 2004; Perlès 2005; Weninger *et al.* 2006; Colledge and Conolly 2007). Differing degrees and tempos of population interaction and movement in the centuries after about 7200 BC go some way towards explaining the north-south variability in the archaeological record of early Greek farming communities, with southern communities seemingly having stronger links with the Levant and the southwestern Anatolian littoral, and northern sites possessing clearer relationships with central Anatolia (Perlès 2005: 280). However, if the ultimate goal of the study of neolithization is to explain how and why such fundamental changes in human ecology and social life took place, rather than a preoccupation with defining 'sources' and 'origins' (cf. Kotsakis 2002), then we need more multiscalar research of late hunter-gatherer and early farming settlements and landscapes to allow us to test (and to develop further) local and regional models of social interaction, population history and cultural geography. As Knossos is one of only two or three sites providing direct evidence about the context of the earliest farming societies in the southern Aegean, it demands intensive investigation.

Considerable interrogation of the extent and nature of the earliest ('Aceramic') deposits at Knossos, first excavated by John Evans in the late 1950s, has led to a current consensus that the first occupation at Knossos consisted of a small community (of ca. 50 people – Broodbank and Strasser 1991) of agro-pastoralists who arrived via sea-craft from, presumably, a coastal region of southwestern Anatolia soon after 7000 BC (Broodbank 1992; van Andel and Runnels 1995). However, this picture is only a rough sketch; much remains obscure about the relationship between Crete's earliest farmers and other communities in the Aegean, and the socio-ecological processes that, over the subsequent two millennia, transformed these landscapes into large-scale agrarian endeavours. In short, building understanding of the origins and social context of early farming in the Aegean is a challenging task that requires the integration of site, regional, and inter-regional studies, as exemplified by Perlès' synthesis of the Early Neolithic (2001).

Knapped stone tools have long been established as an important body of evidence for understanding the dynamics of Greek 'neolithization' (see, in particular, Perlès 1992; 2001: 201–10). There is, however, little published detail about the specifics of knapped stone at Knossos beyond the summary information and a few photographs in the Neolithic excavation reports by John Evans (1964; 1968). This is a large and serious gap in our knowledge, and one exacerbated by the earliest levels of Knossos being aceramic, thus depriving Aegean prehistorians of their usual yardstick for establishing chronology and relationships between contemporaneous communities. The purpose of this paper is thus to provide some detailed information on the first phases of the knapped-stone industry at Knossos, and to relate it, where possible, to contemporary industries in the Aegean. This is not intended as a full technical report and it will discuss summary elements of the industry that are of relevance to the stated purpose: complete publication will follow when the final morphometric and trace-element analysis is complete.

Context

Traditionally, the sequence of Neolithic occupation at Knossos, described initially on the basis of pottery change by Mackenzie (1903), subsequently refined by Furness (1953), and then followed by John Evans (1964), divides the (pottery-using) Neolithic into four periods (EN I, EN II, MN, LN). An 'Aceramic' phase was added to this chronology when a relatively shallow but extensive layer – Stratum X – was discovered underlying the EN I layers and immediately above bedrock (Evans 1964). The EN I phase at Knossos is not the equivalent of EN in Greece, but covers a period from EN through LN I (see Tomkins this volume). Following a recent review of stratigraphy and ceramic development at Knossos, a new chronology for Crete has now been proposed that is fully integrated with that in use in the rest of Greece (Tomkins 2007; this volume, table 3.1). Subsequent references to chronological phases use this new chronology.

The 1957–60 excavations by John Evans initially concentrated in the Central Court of the Palace (Areas A–F), although in 1960 a small area to the north of the palace at the edge of the hill was opened (Area XY). Areas A and C (combined to form AC in 1960 by the removal of the common baulk) were the deepest trenches, with around seven metres of Neolithic deposits. Area AC exhibited a shallow 'Aceramic' level at the bottom, lying on bedrock (Evans 1964; 1994; this volume). Excavations by Evans a decade later (1969–70) opened several trenches both on and off the Central Court in order to define better the spatial extent of the Neolithic settlement and to uncover more completely a Neolithic structure discovered in the earlier seasons. Neolithic levels with no ceramic vessels were discovered in two small soundings, one just at the southern edge of the Central Court (sounding X) and one to its south (sounding ZE). A further eleven soundings were made around the periphery of the Palace, in order to define the extent and depth of the various phases of Neolithic settlement (Evans 1994: 3, fig. 1). A series of nineteen dates places the 'Aceramic' to FN IB sequence between the late eighth/early seventh millennium BC and the end of the fifth millennium BC; no dates are yet available from the remaining FN II–IV phases of the Neolithic sequence (Evans 1994: 20, table II; Tomkins 2007).

At this point, it is worth noting briefly the debate concerning the validity of a *properly Aceramic* phase at Knossos and the small handful of mainland Neolithic sites where such a phase has been claimed (see Bloedow 1991: 39–40 and Perlès 2001: 64–97 for an extended and thorough discussion). In sum, the arguments rest principally on whether any ceramic materials were actually recovered from supposedly aceramic levels and what these levels represent in terms of human activities. Recent re-examination of the evidence from Knossos, Franchthi and Argissa by Perlès (2001: 84–95) has concluded that there is a distinct phase that is characterized by the absence, or scarcity, of ceramic vessels that dates to circa 7200–6500 BC. However, in the context of the following discussion, whether occupation levels dating approximately to the beginning of the seventh millennium BC are aceramic *sensu stricto* is irrelevant – I am here more concerned with the chronology in order to draw meaningful comparisons between roughly contemporaneous assemblages in the Aegean. What is more pertinent is that there are at least three sites – Knossos, Franchthi, Argissa – with deposits of approximately the same date from, respectively, Crete, the Argolid and Thessaly, allowing for a broader regional comparison of lithic technological practices at the onset of farming societies in Greece. I thus follow Perlès in referring to the initial phases of Neolithic settlement, which date to the first centuries of the seventh millennium BC, and which have limited or no evidence of ceramics, as the Initial Neolithic (IN) rather than the Aceramic.

The IN Assemblage: Raw Material, Debitage Techniques and Tools

A total of 394 knapped-stone objects, weighing 653.8 g were available for analysis from IN contexts.[1] By count, obsidian is the preferred raw material (n=276, or 70.1%), but by weight it is in a minority to local materials (310.9 g, or 47.4% of all worked siliceous stone). Other, locally available, worked materials include silicates of varying colours and coarseness (from red-veined coarse green, through finer grained grey, to fine yellow-white translucent), radiolarite, one or two pieces of hard limestone, green quartz, and a number of pieces of milky-white quartz. With the exception of a large flake of quartz, the vast majority of local materials are very small and nodular and most, including the quartz flake, are of poor-quality. The majority (nearly 80%) of the obsidian artefacts are small, broken or fragmentary flakes (*i.e.*, flakes where the striking platform is missing and/or the edges are broken), or small pieces of shatter, where a single ventral surface could not be identified.

Debitage Techniques

The majority of the IN assemblage can be attributed to very intensive flake core reduction using both multi-platform and opposed platform bipolar cores. There are very few complete flakes (n=62, 15.7%). Blades, although present, are equally few in number (n=13, 3.3%). The intensity of reduction suggests that there was an element of resource stress in terms of the availability of this essential raw material. Table 5.1 provides totals for each of the debitage categories for obsidian (upper section) and silicates (lower section).

Cores

A single possible obsidian blade core and one small radiolarite flake core (Figure 5.1) with two or three removals that appear to be the result of investigative knapping were also recovered. Both cores are small (<3.5 cm in maximum dimension), and the bipolar reduction method on the obsidian artefact is technologically similar to that seen on the numerous *pièces esquillées*. The few removal scars that remain on its surface show that at its later stages it would have been producing very thin blade blanks of no more than 10 or 20 mm in length and less than 5 mm wide.

Pièces esquillées

Pièces esquillées are small, thin, and most often square or rectangular objects that possess bipolar flaking and crushing on two opposite edges (although this can at times be restricted to a single edge and occasionally appears on both lateral and polar edges) (Figure 5.2). The *pièces esquillées* from IN levels at Knossos are usually small (the average size is about 2 cm in length), although a few larger pieces (up to ca. 4 cm) are also present (Figure 5.3). The original blank shape is extremely difficult to reconstruct, although most appear originally to have been small flakes or small pieces of elongated shatter that were then subject to repeated impacts on two opposite ends, causing extensive bifacial flaking and crushing along the full extent of each edge in the manner described by Tixier (1963). At least two, and possibly three or four, blade segments appear to have been modified in a like manner, causing similar bipolar crushing and flaking (as is the case with the two prismatic examples shown in Figure 5.6).

A longstanding debate surrounds the question of whether these are cores, insofar as their reduction was undertaken to produce flakes then used for other purposes, or whether they are tools in their own right (Shott 1981; LeBlanc 1992). Experimental use-wear conducted by Ataman (1989), using a sample of *pièces esquillées* from the Pre-Pottery Neolithic site of Çan Hasan III in Central Anatolia, could not refute the hypothesis that they were most likely used to split and shape hard materials such as bone and/or wood. Use wear analysis by Kozlowski *et al.* (1996) of EN *pièces esquillées* from Lerna in the Argolid also concluded that they were probably used in the working of hard materials. Having said this, some of the larger examples from Knossos have removal scars upwards of 3–4 mm in maximum dimension, and thus may have been useful blanks in composite tools. Essentially, it is impossible to draw a dividing line between those *pièces*

obsidian	<1 cm	1–2 cm	2–4 cm	>4 cm	total	%
percussion blades						
complete			2	4	6	2.2
proximal				1	1	0.4
medial			2		2	0.7
pressure blades						
medial		1	1		2	0.7
flakes						
complete	3	17	17	2	39	14.1
proximal fragments		15	9	1	25	9.1
medial/distal fragments	5	58	26	3	92	33.3
cores						
pièces esquillées		32	22	1	55	19.9
blade				1	1	0.4
other						
maintenance flakes			2		2	0.7
shatter	6	30	12		48	17.4
chips	3				3	1.1
Total	**17**	**153**	**93**	**13**	**276**	**100**

local silicates	<1 cm	1–2 cm	2–4 cm	>4 cm	total	%
percussion blades						
proximal			1		1	0.8
medial/distal			1		1	0.8
flakes						
complete	1	7	8	5	21	17.8
broken		4	13	1	18	15.3
fragments	1	22	15		38	32.2
cores						
pièces esquillées			4		4	3.4
flake			1		1	0.8
other						
shatter/fragments	1	14	11	6	32	27.1
indeterminable			2		2	1.7
Total	**3**	**47**	**56**	**12**	**118**	**100**

Table 5.1. Initial Neolithic debitage totals.

esquillées that may have been cores for small blank production and those that may have been wedge tools. Metric analysis does not help distinguish categories either: analysis of size shows a normal distribution (Figure 5.4). One likely possibility is that the objects were initially subject to intensive bipolar reduction for the production of blanks, but when they became too small for this, were used as chisels or wedges.

Blades

Eleven obsidian blade fragments were recovered, excluding those classified as *pièces esquillées*, and their characteristics suggest that nine were produced using percussion methods, and two possibly by pressure techniques. The former (Figure 5.5) are extremely unstandardized and certainly do not represent a coherent approach to blade debitage, but nevertheless provide evidence that blades were occasionally achievable (or obtainable; there is no evidence for their on-site production).

2 cm

Figure 5.1. Cores (a: obsidian, possible pièces esquillées, *34.8×13.7×7.5 mm, X-22; b: chert, 34.3×25.2×17.9 mm, ZE-7).*

2 cm

Figure 5.2. Pièces esquillées *(upper row X-24, lower row X-25).*

The widths of those pieces, still recognizable as blades, range between 11.5 and 22.3 mm, although the majority of the eleven fall between 14 and 17 mm. One segment is almost certainly from a bipolar core, and two others might be. In all three cases, however, the nature of production seems to have been *ad-hoc* and opportunistic. The other blades appear to be single-platform blade cores of varying shapes and sizes, with one or two examples displaying a more structured

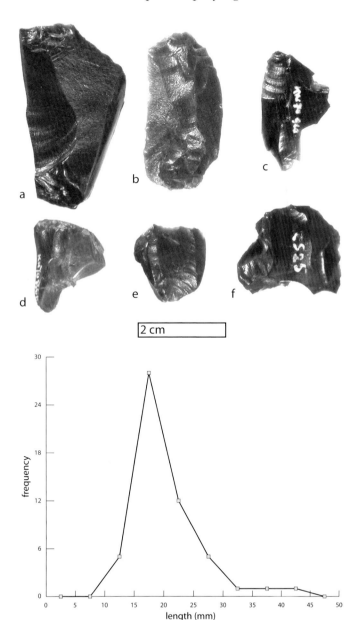

Figure 5.3. Bipolar cores/ pièces esquillées *(a–b: X-19, c: X-24, d: X-25, e–f: AC-26).*

Figure 5.4. Frequency distribution of pièces esquillées *length.*

approach to blade production. Examination of the platforms on the five blades where they are still intact shows similar variability: platform sizes range between 11 mm wide by 6 mm deep and 4 mm wide by 1 mm deep. Core striking platform angles also vary from about 60 to nearly 90 degrees and they are either plain or facetted. In short, the variability in preparation and extraction gives the impression of opportunism rather than strategy. It appears that when material for elongated debitage was available, rough blades were extracted from either single or opposed platforms. In the case of the latter, it appears that bipolar percussion (*i.e.* the placing of one end of a core on a hard surface when striking the other) was also used to extract blanks. While no true blades produced from this technique could be identified – although the core in Figure 5.1 shows that it was used for blade reduction – there are many elongated flakes (see below) that can be attributed to this type of technique.

The two possible pressure blades (Figure 5.6) are small (17.1 × 9.8 × 3.4 mm and 27.5 × 12.3 × 5.2 mm) medial fragments and are extensively retouched, but both possess characteristics of pressure debitage insofar as they are prismatic and have two parallel ridges running down their dorsal surfaces. Admittedly this evidence is slim and one cannot claim with conviction that pressure-debitage was the method used to produce these blades on the basis of two medial fragments. Nevertheless these pieces could be the products of this rather specialized technique. As there is no evidence for local use of this technology, it seems likely that they have been introduced or obtained from elsewhere. The closest known site with similar products is Franchthi, although as discussed

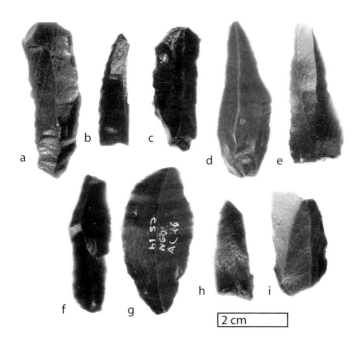

Figure 5.5. Percussion blades (a: X-24, b: X-24, c: X-24, d: AC-26, e: ZE-3, f: X-24, g: AC-26, h: AC-26, i: ZE-3).

below, this form of blade technology does not become well established there until EN (Perlès 2001: 204, fig. 10.1).

Evidence for blade extraction from locally available materials is more limited: the quartz core has elongated flake removals and, on radiolarite, a medial fragment of a possible bipolar blade, and a proximal fragment of what may also have been a blade, were identified. This is limited evidence that the inhabitants of IN Knossos were attempting to extract blades from locally available materials.

Flakes
Although flakes constitute the major class of obsidian artefact (n=178, 64.5%), no definite obsidian flake cores were found in the IN levels. Two core maintenance flakes suggest that flake production involved a considerable degree of bipolar crushing. The outcome of this technique is reflected in the large number of flakes that have evidence of bipolar and multidirectional dorsal scars.

In the absence of flake cores, it is obviously difficult to reconstruct confidently flake reduction methods and techniques, but the available evidence suggests that a combination of bipolar percussion and direct percussion on cores that had little or no preplanning or organization was practised. While there are a few larger and 'cleaner' flakes in the assemblage (*i.e.* complete, 3 cm or larger, with three or fewer dorsal scars), the otherwise usually small size of the flakes (56% are in the 12 cm range), together with the fact that, of these, 68% are fragmentary, is indicative of intensively reduced material. The large numbers of small pieces of shatter also support this theory: bipolar crushing of small cores can produce a good number of small, unstandardized flakes, but it will also produce a large quantity of broken and fragmentary flakes, together with a large amount of shatter. The assemblage also contains a number of 'blade-flakes' from bipolar reduction techniques (Figure 5.7).

As with the obsidian, the vast majority of the IN silicate assemblage (65%) consists of flakes most of which are small and fragmented. The method and technique of flake production resembles that observed for obsidian. The single silicate core is small and battered and shows very well how poor the local material is: its coarseness and internal flaws would render anything except the simplest knapping methods and techniques all but impossible. Indeed, with most of the silicate assemblage, the debitage products appear to be the result

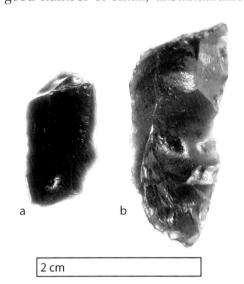

2 cm

Figure 5.6. Possible pressure blade segments (a: X-25, b: X-22).

ol experimental and investigative knapping employed to explore the potential of local sources.

Silicate flakes are on average larger than obsidian (on the basis of frequency of membership in size categories: $C^2 = 14.6$, df = 3, $p = 0.002$) and there are significant variations in the proportion of flake categories between the two materials. The source of these differences is in all probability a combination of three factors: (i) local silicate cores were likely larger than obsidian cores when they entered the reduction sequence; (ii) obsidian cores were more intensively reduced, resulting in larger numbers of smaller debitage; and (iii) the mechanical properties of obsidian result in greater flake fragmentation than is the case for the silicates. This is not meant to imply, however, that the technical approaches to obsidian and silicate core reduction were significantly different. In fact, despite these basic differences in flake form and size, the modal reduction strategy, notwithstanding that there are hints of more organized approaches on both materials, is best described as unstandardized, using either multi-platform or bipolar cores. The major difference in debitage composition between obsidian and silicate is really only a product of the intensity of reduction and the size and quality of the raw material, rather than a result of alternative strategies for local and exotic materials.

Tools

A total of 100 silicate and obsidian artefacts, or 25.4% of the IN assemblage, show evidence of use or retouch. Of these, 88 are obsidian and 12 are silicates. 31.8% of the obsidian artefacts and 10.2% of the silicate artefacts show evidence of retouch. Both percentages are relatively high, although obsidian obviously shows greater intensity of use. There is no clear or consistent morphological patterning of retouched pieces at Knossos, and most appear to have been produced 'at need'. Three very general categories were used to describe the variability: re-touched flakes, retouched blades and *pièces esquillées* (with the latter category possibly containing what were technically cores, rather than tools, as explained previously).

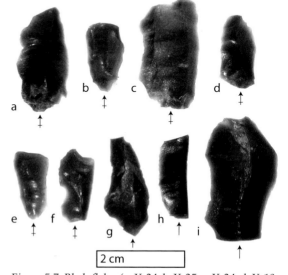

Figure 5.7. Blade flakes (a: X-24, b: X-25, c: X-24, d: X-19, e–i: X-24).

Retouched Flakes (n=28)

The most unstandardized category of stone tool are the retouched flakes. Not readily assignable to any specific use task, these tools are most likely expedient (or *ad-hoc*) light cutting/scraping tools, and it is not always clear whether the 'retouch' is intentional or a by-product of use (Figure 5.8). Most of these tools are extremely small: the majority cluster around 2 cm in maximum length, although several are smaller and the largest is just over 5 cm long. Some examples appear to be broken fragments of larger tools. In the majority of cases, retouch is very marginal and does not significantly alter the original blank edge morphology. The range of shapes in the working edges of these tools is considerable, and several pieces have more than one area of retouch. The most common type of retouch is denticulation (n=14), followed by linear retouch (n=6). Fewer have evidence of abrupt convex/scraper retouch (n=4) or concave retouch (n=2). There are also two notched pieces.

Retouched Blades (n=10)

The blades are irregular and not retouched in a consistent location or manner (see Figure 5.5). Two blades have backing retouch, which extends on to the distal end and becomes less abrupt to form a scraper-like working edge. A further five blades have small amounts of marginal retouch along their lateral edges and were probably simple cutting tools. Two have small amounts of alternating retouch, while one has substantial bifacial retouch and appears to be a fragment of a larger piece.

Ornament?

Finally, there is an obsidian artefact (from Area X, level 25) that shows evidence of having been cut to an intentional shape (Figure 5.9). I note it here only as an unusual object that to my knowledge has no parallel in the Neolithic Aegean.

Comparative Analysis

The IN lithic assemblage at Knossos can be summarily characterized in six points:
1. A preference for obsidian, although experimentation with a variety of local materials is very much in evidence.
2. Use of small bipolar cores for flake, and elongated flake production. Larger percussion blades were used, although evidence for their production is missing.
3. Abundant *pièces esquillées*. Over half of the modified pieces belong to this category. The two alternative (but not mutually exclusive) interpretations see these objects as either intensively reduced bipolar cores, or as small chisels or wedges for wood and bone working.

4. Very intensive use of stone, suggesting resource stress. The majority of the assemblage consists of very small pieces and there is a high proportion of retouched flakes.
5. A lack of standardized tool forms. Retouch is often marginal and rarely appears to have altered the natural profile of the blank's edge significantly. Most retouched forms consist of denticulated or regular (cutting) edges, with fewer instances of convex, concave and notched forms. No microlithic elements (*e.g.*, truncations or trapezes) were identified.
6. Two possible prismatic blade fragments (both of which have been heavily reworked) provide some circumstantial evidence for movement of finished products, possibly via the Peloponnese.

The best comparative sample for placing the Knossos knapped stone in a regional context is the assemblage from the well-known Peloponnesian site of Franchthi Cave studied by Perlès (1990). Some of her more important observations are that there is an increase in the use of obsidian from ca. 3% in the Final Mesolithic to ca. 10% in the IN, and that there are two technological approaches within the IN Franchthi assemblage: a high intensity unstandardized flake industry and a more standardized and technologically sophisticated blade industry. The former accounts for the majority of the IN assemblage, consisting of small (80% are less than 1.5 cm in length) unretouched flakes derived from the 'crushing' (*écrasantes*) of small cores. Blades, both unretouched and retouched, form 10% of the total assemblage, up from 4.5% in the Final Mesolithic. Roughly 12% of all local artefacts and 27% of all obsidian artefacts show signs of modification. The majority of the modified pieces consist of unstandardized flake tools (in descending order of prevalence: notches; linear retouched pieces; *pièces esquillées*; perforators; backed pieces; denticulates; and scrapers). Although fewer in number, the blades and blade tools show a significantly higher technological

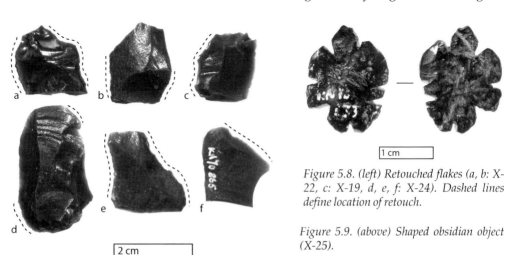

Figure 5.8. (left) Retouched flakes (a, b: X-22, c: X-19, d, e, f: X-24). Dashed lines define location of retouch.

Figure 5.9. (above) Shaped obsidian object (X-25).

investment, and were used as blanks for trapezes, truncations, and points. Elements of the blade assemblage are new to the IN although the microlithic tools and the unstandardized flake tools have a much longer history at Franchthi and provide evidence of continuity with both the Lower (Lithique VII) and Upper (Lithique VIII) Mesolithic (Perlès 1990: 94–105, 130). The appearance of the blade and bladelet component is used by Perlès as evidence that Franchthi was at the southernmost edge of the European-wide occurrence of these types of tools during the early Holocene (Perlès 1990: 130).

The Franchthi assemblage can be contrasted to the roughly contemporary earliest Neolithic levels at Argissa in Thessaly, to which it is very dissimilar. Large obsidian pressure blades are present in the earliest 'Aceramic' levels at the former (Perlès 2001: 89, fig. 5.3), including blades showing evidence of having been used to cut siliceous plants. This, and the lack of a microlithic and expedient flake industry, has been used to argue that the processes of neolithization in Thessaly and the Argolid were different (Perlès 2001: 46). In essence, Perlès has proposed that the indigenous inhabitants of Franchthi Cave might have adopted selected components of the earliest Neolithic economy, while maintaining their technological traditions shared with European hunter-gatherers (Perlès 1990: 130). Conversely, the absence of evidence for a 'Mesolithic' lithic tradition in Neolithic Thessaly (Perlès 1990: 135) suggested that farmers in this area were more clearly of exogenous origin.

Perhaps not surprisingly, given its relative proximity, the IN assemblage from Knossos has much common with the IN Franchthi Cave assemblage. Points of correspondence include the high number of small flakes (under 1.5 cm), and the high rate of crushing and intense reduction, particularly on obsidian. The range and type of tools, especially the numerous denticulates, notches and scrapers, and the high number of *pièces esquillées* are similar to Franchthi. There are, however, also some important differences, of which the most significant are the difference in technical quality, the proportion of blades and blade tools (ca. 2% at Knossos vs. ca. 10% at Franchthi) and the absence of microliths in the IN at Knossos. In this latter respect, it may be safely argued that Knossos lay on the periphery of the sphere of influence that saw the introduction of small blade tools to Franchthi in the IN, and does not appear to be part of the same Mesolithic tradition.

The correspondence between the flake components of the two assemblages is not, however, so easily explained. Perlès proposes that, at Franchthi, these components provide evidence of cultural continuity with the preceding Meso-lithic. At IN Knossos, the assemblage is clearly similar to the flake industry at Franchthi, and has very little evidence for the more sophisticated blade industry. However, given that IN Knossos represents the colonization of new territory by farmers equipped with domestic crops and animals not previously observed in Greece (*e.g.*, *Triticum aestivum*), any Mesolithic elements in the assemblage seem unlikely to be the product of cultural continuity with mainland Aegean in-digenous hunter-gatherers.

Two possible hypotheses to account for the similarities are thus proposed: (i) the similarities between the IN tool kits of Knossos and Franchthi are not the result of any direct cultural transmission, but the result of similar functionally derived technical strategies, chosen to solve the parallel geographical and environmental contexts of the Argolid and central Crete; (ii) the similarities are a product of limited cultural transmission between local (indigenous) hunter-gatherers, as represented at Franchthi, and exogenous farmers as represented at Knossos, with the incomers modifying their technology in response to local constraints. Less attractive are the two alternates to these proposals: (iii) the small flake tool tradition evident at IN Franchthi is, *contra* Perlès, not the result of cultural continuity from earlier populations, but represents a newly introduced industry (*i.e.* cultural transmission in the direction opposite to what I suggest above), or; (iv) there is evidence of cultural continuity with the Final Mesolithic in the IN Knossos assemblage.

Given these four choices, the first is the easiest to defend, given: (a) the absence of evidence for other Mesolithic traits in the Knossos assemblage; (b) that there is unambiguous evidence of small informal flake tools used during the Mesolithic; (c) there is as yet no evidence for Mesolithic activity on Crete and the subsistence package introduced in the IN at Knossos points clearly to an exogenous, rather than indigenous, provenance for the first settlers of Knossos.

This leaves the very pronounced differences between Knossos and the Thessalian IN lithic industry, typified by the Argissa assemblage. As with Perlès, I interpret this discrepancy as a result of the settling of Knossos by a community with different technological strategies to those of the Thessalian settlers. This conclusion is compatible with results from recent analysis of material culture (Perlès 2005) and subsistence practices (Colledge *et al.* 2004; Colledge and Conolly 2007). Compounding this source of technical divergence, Knossos was, from the beginning of its settlement until later in the Neolithic, relatively isolated from the circulation of (off-island?) raw and finished materials resulting in limited cultural transmission.

Of course, the other notable outlier in the IN Aegean interaction sphere was Franchthi. This changes by the EN, when cultural continuity with the Mesolithic is no longer evident and there was a shift in settlement to outside the cave. From the EN, Franchthi shows evidence of participation in regional goods and knowledge exchange networks. As is the case with EN Thessalian sites, Melian obsidian becomes the most commonly used raw material, and obsidian pressure blade technology assumes a dominant role. There is a corresponding increase in the number of retouched blades, and a decline in the irregularly retouched components such as notches, denticulates and *pièces esquillées* (Perlès 2001: 205). The EN levels from Lerna (Kozlowski *et al.* 1996) also share many characteristics with Franchthi, and EN lithic assemblages from the Peloponnese to Thessaly show a preponderance of obsidian blades, often manufactured using pressure techniques. In Greece and Anatolia the emergence of pressure blade technology is associated with specialized production (Conolly 1999; Perlès and Vitelli 1999), and Perlès has argued that in the Aegean these products were probably distributed via specialized seafarers and/or itinerant craftspeople (Perlès 1992).

However, the EN–LN I assemblage from Knossos, which I will report on more fully elsewhere, continues to stand somewhat apart from these mainland developments. Unlike Franchthi, there is considerable continuity between IN and EN at Knossos. Differences are largely restricted to the decline in the use of local materials and a small increase in the number of blades in the assemblage (from ca. 2% to 6%). A reasonable working hypothesis to account for the absence of mainland traits in both the IN and EN is that Knossos was not a significant participant in the Aegean-wide circulation of knowledge, raw materials and finished goods that is seen between mainland sites during EN (Perlès 1992). This conclusion is additionally supported by the ceramic analysis conducted by Tomkins and Day (2001), which showed that off-island imports at EN Knossos constitute only a very small part of the ceramic assemblage (Tomkins 2004: 48; Tomkins *et al.* 2004).

Summary

Although often overlooked in favour of the more ubiquitous ceramic sherds, stone tools were a core element of the toolkit of the earliest Neolithic inhabitants of the Aegean and provide much essential information about economic organisation, subsistence, trade and exchange. The Knossos assemblage is no exception, and its analysis has resulted in a number of significant observations. First, the IN and EN Knossos assemblage was very intensely worked and shows evidence of 'resource stress'. Secondly, there are some parallels but also significant differences with the IN Franchthi assemblage, suggesting different processes of neolithization for different areas of the southern Aegean. Thirdly, and unlike Franchthi, the EN assemblage at Knossos shows much continuity with no obvious break in tradition from the IN. Fourthly, there is some limited evidence for minor participation of Knossos in the well-documented exchange of specialized obsidian blade products and finished tools between EN mainland sites. In conclusion, I trust that this analysis has both reinforced the important role that lithic analysis can play in Aegean prehistory, and that some useful insights have been contributed to the earliest phase of Crete's human past and thus also the earliest stages of farming in the Aegean.

Acknowledgements

I would like to thank Professor J. D. Evans and the British School at Athens for providing me with, respectively, permission and a permit to work on the Knossos material. In addition, Valasia Isaakidou, Peter Tomkins and Todd Whitelaw were all very generous with their time and clarified many details about the Neolithic phasing, for which I am grateful. This research was funded by the Institute of Aegean Prehistory and The British Academy, and to both organizations I record my thanks.

Notes
1   Note that my counts differ very slightly from those originally published by John Evans. In the intervening 30 years some plastic bags have disintegrated, and some material, originally recorded as unworked, I have reclassified as worked.

Bibliography

van Andel, T. and C. Runnels
    1995   The earliest farmers in Europe. *Antiquity* 69: 481–500.
Ataman, K.
    1989   *The Chipped Stone Assemblage from Can Hasan III: A Study in Typology, Technology and Function*. PhD dissertation, University of London.
Bloedow, E.
    1991   The 'Aceramic' Neolithic phase in Greece reconsidered. *Mediterranean Archaeology*: 4–44.
Broodbank, C.
    1992   The Neolithic labyrinth: social change at Knossos before the Bronze Age. *JMA* 5: 39–75.
Broodbank, C. and T. F. Strasser
    1991   Migrant farmers and the Neolithic colonization of Crete. *Antiquity* 65: 233–45.
Colledge, S. and J. Conolly
    2007   A review and synthesis of the evidence for the origins of farming on Cyprus and Crete. In S. Colledge and J. Conolly (eds.), *The Origins and Spread of Domestic Plants in Southwest Asia and Europe*: 53–74. Walnut Creek, CA: Left Coast Press.
Colledge, S., J. Conolly and S. Shennan
    2004   Archaeobotanical evidence for the spread of farming in the eastern Mediterranean. *Current Anthropology* 45: S35–S58.
Conolly, J.
    1999   Technical strategies and technical change at Neolithic Çatalhöyük, Turkey. *Antiquity* 73: 791–800.
Evans, J. D.
    1964   Excavations in the Neolithic settlement of Knossos 1957–1960, part I. *BSA* 59: 132–240.
    1968   Knossos Neolithic, part II: summary and conclusions. *BSA* 63: 267–76.
    1994   The early millennia: continuity and change in a farming settlement. In D. Evely, H. Hughes-Brock and N. Momigliano (eds.), *Knossos: A Labyrinth of History. Papers Presented in Honour of Sinclair Hood*: 1–20. London: British School at Athens.
Furness, A.
    1953   The Neolithic pottery of Knossos. *BSA* 48: 94–134.
Kotsakis, K.
    2002   Review of 'The Early Neolithic in Greece', by Catherine Perlès. *European Journal of Archaeology* 5: 373–77.

Kozlowski, J. K., M. Kaczanowska and M. Pawlikowski
    1996   Chipped-stone industries from Neolithic levels at Lerna. *Hesperia* 65: 295–372.
LeBlanc, R.
    1992   Wedges, pièces esquillées, bipolar cores, and other things: An alternative to Shott's view of bipolar industries. *North American Archaeologist* 13: 1–14.
Mackenzie, D.
    1903   The pottery of Knossos. *JHS* 23: 157–205.
Perlès, C.
    1990   *Les Industries lithiques taillées de Franchthi (Argolide, Grèce). Tome II: Les Indusries du Mésolithique et du Néolithique Initial.* (Excavations at Franchthi Cave, Greece, Vol. V). Bloomington: Indiana University Press.
    1992   Systems of exchange and organization of production in Neolithic Greece. *JMA*: 115–64.
    2001   *The Early Neolithic of Greece*. Cambridge: Cambridge University Press.
    2005   From the Near East to Greece: Let's reverse the focus. Cultural elements that didn't transfer. In C. Lichter (ed.), *How did Farming Reach Europe?*: 275–90. Istanbul: Ege Yayınları.
Perlès, C. and K. Vitelli
    1999   Craft specialization in the Greek Neolithic. In P. Halstead (ed.), *Neolithic Society in Greece* (SSAA 2): 96–107. Sheffield: Sheffield Academic Press.
Shott, M.
    1981   Bipolar industries: Ethnographic evidence and archaeological implications. *North American Archaeologist* 10: 1–24.
Tixier, J.
    1963   *Typologie de l'Epipaléolithique du Maghreb.* Mémoires du Centre de Recherches Anthropologiques Préhistoriques, Alger. Paris: Arts et métiers graphiques.
Tomkins, P.
    2004   Filling in the 'Neolithic background': social life and social transformation in the Aegean before the Bronze Age. In J. Barrett and P. Halstead (eds.), *The Emergence of Civilisation Revisited* (SSAA 6): 38–63. Oxford: Oxbow Books.
    2007   Neolithic: Strata IX–VIII, VII–VIB, VIA–V, IV, IIIB, IIIA, IIB, IIA and IC Groups. In N. Momigliano (ed.), *Knossos Pottery Handbook: Neolithic and Bronze Age (Minoan)* (British School at Athens Studies no. 14): 9–48. London: British School at Athens.
Tomkins, P. and P. M. Day
    2001   Production and exchange of the earliest ceramic vessels in the Aegean: a view from Early Neolithic Knossos, Crete. *Antiquity* 75: 259–60.
Tomkins, P., P. M. Day and V. Kilikoglou
    2004   Knossos and the Early Neolithic Landscape of the Herakleion Basin. In G. Cadogan, E. Hatzaki and A. Vasilakis (eds.), *Knossos: Palace, City, State*: 51–59. London: British School at Athens.
Weninger, B., E. Alram-Stern, E. Bauer, L. Clare, U. Danzeglocke, O. Jöris, C. Kubatzki, G. Rollefson, H. Todorova and T. van Andel
    2006   Climate forcing due to the 8200 cal yr BP event observed at Early Neolithic sites in the eastern Mediterranean. *Quaternary Research* 66: 401–20.

6

'The Fauna and Economy of Neolithic Knossos' Revisited

Valasia Isaakidou

Introduction

The importance accorded to bioarchaeology by John Evans was manifest in the collection of plant and faunal remains already in his first Knossian campaign (1958–60) and later in his collaboration with Eric Higgs' *Early History of Agriculture* project. During the 1969–70 campaign, project members M. and H. Jarman inaugurated one of the earliest programmes in Greece for *systematic* recovery of bioarchaeological remains by flotation and sieving. Prior to this, the Jarmans had undertaken analysis of the faunal remains collected during Evans' first campaign. Although results of their work at Knossos were never fully reported, preliminary accounts underlined the importance of the earliest levels at Knossos for understanding the origins and spread of farming (Higgs and Jarman 1969) and drew attention to changes through the Neolithic in the relative frequencies of the major domestic taxa (henceforth MDT) (Jarman and Jarman 1968; Jarman *et al.* 1982: 147). The latter, involving long-term increase in the proportion of cattle, was variously interpreted by the Jarmans themselves, and subsequently by Halstead (1981) and Broodbank (1992), in terms of changing landscape, land use, animal management, consumption and symbolism, but has been regarded by others as a taphonomic artefact (Winder 1986; 1991; Whitelaw 1992).

This chapter presents a re-analysis of changing MDT frequencies through the Neolithic at Knossos, based on re-study of the faunal assemblage, and re-interpretation of these trends in the light of ethnographic investigation of non-mechanised farming in Mediterranean Europe. It is argued that, with due allowance for taphonomic distortion, trends in MDT frequencies are real and can be understood in terms of the increasing importance of *female* draught cattle, both in underpinning intensive cultivation ('gardening with cows'), as the settlement at Knossos expanded, and ultimately perhaps in promoting social competition. The trends in MDT frequencies are thus related to changes in land use, that are in turn linked to demographic and social changes at Knossos. Before embarking on this re-interpretation, the chapter begins with a summary of previous research on the Knossos faunal assemblage and with the rationale for its re-study. The new chronological scheme used by Tomkins (2007; this volume) is followed throughout the paper; the old chronology is noted in parenthesis, when older sources are discussed.

The Knossos Faunal Assemblage: Previous Research and the Rationale for Re-study

In their original discussion of the Knossos assemblage, the Jarmans interpreted the relative frequencies of the MDT in terms of their different feeding habits and 'ideal' habitats: goats on 'cliff faces and the rockier, more barren hills', sheep 'in woodless areas of lower-lying ground and piedmont', pigs 'in human habitations and wooded areas' and cattle on 'open vegetation' (Jarman and Jarman 1968: 261). The pristine ecosystem, supposedly in existence when the first colonists arrived, was argued to have provided suitable niches for the first three species, but not for the initially scarce cattle. Thereafter, pigs would have cleared undergrowth and retarded regeneration of larger trees and so eaten their way out of Knossian Neolithic husbandry. The increase in percentage of cattle from EN to early FN (EN to MN in old chronology) was seen as a result of pig-induced deforestation and expansion of open land, but also as evidence of an improving husbandry regime, in which initial reliance on the faster reproducing pigs gave way to 'the slower maturing species' (Jarman and Jarman 1968: 260). When MDT frequencies were 'corrected' for the different meat yields of each taxon, the increasing importance of cattle as a source of meat protein was accentuated even further (Jarman and Jarman 1968: 261, table 13).

In a later synthesis based on additional data from the second campaign – not presented in the publication – Jarman et al. confirmed the increase in cattle from EN to early FN (EN–MN), when they accounted for 50% of MDT, but detected a reversal of this trend in the later FN (LN) (Jarman et al. 1982: 147). The increase in cattle was considered unusual, on the grounds that sheep and goats are better adapted to the Cretan ecosystem. The possibility that this anomaly reflected a precocious 'political' predominance of Knossos, allowing selective consumption of produce from a wider area, was rejected on the grounds that a high proportion of cattle was not also seen in the assemblage from the later Bronze Age, when the regional predominance of Knossos was beyond doubt (Jarman et al. 1982: 147). The authors were more comfortable with the explanation that, in the 'buffered and protected environment' of Neolithic Crete, with no known pre-Neolithic human presence, 'the inhabitants were able to indulge a preference for beef for as long as 2500 years, before being forced in Late Neolithic times to adjust more closely to basic ecological constraints' (Jarman et al. 1982: 147).

Again adopting an ecological perspective, Halstead (1981) argued that the initial predominance of sheep at Knossos and other long-lived Neolithic sites in Greece, in a predominantly wooded landscape, represented concentration of domestic animals on stubble and fallow fields. The common long-term trend through the Neolithic to increasing proportions of cattle, pigs or goats, at the expense of sheep, was interpreted in terms of progressive opening up and exploitation of the non-arable parts of the landscape, while the eventual reversal of this trend in favour of sheep was attributed to increasing importance of wool (Halstead 1981: 328).

Unconvinced by ecological arguments, Broodbank drew on material culture as well as faunal remains to argue for a LN–early FN (ENII–MN) 'cultural revolution' at Knossos (Broodbank 1992). He noted that the 'anomalous' increase of cattle coincided with the first appearance at Knossos of spinning and weaving equipment (spindle whorls and possible loom weights), which would have been more compatible with an increase in the importance of sheep and goats (as providers of wool and hair). The predominance of cattle among animal figurines, on the other hand, suggested to Broodbank increased *cultural* rather than *economic* importance of cattle. Thus, cattle in LN–early FN Knossos could have acted 'as symbols, possessions, and prestige food for conspicuous on-site butchery, consumption and discard' (Broodbank 1992: 62).

Broodbank's conclusions were challenged by Whitelaw (1992) based, in the case of the faunal evidence, on work by Winder (1986). In the context of his doctoral research, Winder had collected and statistically re-analysed all the Jarman *data* from Knossos. He concluded that patterns of body part representation demonstrated severe impact of post-depositional processes that would have seriously affected taxonomic composition. It followed that animal management and consumption practices could not be inferred from changing frequencies of MDT (Winder 1986: 144–45).

The conflicting interpretations of changing MDT proportions at Knossos, and likewise Winder's pessimistic assessment of the data underpinning these changes, are in large measure attributable to the limitations of zooarchaeological methodology in the 1960s. The limited range and precision of the information recorded by the Jarmans pose two problems: first, they enforce excessive reliance on taxonomic composition for exploring animal management and consumption; and secondly, they do not allow the effects of post-depositional processes to be identified and filtered out. The first problem perhaps explains the Jarmans' emphasis on animal ecology and ethology, but all four MDT have broad tolerances and the limitations of this approach are arguably evident in the widely differing interpretations offered in the Jarmans' 1968 and 1982 syntheses. The second problem was exacerbated by the Jarmans' method of quantification in terms of numbers of identified specimens (NISP). This method has been severely criticised by zooarchaeologists (*e.g.*, Uerpmann 1979; Watson 1979), as it fails to control for differential fragmentation between body parts, taxa and age groups: NISP exaggerates the frequency of larger animals (*e.g.*, Payne 1972) for reasons of (a) visibility and thus recovery, and (b) robusticity and hence resilience to mechanical damage (*e.g.*, scavenger attrition, trampling). In the case of the Jarman study, these effects were exacerbated by: (a) post-excavation damage suffered by the 1957–60 material and failure to mend resulting (very common) fresh breaks (Isaakidou 2004: 116–19); and (b) ancient human-induced differential fragment-ation between taxa. Winder did not identify these analytical problems, as he was able to locate and re-examine only a fraction of the assemblage itself (Winder 1986). Thus, the data generated by the Jarmans should not be used to answer questions related either to animal exploitation at Knossos or to post-depositional alteration of the assemblage.

The Knossos Neolithic faunal assemblage is important for several reasons: its size (many thousands of identifiable bones); its diachronic character (a very rare example of a site with continuous occupation from the earliest Neolithic to the end of the Bronze Age); and its derivation from a settlement that grew significantly through the Neolithic and eventually developed into a major Bronze Age centre. Given the limitations of the Jarmans' original study, therefore, re-examination of the assemblage with more modern methods was desirable.

Re-analysis: Methods and Results

Methods

In order to shed light on animal exploitation and, also, to filter out the effects of post-depositional processes, ancient and modern, an array of variables was recorded. First, a different quantification method was employed, Minimum Number of Anatomical Units (MinAU – Halstead 1992; in press) designed to minimise the effects of differential fragmentation between different species and body parts. Presence/absence of gnawing marks and fragment morphology (following Binford 1981) were recorded to serve as independent measures of the frequency and intensity of scavenger attrition and anthropogenic bone breakage. Thus, it was possible to assess the effects of post-depositional processes using a *number* of variables, rather than having to rely *solely* on body part representation (in contrast with Winder 1986).

Management and consumption were explored using techniques for the identification and interpretation of species, age, sex, life history (pathology), and butchery that were mostly unavailable to the original researchers. Improved methods of sheep and goat speciation, enabling generation of separate mortality curves for sheep and goats, provided a clearer picture of animal husbandry, which is of great importance given the potential differences in feeding habits and productive potential of these two species, and hence in their role in the farming regime. Moreover, thanks to Tomkins' revised chronological scheme, the faunal assemblage is now more finely dated, and so more amenable to diachronic analysis, than was hitherto the case.

Exploring Taxonomic Composition

The *presence* of all four MDT from the earliest, basal levels has already been noted (Jarman and Jarman 1968), but relative frequencies according to the Jarmans and the recent re-analysis differ considerably (Figure 6.1). According to the Jarman data, cattle increase steadily through the Neolithic, becoming the predominant taxon in early FN. According to the re-analysis, cattle increase from the Aceramic to LN, but *sheep* remain the *dominant* taxon throughout the Neolithic. The most economical explanation for this discrepancy is the use of different quantification methods (see above). Nevertheless, the present study concurs with the Jarmans in identifying an increasing frequency of cattle remains in successive phases of the Neolithic (Figure 6.2).

Before interpreting this trend in terms of animal management or consumption, the potential effect of post-depositional processes must be considered. First, soil chemistry as an important agent of bone destruction at Knossos can be dismissed, given the nature of the soils on the Kephala hill. On the contrary, the pristine condition of the apparently rapidly buried bone of Aceramic-EN date (smooth surfaces, no signs of chemical etching) shows that Knossian soils are conducive to good bone preservation. Secondly, if carnivore attrition were the primary agent affecting the taxonomic composition of the assemblage, an increase in the frequency of larger animals (cattle) and decrease of the smaller ones (sheep, and to a lesser degree the slightly larger pigs and goats) should be accompanied by a rise in the incidence of gnawing. Figure 6.2 clearly shows this not to be the case. Both incidence of gnawing and proportion of cattle increase from the Aceramic to EN and MN, but sheep decrease only in MN. Moreover, the frequency of cattle increases most dramatically when gnawing decreases slightly between MN and LN. Finally, the fluctuations of the other two medium-sized taxa, pigs and goats, are not plausibly explained by carnivore attrition, as they do not follow the pattern observed for sheep. Evidently, carnivore attrition does not

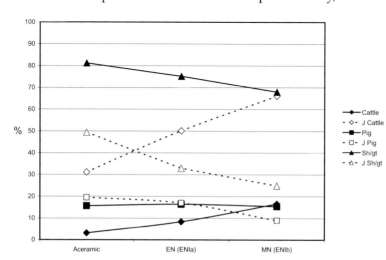

Figure 6.1. Taxonomic composition according to Jarman and Jarman 1968 (dashed line) and Isaakidou 2004 (solid line), based on NISP and MinAU counts respectively.

provide a satisfactory explanation for changes in taxonomic composition. Likewise, while relative frequencies of the MDT are affected by variations in the quality of bone retrieval during excavation (more sieving of the lowest levels) and perhaps in the intensity of butchery, these do not undermine the trend to increasing proportions of cattle identified by the Jarmans (Isaakidou 2004).

The suggestion by Winder that the increase in cattle is an artefact of taphonomic processes is thus unfounded, but the interpretations of this trend by the Jarmans and Broodbank are also problematic. As has already been noted, all four MDT have broad ecological tolerances and in any case, availability of different forms of pasture will partly have depended on the scale of both herding and arable farming. Nonetheless, there seems to be no basis for the claim that cattle were less suited than pigs, sheep or goats to the landscape around Neolithic Knossos. On the contrary, sheep are the best adapted of the MDT to grazing arable land and so should arguably have been *least* suited to the initial 'pristine' environment of EN Knossos, but perhaps favoured thereafter by progressive clearance. If relative proportions of the four MDT are shaped by environmental constraints, therefore, this was arguably because livestock were closely integrated with crop husbandry. Broodbank's model of 'conspicuous consumption' of cattle can also be questioned on the basis of re-study of the assemblage. Throughout the Neolithic at Knossos, carcasses of all four MDT seem to have been widely shared out, but butchery marks coupled with bone fragmentation and dispersal offer no evidence of large-scale *commensality*. Indeed, the carcasses of cattle were

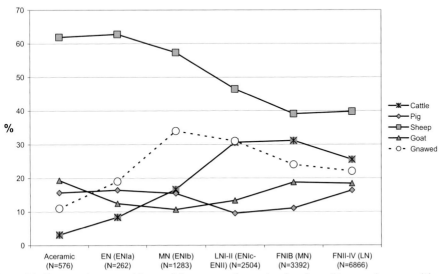

Figure 6.2. Taxonomic composition and frequency of gnawing by phase. Taxonomic composition based on MinAU counts, excluding parts of the skeleton particularly prone to taphonomic and recovery biases – cranial specimens and phalanges; gnawing based on MaxAU counts; phasing follows Tomkins 2007 (in parenthesis: the traditional chronology, with EN subdivisions following Tomkins 2001).

exploited *more intensively* than those of the other MDT (Isaakidou 2007), suggesting no wasteful conspicuous consumption of this species.

Previous studies have perhaps sought to accommodate evidence for changing *taxonomic composition* to the polar alternatives of ecological constraints (Jarman and Jarman 1968) and indulgent or conspicuous consumption (Jarman *et al.* 1986; Broodbank 1992). Choices between livestock species are also shaped, however, by goals other than meat production and, as argued above, by the embedding of domestic animals in broader practices of crop husbandry and land use. These possibilities are discussed below with reference to recent farming practices, but are first evaluated by introducing other lines of evidence for animal management at Neolithic Knossos.

Demographic Profiles and 'Occupational Stresses'

Age, sex and metrical data for sheep, cattle and goats from Knossos show that, throughout the Neolithic, husbandry practices were stable and consistent with a 'meat' strategy of production in which males tended to be culled as juveniles or sub-adults and females as adults (Isaakidou 2006: 101–3, figs. 8.2–4). This strategy does not preclude *non-intensive/non-specialised* management for secondary products (wool, traction, milk) and indeed could have ensured (but is not evidence *for*) a balanced supply of meat *and* secondary products (Halstead 1998).

In the case of cattle, however, evidence of *actual* rather than *potential* exploitation for secondary products was afforded by osteoarthritic pathological conditions on skeletal material. They are manifested as remodelling of articular surfaces (*e.g.*, lipping, condyle extension, *etc.*), development of osteophytes, and grooving of articular surfaces, overwhelmingly on phalanges and distal meta-podials, and eburnation of hip joints (*caput femoris* and *acetabulum pelvis*) (Isaakidou 2006). These conditions, a result of repetitive trauma or stress on the joints, may plausibly be attributed, based on examination of modern carcasses of animals with known life histories, to injuries incurred in *traction* (*e.g.*, Baker and Brothwell 1980; Bartosiewicz *et al.* 1997; de Cupere *et al.* 2000; Isaakidou 2006: 104–8). Such 'traction pathologies' are well represented in MN–FN, while their scarcity in the Aceramic and EN may well be due to the small size of the samples of cattle bones in the earliest phases. A number of these pathological conditions, ranging in date from EN to FN, were observed on *sexable* body parts (pelves) and these were, *with a single exception*, from adult *breeding females* (Isaakidou 2006: 107, table 8.4). Traction pathologies were also found in the modest sample of EM cattle bones and, although none of these was observed on a sexable pelvis, the proportion of males surviving into adulthood appears to have been higher than in the Neolithic, raising the possibility that – as well as or instead of cows – oxen were now used as draught animals (Isaakidou 2006: 106, table 8.3).

Percentages of Deadstock and Numbers of Livestock

Before attempting to explore the relationship between Neolithic use of cows for traction and the long-term increase in the proportion of the Knossos faunal assemblage made up by cattle, it is necessary to clarify what this latter trend actually means. First, as has already been noted, taphonomic processes have affected the bones of the four MDT to varying degrees. The method of quantification used here (which lowered the proportional representation of cattle in favour of sheep/goats) has to some extent filtered out such biases. Secondly, a faunal assemblage is a record of *dead*stock proportions, whereas previous attempts to interpret Knossos MDT figures have mostly been concerned – implicitly rather than explicitly – with *live*stock. Large samples of ageable mandibles from Knossos do not indicate significant change through the Neolithic in MDT mortality patterns, so changing MDT proportions apparently do reflect changing *live*stock proportions and not merely changes in the age at which one or more species was culled (for the distinction between *live*stock and *dead*stock proportions, see Albarella 1999; Halstead 2002). Thirdly, some interpretations of Knossian taxonomic composition (*e.g.*, the recursive relationship between local landscape and MDT proportional representation) are arguably concerned with *absolute* rather than *relative* numbers of livestock. The rising percentage of cattle among MDT, however, could equally result from, for example, increasing absolute numbers of cattle or decreasing absolute numbers of other domesticates. This issue cannot be resolved definitively, but an increase in absolute numbers of cattle alone would have resulted in a lower percentage of sheep, goats and pigs, whereas the EN–LN increase in proportion of cattle is essentially at the expense of sheep (Figure 6.2). If, following Halstead (1981), sheep was the species most closely tied to grazing of arable plots, then their absolute numbers may very broadly have been proportional to the extent of arable land and thus even more loosely proportional to the size of the human population of Knossos. On this basis, it may very tentatively be suggested that the rising percentage of cattle at Knossos represented an increase in the numbers of this species and perhaps decrease in sheep numbers, in each case relative to human population and arable land. The proportion of cattle made up by draught cows in each phase cannot be estimated, because traction does not inevitably result in distinctive pathology (Johannsen 2005) and anyway the incidence of pathological specimens is partly a function of the variable representation and preservation of different body parts of adult cattle. There is no reason, however, to doubt that draught cows contributed to the EN–LN increase in cattle. If this increase was indeed accompanied by a decline in sheep numbers, as suggested here, then cattle may also have played an increasing role during EN–LN in grazing and/or manuring arable land.

The remainder of this chapter considers the implications of Neolithic use of draught cows for the nature of the farming regime and, more broadly, for the size and organisation of the human community at Knossos.

Early Farming at Knossos

Models of Early Farming in the Aegean

Traditional extensive agriculture (cereal growing in alternation with bare fallow, specialisation in olives or vines) and herding (transhumant pastoralism) in the Mediterranean have long served as models for past land use in the Aegean (*e.g.*, Semple 1922; Renfrew 1972; Jarman *et al.* 1982), but a series of studies in the last 20 years has shown that such practices are shaped as much by inequalities of land ownership or the existence of markets, as by climatic constraints (*e.g.*, Halstead 1987; 2000; Cherry 1988; Forbes 1993).

On this basis, it has been argued that extensive cereal/fallow agriculture, with tillage by ox-drawn ards, occurred in the highly inegalitarian context of the later Bronze Age palaces of southern Greece (*e.g.*, Halstead 1995a), but that Neolithic cultivation would have resembled the more *intensive* practices of recent small-scale farmers. The small size of most Neolithic settlements, and consequently short distance to cultivated plots, would greatly have facilitated such intensive husbandry (Halstead 1981). More specifically, using a combination of analogical reasoning and archaeological evidence, Halstead has developed a model of Neolithic land use in which cereals and pulses were grown in similar quantities and perhaps in rotation, employing intensive methods such as hand tillage, manuring, weeding, and possibly watering (*e.g.*, Halstead 1981; 2000). This horticultural regime was closely integrated with small scale herding, on cultivated land, of *sheep*, which fertilised soils, consumed weeds and controlled lodging of cereals (Halstead 1996b; 2006). The model has received support from Bogaard's recent study of Central European archaeobotanical evidence, which showed that such an intensive gardening regime prevailed in the earlier Neolithic of this area (Bogaard 2004), and from a synthesis of bioarchaeological evidence arguing the inception of this regime in the earlier Neolithic of the Near East and Anatolia (Bogaard 2005). Finally, the model is compatible with, and to some extent an elaboration upon, Sherratt's argument that use of the ard (or scratch-plough), pulled by yoked cattle, first diffused into Europe in the fourth-third millennia BC and that cultivation was previously carried out with some form of hoe or digging stick (Sherratt 1981). The evidence from Knossos, however, indicates use of cattle for traction possibly from the late seventh-mid sixth millennium BC – about three millennia earlier than anticipated by Sherratt – and suggests that a variant of Halstead's model of Neolithic cultivation may have been practised, at least at Knossos. To this latter end, it is instructive to consider the role of draught cows in recent Mediterranean farming and, particularly, in an *intensive* cultivation regime.

Farming by Analogy

Surprisingly for a modern city-dweller with limited knowledge of pre-mechanised farming practices, use of *female* cattle as draught animals was widespread in southern Europe even within living memory. The explanation normally offered by elderly farmers is that, whereas oxen (castrated males) only provide muscle power, cows are multi-purpose animals, able to provide milk and calves (for sale or to rear as future breeding/work animals), as well as labour. Cows were thus well suited to the small-scale, largely self-sufficient agriculture practised by many households around the Mediterranean in the recent past. On the other hand, as informants also routinely emphasise, with the exception of recent improved breeds that were demanding of fodder, cows ploughed more slowly, less effectively and for shorter periods of time than oxen and so were unsuitable for large-scale cultivation. Likewise, cows could pull smaller loads over shorter distances than oxen and so tended to be used to bring in the harvest or to fetch wood for the household, rather than for commercial transport. Those unable to maintain even two draught *cows* variously yoked a single cow or donkey to that of a neighbour, hired (or exchanged human labour for) a plough team, or worked their land by hand. Each of these solutions limited yet further the scale of cultivation possible and also meant that sowing was unlikely to be timely and the harvest thus less reliable. This last point may have been particularly critical in the semi-arid lowlands of the southern Aegean, where a sharply seasonal climate results in a narrow 'window' for autumn ploughing and sowing (Figure 6.3). The severity of summer drought means that tillage and sowing cannot begin until the autumn rains have softened and moistened the ground and then farmers must wait for the surface to dry out enough to allow creation of an even tilth. On the other hand, because the summer drought sets in very early and very rapidly, crops sown *late* are dependent for success on highly unreliable spring rainfall and so are avoided where possible. In ideal circumstances (early and moderate rainfall), the autumn sowing season might last three months (usually November–January), but elderly central Cretan farmers emphasise that it was often abbreviated if the rains started late and/or were too heavy or too sustained for the ground to dry out (Halstead field notes, Knossos, Kalo Khorio Pediados). In the face of such time stress, ploughing – even with cows – entailed a much lower risk of sowing crops too late or on an insufficient scale than did manual tillage.

Although draught cows were mostly used by recent Mediterranean farmers in the context of *extensive* (in the sense of modest labour-inputs and area-yields rather than large-scale) agriculture, they could also support *intensive* farming. Farmers in upland villages in the Asturias region of northern Spain grew 'primitive' emmer and spelt wheat in rotation with maize and potatoes, in small plots (of ca. 0.04–0.3 ha) within 20–30 minutes walk from the house. Each family cultivated up to 0.5–1.5 ha, of which only 0.2–0.5 ha were used for wheat. Despite the small size of the areas cultivated, yields were high, ranging from ca. 1 ton/ha of clean grain in bad years to 2.5 tons/ha in good years. This was achieved by the implementation of methods of husbandry normally employed in intensive 'garden' cultivation, namely *hand-weeding* and *heavy manuring*. Cows played a multiple role in this regime, not only providing tillage, as in other areas of southern Europe, but also producing the stall-manure that ensured high yields per unit area and pulling the sledges (Figure 6.4) that transported both manure to the fields and hay to the byres (Halstead field notes).

In Asturias, therefore, draught cattle were integral to intensive cultivation as sources of manure and of labour for tillage and transport. These roles enabled a 'horticultural' regime to be maintained over *much greater distances* (≤1 km) than would otherwise have been practicable. By contrast, where recent 'garden' cultivation in the Mediterranean relied solely on human labour, it was typically restricted to the immediate vicinity of the village and practised on a very small scale, for the growing of pulses and vegetables (*e.g.*, Jones *et al.* 1999). Asturian farming practices were of course linked to particular historical circumstances (*e.g.*, scarcity of land due to the existence of rich absentee landowners, opportunities for wage labour in the mines and to sell calves in urban markets) and so are unlikely to be directly comparable to Neolithic Crete. They represent a viable alternative, however, to current models of intensive manual or extensive ox-based cultivation and so may have heuristic value for understanding the zooarchaeological evidence from Knossos.

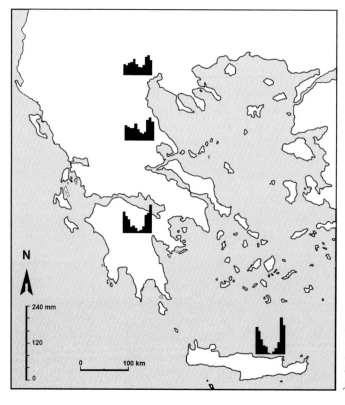

Figure 6.3. Mean monthly rainfall 1894–1929 for Thessaloniki, Larisa, Nafplio and Heraklio (north to south) (after Admiralty 1944: 94, fig. 58).

Figure 6.4. Asturias: basket mounted on sledge used for transporting manure (left) and manure piles in field (each representing a sledge-load) (photos by author, January 2006).

The Use of Draught Cows at Neolithic Knossos

As noted above, recent Mediterranean farmers used draught cattle both to plough and to pull carts or sledges. The pathological evidence from Knossos offers no indication of whether draught cows were used for ploughing or transport or both, but neither role required any great technological breakthrough. In recent times, many farmers made their own wooden ards (choice of suitably shaped raw materials was more crucial than carpentry skills) (Halstead field notes) and the relatively complex task of making wheeled vehicles could have been avoided by using sledges for transport. There is no reason, therefore, why draught cows at Knossos should not have been used for both tillage and transport.

Whether draught cows were used in small-scale but extensive agriculture, such as was widespread in Crete in the recent past, or in intensive cultivation like that practised in Asturias, is not yet clear. Once a much richer archaeo-botanical assemblage is available from Knossos, the issue should be resolved by isotopic evidence for or against manuring (Bogaard *et al.* 2007) and by weed ecological evidence for level of fertility and intensity of tillage of crops (Bogaard *et al.* 2000). As noted above, however, archaeobotanical data from EN (sixth millennium BC) central Europe indicates an intensive regime and there is some faunal evidence that this may have been associated with use of draught cattle (Bogaard 2004). For Knossos, in the absence of direct evidence, we can do no more than consider whether extensive or intensive cultivation seems more likely. The *potential* for intensive husbandry is largely a function of the availability of labour and this is in turn partly determined by the scale of cultivation (*e.g.*, self-sufficiency versus surplus production) and the distance between place of residence and cultivation plots. The latter parameter can be modelled by considering the size of the Neolithic community at Knossos and estimating the scale of cultivation needed to support it.

The main aim of John Evans' second field campaign at Knossos was to

	after JD Evans				after Tomkins			
	Site area (ha)	No. of inhabitants			Site area (ha)	No. of inhabitants		
		@ 100/ha	@ 200/ha	@ 300/ha		@ 100/ha	@ 200/ha	@ 300/ha
Aceramic	0.25	25	50	75	0.25–0.35	25–35	50–70	75–105
EN					0.25–0.35	25–35	50–70	75–105
MN	2	200	400	600	0.7–0.8	70–80	140–160	210–240
LNI					1.4–1.75	140–175	280–350	420–525
LNII	3	300	600	900	1.75–2.5	175–250	350–500	525–750
FNIII–IV	5	500	1000	1500	1.75–2.5	175–250	350–500	525–750

Table 6.1. Population estimates for Neolithic Knossos based on site-size estimates after Evans (1971) and Tomkins (this volume: table 3.2).

explore, through multiple soundings across the Kephala hill, the growth of the settlement during the Neolithic. His resulting estimates of settlement size in successive phases of the Neolithic (Evans 1971: 96, fig. 1) formed the basis for Broodbank's attempt, discussed at the outset of this chapter, to link population growth to social complexity and to increasing importance of cattle (Broodbank 1992). On the basis of re-study of data from both John and Arthur Evans' excavations, Tomkins (this volume; in prep.) has offered estimates of settlement size that are chronologically finer and also imply rather slower growth, although ongoing intensive survey by Vasilakis and Whitelaw may yet lend support to the higher figures (Whitelaw pers. comm.). Tomkins' more conservative figures are adopted in the following discussion, but – to aid comparison – Table 6.1 shows both sets of estimates of settlement size in successive phases and, in each case, calculates the implied number of inhabitants for a range of habitation densities.

The initial Aceramic settlement at Knossos was small and grew slowly through EN, reaching the size of many early Thessalian tells (0.75 ha – Halstead 1984) in MN and thereafter expanding to 1.75–2.5 ha in LN II, a size not exceeded during FN (Tomkins this volume; in prep.; *contra* Evans 1971). In LN, the community at Knossos may (depending on the habitation density adopted) have reached the required size for long-term demographic viability (>500 people, Wobst 1974) and the threshold above which egalitarian communities tend to fission (>400 people – Forge 1972; Whitelaw 1983: 340) or develop more complex social mechanisms for resolving internal conflict. By EM I–II the settlement may have covered 5 ha, with a population of perhaps 1000 – well above the thresholds for both demographic self-sufficiency and hierarchical organisation (Whitelaw 1983; 2004). These social implications of settlement growth are further discussed below.

Table 6.2 calculates the area of cultivated land required in successive phases to produce staple grain crops, assuming a habitation density of 200/ha (the maximum favoured by Broodbank 1992) and a grain requirement of 250 kg/head/year (cf. Halstead 1981: 317 [200 kg] and Bogaard 2005: 43 [300 kg]). The area required is calculated for both intensive and extensive husbandry regimes,

Phase	Grain (250 kg/person)	Intensive farming (1500 kg/ha annual yield)		Extensive farming (1000 kg/ha)	
		Land (ha)	Radius (m)	Land (ha)	Radius (m)
Aceramic	12500–17500	8.3–11.7	165–196	25–35	284–334
EN	12500–17500	8.3–11.7	165–196	25–35	284–334
MN	35000–40000	23.3–26.7	276.5–296	70–80	474.5–507
LNI	70000–87500	46.7–58.3	391–437	140–175	671–750
LNII–FN	87500–125000	58.3–83.3	437–523	175–250	750–897
EM	375000	166.7	739	500	1268

Table 6.2. Land requirements and radius to edge of cultivated land from centre of site with settlement area added; calculations based on Tomkins' estimates for site size (Tomkins this volume: table 3.2).

assuming annual cropping and average yields of 1500 kg/ha under *intensive* farming (Charles *et al.* 2002; Bogaard 2004: 24, table 2.1; Halstead field notes – Asturias) and biennial fallowing and average yields of 1000 kg/ha under *extensive* farming (*e.g.*, Halstead 1981: 318; cf. Broodbank 1992). The radius of the area within which both settlement and cultivated land could be accommodated is also calculated (cf. Halstead 1981: 219, table 11.3), ignoring (for the sake of simplicity) the obvious heterogeneity of land around Knossos in terms of both agricultural potential and ease of access. In this latter respect, the tabulated distances to furthest fields will be underestimates, but to attempt greater precision, in the absence of geoarchaeological evidence for landscape change and of archaeobotanical or surface survey evidence for areas cultivated, is arguably pointless at this point.

In the Aceramic Neolithic, the projected distance to furthest fields, even if an extensive regime is assumed, is less than 300 m and so falls comfortably within the distances walked to intensively hand-cultivated plots in the recent past in various parts of Greece (*e.g.*, Jones *et al.* 1999) and in Asturias (Halstead field notes). In practice, an extensive regime is implausible, if not inviable, without draught cattle to help break fallowed plots, but it is possible that evidence of traction pathologies will be found if and when a larger sample of Aceramic cattle bones is available. On the other hand, it is highly likely that plots so close to the settlement were fertilised by disposal of domestic waste and the penning of animals (the latter practice facilitated by absence of large predators – Isaakidou 2004), weeded in the course of collecting greens for human consumption or to feed to animals kept around the house, and dug over by foraging domestic pigs. Moreover, yields on previously uncultivated soils will initially have been high and sheep, initially the dominant MDT, probably grazed on arable land and so helped to maintain fertility. Around the small earliest settlement at Knossos, therefore, cultivation was arguably intensive by default (cf. Halstead 1981: 319). If the high area yields of an intensive regime are accepted, the distance to furthest fields will have remained below 300 m in EN and MN, when evidence of traction pathologies suggests that working cattle will have contributed to soil fertility by grazing arable plots and perhaps by producing and transporting stall manure. Recent farmers in northern Greece tended to spread stall manure on fields within a ca. 500 m radius because of the difficulty of carting it further – even with the help of draught cattle. Even in LN II–FN, the cultivated land of Knossos may have fallen within a radius of ca. 500 m and thus near enough for intensive manuring. The use of draught cattle at Knossos probably began, therefore, in the context of intensive crop husbandry and at no point in the Neolithic need settlement growth have enforced the use of cattle traction to support extensive agriculture. On the contrary, draught cattle may have enabled the continuation of intensive husbandry even when the settlement reached an estimated population of up to 500 in LN II and FN. In EM I–II, however, an estimated population of 1000 would have required fields more than 700 m away (even assuming high yields) and, at this distance, it is unjustifiable to treat land in all directions as equally fertile and equally accessible. At this stage, the combination of distant fields and variable terrain is likely to have forced the inhabitants of Knossos into increasing reliance on extensive cultivation (Isaakidou in prep.).

This attempt to model land use at Knossos, and the role therein of draught cattle, must obviously be treated with caution: distance alone does not determine the intensity of crop husbandry, and the figures adopted for site size, for habitation density and for crop yields are all open to challenge. Nonetheless, current estimates of the size and density of habitation of the EN settlement would have to be revised upwards very dramatically to support an argument that draught cattle were first used at Knossos because settlement growth had enforced extensive crop husbandry. On the contrary, it seems that draught cattle were initially used under an intensive regime, perhaps as a local response to time stress in the sowing period (because of the sharply seasonal Cretan climate) (Figure 6.3) or perhaps as a more widespread but largely unrecognised feature of early farming. Equally, although a case could be made for extensive agriculture before EM by revising upwards the estimates for site area and habitation density in LN or FN, it seems clear that the early use of draught cattle did not trigger marked settlement growth.

Cows and Complexity at Knossos?

Draught cows arguably enabled the growth in size of Neolithic Knossos, by making intensive crop husbandry viable on a larger scale and so tipping the balance in favour of local growth over the foundation of new settlements. Whatever the reasons for the growth of Neolithic Knossos, Tomkins' estimates of site size suggest that growth stopped or slowed down for a considerable period during the later Neolithic, perhaps because the threshold for 'egalitarian' organisation had been reached. Renewed settlement growth in EM may then have been triggered, or at any rate enabled, by the emergence towards the end of the Neolithic of more marked social hierarchy. Might the use of draught animals have contributed to emerging social inequality, as others have previously argued (*e.g.*, Goody 1976; Gilman 1981; Sherratt 1981; Bogucki 1993; Halstead 1995a)?

Draught cows may have contributed to the survival, cohesion and equality of the Neolithic community at Knossos. By reducing time stress during the autumn sowing period, they may have reduced significantly the risk of inadequate harvests and facilitated overproduction of a 'normal surplus' that could be stored as insurance against future crop failure. By relieving humans of the most arduous tillage and transport tasks, they may have reduced the risk of injury (including, in the case of women, miscarriages) and so improved human fitness for both work and reproduction. And by extending the distance over which intensive husbandry (including heavy manuring) was practicable, they may have delayed the emergence of inequality between holders of fertile and well-worked infield plots and others with access only to less fertile and more poorly tilled plots further from the settlement.

On the other hand, cattle reproduce more slowly than the other MDT and must be reared to two (preferably three or four) years of age before they are put to work (Halstead field notes Greece, Spain; also Johannsen 2005), so ownership of a working pair significantly increases the capital costs of farming. Moreover, because cattle often learn to work only on the left or on the right side of the pair (Halstead field notes), maintenance of one replacement trained to the yoke may have been insufficient insurance against injury or premature death of a draught-animal. Even if animals suitable for yoking were readily available, draught cattle work ineffectively unless fed grain or nutritious gathered fodder in addition to coarse crop residues. As in the recent past, it is likely that the inhabitants of Neolithic Knossos varied in their ability to spare land for fodder crops or to mobilise labour for collection of wild fodder. If access to draught cattle was uneven, then the ability to sow promptly, to cultivate distant plots intensively and to produce normal surplus will also have been unequal. Any such inequality was doubtless to some degree smoothed out by mutual assistance or exchange and Tomkins has argued that the stylistic uniformity of EN–MN ceramics at Knossos betrays a concern for the promotion of a strong collective identity (Tomkins 2004: 46–48). In recent farming communities, however, mutual assistance is *not* unconditional (*e.g.*, Sahlins 1972) and plough animals or food are often loaned in return for labour, rather than given (*e.g.*, in C. Italy – M. Forte field notes – and both northern and southern Greece – Halstead field notes). Such exchanges provide short-term relief to the needy, but may in the long-term lead to a cycle of increasing inequality. Much depends on the extent to which land and draught cows were in collective or domestic ownership at Knossos and on how conditional was any obligation to help needy neighbours.

In highland New Guinea (Brown 1978: 78–81), and for that matter in recent rural Greece (Petropoulos 1943–44), land may be cleared and defended collectively, but the right to harvest crops lies with the individual(s) who has planted and tended them. The amount of labour invested in intensive cultivation, of the sort suggested here for Neolithic Knossos, implies therefore that not only individual crop stands, but arguably also, on a longer time-scale, individual plots of land would have been viewed as private property at least to the extent that those who invested their labour had preferential access to its fruits. Moreover, it would have been difficult to ensure timely and careful execution of the multiple agricultural tasks to be performed, if one or a few individuals did not have control over each plot. There are possible hints of the existence of concepts of private property *within* the settlement: the three consecutive architectural phases of the LN (II) house in area AABB, remodelled, but with walls re-built on the same spot and on the same alignment (Figure 6.5) (see also Evans 1971: 107 and fig. 4; 1994: figs. 5 and 6); and the modifications and rebuilding between LN and early FN of the house in area XY (Evans 1971: 107; Tomkins in prep.) (cf. for Thessaly, Halstead this volume; Kotsakis 2006). This continuity does not seem to have been imposed by constraints on space, as excavation has revealed substantial open areas between houses in this and later periods (Evans 1964; 1971). For earlier periods (pre-LN II), exposures are too limited to provide a clear picture of settlement organisation.

Private ownership of house-plots, however, need not necessarily have been extended to arable land and anyway it is likely that ownership of both was communal at least to the extent that land could be redistributed if demographic or economic accident left some plots ownerless. The growth of the settlement may have played an interesting role here. The Aceramic–MN settlement was too small to be demographically self-sufficient and, if the norm for marriage involved uxorilocal or virilocal residence, then exogamy would have increased the probability both of ownerless plots and of landless (or land-poor) households. By LN II, the settlement may have reached or approached a size where exogamy became unnecessary and it may not be coincidental that the frequency of 'non-local' fabrics decreases dramatically from half of the ceramic assemblage in EN–MN to below 20% in LN I–II (Tomkins 2004; Tomkins *et al.* 2004). If the abundance of non-local EN–MN pottery reflects exchange linked to the maintenance of ties with affinal kin in archaeologically invisible communities (cf. Tomkins this volume), their sharp decline in LN might reflect a preference for local endogamy. Endogamy should have reduced the probability of ownerless plots being subject to collective redistribution and so may have been favoured as a means of retaining family or lineage control over prime land that will have become increasingly scarce as Knossos grew in size. At any rate, it is intriguing that the marked uniformity of EN–MN ceramics gives way to a much greater diversity in LN (Broodbank 1992: 53), despite the sharp decline in the proportion of non-local vessels. If EN–MN uniformity indeed reflects a strong *collective ideology*, then LN diversity suggests growing legitimacy for *competition* (cf. Halstead 1995b; Tomkins 2004).

Rights to the services of draught cattle are not directly amenable to archaeological investigation. The draught cows at Neolithic Knossos were

Figure 6.5. Walls in Area AA/BB (after Evans 1971: 104, fig. 4 'Section of the east face of AA/BB').

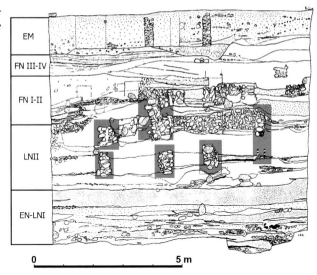

EM

FN III-IV

FN I-II

LNII

EN-LNI

0   5 m

eventually slaughtered and eaten, but after several years of calving and working, so someone evidently exercised effective control over the competing uses of the animals. By the same logic, those who reared, trained and fed such animals probably had first call on their labour and so would have been best placed to ensure timely and rapid exploitation of conditions suitable for tillage and sowing, even if they subsequently loaned the animals to others. It has been argued above that the increasing proportion of cattle from EN to LN probably did represent an increase in the ratio of cattle to humans at Knossos and hence increased availability of draught cows for tillage. On this basis, the rearing of draught cattle may have been restricted in EN and MN to the largest, most ambitious or most innovative 'households', but may have been more widespread in LN, when expansion of the settlement arguably made animal traction a prerequisite of successful intensive farming. How widespread was LN access to draught cows cannot be gauged from the faunal remains because their contextual resolution is low and anyway carcasses seem to have been widely shared during consumption (Isaakidou 2007). The labour costs of rearing and feeding such animals, however, probably prevented universal ownership. If the diversity of LN ceramics does signal acceptance of greater competition, then any households without access to their own draught cows may have borrowed those of more successful neighbours on a basis that led to a spiral of growing inequality. The reduced proportion of cattle, and commensurate increase in sheep, in FN may indicate a subsequent decline in ownership of cattle and so growing inequality, although the continued reliance on *cows* (rather than *oxen*) for traction suggests that any inequality in productive capacity was limited in scale. Only in EM may the, as yet slender, evidence for draught *oxen* signal the emergence of radical inequalities in agricultural production.

Conclusions

The excavations of John Evans in the Neolithic mound at Knossos, coupled with those of others in the Bronze Age levels above, have produced what is probably Europe's longest diachronic faunal record of domestic animal husbandry. Initial study of this record 40 years ago detected an increasing proportion of cattle bones through the Neolithic that has variously been interpreted as the outcome of ecological/economic (Jarman and Jarman 1968; Halstead 1981; Jarman *et al.* 1982) or social (Broodbank 1992) processes or as a taphonomic artefact (Winder 1986; Whitelaw 1992). Re-study of the assemblage, including more rigorous methods of quantification and the recording of a much wider range of variables, confirms this increasing trend in the proportion of cattle bones and demonstrates that it is independent of the considerable and varied taphonomic distortion that has occurred. Furthermore, detailed consideration of butchery traces and bone fragmentation suggests that cattle were not the focus of conspicuous consumption (as suggested by Broodbank). A combination of demographic, biometric and pathological evidence, however, indicates use of adult breeding cows for draught purposes.

Given the broad ecological tolerances of the early Knossian domestic animals, the increasing proportion of cattle is more usefully considered in relation to local patterns of land use rather than regional landscape. The small size of the initial Neolithic settlement at Knossos, it is argued, would by default have favoured intensive 'garden' cultivation, such as has been demonstrated archaeobotanically elsewhere in Europe, rather than an extensive 'field' regime. Prevailing models of Neolithic farming tend to link such 'garden' cultivation with manual tillage, but recent intensive cultivation in the Asturias region of northern Spain was reliant on draught cows both for tillage (together with manual labour) and for the production and transport of manure. Draught cows were probably first used at Knossos, therefore, in the context of intensive crop husbandry and the rising proportion of cattle through much of the Neolithic arguably reflects increasing reliance on their labour as the settlement grew in size and, presumably, fields were cultivated at a greater distance. Cows were apparently first used for draught when Knossos was very small, however, perhaps to facilitate competitive overproduction and/or to reduce the risks posed by time stress in the sowing period. Heavy use of draught cows is not as yet attested at Neolithic sites on the Greek mainland, for example in Thessaly, inviting speculation that early reliance on draught cattle may have been especially favoured at Knossos by the acutely seasonal climate of the southern Aegean, which will have exacerbated problems of time stress during the sowing period. During LN, Knossos seems to have reached a size well in excess of the *suggested* norm for Neolithic communities in Thessaly, implying that this heavy use of draught cows facilitated the significant growth exhibited by the Knossos settlement – perhaps by making intensive cultivation feasible on a larger scale and so reducing some of the practical pressures in favour of the fissioning of the community.

If draught cows did indeed facilitate settlement growth, their use perhaps did have profound significance for Knossian society. By LN II, Knossos may have grown to a size that offered relative demographic self-sufficiency and above which further growth (rather than fission) was only possible with the development of institutionalised hierarchy. On present evidence, it seems that further expansion of the settlement did not take place until the EM period and, therefore, that draught cows enabled but did not drive settlement growth. To some extent, draught cows may have contributed to the maintenance of a relatively egalitarian community, by reducing the risks of time stress in the sowing period and enabling those cultivating near and distant fields alike to pursue an intensive regime of crop husbandry. If draught cows were in some form of 'private' rather than collective ownership, however, as has been argued here to be likely, the difficulties of rearing and maintaining working cattle will surely have led to unequal access to their labour and thus to inequality in the production of staple grain crops. The long-term consequences of such inequality depend to a great extent on whether producers of staple deficits were helped by kin and neighbours unconditionally or were expected to reciprocate assistance with labour or other resources. The contrast between a remarkably uniform EN–MN ceramic assemblage and the more diverse LN repertoire may, as Tomkins has argued, signal a shift from a strongly communal ideology to greater tolerance of more competitive behaviour. Equally, the LN growth of the settlement and increased distance to fields must have made farmers without access to work animals increasingly vulnerable to economic failure and social subordination – perhaps accounting for the symbolic emphasis on cattle discussed by Broodbank. The subsequent FN decline in the proportion of cattle may reflect increasingly restricted ownership of and access to working animals, but the continued use of cows for draught purposes suggests that any overproduction by a putative emerging elite was modest, and far below the massive levels achieved with male oxen in later palatial societies.

Cattle arguably played an important and diverse role in the development of farming, settlement and society at Neolithic Knossos. This chapter has attempted to explore this role by using a diversity of new faunal data and by placing the exploitation of Knossian cattle in both its ecological/economic and social context. In this latter respect it could be concluded that the work of both the Jarmans and Broodbank has been vindicated, while the control of taphonomic distortion – emphasised by Winder and Whitelaw – was also fundamental to re-analysis of the faunal assemblage. High priorities for further faunal analysis at Knossos should be systematic retrieval and analysis of much larger Aceramic-EN and EM assemblages, to clarify whether use of draught cows is as old as the settlement and to determine when male cattle started to be kept in large numbers for traction.

In concluding, the evidence for early use of draught cows at Knossos should be placed in a wider context. Evidence for use of draught cattle from *at least the sixth* millennium BC pushes back this component of Andrew Sherratt's 4–3m BC 'secondary products revolution' (Sherratt 1981) by perhaps *two* millennia. Nor were draught cattle at Knossos very revolutionary, in that they appear not to have triggered immediate settlement growth or any other rapid changes. On the other hand, the model proposed here for 'gardening with cows' at Knossos follows Sherratt's perceptive lead in emphasising the role of draught cattle in transport as well as tillage. Moreover, even if draught cattle did not trigger revolutionary social change they are likely to have been an important element in the dynamic social environment of early Knossian farmers, exercising a strong influence over their prospects both of achieving subsistence security and of gaining access to the labour and allegiance of less fortunate neighbours. Finally, the early dates for draught animals at Knossos undermine the suggested link between the adoption of ploughing and FN marginal colonisation on Crete (*e.g.*, Watrous 1994). Available evidence from Knossos suggests that the role of draught cattle, if any, in marginal colonisation may have been to facilitate surplus production at older settlements in favourable locations and thus dependence of marginal sites on exchange.

Acknowledgements

This paper benefited enormously from long discussions with Paul Halstead, Peter Tomkins and Amy Bogaard. Paul and Peter provided incisive comments on an earlier draft. I also thank both for being so generous with their unpublished work over the years. Nick Winder provided crucial information and a copy of his thesis when I first embarked on this rather risky voyage of the re-discovery and re-analysis of the Neolithic faunal remains. Warmest thanks are due to John Evans, the excavator of Neolithic Knossos, who provided permission and vital information for this study, and the funding bodies (AHRB, INSTAP, BSA) whose support made it all possible.

Bibliography

Admiralty
   1944   *Greece, 1: Physical Geography, History, Administration and Peoples (Geographical Handbook Series)*. Andover: Admiralty, Naval Intelligence Division.
Albarella, U.
   1999   'The mystery of husbandry': medieval animals and the problem of integrating historical and archaeological evidence. *Antiquity* 73: 867–75.
Baker, J. and D. Brothwell
   1980   *Animal Diseases in Archaeology*. New York: Academic Press.
Bartosiewicz, L., W. van Neer and A. Lentacker
   1997   *Draught Cattle: Their Osteological Identification and History*. Tervuren (Belgium): Musée Royal de l'Afrique Centrale.
Binford, L. R.
   1981   *Bones: Ancient Men and Modern Myths*. New York: Academic Press.

Bogaard, A.
  2004   *Neolithic Farming in Central Europe*. London: Routledge.
  2005   'Garden agriculture' and the nature of early farming in Europe and the Near East. *World Archaeology* 37: 177–96.
Bogaard, A., M. Charles, P. Halstead and G. Jones
  2000   The scale and intensity of cultivation: evidence from weed ecology. In P. Halstead and C. Frederick (eds.), *Landscape and Land Use in Postglacial Greece* (SSAA 3): 129–34. Sheffield: Sheffield Academic Press.
Bogaard, A., T. H. E. Heaton, P. Poulton and I. Merbach
  2007   The impact of manuring on nitrogen isotope ratios in cereals: archaeological implications for reconstruction of diet and crop management practices. *Journal of Archaeological Science* 24: 335–43.
Bogucki, P.
  1993   Animal traction and household economies in Neolithic Europe. *Antiquity* 67: 492–503.
Broodbank, C.
  1992   The Neolithic labyrinth: social change at Knossos before the Bronze Age. *JMA* 5: 39–75.
Brown, P.
  1978   *Highland Peoples of New Guinea*. Cambridge: Cambridge University Press.
Charles, M., A. Bogaard, G. Jones, J. Hodgson and P. Halstead
  2002   Towards the archaeobotanical identification of intensive cereal cultivation: present-day ecological investigation in the mountains of Asturias, northwest Spain. *Vegetation History and Archaeobotany* 11: 133–42.
Cherry, J. F.
  1988   Pastoralism and the role of animals in the pre- and proto-historic economies of the Aegean. In C. R. Whittaker (ed.), *Pastoral Economies in Classical Antiquity*: 6–34. Cambridge: Cambridge Philological Society.
de Cupere, A., A. Lentacker, W. van Neer, M. Waelkens and L. Verslype
  2000   Osteological evidence for the draught exploitation of cattle: first applications of a new methodology. *International Journal of Osteoarchaeology* 10: 254–67.
Evans, J. D.
  1964   Excavations in the Neolithic settlement of Knossos 1957–1960, part I. *BSA* 59: 132–240.
  1971   Neolithic Knossos: the growth of a settlement. *PPS* 37: 95–117.
  1994   The early millennia: continuity and change in a farming settlement. In D. Evely, H. Hughes-Brock and N. Momigliano (eds.), *Knossos, a Labyrinth of History. Papers Presented in Honour of Sinclair Hood*: 1–20. London: British School at Athens.
Forbes, H.
  1993   Ethnoarchaeology and the place of the olive in the economy of the southern Argolid, Greece. In M.-C. Amouretti and J.-P. Brun (eds.), *Oil and Wine Production in the Mediterranean Area*: 213–26. Athènes: École Française d'Athènes.
Forge, A.
  1972   Normative factors in the settlement size of neolithic cultivators (New Guinea). In P. J. Ucko, R. Tringham and G. W. Dimbleby (eds.), *Man, Settlement and Urbanism*: 363–76. London: Duckworth.
Gilman, A.
  1981   The development of social stratification in Bronze Age Europe. *Current Anthropology* 22: 1–8.
Goody, J.
  1976   *Production and Reproduction: a Comparative Study of the Domestic Domain*. Cambridge: Cambridge University Press.

Halstead, P.
1981   Counting sheep in neolithic and bronze age Greece. In I. Hodder, G. Isaac and N. Hammond (eds.), *Pattern of the Past: Studies in Honour of David Clarke*: 307–39. Cambridge: Cambridge University Press.
1984   *Strategies for Survival: an Ecological Approach to Social and Economic Change in the Early Farming Communities of Thessaly, N. Greece*. PhD dissertation, University of Cambridge.
1987   Traditional and ancient rural economy in Mediterranean Europe: plus ça change? *JHS* 107: 77–87.
1992   Dimini and the 'DMP': faunal remains and animal exploitation in Late Neolithic Thessaly. *BSA* 87: 29–59.
1995a   Plough and power: the economic and social significance of cultivation with the ox-drawn ard in the Mediterranean. *Bulletin on Sumerian Agriculture* 8: 11–22.
1995b   From sharing to hoarding: the neolithic foundations of Aegean Bronze Age society? In R. Laffineur and W.-D. Niemeier (eds.), *POLITEIA: Society and State in the Aegean Bronze Age* (Aegaeum 5): 11–20. Liège: University of Liège.
1996a   The development of agriculture and pastoralism in Greece: when, how, who and what? In D. R. Harris (ed.), *The Origins and Spread of Agriculture and Pastoralism in Eurasia*: 296–309. London: University College London Press.
1996b   Pastoralism or household herding? Problems of scale and specialisation in early Greek animal husbandry. *World Archaeology* 28: 20–42.
1998   Mortality models and milking: problems of uniformitarianism, optimality and equifinality reconsidered. *Anthropozoologica* 27: 3–20.
2000   Land use in postglacial Greece: cultural causes and environmental effects. In P. Halstead and C. Frederick (eds.), *Landscape and Land Use in Postglacial Greece* (SSAA 3): 110–28. Sheffield: Sheffield Academic Press.
2002   Texts, bones and herders: approaches to animal husbandry in late bronze age Greece. In J. Bennet and J. Driessen (eds.) *A-NA-QO-TA: Studies Presented to John T. Killen*. *Minos* 33–34 [1998–99]: 149–89.
2006   Sheep in the garden: the integration of crop and livestock husbandry in early farming regimes of Greece and southern Europe. In D. Serjeantson and D. Field (eds.), *Animals in the Neolithic of Britain and Europe*: 42–55. Oxford: Oxbow Books.
in press Faunal remains from FN-EH Nemea Tsoungiza: husbandry, butchery, consumption and discard of animals. In D. Pullen, with contributions by P. Halstead, A. Karabatsoli, J. Hansen, S. Allen, K. Krattenmaker, Z. Stos-Gale, M. Kayafa and N. Gale, *Nemea Valley Archaeological Project I: The Early Bronze Age Village on Tsoungiza Hill*. Princeton: American School of Classical Studies at Athens.
Higgs, E. S. and M. R. Jarman
1969   The origins of agriculture: a reconsideration. *Antiquity* 43: 31–41.
Isaakidou, V.
2004   *Bones from the Labyrinth: Faunal Evidence for the Management and Consumption of Animals at Neolithic and Bronze Age Knossos, Crete*. PhD dissertation, University College London.
2006   Ploughing with cows: Knossos and the 'secondary products revolution'. In D. Serjeantson and D. Field (eds.), *Animals in the Neolithic of Britain and Europe*: 95–112. Oxford: Oxbow Books.
2007   Cooking in the labyrinth: exploring 'cuisine' at Bronze Age Knossos. In C. Mee and J. Renard (eds.), *Cooking Up the Past: Food and Culinary Practices in the Neolithic and Bronze Age Aegean*: 5–24. Oxford: Oxbow Books.
Jarman, M. R. and H. N. Jarman
1968   The fauna and economy of Neolithic Knossos. *BSA* 63: 241–64.

Jarman, M. R., G. N. Bailey and H. N. Jarman
  1982   *Early European Agriculture: Its Foundation and Development*. Cambridge: Cambridge University Press.
Johannsen, N.
  2005   Palaeopathology and Neolithic cattle traction: methodological issues and archaeological perspectives. In J. Davies, M. Fabis, I. Mainland, M. Richards and R. Thomas (eds.) *Diet and Health in Past Animal Populations: Current Research and Future Directions*: 39–51. Oxford: Oxbow Books.
Jones, G., A. Bogaard, P. Halstead, M. Charles and H. Smith
  1999   Identifying the intensity of crop husbandry practices on the basis of weed floras. *BSA* 94: 167–89.
Kotsakis, K.
  2006   Settlement of discord: Sesklo and the emerging household. In N. Tasić and C. Grozdanov (eds.), *Homage to Milutin Garašanin*: 207–20. Belgrade: Serbian Academy of Sciences and Arts, Macedonian Academy of Sciences and Arts.
Payne, S.
  1972   Partial recovery and sample bias: the results of some sieving experiments. In E. S. Higgs (ed.), *Papers in Economic Prehistory*: 49–64. London: Cambridge University Press.
Petropoulos, D. A.
  1943–4 Ethima sinergasias kai allilovoithias tou Ellinikou laou. *Epetiris Laografikou Arkhiou*: 59–85.
Renfrew, C.
  1972   *The Emergence of Civilisation*. London: Methuen.
Sahlins, M.
  1972   *Stone Age Economics*. New York: Aldine de Gruyter.
Semple, E. C.
  1922   The influence of geographic conditions upon ancient Mediterranean stock-raising. *Annals of the Association of American Geographers* 12: 3–38.
Sherratt, A.
  1981   Plough and pastoralism: aspects of the secondary products revolution. In I. Hodder, G. Isaac and N. Hammond (eds.), *Pattern of the Past: Studies in Honour of David Clarke*: 261–305. Cambridge: Cambridge University Press.
Tomkins, P.
  2001   *The Production, Circulation and Consumption of Ceramic Vessels at Early Neolithic Knossos, Crete*. PhD dissertation, University of Sheffield.
  2004   Filling in the 'Neolithic background': social life and social transformation in the Aegean before the Bronze Age. In J. Barrett and P. Halstead (eds.), *The Emergence of Civilisation Revisited* (SSAA 6): 38–63. Oxford: Oxbow Books.
  2007   Neolithic: Strata IX–VIII, VII–VIB, VIA–V, IV, IIIB, IIIA, IIB, IIA and IC Groups. In N. Momigliano (ed.), *Knossos Pottery Handbook: Neolithic and Bronze Age (Minoan)*: 9–48. London: British School at Athens.
Tomkins, P., P. M. Day and V. Kilikoglou
  2004   Knossos and the Early Neolithic Landscape of the Herakleion Basin. In G. Cadogan, E. Hatzaki and A. Vasilakis (eds.), *Knossos: Palace, City, State*: 51–59. London: British School at Athens.
Uerpmann, H. P.
  1979   Animal bone finds and economic archaeology: a critical study of 'osteo-archaeological' method. *World Archaeology* 4: 307–22.

Walrous, V.
  1994   Review of Aegean Prehistory 3: Crete from earliest prehistory through the Proto-palatial period. *AJA* 98: 695–753.
Watson, J. P. N.
  1979   The estimation of the relative frequencies of mammalian species: Khirokitia. *Journal of Archaeological Science* 6: 127–37.
Whitelaw, T. M.
  1983   The settlement at Fournou Korifi, Myrtos and aspects of Early Minoan social organization. In O. Krzyszkowska and L. Nixon (eds.), *Minoan Society*: 323–45. Bristol: Bristol Classical Press.
  1992   Lost in the labyrinth? Comments on Broodbank's 'Social change at Knossos before the Bronze Age'. *JMA* 15: 225–38.
  2004   Estimating the population of Neopalatial Knossos. In G. Cadogan, E. Hatzaki and A. Vasilakis (eds.), *Knossos: Palace, City, State*: 147–58. London: British School at Athens.
Winder, N. P.
  1986   *Faunal Analysis; Studies in the Analysis and Interpretation of Animal Bones from Large, Multi-Phase Archaeological Excavations.* PhD dissertation, University of Southampton.
  1991   Interpreting a site: the case for a reassessment of the Knossos Neolithic. *Archaeological Reviews from Cambridge* 10: 37–52.
Wobst, H. M.
  1974   Boundary conditions for Paleolithic social systems: a simulation approach. *American Antiquity* 39: 147–78.

7

Figurin' Out Cretan Neolithic Society: Anthropomorphic Figurines, Symbolism and Gender Dialectics

Maria Mina

A Few Words on Scope, Theory and Methodology

Cretan Neolithic figurines came to the forefront of research thanks mainly to the work of Peter Ucko in 1968, which opened up new avenues of interpretation beyond the Mother-Goddess theory. Their analysis, however, still remains largely divorced from that of other Aegean assemblages. The first aim of the present paper is to address this lacuna in research, by attempting a comparative study of Cretan figurines within their wider Aegean context, aiming at a more comprehensive understanding of 'Neolithization' and social organisation in the Neolithic Aegean. The second aim of the paper is to explore Neolithic society through the prism of gender, a parameter that may prove highly enlightening for aspects of social and economic organisation and, in turn, governing ideological principles. Although studies of gender in relation to figurines have been conducted recently in the field of Aegean prehistory (Orphanidi-Georgiadi 1992; Talalay 1993; 2000; 2005; Hitchcock 1997; Kokkinidou and Nikolaidou 1997; Hamilton 2000), there is a need for comparative analyses that examine processes of social change in different regions of the Aegean and beyond. Such studies may offer a high resolution analysis that can serve to deconstruct broad socio-economic models.

Some Issues of Theory and Method

Figurines should not be treated differently from other categories of artefacts. More specifically, we must free ourselves of the aesthetic value judgements of traditional art-historical approaches and avoid semiotic approaches that lock figurines in static frames. A more fruitful context for the analysis of anthropomorphic figurines may be offered by the anthropology of art, in its attempts to elucidate the 'way of seeing' of a cultural system (Gell 1998: 2) and its emphasis on the ways in which art forms assume an active position in relation to the world around them (Gell 1998: 6). The dynamic role played by artefacts has been discussed by a number of scholars (Richardson 1989; Tilley 1989; 1999; Beaudry *et al.* 1991, Layton 1991, Wolff 1993, Gell 1998; Knappett 2002; 2006; Gosden 2005; Lele 2006), who have highlighted the ways in which objects and humans are bound together in mutually affecting relationships. It follows that anthropomorphic figurines, as artefacts, are similarly part of the web that binds together humans and material forms through agent-patient relationships and, as such, have the potential to deceive social actors and maintain or challenge the existing social order (Hatcher 1985; Tilley 1989: 189; Wolff 1993; Gosden 2005).

In order to understand fully the dynamic potential of figurines in the construction of social and gender identity, we need to consider the ways in which objects and humans are co-dependent (Knappett 2002: 98–99; Lele 2006: 54–55). The human mind is part of the human body, which, in turn, is part of the wider environment. Through intentional contact with the body, matter transformed into a figurine is imbued with the intention of the producer as well as the properties of the material (clay or stone) (Knappett 2006: 240). Rather than contrasting agents and objects, therefore, it is more productive to think of agency as being distributed across networks of human and non-human entities (including artefacts) shifting through networks of production and consumption (Knappett 2002: 100–1). Personhood is not restricted to the confines of the physical body, and the articulation of body, mind and matter into a co-dependent whole is made possible through layering and networking, the two artefactual and bodily processes through which cognition and agency extend beyond the physical body (Knappett 2006). Anthropomorphic figurines, therefore, afford insights into the way agency and cognition operated in the construction of personhood, and of social and gender identity in the context of the Aegean Neolithic.

So far, we have seen how Neolithic figurines can be understood as indices that make up and testify to prehistoric personhood (Gell 1998: 222). Another relevant parameter, through which meaning is constructed, is the quality of prehistoric figurines as symbols (cf. Knappett 2002; Lele 2006). Although some regard prehistoric figurines as iconic representations of actual people or ancestral figures (Ucko 1968; Kokkinidou and Nikolaidou 1993; Talalay 1993; Gallis 2001; Bailey 2005), the symbolic qualities of figurines should also be acknowledged for the following reasons. The physical human body constitutes a common metaphor through which people order and understand the world around them – the social body (Tilley 1999). Moreover, the representation of embodied identities may be understood in terms of human preoccupation with important events such as conception, birth, growth and death, which are often explained by drawing parallels between the physical functions of the human body and natural cycles and phenomena, such as the changing seasons or celestial movements (Haaland and Haaland 1996).

Symbolic ideas also find expression in figurines through the use of decorative motifs or modelling of posture and through the social and ideological meaning that these encompassed and communicated to a prehistoric audience. Stages of manufacture (*chaîne opératoire*) are another locus for symbolic discourse and negotiation of gender identities, as has been demonstrated in relation to pottery production in Sub-Saharan Africa (Gosselain 1999). Similarly, the fundamental role of figurines in the symbolic construction of social identities and order is evident in the special status of those who make figurines in relation to rituals, in the metaphorical link between giving birth and shaping a figurine from clay and in their relationship to human experience and rites of passage. Symbolic meaning generated by figurines may also have been expressed through prohibition on the involvement of certain gender and age categories in their production, the pyrotechnical aspects of manufacture and symbolic associations with fire, 'hot' and 'cold' activities and things, and through the parallel treatment of the clay and physical body as in the application of decoration. Several scholars have already interpreted Neolithic anthropomorphic figurines as symbols of fertility or lineage histories (Ucko 1968; Kokkinidou and Nikolaidou 1993: 60; 1997; Talalay 1993; Gallis 2001; Bailey 2005).

Emphasis is placed here on representation of the physical body, especially in relation to sexual anatomy, not because universal gender roles are assumed, but because of overwhelming ethnographic evidence that the physical body plays a fundamental categorising role in the construction of social and hence gender identities (Herdt 1994: 80). Social and cultural context is of paramount importance in social conditioning and in shaping the way in which gender is performed and expressed through the body (MacRae 1975; Gatens 1992: 298; Aalten 1997; Lindemann 1997), but the dynamic ability of physical bodies to serve as powerful media of resistance, through constant re-interpretation of dominant discourses (Moore 1994: 325), also needs to be acknowledged. The performance of gender identity through physical bodies is obvious, but in the case of figurines we need to think in terms of the represented embodied identities and practices which operated at a social and symbolic level. Analysis of aspects of gender embodiment can offer us valuable insights into gender construction, although the precise meaning of associated symbolic concepts is less accessible to us today. Metaphorical embodiment, therefore, as revealed through the representation of the physical body of figurines, is relevant at two cognitive levels: that of the manufacturer and that of the user, who may or may not have been the same person.

Because of the key role of the physical body in structuring the attribution of gender and the metaphorical categorisation of social order, the analytical categories employed here are based on the presence or absence of primary and secondary anatomical characteristics. Far from assuming *a priori*, for prehistoric actors or figurines, a correspondence of sex and gender on a bi-polar axis, the categories emerged from observation of the emphasis or omission of physical attributes. These, combined with additional attributes (the next stage of analysis), finally drew the more complex canvas of represented gender identities and ideas. In brief, the categories employed are:

(a) *Female figurines*, with clearly modelled female genitalia and/or breasts;
(b) *Probably Female figurines*, with the above attributes not easily discernible

mainly due to unclear modelling of genitalia and/or breasts, weathering or
partial damage;
(c) *Female form figurines*, with the hourglass outline of the female body and/or
accentuated buttocks, but lacking the anatomical attributes characteristic of
the *Female* category;
(d) *Probably Female form figurines*, that are too fragmentary to be categorised with
certainty as *Female form*;
(e) *Male* figurines, with clearly modelled male genitalia;
(f) *Probably Male* figurines, with unclear male genitalia due to unclear modelling
or weathering;
(g) *Asexual* figurines, lacking any form of primary or secondary anatomical
attributes;
(h) *Probably Asexual* figurines, represented by 'asexual' upper or lower body
fragments which cannot be categorised with certainty as *Asexual* because of
their partial state;
(i) *Ambiguous* figurines with both female and male anatomical attributes
(presence of breasts and male genitalia), or with modelled genitalia that bear
male and female traits.

As the aim of this paper is to discuss Cretan Neolithic figurines within a wider
Aegean context, patterns are first identified in the *published* corpus from the
Aegean as a whole (Mina 2005), before undertaking comparison with data from
Crete. I should also state at this point that the regions discussed coincide with
the borders of the modern state of Greece and that for Crete I follow the dating
scheme proposed by Tomkins (2007) which serves well the comparative analysis
between Crete and the rest of the Aegean undertaken here. In addition, the
analysis focuses selectively on aspects of symbolic representation in figurines
that seem particularly informative for Neolithic gender and society in the Aegean.

Analysis

The Sample

Figure 7.1 summarises the results of analysis of 1,086 *published* figurines from the
Aegean as a whole, of which 110 are from Crete (Mina in press). Thessaly and
Macedonia dominate the sample, with Crete in third place (10%), while other
areas are less well represented. The uneven geographical distribution of *published*
figurines may partly reflect regional contrasts in production and consumption,
but this is difficult to assess given the very variable number and scale of
excavations, the sometimes significant contribution of surface collections, and
uneven publication. Figure 7.2 also demonstrates that the samples from the three
areas are not evenly distributed in terms of chronology (especially for Macedonia),
an added parameter that needs to be addressed when comparing figurine

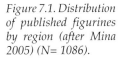

Figure 7.1. Distribution of published figurines by region (after Mina 2005) (N= 1086).

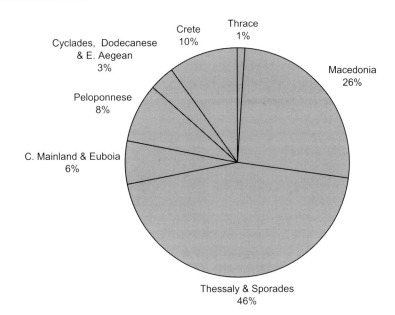

production at a regional scale. Nevertheless, anthropomorphic figurines emerge as a class of material culture that, from the earliest Neolithic, expressed ideas about society and ideology in different parts of the Aegean.

On Crete, anthropomorphic figurines are represented in the earliest (Initial Neolithic) levels at Knossos (Figure 7.2), but the vast majority are of LN date (Figure 7.3) (Evans 1961; 1964; Ucko 1968; Broodbank 1992). A few similar examples from the sites of Gerani (Orphanidi 1998), Gortyn (Ucko 1968), Pelekita cave (Orphanidi 1998) and Phaistos (Ucko 1968) mirror the apparently belated dispersal of population in the Cretan landscape (Watrous 2001: 162), but also indicate that the associated gender symbolism was equally relevant to people at the large site of Knossos and to their counterparts in other, much smaller communities. In the case of one FN figurine from Knossos, its possible Anatolian parallels may even indicate the importation of gender-related objects from outside regions. Finally, two important points should be made: (1) not all figurines excavated at Knossos are included in the present study (more figurines, unpublished to-date, are mentioned in both Arthur and John Evans' notebooks, but are currently inaccessible due to the large-scale refurbishment of Herakleion Museum, currently under way), and (2) more of the LN–FN settlement has been exposed by modern excavation than the EN–MN settlement (Evans 1964; 1971). Future research, therefore, could elucidate further the role of anthropomorphic figurines from Neolithic Knossos.

Representation of Sex and Gender Symbolism

As a first step towards exploring the issue of gender, Figure 7.4 presents the

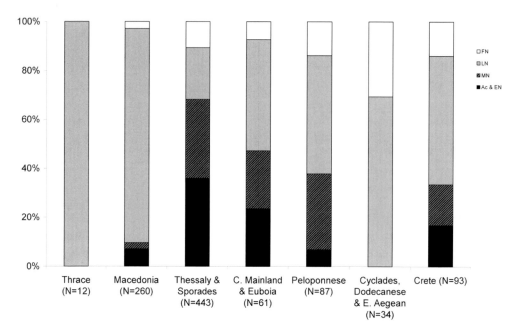

Figure 7.2. Distribution of figurines by region and chronological period (after Mina 2005).

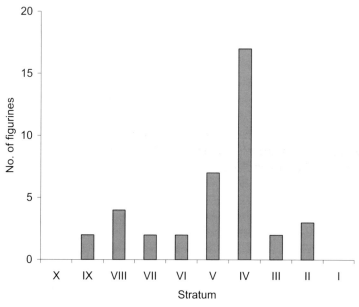

Figure 7.3. Distribution by stratum of anthropomorphic figurines from the 1957–60 excavations at Knossos (after Broodbank 1992: 58, fig. 6) (N=39).

proportion of figurines, in each of the categories of represented sex defined above, in the sample from the Neolithic of the Aegean as a whole (Mina in press). The *Female* and *Female*-related (*Probably Female, Female form, Probably Female form*) categories are clearly predominant (67%), followed by *Asexual* figurines (18%), while *Male* (2%) and *Ambiguous* (1%) figurines are rare. Significantly, the basic pattern (Female > Asexual >> Male/Ambiguous) is replicated in Macedonia, Thessaly and Crete, when the three regions with the largest samples are examined separately (Figure 7.5) and also in the four main chronological subdivisions of the Neolithic, although Asexual figurines gain some ground at the expense of the Female categories from EN/MN to LN/FN (Figure 7.6). The apparently pervasive preoccupation of Aegean Neolithic society with symbolic constructs related to the female body contrasts sharply with the limited representation of the male body. *Asexual* and *Ambiguous* figurines, on the other hand, the makers of which chose to omit or subvert anatomical features, pose interesting questions concerning the embodiment and construction of gender. The extent to which these anatomically based categories match gender constructs may now be explored further by considering other variables.

Decorative Motifs

Decoration is one of the variables that can afford crucial insights into the construction and embodiment of gender and social identity. Thus, the presence of incised, punctured or painted decoration on figurines was recorded and

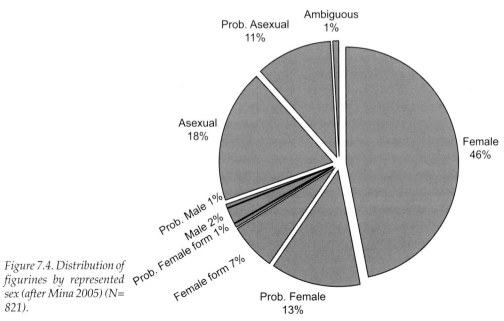

Figure 7.4. Distribution of figurines by represented sex (after Mina 2005) (N= 821).

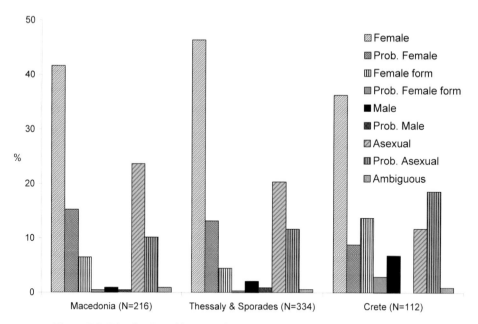

Figure 7.5. Distribution of figurines by represented sex and region (after Mina 2005).

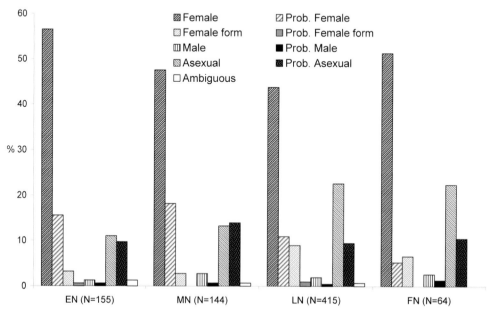

Figure 7.6. Distribution of figurines by represented sex and chronological period (after Mina 2005).

decorative motifs were categorised according to three main thematic categories of 'body decoration', 'attire' and 'jewellery'. Their systematic study has revealed symbolic overlap between the categories of *Female* and *Female form* figurines, and *Female* and *Asexual* figurines (Mina 2007; in press), examples of which can be seen in Figures 7.7 and 7.8. More specifically, this overlap is apparent in the application of decorative motifs and colour to specific parts of the body (discussed in detail in the following paragraphs), which in turn indicates a convergence at the level of the expressed gender symbolisms. It may plausibly be proposed, therefore, that *Female form* and at least some *Asexual* figurines represented different forms of female identity, perhaps related to stages in a person's life (*e.g.*, pre-pubescent, pubescent, mature). Among *Male* figurines, on the other hand, decoration is rare and neither placement nor form of motifs indicates symbolic overlap with *Female* or *Female form* or *Asexual* figurines. It is possible, therefore, that some undecorated *Asexual* figurines represented men. Finally, *Ambiguous* figurines may represent an ideological construct or even an actual third gender. Both on Crete and in the Aegean as a whole, therefore, preoccupation with female-related symbolism (relating to the physical, social and ideological body) suggests that gender played a significant role in the organisation of society, while the multiple forms that female figurines took in terms of anatomical modelling and decoration suggest that the construction of at least female gender identity was closely related to age.

Closer examination and analysis of the repertoire of decoration reveal three main thematic categories (Mina in press). A number of motifs seem to depict body decoration by painting, tattooing or scarring (Figure 7.9). The practice of body decoration thus arguably played a part in the construction of gender identity, perhaps through the performance of rituals intended to perpetuate culturally accepted gender roles and behaviours (cf. Hodder 1982; David *et al.* 1988: 378; Turner 1995; Joyce 2002; Rainbird 2002). Two other classes of motifs

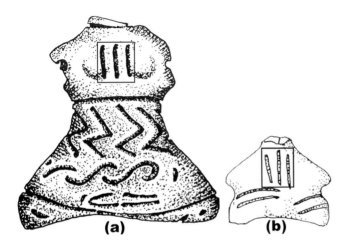

(a)   **(b)**

Figure 7.7. Shared motifs between Female (a) and Female form (b) figurines from LN Sitagroi (after Renfrew et al. 1986: 232, fig. 9.12; 268, fig. 9.92).

represented attire and jewellery (Figures 7.10 and 7.11). These include garments that covered the whole or part of the body and occasionally jewellery such as necklaces or amulets, while plastic or incised features indicated headdresses and forms of coiffure, as well as implicit modelling of earrings or ear-studs. It seems that body decoration, clothing and jewellery were all important for the effective communication of gender-related symbolism. Surviving artefacts related to personal modification (*i.e.*, clothing and ornaments) (Perlès 2001: 288) suggest parallel practices of gender embodiment to those implied by figurines. Motifs denoting body decoration were mainly applied to *Female* figurines which may indicate that female bodies held a central place in the practices and symbolic constructs that marked gender and cultural identity in Neolithic society (Mina in press). Moreover, a shift during LN and FN from body decoration motifs to attire and jewellery-related decoration implies diachronic change in the way gender

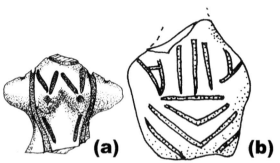

Figure 7.8. Shared motifs between Female (a) and Asexual (b) figurines from LN Sitagroi (after Renfrew et al. 1986: 275, fig. 9.121; 243, fig. 9.34).

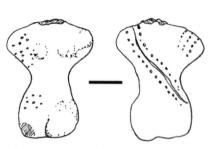

Figure 7.9. Motifs denoting body decoration from MN Knossos (after Ucko 1968: fig. 121).

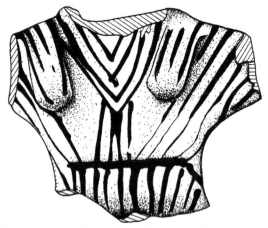

Figure 7.10. Motifs denoting attire from MN Franchthi (after Talalay 1993: 155, pl. 2:a).

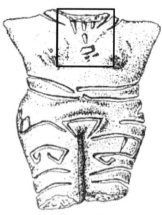

Figure 7.11. Motif denoting jewellery from LN Makriyalos (after Besios and Pappa 1998: fig. 12).

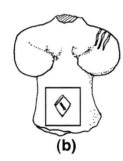

Figure 7.12. Motifs denoting body decoration on Female *figurines from LN Knossos (after Ucko 1968: figs. 84 (a) and 130 (b)).*

(a)   **(b)**

was constructed through embodied practices. The manipulation of these added layers of gender symbolism reveals potential for increased complexity in the way gender identity and associated symbolism were communicated. Moreover, if we consider that the use of materials, such as fabrics or jewellery, may have been the preserve of a certain social group, then construction of gender towards the end of the Neolithic may have also become more complex through its connection with access to material wealth.

When the repertoire of motifs is examined by region, Crete resembles the rest of the Aegean during EN and MN, in that motifs are mainly applied to *Female* figurines and represent body decoration. LN and FN material from Crete is distinctive, however, both in lacking the variety of motifs representing attire and jewellery in Macedonia and Thessaly and even in the smaller sample from the Peloponnese, and in continued association with the same motifs of body-decoration as in earlier periods. Perhaps this reflects particular conservatism in social organisation and ideological constructs on Neolithic Crete and a desire of the community to comply with, rather than openly challenge, older social norms. At any rate, it seems that women in Crete continued through to the later Neolithic to express gender identity through manipulation of their physical appearance by scarring, tattooing or body painting. Two *Female* figurines from Crete, with motifs marking the breast and abdomen area (Figure 7.12), may additionally indicate that particular attention was paid to reproduction in the construction of female identity.

Body decoration is also known anthropologically to demarcate and communicate social and group identity (Hodder 1982; David *et al.* 1988: 378; Turner 1995: 146) and the strong association of such motifs with *Female* and *Female*-related figurines, and conversely the rarity of decoration on *Male* figurines, may indicate that men on Crete and elsewhere in the Neolithic Aegean were less involved in the preservation and communication of social and cultural identity. The existence, however, of one *Male* figurine from Gerani, which bears a motif resembling a tattooed motif on the abdomen area, suggests that we cannot exclude men from such embodying practices. Nonetheless, and in spite of the observed contrast between Crete and other regions in LN–FN decorative repertoire, some striking specific parallels deserve discussion. Perhaps ten of the Cretan motifs denoting body decoration are paralleled in other regions, although they do not always coincide chronologically (Mina in press). A few examples are shown here in Figures 7.13 and 7.14. The parallels, which extend to similar associations with represented sex, suggest a shared 'vocabulary' of gender symbolism (despite general typological differences that argue against imports) and thus point to significant cultural contacts between Crete and other Aegean areas.

The Use of Colour

Neolithic figurines were decorated with pigments, deliberate use of which to express symbolic notions is well attested ethnographically (Walisewska 1991; Chapman 2002). The range of colours detected throughout the Neolithic is black, red and white in EN, black and red in MN, black, red, red on white and white in LN, and, black, blue, green and white in FN (Mina in press). Although there are few examples of surviving pigment, we might speculate that the new combination of colours in LN and the introduction of new colours in FN are indicative of a new social and material order. Anthropological studies suggest that use of new colours and new colour combinations is related to the development of new material culture forms and new classificatory categories at the level of society (cf. Chapman 2002: 67). The use of new colours in relation to anthropomorphic figurines from LN may indicate the emergence in the Aegean of new symbolism of gender embodiment and associated ideology. More specifically, the consistent application of specific colours in relation to selected anatomical parts (such as breasts, chest area, the abdomen and pubic region) of mainly *Female* and *Female*-related figurines indicates such changes at the level of gender. Moreover, the close correspondence of the same palette with that used on pottery alludes to the symbolic use of colour and gender associations in material culture domains that extend beyond that of figurines (Talalay 1993: 35).

In the case of Cretan figurines, the use of pigment is restricted to *Female* and *Female*-related figurines, of mainly LN date. The repertoire of colours (red, white, red on white, and black for rendering of hair) parallels that of the rest of the Aegean. Figure 7.15 shows two such examples of *Female* figurines decorated with white on red pigment on the chest area. Again pigment emphasises fertility-related parts, such as the pubic and breast area and the abdomen, although on Crete there is a preference for white rather than red. Although a universal 'language' of colour symbolism cannot be assumed (Layton 1991: 118), ethno-graphic studies have shown a tendency for societies to link colours to certain substances, such as bodily fluids and related symbolic notions (Walisewska 1991). On this basis, the colour white may have symbolised bodily fluids such as milk or semen, and its use on *Female* figurines on the abdomen and pubic area may have constituted a symbolic reference to pregnancy, breast-feeding, *etc.*, which in turn may have acted as a metaphor for the natural life cycle. As well as underlining the emphasis on female bodies in the construction and com-munication of gender and group identity, the suggested link between women

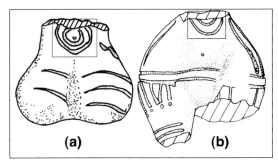

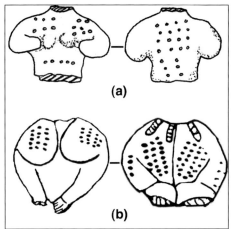

(a)

(b)

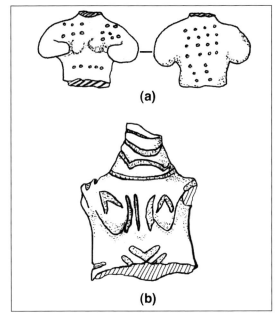

(a)

(b)

Figure 7.13. (top left) Motifs shared between Crete and Macedonia: (a) from MN Knossos (after Ucko 1968: fig. 123) and (b) from LN Sitagroi (from Renfrew et al. 1986: 236, fig. 9.21).

Figure 7.14. (above) Motifs shared between Crete and Central Mainland: (a) from LN Knossos (after Ucko 1968: fig. 128) and (b) from LN Chaeroneia (after Orphanidi 1998: 140, pl. 60).

Figure 7.15. (Bottom left) Female figurines with red on white pigment demarcating chest area: (a) LN Knossos (after Ucko 1968: fig. 128) and (b) LN Sitagroi (after Renfrew et al. 1986: 243, fig. 9.35).

and decoration also indicates the central role played by women's bodies in the ordering of the natural and social cosmos. *Male* figurines, on the other hand, were rarely decorated with the use of motifs or pigment, and statistical analysis confirms that the application of decoration was in fact closely related to the represented sex (Mina in press). It would appear, therefore, that male bodies did not operate to the same extent or in the same way as categorising symbolic constructs in Neolithic Aegean society, although the FN specimen from Gerani indicates that men were not excluded from such practices, at least on Crete.

Posture

In EN, the preferred modelled postures appear to be specific to *Female* figurines with some similarity to *Female form* figurines, for instance, in the placing of

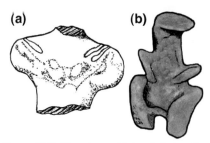

(a)   **(b)**

Figure 7.16. Figurines with hands below the breast area: (a) Female from EN Knossos (after Ucko 1968: fig. 144) and (b) Female form from EN Knossos (after Rethemiotakis 1996: 322, pl. 248).

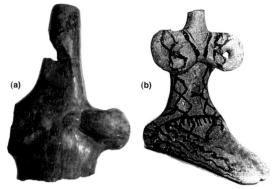

(a)   (b)

Figure 7.17. Female figurines with hands on the breast area: (a) LN Knossos (photo by author) and (b) LN Franchthi (Source: Talalay 1993: 153, pl. 1).

hands on or below the breast area (Figure 7.16). A *Male* figurine, however, with the hands resting on the chest area (Ucko 1968: fig. 85) may indicate some degree of similarity with postures preferred for its female counterparts. In MN, the range of postures decreases and exhibits overlap between *Female* and *Asexual* figurines. In LN, the same overlap is observed between *Female* and *Asexual* figurines, which do not draw emphasis to parts of the body, such as the chest or genital region. The posture of *Female* figurines that draws attention to the breast area is also shared between Crete and the rest of the Aegean (Figure 7.17). In FN, however, the variety of postures emphasising sex-related anatomical attributes does not appear to continue (Mina 2005; cf. Nanoglou 2005 for Thessaly). As far as the Cretan postural repertoire is concerned, the same postures, or variations thereof, are also repeated on the few FN figurines outside Knossos with no indication of gender differentiation.

A number of conclusions can be drawn from the Cretan postural repertoire in relation to other regions of the Aegean. Starting with the similarities, *Female* figurines with an emphasis on the breast area have also been recovered elsewhere. The fact that such postures are exclusively associated with female representations suggests an emphasis placed on the physical body (and more specifically the breasts), while the inferences we can draw in relation to fertility and motherhood indicate that they were central notions for the construction of female gender identity and ideology in a wider Aegean context. Another posture, which has important implications for the understanding of gender identity in relation to social status, is that of seated figurines, which implies elevated social status (see Wason 1994: 105). Interestingly, *Male* figurines represented as seated on stools have been recovered from Crete, but also other parts of the Aegean. A number of postures, however, imply differentiation in relation to other regions at the level of the represented gender embodiment and the associated symbolisms. No examples from Crete are known to date to be modelled as pregnant and no seated figurines on stools or chairs represented *Female, Asexual* and *Ambiguous* examples.

The implications of the expression of gender through the postural embodiment of figurines allow crucial insights into performed gender roles and status at one level, and ideological allusions on another. The process of gender negotiation is social, as well as political, because it involves the definition of rights and understanding of normative practices (which themselves constitute political definitions), but also because negotiation of rights and obligations related to gender identity has material consequences (Sørensen 2000: 62–63 quoting Moore 1994). One such expression of the process of gender negotiation was perhaps demonstrated by the modelling of *Male, Female* and *Ambiguous* seated figurines, which may be interpreted as a mechanism of shifting social status between genders with consequences relating to access to economic resources. This is a possible indication of a purposeful attempt by social actors to erode and subvert socially accepted gender status, which may explain the *Ambiguous* seated specimens. The fact that one *Male* example is known from Crete would suggest that Crete and other Aegean regions converged at the level of emerging hierarchy. On the other hand, the absence of *Female* or other types of seated figurine may be provisionally interpreted as an indication that the achievement of social status by (some) men was left unchallenged by other gender groupings, or that the social status of women was attained through their association with other practices, such as tattooing and body decoration.

The Cretan sample also lacked figurines stressing selective anatomical parts and the increased complexity in relation to gender embodiment and manipulation of attire identified in other Aegean assemblages, perhaps implying less marked transformation and thus polarisation, at least at the level of gender relations. The absence from the Cretan assemblage of figurines heavily decorated with motifs denoting clothing or jewellery, which can be interpreted as probable status insignia, highlights further differences with Thessaly and Macedonia in terms of social organisation. The lack of such figurines from Crete – Knossos especially – could be interpreted as either deliberate 'silencing' of social differences, or as an alternative path in constructing gender and social status. The choices made on Crete gain special significance against the backdrop of socio-economic transformations taking place in LN when there is evidence of increased competition between households for economic and social power (Broodbank 1992: 66; Tomkins 2004: 50–55). The element of relative continuity evident in the figurine sample of Crete may indicate an attempt to maintain social norms regarding gender and social status at a time when earlier communal values were being renegotiated (Tomkins 2004: 54). The presence of the LN seated figurine, however, may attest to newly emerging social competition. Regarding gender dynamics, the lack of other evidence that would support the existence of gender inequality may indicate that figurines were possibly employed as media that emphasised or underplayed social values accordingly. The circulation of figurines in the sphere of ideology would have enabled prescribed norms to be highly effective in the communication and impact of the desired ideas. Finally, the comparison of Crete with other regions, such as Thessaly and Macedonia, where some unparalleled new patterns of figurine modelling in the LN suggest increased complexity in the construction of gender, implies alternative strategies adopted by Aegean societies as they chose to maintain or reject earlier norms.

Concluding Remarks

The 'leap' from analysis of represented sex to recognition of gender categories is neither self-evident nor predetermined. Analysis of added layers of meaning, represented by modelled posture and decoration, has helped define gender categories beyond the recorded anatomical features, and has demonstrated how the body operated at a symbolic level. Furthermore, decoration or posture may reveal overlap between or differentiation within the genders represented and the concepts that they stood for. For instance, representational and symbolic overlap between *Female, Female form* and *Asexual* figurines suggests that age played an important role in the construction of gender (female gender in particular) (Mina in press). The recovery of *articulated infant* burials and *disarticulated adult* remains at Knossos suggests differential treatment between age groups and thus offers additional support for the underlying role of age in the construction of identity. Such distinct attitudes towards one segment of the population indicates that age played an underlying role in the process of reaching full personhood and gender status among community members (Triantaphyllou 1999; 2001; this volume; Lucy 2005: 63), and was perhaps linked to the recognition of individuals as economic contributors (Sofaer Derevenski 1997: 887; Scott 1999: 99).

Anthropomorphic figurines may have been produced in the context of rituals, performed to mark stages in a person's life (*i.e.*, coming of age, 'marriage' or childbirth), which would explain the varied forms given to figurines. It is also possible that they were used in ceremonies related to natural cycles of production, seasons, or production and consumption practices. These images were symbolically loaded with cultural and ideological notions related to gender, but at the same time they may have served to 'educate' (Ucko 1968; Kokkinidou and Nikolaidou 1993: 60; 1997) and structure gender relationships and roles. The widespread occurrence of female representations in most regions of the Aegean attests to a preoccupation of Neolithic society with aspects of female gender (though not exclusively), perhaps tied to symbolic notions of fertility and propagation, though female (as male) social status was constituted in manifold ways and should not be seen as exclusively tied to reproductive capacity. Although we cannot give definitive answers regarding figurine manufacture and gender attribution, the contrast with the highly standardised Early Bronze Age figurines implies a relatively high degree of individualism (possibly as a result of a degree of self-projection) for the modelling of Neolithic figurines. Even if we assume that one gender was more closely associated with the modelling of one or more figurine sex categories or with particular stages of figurine production, we need to bear in mind that such symbolic representations were nevertheless equally relevant to other gender groups, since gender and associated notions are constructed on a dialectic and interactive basis.

Comparative study of figurine material from both sides of the Aegean would have provided, without doubt, further insights into gender and social organisation, but consideration of Anatolian evidence has not been attempted in the present study. Regarding the analysis presented in the present paper, future study of the whole excavated corpus of figurines from Knossos will help elucidate further the degree to which bias may have affected the sample under study. Nevertheless, the detected patterns deserve consideration, which will instigate a productive discussion around the possible insights that anthropomorphic figurines afford us into social organisation of Neolithic Crete. In fact, the comparison of Neolithic Crete with the rest of the Aegean has revealed striking parallels and divergences in terms of gender construction and social relations. The similarities relate to the classification model of gender categories, indicating a complex mechanism of social organisation away from bi-polar models, an emphasis on women's reproduction and involvement in ritual customs and the communication of gender and cultural identity in the wider ideological context of Neolithic culture. Evidence from Crete and other regions of the Aegean indicates that gender was also implicated in the negotiation of social status. On the other hand, the evidence for increasing complexity in embodied practices related to gender, and the emergence of more standardised and dichotomous ways in which men and women experienced their gender identity in LN, are absent from Crete. The example of Knossos, therefore, poses interesting questions about the avenues of social organisation followed in the Neolithic Aegean and the validity of preconceived models for understanding of social complexity, gender roles and status. Finally, the study of figurines has demonstrated that the Aegean in the Neolithic period was characterised by varied and fluctuating rhythms of complexity.

Acknowledgements

I thank the organisers for inviting me to participate in the 10th Sheffield Round Table, as well as Professor John Bennet and Debi Harlan for their generous hospitality. I am grateful to Professor John Evans for granting me permission to study the unpublished figurines from his 1969–1970 excavations at Knossos, and to Dr V. Isaakidou for drawing my attention to their existence. I would also like to thank Drs. P. Halstead, V. Isaakidou and P. Tomkins who provided useful comments and suggestions on an earlier draft of this paper. Professor C. Renfrew,

Dr L. Talalay, M. Besios and M. Pappa have kindly granted permission to reproduce illustrations from their publications. Last, but not least, thanks are due to my supervisors, Professor R. Whitehouse and Dr C. Broodbank, for their constructive comments on my doctoral thesis that the present paper draws upon.

Bibliography

Aalten, A.
   1997   Performing the body, creating culture. In K. Davis (ed.), *Embodied Practices: Feminist Perspectives on the Body*: 41–58. London: Sage.
Bailey, D.
   2005   *Prehistoric Figurines: Representation and Corporeality in the Neolithic*. London: Routledge.
Beaudry, M. C., L. J. Cook and A. Mrozowski
   1991   Artefacts and active voices: material culture as social discourse. In R. H. McGuire and R. Paynter (eds.), *The Archaeology of Inequality*: 150–91. Oxford: Blackwell.
Besios, M. and M. Pappa
   1998   Neolithikos oikismos Makriyalou, 1995. *AEMTh* 9: 173–78.
Broodbank, C.
   1992   The Neolithic Labyrinth: social change at Knossos before the Bronze Age. *JMA* 5: 39–75.
Chapman, J.
   2002   Colourful prehistories: The problem with the Berlin and Kay colour paradigm. In A. Jones and G. MacGregor (eds.), *Colouring the Past: The Significance of Colour in Archaeological Research*: 45–72. Oxford: Berg.
David, N., J. Sterner and K. Gavua
   1988   Why pots are decorated. *Current Anthropology* 29: 365–89.
Evans, J. D.
   1961   Knossos before Minos. Neolithic houses below the palace court and a marble figurine of outstanding beauty. *The Illustrated London News* 239: 60–61.
   1964   Excavations in the Neolithic settlement at Knossos, 1957–1960, Part I. *BSA* 59: 132–240.
Gallis, K.
   2001   Tracing the relation of a Neolithic figurine to a specific individual of the Neolithic society of Thessaly (Greece). In R. N. Boehmer and J. Maran (eds.), *Lux Orientis: Archäologie zwischen Asien und Europa* (Festschrift für Harald Hauptmann zum 65 Geburtstag): 139–43. Rahden/Westf: Verlag Marie Leidorf.
Gatens, M.
   1992   Power bodies and difference. In M. Barrett and A. Phillips (eds.), *Destabilizing Theory: Contemporary Feminist Debates*: 120–37. Cambridge: Polity Press in association with Blackwell Publishers.
Gell, A.
   1998   *Art and Agency: An Anthropological Theory*. Oxford: Clarendon Press.
Gosden, C.
   2005   What do objects want? *Journal of Archaeological Method and Theory* 12: 193–211.
Gosselain, O. P.
   1999   In pots we trust: the processing of clay and symbols in Sub-Saharan Africa. *Journal of Material Culture* 4: 205–30.

Haaland, G. and R. Haaland
   1996   Levels of meaning in symbolic objects. In N. Hamilton, J. Marcus, D. Bailey, G. R. Haaland and P. Ucko, Viewpoint: can we interpret figurines? *CAJ* 6: 295–300.
Hamilton, N.
   2000   Ungendering archaeology: concepts of sex and gender in figurine studies in prehistory. In M. Donald and L. Hurcombe (eds.), *Representations of Gender from Prehistory to the Present*: 17–30. London: Macmillan.
Hatcher, E. P.
   1985   *Art as Culture: an Introduction to the Anthropology of Art*. Lanham and London: University Press of America.
Herdt, G.
   1994   Introduction: third sexes and third genders. In G. Herdt (ed.), *Third Sex, Third Gender: Beyond Sexual Dimorphism in Culture and History*: 21–81. New York: Zone Books.
Hitchcock, L. A.
   1997   Engendering domination: a structural and contextual analysis of Minoan Neopalatial bronze figurines. In J. Moore and E. Scott (eds.), *Invisible People and Processes: Writing Gender and Childhood into European Archaeology*: 113–30. London: Leicester University Press.
Hodder, I.
   1982   *Symbols in Action: Ethnoarchaeological Studies of Material Culture*. Cambridge: Cambridge University Press.
Joyce, R.
   2002   Beauty, sexuality, body ornamentation and gender in Ancient Mesoamerica. In S. M. Nelson and M. Rosen-Ayalon (eds.), *In Pursuit of Gender: Worldwide Archaeological Approaches*: 81–91. Walnut Creek: Altamira Press.
Knappett, C.
   2002   Photographs, skeuomorphs and marionettes: some thoughts on mind, agency and object. *Journal of Material Culture* 7: 97–117.
   2006   Beyond skin: layering and networking in art and archaeology. *CAJ* 16: 239–51.
Kokkinidou, D. and M. Nikolaidou
   1993   *H Archaiologia kai i Koinoniki Tautotita tou Phylou: Prosengiseis stin Agrotiki Proistoria*. Thessaloniki: Vanias.
   1997   Body imagery in the Aegean Neolithic: ideological implications of anthropomorphic figurines. In J. Moore and E. Scott (eds.), *Invisible People and Processes: Writing Gender and Childhood into European Archaeology*: 88–112. London: Leicester University Press.
Layton, R.
   1991   *The Anthropology of Art*. Cambridge: Cambridge University Press, 2nd edn.
Lele, V. P.
   2006   Material habits, identity, semeiotic. *Journal of Social Archaeology* 6: 48–70.
Lindemann, G.
   1997   The body of gender difference. In K. Davis (ed.), *Embodied Practices: Feminist Perspectives on the Body*: 73–92. London: Sage.
Lucy, A.
   2005   The archaeology of age. In M. Díaz-Andreu, S. Lucy, S. Babis and D. N. Edwards (eds.), *The Archaeology of Identity: Approaches to Gender, Age, Status, Ethnicity and Religion*: 43–66. London: Routledge.
MacRae, D. G.
   1975   The body and social metaphor. In J. Benthall and T. Polhemus (eds.), *The Body as a Medium of Expression*: 59–73. London: Allen Lane.

Mina, M.
   2005   *Anthropomorphic Figurines from the Neolithic and Early Bronze Age Aegean: Gender Dynamics and Implications for the Understanding of Aegean Prehistory*. PhD dissertation, University College London.
   2007   Figurines without sex; people without gender. In S. Hamilton, R. Whitehouse and K. Wright (eds.), *Archaeology and Women: Ancient and Modern Issues*: 263–82. Oxford: Berg.
   in press *Anthropomorphic Figurines from the Neolithic and Early Bronze Age Aegean: Gender Dynamics and Implications for the Understanding of Aegean Prehistory* (BAR International Series). Oxford: British Archaeological Reports.
Moore, H. L.
   1994   *A Passion for Difference*. Cambridge: Polity Press.
Nanoglou, S.
   2005   Subjectivity and material culture in Thessaly, Greece: the case of Neolithic anthropomorphic imagery. *CAJ* 15: 141–56.
Orphanidi-Georgiadi, L.
   1992   Thoughts on the Neolithic figurines of the Aegean. *SMEA* 30: 165–78.
Orphanidi, L.
   1998   *Eisagogi sti Neolithiki Eidoloplastiki; Notioanatoliki Europi kai Anatoliki Mesogeios*. Athens: Academia Athenon, Kentron Ereunas tis Archaiotitos.
Perlès, C.
   2001   *The Early Neolithic in Greece: The First Farming Communities in Europe*. Cambridge: Cambridge University Press.
Rainbird, P.
   2002   Marking the body, marking the land; body as history land as history: tattooing and engraving in Oceania. In Y. Hamilakis (ed.), *Thinking through the Body: Archaeologies of Corporeality*: 233–47. New York: Kluwer Academic/Plenum Publishers.
Renfrew, C., M. Gimbutas and E. S. Elster (eds.)
   1986   *Excavations at Sitagroi: A Prehistoric Village in Northeast Greece, 1*. Los Angeles: UCLA Institute of Archaeology.
Rethemiotakis, G.
   1996   Anthropomorphic figurines: Crete. In G. Papathanassopoulos (ed.), *Neolithic Culture in Greece*: 158. Athens: Goulandris Foundation, Museum of Cycladic Art.
Richardson, M.
   1989   The artefact as abbreviated act: a social interpretation of material culture. In I. Hodder (ed.), *The Archaeology of Contextual Meanings*: 172–77. Cambridge: Cambridge University Press.
Scott, E.
   1999   *The Archaeology of Infancy and Infant Death*. (BAR International Series 819). Oxford: British Archaeological Reports.
Sofaer Derevenski, J.
   1997   Age and gender at the site of the Tiszapolgár-Basatanya, Hungary. *Antiquity* 71: 875–89.
Sørensen, M. L. S.
   2000   *Gender Archaeology*. Cambridge: Polity Press.
Talalay, L. E.
   1993   *Deities, Dolls, and Devices: Neolithic Figurines from Franchthi Cave, Greece*. Bloomington and Indianapolis: Indiana University Press.
   2000   Archaeological misconceptions: contemplating gender and power in the Greek Neolithic. In M. Donald and L. Hurcombe (eds.), *Representations of Gender from Prehistory to the Present*: 3–16. London: Macmillan.

2005   The gendered sea: iconography, gender and Mediterranean prehistory. In E. Blake and A. B. Knapp (eds.), *The Archaeology of Mediterranean Prehistory*: 130–55. Oxford: Blackwell.

Tanner, J.
   1992   Art as expressive symbolism: civic portraits in Classical Athens. *CAJ* 2: 167–90.

Tilley, C.
   1989   Interpreting material culture. In I. Hodder (ed.), *The Meanings of Things: Material Culture and Symbolic Expression*: 185–94. London: Unwin Hyman.
   1999   *Metaphor and Material Culture*. Oxford: Blackwell.

Tomkins, P.
   2001   *The Production, Circulation and Consumption of Ceramic Vessels at Early Neolithic Knossos, Crete*. PhD dissertation, University of Sheffield.
   2004   Filling in the 'neolithic background': social life and social transformation in the Aegean before the Bronze Age. In J. C. Barrett and P. Halstead (eds.), *The Emergence of Civilisation Revisited* (SSAA 6): 38–63. Oxford: Oxbow Books.
   2007   Neolithic: Strata IX–VIII, VII–VIB, VIA–V, IV, IIIB, IIIA, IIB, IIA and IC Groups. In N. Momigliano (ed.), *Knossos Pottery Handbook: Neolithic and Bronze Age (Minoan)*: 9–48. London: British School at Athens.

Triantaphyllou, S.
   1999   Prehistoric Makriyalos: a story from the fragments. In P. Halstead (ed.), *Neolithic Society in Greece* (SSAA 1): 128–35. Sheffield: Sheffield Academic Press.
   2001   *A Bioarchaeological Approach to Prehistoric Cemetery Populations from Central and Western Greek Macedonia*. ((BAR International Series 976). Oxford: British Archaeological Reports.

Turner, B.
   1995   Body and society: an introduction. In M. Featherstone and B. Turner (eds.), *Body and Society*: 1–12. London: Sage.

Ucko, P. J.
   1968   *Anthropomorphic Figurines of Predynastic Egypt and Neolithic Crete with Comparative Material from the Prehistoric Near East and Mainland Greece*. London: Andrew Szmidla.

Walisewska, E.
   1991   Archaeology of religion: colours as symbolic markers dividing sacred from profane. *Journal of Prehistoric Religion* 5: 36–41.

Wason, P. K.
   1994   *The Archaeology of Rank*. Cambridge: Cambridge University Press.

Watrous, L. V.
   2001   Crete from the earliest prehistory through the Protopalatial period. Addendum: 1994–1999. In T. Cullen (ed.), *Aegean Prehistory: A Review*: 157–223. Boston: Archaeological Institute of America.

Wolff, J.
   1993   *The Social Production of Art*. London: Macmillan.

8

Living with the Dead: a Re-Consideration of Mortuary Practices in the Greek Neolithic

Sevi Triantaphyllou

In a review, 35 years ago, of Neolithic burial customs in Greece, Hourmouziadis (1973) drew attention to the scarcity and diversity of the evidence. Individual or group inhumations in simple pits within thc settlement were predominant, but burials in pots and stone-lined graves were also known, as were cremations. Hourmouziadis himself had found one clear case of secondary burial – a group of skulls and other bones found under an EN house floor at Prodromos in Thessaly – and LN curation of skulls was also observed at Alepotrypa cave in the Peloponnese, but scattered bones at the latter site had been interpreted by the excavator as a result of post-depositional disturbance. Most sites (including Knossos) had yielded few (if any) burials and grave goods were scarce or absent, while the rare groups of burials that might be labelled 'cemeteries' were restricted to the later Neolithic. The available information was drawn almost entirely from excavators' reports, without detailed osteological study, and occasional reports of stray human bones in faunal assemblages (*e.g.*, in LN deposits at Argissa in Thessaly – Boessneck 1962: 58, table 1) attracted little attention. Over the following two decades, the volume of material grew and the diversity of burial practice was reinforced by new discoveries: of groups of cremations at EN Soufli and LN Zarko in Thessaly, the latter – significantly – forming a cemetery at some distance from the settlement (Gallis 1982); of intramural infant burials at LN Dimini in Thessaly (Hourmouziadis 1978); and of differential treatment of infants and older individuals (see below) at LN–FN Kalythies cave on Rhodes (Halstead and Jones 1987). The sparseness of the burial record and modest nature of any accompanying grave goods, however, continued to suggest only limited interest in mortuary display and provided no evidence of social inequality, while EN–MN funerary rituals at least 'occurred within the context of the family and were not yet a means of integrating the whole community' (Demoule and Perlès 1993: 385).

Over the last 10–15 years, the picture has changed dramatically in three ways. First, large-scale excavations at LN Makriyalos (Pappa and Bessios 1999) in central Macedonia, at LN Toumba Kremastis-Koiladas in western Macedonia (Hondrogianni-Metoki 2001), and at LN Profitis Ilias-Mandras in Thessaly (Toufexis and Manolis in press) have yielded large assemblages of human remains, especially disarticulated remains. Secondly, new (*e.g.*, Makriyalos – Triantaphyllou 2001) and some older assemblages (*e.g.*, Alepotrypa cave – Papathanasiou 2001) have been the subject of systematic osteological studies that have shed important light on treatment of the body and its relationship to age and sex. And thirdly, discussion of Neolithic mortuary evidence from Greece has increasingly been informed by an anthropological perspective (Fowler 2004) and by comparison with finds from the Balkans and other parts of Europe, with the result that these human remains are viewed as active elements in negotiations between the living and the dead or amongst the living (cf. Barrett 1988; Parker Pearson 1993; 1999; Robb 1994; 1999; Radovanović 1996; 2000; Whittle and Wysocki 1998; Chapman 2000; Wysocki and Whittle 2000; Borić and Stefanović 2004). As a result of all three developments, there has been growing awareness of the significance of disarticulated human remains in the Neolithic of Greece, exemplified by Cullen's work on the bone scatters from Franchthi cave in the Peloponnese (Cullen 1999), Talalay's comparative study of the evidence for secondary treatment of skulls in Anatolia and Greece (Talalay 2002) and arguments for the role of commingled human remains in negotiating collective solidarity at Makriyalos (Triantaphyllou 1999; 2001; Kotsakis 1999). As Perlès has recently admitted, previous suggestions as to the domestic character of mortuary practices and the lack of emphasis on death rituals are no longer tenable (Perlès 2001: 273, 281).

This chapter explores this growing body of evidence for the treatment of human remains in the Greek Neolithic, drawing both on recently published studies and on preliminary results from ongoing study of assemblages from Macedonia and from re-study of the material from Knossos. It is argued that some patterning can now be discerned in the diversity of the mortuary record and that this may relate to the tension, alluded to by Demoule and Perlès (1993) between family/domestic and communal scales of social integration.

Diversity in death: the manipulation of the deceased in Neolithic Greece

A recent summary of the evidence for manipulation of the deceased in the Neolithic of Greece (Milka 2003) to a large extent confirmed the patterns discerned in the earlier syntheses of Hourmouziadis (1973) and Demoule and Perlès (1993). Evidence is much more abundant from the LN–FN than EN–MN, but the later Neolithic has a wider geographical distribution and longer temporal span than EN–MN and has been the focus of more and larger-scale excavations. Despite the differences between periods in sample size, however, the *diversity* of burial forms remains essentially unchanged: primary and secondary inhumations, scattered bones and cremations are represented throughout the Neolithic within open-air settlements, in caves and in organised cemeteries. Primary inhumations remain the most widespread form of burial throughout, albeit less clearly

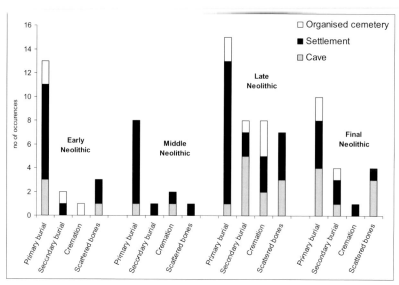

Figure 8.1. Distribution of types of disposal in the Neolithic Aegean.

predominant in LN–FN than EN–MN. The most striking change since the earlier syntheses, however, in the nature (as opposed to quantity) of the evidence, is the abundance of scattered and selectively manipulated human remains (Figure 8.1).

The caves of Alepotrypa, Franchthi, Skoteini and Kalythies

There is growing evidence from cave sites for such differential mortuary treatment. At Franchthi, EN scattered bones as well as primary inhumations have been found both inside the cave (142 scattered bones and 13 inhumations) and on the associated Paralia open-air site (127 scattered bones and 18 inhumations) (Jacobsen and Cullen 1981; Cullen 1999). Primary burials and bone scatters differ in the representation of age groups: there is a higher incidence of infants (0–2 years) and juveniles (2–12 years) in the burials and relative scarcity of young children (0–12 years) in the scattered material (after Cullen 1999: 166). At LN–FN Alepotrypa cave in the southern Peloponnese, primary inhumations and secondary burials are accompanied by evidence for differential treatment of skulls (Papathanass-opoulos 1971; 1996; Papathanasiou 2001). There is also evident spatial segregation between primary burials, located in the inhabited areas of the cave, and secondary burials and ossuaries, located in areas reserved for successive interments over a long period of time. LN–FN Skoteini cave, on Evvia in central Greece, yielded scattered human bones from perhaps 14 infants, children, pre-adolescents and young adults, while six pits in the nearby open-air cemetery contained parts (with long bones under-represented) of 24 individuals, of whom 17 were mature adults (Stravopodi 1993). At LN–FN Kalythies cave on Rhodes, scattered human remains found in the animal bone assemblage included long bones of infants, possibly representing disturbed or unrecognised primary burials, and hand/foot bones and loose teeth of older individuals who had presumably been interred in the cave and then removed for secondary burial elsewhere (Halstead and Jones 1987).

Open-air sites in Macedonia: Makriyalos, Toumba Kremastis-Koiladas and Paliambela-Kolindrou

Scattered bones have also been found in large quantities, again mostly mixed in with the faunal assemblage, from recent excavations of open-air sites in Macedonia at LN Makriyalos, LN Toumba Kremastis-Koiladas and MN Paliam-bela-Kolindrou. Makriyialos is a 'flat-extended' settlement (Pappa and Besios 1999), while Toumba Kremastis-Koiladas (Hondrogianni-Metoki 2001) and Paliambela-Kolindrou (Kotsakis and Halstead 2004) have both tell and flat-extended components. At Makriyalos, two phases of LN occupation have been distinguished (early LN phase I and late LN phase II), which barely overlap spatially – in sharp contrast with the relative spatial stability of habitation typical of tell sites. In addition to groups of 'habitation' pits, Makriyalos I comprises large borrow pits, filled with the debris from what appear to have been major feasting episodes, and three ditches, of which two (the deep inner Ditch Alpha and the shallow outer Ditch Beta) enclosed and a third (Ditch Gamma) perhaps sub-divided the settlement area. The excavated part of the phase II settlement comprises a dense scatter of 'habitation' pits and traces of above ground rectangular buildings, borrow pits and a short stretch of a relatively insubstantial ditch (Pappa and Besios 1999; Pappa *et al.* 2004). In common with faunal remains and ceramics, human skeletal material is far more abundant in phase I than in phase II deposits (Triantaphyllou 1999; 2001). Articulated inhumations were found only in phase I: 19 in Ditch Alpha (including 7 part-skeletons possibly disturbed unintentionally by repeated digging in the ditch) and one in borrow pit 214. Disarticulated human bones from phase I were likewise concentrated in Ditch Alpha (parts of 38 individuals), but were also found scattered in smaller numbers (representing 13 individuals) in Ditches Beta and Gamma, in borrow pit 214 and in habitation features (Figure 8.2). The significance of this uneven distribution of disarticulated remains is underlined by the fact that Ditch A yielded less than a fifth of the phase I faunal assemblage. Phase II disarticulated remains were found in habitation contexts and in a large borrow pit in excavation sector Xi (representing 9 and 2 individuals, respectively).

For Makriyalos I, it seems likely that Ditch Alpha was the main locus for primary inhumation and that most burials were subsequently disinterred and body parts re-deposited there or elsewhere; there is no evidence (*e.g.*, weathering of bone surfaces) that disarticulated remains had initially been exposed rather than buried (cf. Byers 2002: 103–21). For phase II, the same practice may be

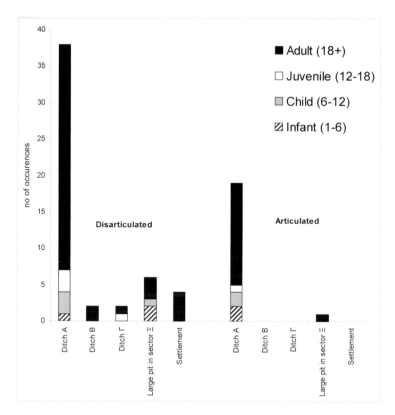

Figure 8.2. LN Makriyalos: Distribution of age groups.

inferred, but there is no evidence as to where primary inhumation took place. Some of the articulated skeletons were evidently buried in a simple pit or laid out with care or deposited with artefacts. By comparison with Alepotrypa and Skoteini caves, the detection of selective treatment of disarticulated body parts is complex. The under-representation, among both articulated and disarticulated remains, of small hand/foot bones, ribs and vertebrae and, to a lesser extent, flat bones (pelvis and scapula) (Triantaphyllou 2001: 49–51) can plausibly be attributed to a combination of poor survival of fragile elements (compounded by non-recognition during preliminary sorting of faunal material) and partial retrieval of small elements under rescue excavation conditions. This interpretation is supported by the fact that, among *articulated* remains, the relative proportions of cranial material, teeth and long bones are roughly as expected in complete skeletons. Among *disarticulated* material in Ditch Alpha, however, long bones (which are large, durable and easily recognised) are strikingly under-represented, suggesting that they were preferentially removed when primary burials were disinterred. The sample of disarticulated material from other phase I contexts is not large enough for certainty, but is dominated by long bones and so is certainly consistent with the hypothesis that secondary burial involved preferential removal from Ditch Alpha of long bones and their re-deposition elsewhere. In terms of age groups, infants, children, juveniles and adults are all represented among both articulated and disarticulated remains and the under-representation of young age groups and absence of neonates are again probably due, at least in part, to their fragility and to partial retrieval (Figure 8.2). Females outnumber males, however, among both articulated and disarticulated remains (Trianta-phyllou 2001: 53, table 5.7) and, although sample size again indicates the need for caution, the greater fragility of female skeletons (Weiss 1972) suggests their over-representation may be significant. If so, the implication is that some men were ultimately disposed of elsewhere and that the recognised mortuary contexts at Makriyalos catered for only part of the community.

Study of both Toumba Kremastis-Koiladas and Paliambela-Kolindrou is ongoing and thus both osteological data and contextual information are incomplete. At the former site, excavation beyond the limits of the tell site exposed stretches of ditch and some 400 pits, all of early LN date (Hondrogianni-Metoki 2001). As at Makriyalos, therefore, the excavated area exhibits no continuity of occupation. Some of these pits yielded clear evidence of structured deposition of ceramics, figurines and animal bones. In anatomical composition, the 123 disarticulated human remains recorded resemble the equivalent material from contexts *other than* Ditch Alpha at Makriyalos (Figure 8.3): hand/foot bones, flat bones, ribs and vertebrae are under-represented and long bones strongly outnumber cranial fragments and teeth. The lack of evidence for weathering or animal scavenging again argues against initial exposure of bodies. The dis-articulated fragments thus seem to represent selective secondary deposition of long bones long enough after primary inhumation for decomposition of the body to have been more or less complete (a few finds of adjacent elements might indicate incomplete decomposition). The minimum number of individuals represented by the disarticulated material has been estimated at 14 and includes all age groups (11 adult, 1 juvenile, 1 child and 1 neonate) and both sexes (4 male, 1 female and 6 indeterminate adults), but adults and younger individuals clearly differed in terms of both the treatment of the body and the context of final deposition. Most of the disarticulated human material found in the pits belongs to adults and no articulated adults have yet been found. On the other hand, two articulated (and a third disarticulated) neonates were found in the ditches and articulated skeletons of two further subadult individuals in pits: a 12 year-old child (together with clear structured deposition of animal bones, ceramics and figurines) in the large pit 76 and a 4 year-old infant in the smaller burial pit 24.

At Paliambela-Kolindrou, excavation has so far focussed mainly on the low tell rather than flat-extended component of the site, but deposits are thin and habitation on any one part of the tell appears discontinuous (P. Halstead, K. Kotsakis and D. Urem-Kotsou pers. comm.). A small assemblage of disarticulated human remains of MN and LN date is under study. Most of this material is

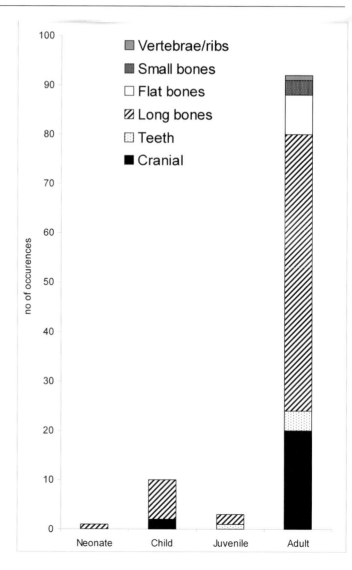

Figure 8.3. Toumba Koiladas-Kremastis: Representation of scattered bones by age category.

derived from an MN enclosure ditch on the southeast margin of the tell and is comprised almost exclusively of cranial fragments of at least one child, one juvenile and two adults (the latter including a probable male and a probable female). Despite wholesale dry-sieving of the deposit, no small hand or foot bones were recovered, suggesting that the ditch was the locus for secondary deposition of skulls rather than for primary inhumation of bodies which, after decomposition, were selectively disinterred for secondary treatment elsewhere. Conversely, two MN ditches on the north and northwest margins of the tell have so far yielded only scattered *postcranial* remains, including small hand/foot bones, of at least two (one neonate and one adult) and three (one infant, one juvenile and one adult) individuals, respectively and so might represent the locus of temporary primary inhumation, but these latter samples are as yet very small.

Coordination of human osteological and zooarchaeological research at these three recent excavations of open-air sites in Macedonia has dramatically increased the corpus of Neolithic human skeletal data from Greece and, especially, the evidence of disarticulated human remains. At each site, there is evidence, of varying strength, that disarticulation was at least partly the result of the selective removal of body parts, of long bones at LN Makriyalos and Toumba Kremastis-Koiladas and of skulls at MN Paliambela, during secondary manipulation of the deceased. This secondary manipulation took place long enough (perhaps 3–5 years – Rodriguez and Bass 1985) after primary inhumation (not exposure) for bodies to have decomposed more or less fully. At Makriyalos I, there is evidence that male and female adults were treated differently, with males underrepresented among both articulated and disarticulated material, while the samples from Toumba Kremastis-Koiladas and Paliambela-Kolindrou are as yet too small to explore this issue. At Toumba Kremastis-Koiladas, there are indications that the full mortuary programme including secondary disarticulation was performed preferentially on adults, while the remains of younger individuals were manipulated less intensively. This distinction was not observed at Makriyalos, although articulated child burials are probably less likely to be recognised as such in excavation than those of adults and so, with partial retrieval, are more likely to have been misclassified as disarticulated. Moreover, unless the under-representation of young individuals at Makriyalos is entirely an artefact of taphonomic and retrieval biases, differential mortuary treatment on the basis of age was also taking place at this site. Mortuary treatment at these three sites was thus far from simple, but instead comprised at least two stages of ritual, separated in both time and space, and involved spatial and/or anatomical differentiation between individuals on the basis of age and perhaps sex.

Knossos

From his excavations at Neolithic Knossos on Crete, John Evans reported no adult human remains but several 'intramural' child burials (Evans 1964; 1971). Of seven such burials reported from the first excavation campaign (1957–60) in area AC under the Central Court and initially dated to the Aceramic (Evans 1964: 140), burial G is now assigned to the Aceramic and the remainder to EN on the basis of re-study of ceramics and excavation notebooks (Tomkins pers. comm.). Five of these skeletons were recently relocated and re-studied, yielding the following age estimates: burial A – neonate, burial D – foetus/neonate, burial E – foetus, burial F – neonate, burial G – 3 year-old infant. These estimates closely match those reported by Evans (1964: 142), who in addition attributed burial B to a 6–7 year old and burial C to a 2–3 year old. Burials A to F were found articulated in a flexed position and on the same orientation (Evans 1964: figs. 7–8). The

Aceramic burial G was placed in a more obvious pit sealed with an oval stone. An unspecified number of child burials is also reported from the second excavation campaign (1969–70), including two infants in area RS under the Central Court (Evans 1971: 111; also Broodbank 1992: 59), but the latter have now been re-identified as burials of dogs (Isaakidou pers. comm.). On the other hand, a skeleton found under an upturned pot fragment and attributed in excavation to rabbit or hare has been identified by the author as that of a foetal human, buried in a probably disused structure of late MN date (Tomkins pers. comm.).

In addition to the human remains collected during excavation, further material was recognised during recent re-study of the animal bone material (Isaakidou 2004). Sieving in area AA–BB under the West Court had retrieved remains of two neonatal humans, possibly from articulated skeletons not recognised during excavation, that seem to have been associated with a multi-roomed house of FNIA date. A further 16 human fragments were found scattered through the MN–FN deposits. Some chronological issues remain to be resolved and the sample is very small, but it is nonetheless significant, because adults are represented among the fragments, as well as the children, infants and neonates already recognised among articulated burials (Figure 8.4). Adults may have been subject to secondary disarticulation, therefore, as in Macedonia, rather than lying undiscovered in inhumations off-site. Whether the treatment of children changed through time, from burial in open space to burial within houses (Broodbank 1992), is impossible to judge from such a small sample. Nor is the lack of scattered adult bones from the Aceramic and EN surprising, given the relatively small amount of faunal material from the earliest levels (cf. Isaakidou this volume). Differential treatment of adults and young individuals seems a safer inference. The overall scarcity of scattered human remains from Neolithic Knossos is striking, however, given the large scale of excavation. A rough and readily available yardstick for comparing the frequency of scattered human bones at Neolithic Knossos, Toumba Kremastis-Koiladas and Makriyalos is relative to numbers of identifiable animal bones, which are estimated at approximately 50,000, 40,000 and 30,000 respectively (using identical methodology – V. Isaakidou, P. Halstead and V. Tzevelekidi pers. comm.). The frequency of scattered human bones is thus something like 0.3 per 1000 identified animal bones at Knossos, 3/1000 at Toumba Kremastis-Koiladas and 27/1000 at Makriyalos. A similar figure cannot be calculated yet for Paliambela-Kolindrou, because analysis is at an early stage, but human bones were widely encountered in preliminary sorting of faunal remains so the site is expected to resemble its Macedonian neighbours rather than Knossos.

Discussion

Secondary manipulation especially of adult skeletons is now evident for Neolithic Greece at several caves, at three open-air sites in Macedonia and at the Knossos

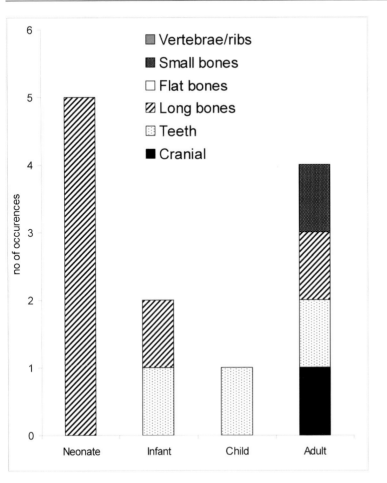

Figure 8.4. Neolithic Knossos: Representation of scattered bones by age category.

tell. Stray human bones are also reported in faunal assemblages from Neolithic levels at other tell sites in northern Greece (see below) and the lack of such reports in other cases cannot be taken as evidence that scattered human bones were absent. Elsewhere in Neolithic Europe, deposits of commingled human bones have been interpreted as evidence that, after death, individuals were subsumed within a collective identity (Shanks and Tilley 1984). At Makriyalos I, this interpretation received support from the concentration of primary burials and disarticulated remains in Ditch A that enclosed and bounded the settlement (Triantaphyllou 1999) and was also surely the product of a massive collective labour project (Kotsakis 1999; Pappa and Besios 1999). Indications from Toumba Kremastis-Koiladas and perhaps Paliambela-Kolindrou, that disarticulation of the deceased was preferentially performed for adults, underline the social significance of this secondary mortuary treatment and are certainly consistent with the idea that it symbolised incorporation into the community of collective dead or ancestors.

Collective identity was also negotiated and reinforced at Makriyalos I in episodes of conspicuous commensality (Pappa *et al.* 2004) using highly standard-ised ceramic serving vessels (Urem-Kotsou and Kotsakis 2007), while traces of flimsy huts at this and other flat-extended sites contrast with the construction on many tell sites of relatively monumental houses (Kotsakis 1982; 1999; 2006). Large and imposing houses emphasised the separation of the household from the wider community, while the gradual erosion of collective obligations may be reflected in a long-term tendency for cooking facilities to be relocated from open 'public' areas to closed yards and indoor 'kitchens' (Halstead 1995; 2006). Tomkins (2004; 2007; this volume) has argued that a broadly similar architectural trend at Knossos is paralleled by a shift in ceramics from relative standardisation in EN–MN to greater diversity in LN–FN (also Broodbank 1992: 52–57). The common element in these various models is the tension between collective and domestic scales of identity and activity in the Neolithic, with suggestions that the collective received greater emphasis in the earlier Neolithic and on flat-extended sites, while the balance had shifted towards the domestic in the later Neolithic and on tell sites. It is tempting to relate variability in mortuary practice to the opposition between flat-extended and tell settlements, given that the evidence for scattered remains is stronger at the former, while primary inhumations are better known from the latter. Such a contrast, however, may be more apparent than real. First, articulated inhumations are rare or unknown on most tell settlements. For example, only one burial of an adult male was reported from MN Tsangli (Wace and Thompson 1912), eight subadult pot burials from LN Dimini (Hourmouziadis 1978) and another two subadult pot burials from LN Rachmani (Wace and Thompson 1912) in Thessaly. Even at EN Nea Nikomedia, where 35 articulated inhumations were found in shallow pits among the EN houses (Rodden 1962; 1965; Angel 1973), the number of such burials is perhaps too few – given the longevity of habitation and the scale of excavation – to have been the normal form of mortuary treatment. Indeed, in light of the previous discussion, it may be suggested that these primary inhumations represent individuals who received an abnormal form of burial (cf. Halstead 1984) because they, or the manner of their death, were in some way unusual (cf. O'Shea 1984). For example, an adult female and two children interred as a group may have died together in an accident or from a contagious illness. Anyway, even more individuals (52) are reported represented by disarticulated remains, although the excavator inter-preted these as the result of (accidentally) disturbed inhumations rather than secondary mortuary treatment, because the bones were well preserved.

The number of stray human remains at Nea Nikomedia cannot yet be compared to the size of the faunal assemblage, but this exercise is possible for some other tell sites in northern Greece: ca 0.8/1000 identified animal bones at EN and LN Argissa in Thessaly (Boessneck 1962: 58, table 1), 5/1000 at MN–LN Dimitra in eastern Macedonia (Yiannouli 1994) and 4/1000 at LN–FN Pevkakia in Thessaly (Jordan 1975: 10, table 1; Hinz 1979). At LN Stavroupoli, which has both tell and flat-extended components, in addition to five primary inhumations and one cremation, 117 scattered human remains (Triantaphyllou 2002; 2004) were recovered in the faunal assemblage of 14,231 identifiable specimens (Yiannouli 2002; 2004), representing a rate of 8 per 1000 animal bones. These figures are all higher than that for Knossos (0.3/1000) and lower than that for Makriyalos (27/1000), but bracket that for Toumba Kremastis-Koiladas (3/1000), so on this basis no simple distinction can be drawn between flat-extended and tell sites in the frequency of disarticulated remains.

Of course, such site-wide figures may be misleading if mortuary deposition was focussed on particular contexts. For example, at Makriyalos I, both articulated inhumations and scattered remains were heavily concentrated in enclosure Ditch Alpha, whereas no human bones were recognised in the massive faunal assemblage from the feasting pit 212 (cf. Pappa *et al.* 2004). It is too early to judge whether primary burial in enclosure ditches is a recurrent feature of flat-extended and not of tell sites. Paliambela-Kolindrou, where primary burial has tentatively been identified in an MN Ditch, unfortunately is not a typical example of either type of site. The LN cremation cemetery located ca 200–300m from Platia Magoula Zarkou (Gallis 1982: 103) might be taken as evidence for an alternative practice at tell sites, but the EN group of cremations at Soufli was found on the edge of the mound (Gallis 1982: 25–26, figs. 2–3a). Anyway, both groups of cremations may have involved burning of decomposed bodies. In each case, at least some cremations apparently contained bone fragments from more than one human individual (nos. 17 and perhaps 14 and 16 at Soufli; nos. 24, 35 and perhaps 15, 20 and 25 at Platia Magoula Zarkou) and also burnt bones of animals. The mixing of individuals and of humans and animals, which is almost certainly under-estimated given the poor preservation of the material, would arguably have occurred more readily if bodies were disarticulated before cremation. Moreover, most of the Soufli cremations included a mix of burnt and unburnt bones (Xirotiris 1982) and, particularly at Soufli, the brown/black colour of burnt bone and lack of marked warping and cracking suggest burning at low temperatures and/or of short duration (cf. Buikstra and Swegle 1989; also Correia 1997). Intact corpses would thus have been only partially burnt and would not easily have been mixed – unless final interment followed exposure or burial for a significant length of time after cremation. These cremations might thus also have been a form of *secondary* mortuary treatment, although both sites have yielded remains of infants, juveniles or young adults and adults.

The search for pattern (whether chronological, geographical or in relation to settlement type) in the small and patchy extant dataset is risky. Secondary mortuary ritual seems to have been fairly ubiquitous and it is possible that future osteological research will provide additional evidence that the oppositions between primary and secondary burial and between dispersal and cremation are primarily related to age and sex and perhaps even life history (*e.g.*, diet, health, occupational stress, cause of death). Nonetheless, stray human bones were encountered in a high proportion of contexts at Makriyalos and Paliambela-

Kolindrou, in start contrast to Knossos; such contextual breakdown of the data is not published for other tell sites. It remains a possibility, therefore, that disarticulated remains are more *widely dispersed* in sites like Makriyalos and Paliambela-Kolindrou than in classic compact tell sites. This suggestion, if confirmed in the future, would have obvious relevance to Kotsakis' argument (1999) that the continuity of habitation and monumentality of building that underpin tell formation are ultimately strategies for asserting domestic over collective rights to land.

Conclusion

As a result of recent large-scale excavations, the volume of human skeletal material from the Neolithic of Greece is growing rapidly. Much of the new material is in the form of disarticulated fragments that were recognised not during excavation but in subsequent analysis of large faunal assemblages, so underlining the need for coordination of human osteological and zooarchaeological study. While some disarticulated remains are probably the result of post-depositional disturbance of primary inhumations, many are the product of deliberate secondary manipulation of skeletons – a phenomenon widely observed in the Neolithic from the Levant and Turkey (*e.g.*, Talalay 2002; Andrews and Bello 2006) to the Balkans (*e.g.*, Chapman 2000: 134–46), Italy (Skeates 1991; 1999; Robb 1994; Beckett and Robb 2006) and Britain (*e.g.*, Shanks and Tilley 1984; Whittle and Wysocki 1998). As elsewhere, the Greek evidence for secondary manipulation of more or less decomposed skeletons implies that the passage of the deceased from the community of the living to that of the dead or ancestors involved rites of passage separated by a transitional period of a few years during which the body decayed. While selective removal of body parts suggests an active role for such relics in prompting memory of the past (cf. Humphreys and King 1981; Bloch and Parry 1982; Metcalf and Huntington 1991), disarticulation and dispersal suggest more effort to remember shared ancestors than the individual founders of particular lineages. Moreover, as osteological analysis of Neolithic human remains becomes more routine in Greece, it is increasingly clear that secondary manipulation was preferentially applied to adults and also possible that males and females were treated differently. Perhaps those who died young were not eligible to join the community of ancestors or their transition to the latter merited less ceremony.

The evidence for secondary manipulation of the deceased in Neolithic Greece is largely derived, to date, from caves and from flat-extended open-air sites in the north of the country. Primary inhumations are better known at tell sites, although usually in numbers so small as to suggest that they might represent exceptional individuals or abnormal deaths. At Neolithic Knossos, John Evans' excavations located several primary inhumations of children, to which study of the faunal assemblage has now added disarticulated remains of both adults and children. The number of disarticulated fragments is very low, given the size of the faunal assemblage, but it is unclear whether this may be a recurrent feature of Neolithic tell as opposed to flat-extended sites. Disarticulated human remains, symbolising collective identity, are less common and less widespread on tell sites, where architectural claims to 'private' space were denser, more monumental and more long lasting (Kotsakis 1999). At the beginning of the Bronze Age, individual graves grouped in cemeteries become the norm in many parts of the Aegean, offering new scope for advertising and perhaps renegotiating the status of deceased individuals (Nakou 1995; Cavanagh and Mee 1998; also Broodbank 2000). Eminent Bronze Age individuals did not bury themselves, however, and claims to elevated status were presumably made by their kin. If the emergence of individual burial does signal increased competition for status between house-holds or lineages, then it represents the culmination of a process of negotiation between collective and domestic identity and rights that had been played out in settlement layout, architecture and ceramic table-wares, as well as mortuary behaviour, throughout the Neolithic.

Acknowledgements

I thank Valasia Isaakidou and Peter Tomkins for inviting me to contribute to this Round Table. Study of the Knossos human remains would have been impossible without Valasia's assistance in locating material in store and Peter's help with contextual and chronological information. I also thank Valasia for sorting out disarticulated human fragments from the Knossos faunal assemblage, and Vasso Tzevelekidi for the same service in the case of Toumba Kremastis-Koiladas. I am grateful to the excavators who entrusted me with the study of material: J. D. Evans for Knossos, Manthos Besios and Maria Pappa for Makriyialos, Paul Halstead and Kostas Kotsakis for Paliambela-Kolindrou, and Areti Hondrogianni-Metoki for Toumba Kremastis-Koiladas. I am also indebted to Vangelio Kiriatzi, Nancy Krahtopoulou and Valasia Isaakidou, for providing me with articles and bibliographical references during my 'exile' in Nafplio; and to Kostas Kotsakis for fruitful discussions on the distinction between tell and flat sites and for access to unpublished work. Paul Halstead helped me structure my ideas, particularly with regard to the possibilities that primary inhumations represent an abnormal form of burial and that cremations in Thessaly were a form of secondary treatment of body parts. Last but not least, study of the human osteological remains from Knossos, Toumba Kremastis-Koiladas and Paliambela-Kolindrou was funded by the Institute of Aegean Prehistory.

Bibliography

Andrews, P. and S. Bello
    2006   Pattern of human burial practices. In R. Gowland and C. Knüsel (eds.), *Social Archaeology of Funerary Remains*: 14–29. Oxford: Oxbow Books.

Angel, J.
    1973   Early Neolithic people of Nea Nikomedeia. In I. Schwidetzky (ed.), *Die Anfänge des Neolithikums vom Orient bis Nordeuropa*: 103–12. Funtamenta B/3, Teil VIIIa, Anthropologie 1.

Barrett, J. C.
    1988   The living, the dead and the ancestors: Neolithic and Early Bronze Age mortuary practices. In J. C. Barrett and I. A. Kinnes (eds.), *The Archaeology of Context in the Neolithic and Bronze Age: Recent Trends*: 30–56. Sheffield: Department of Archaeology and Prehistory, University of Sheffield.

Beckett, J. and J. Robb
    2006   Neolithic burial taphonomy, ritual and interpretation in Britain and Ireland: a review. In R. Gowland and C. Knüsel (eds.), *Social Archaeology of Funerary Remains*: 57–80. Oxford: Oxbow Books.

Bloch, M. and J. Parry
    1982   *Death and the Regeneration of Life*. Cambridge: Cambridge University Press.

Boessneck, J.
    1962   Die Tierreste aus der Argissa-Magula vom präkeramischen Neolithikum bis zur Mittleren Bronzezeit. In V. Milojcic, J. Boessneck and M. Hopf (eds.), *Argissa-Magula 1: das Präkeramische Neolithikum sowie die Tier- und Pflanzenreste (BAM 2)*: 27–99. Bonn: Rudolf Habelt.

Borić, D. and S. Stefanović
    2004   Birth and death: infant burials from Vlasac and Lepenski Vir. *Antiquity* 78: 526–46.

Buikstra, J. and M. Swegle
    1989   Bone modification due to burning: experimental evidence. In R. Bonnichsen and M. H. Sorg (eds.), *Bone Modification*: 247–58. Maine: University of Maine.

Broodbank, C.
    1992   The Neolithic labyrinth: social change at Knossos before the Bronze Age. *JMA* 5: 39–75.
    2000   *An Island Archaeology of the Early Cyclades*. Cambridge: Cambridge University Press.

Byers, S. N.
    2002   *Introduction to Forensic Anthropology: A Textbook*. Boston: Allyn and Bacon.

Cavanagh, W. G and C. Mee
    1998   *A Private Place: Death in Prehistoric Greece*. (SIMA 125). Jonsered: P. Åströms.

Chapman, J.
    2000   *Fragmentation in Archaeology*. London: Routledge.

Correia, P.
    1997   Fire modification of bone: a review of the literature. In U. D. Haglund and M. H. Sorg (eds.), *Forensic Taphonomy: the Postmortem Fate of Human Remains*: 275–93. Boca Raton: CRC Press.

Cullen, T.
    1999   Scattered human bones at Franchthi cave, Greece: remnants of ritual or refuse? In P. Betancourt, V. Karageorghis, R. Laffineur and W.-D. Niemeier (eds.), *MELETEMATA. Studies in Aegean Archaeology presented to Malcolm Wiener as he enters his 65th year* (Aegaeum 20): 165–71. Liège: University of Liège.

Demoule, J. P. and C. Perlès
  1993   The Greek Neolithic: a new review. *Journal of World Prehistory* 7: 355–416.
Evans, J. D.
  1964   Excavations at the Neolithic settlement at Knossos, 1957–60. *BSA* 59: 132–240.
  1971   Neolithic Knossos: the growth of a settlement. *PPS* 37: 95–117.
Fowler, K. D.
  2004   *Neolithic Mortuary Practices in Greece* (BAR International Series S1314). Oxford: British
          Archaeological Reports.
Gallis, K.
  1982   *Kafseis Nekron apo ti Neolithiki Epochi sti Thessalia*. Athens: TAPA.
Halstead, P.
  1984   Strategies for Survival: an Ecological Approach to Social and Economic Change in the
          Early Farming Communities of Thessaly, N. Greece. PhD dissertation, University of
          Cambridge.
  1995   From sharing to hoarding: the Neolithic foundations of Aegean Bronze Age? In R.
          Laffineur and W.-D. Niemeier (eds.), *POLITEIA. Society and State in the Aegean Bronze
          Age* (Aegeum 12): 11–20. Liège: University of Liège.
  2006   What's ours is mine? Village and household in early farming society in Greece (G. H.
          Kroon Memorial Lecture 28). Amsterdam: University of Amsterdam.
Halstead, P. and G. Jones
  1987   Bioarchaeological remains from Kalythies cave, Rhodes. In A. Sampson (ed.), *I Neolithiki
          Periodos sta Dodekanisa*: 135–52. Athens: Ministry of Culture.
Hinz, G.
  1979   *Neue Tierknochenfunde aus der Magula Pevkakia in Thessalien, 1: die Nichtwiederkaüer*. PhD
          dissertation, University of Munich.
Hondrogianni-Metoki, A.
  2001   Egnatia Odos, anaskafi stin proistoriki thesi 'Toumba Kremastis-Koiladas', Nomou
          Kozanis. *AEMTh* 13: 399–413.
Hourmouziadis, G.
  1973   Tafika ethima. In D. R. Theocharis (ed.), *Neolithiki Ellas*: 201–12. Athens: National Bank
          of Greece.
  1978   Eisagogi stis ideologies tis ellinikis proistorias. *Politis* 17: 30–51.
Humphreys, S. C. and H. King (eds.)
  1981   *Mortality and Immortality: the Anthropology and Archaeology of Death*. London: Academic
          Press.
Isaakidou, V.
  2004   Bones from the Labyrinth: Faunal Evidence for the Management and Consumption of
          Animals at Neolithic and Bronze Age Knossos, Crete. PhD dissertation, University
          College London.
Jacobsen, T. and T. Cullen
  1981   A consideration of mortuary practices in Neolithic Greece: burials from Franchthi
          cave. In S. C. Humphreys and H. King (eds.), *Mortality and Immortality: the Anthropology
          and Archaeology of Death*: 79–101. London: Academic Press.
Jordan, B.
  1975   *Tierknochenfunde aus der Magula Pevkakia in Thessalien*. PhD Dissertation, University of
          Munich.
Kotsakis, K.
  1982   Recent research at Sesklo. *Symposia Thracica* A: 265–69.

1999   What tells can tell: social space and settlement in the Greek Neolithic. In P. Halstead (ed.), *Neolithic Society in Greece* (SSAA 2): 66–76. Sheffield: Sheffield Academic Press.

2006   Settlement of discord: Sesklo and the emerging household. In N. Tasić and C. Grozdanov (eds.), *Homage to Milutin Garašanin*: 207–20. Belgrade: Serbian Academy of Sciences and Arts, Macedonian Academy of Sciences and Arts.

Kotsakis, K. and P. Halstead
2004   Anaskafi sta Neolithika Paliambela Kolindrou. *AEMTh* 16: 407–15.

Metcalf, P. and R. Huntington
1991   *Celebrations of Death. The Anthropology of Mortuary Ritual.* Cambridge: Cambridge University Press.

Milka, E.
2003   *Osta, Skeletoi kai Anthropoi: i Metacheirisi ton Nekron sti Neolithiki Ellada.* Thessaloniki: MA dissertation, Aristotle University of Thessaloniki.

Nakou, G.
1995   The cutting edge: a new look at early Aegean metallurgy. *JMA* 8: 1–32.

O' Shea, J. M.
1984   *Mortuary Variability.* New York: Academic Press.

Papathanasiou, A.
2001   *A Bioarchaeological Analysis of Neolithic Alepotrypa Cave, Greece* (BAR International Series S961). Oxford: British Archaeological Reports.

Papathanassopoulos, G.
1971   Spilaia Dirou, 1971. *AAA* 4: 289–304.

1996   Tafika ethima tou Dirou. In G. Papathanasopoulos (ed.), *Neolithikos Politismos stin Ellada*: 175–77. Athens: Goulandris Museum.

Pappa, M. and M. Besios
1999   The Neolithic settlement at Makriyalos, Northern Greece: preliminary report on the 1993–1995 excavations. *Journal of Field Archaeology* 26: 177–95.

Pappa, M., P. Halstead, K. Kotsakis and D. Urem-Kotsou
2004   Evidence for large-scale feasting at Late Neolithic Makriyalos, N. Greece. In P. Halstead and J. Barrett (eds.), *Food, Cuisine and Society in Prehistoric Greece* (SSAA 5): 16–44. Oxford: Oxbow Books.

Parker Pearson, M.
1993   The powerful dead: archaeological relationships between the living and the dead. *CAJ* 3: 203–29.

1999   *The Archaeology of Death and Burial.* England: Sutton Publishing.

Perlès, C.
2001   *The Early Neolithic in Greece.* Cambridge: Cambridge University Press.

Radovanović, I.
1996   *The Iron Gates Mesolithic.* Ann Arbor: International Monographs in Prehistory.

2000   Houses and burials at Lepenski Vir. *European Journal of Archaeology* 3: 330–49.

Robb, J.
1994   Burial and social reproduction in the peninsular Italian Neolithic. *JMA* 7: 27–71.

Rodden, R. J.
1962   Excavation at the Early Neolithic site at Nea Nikomedeia, Greek Macedonia (1961 season). *PPS* 11: 267–88.

1965   An Early Neolithic village in Greece. *Scientific American* 212: 83–92.

Rodriguez, W. C. and W. M. Bass
1985   Decomposition of buried bodies and methods that may aid their location. *Journal of Forensic Sciences* 28: 423–32.

Shanks, M. and C. Tilley
 1984   Ideology, symbolic power and ritual communication: a reinterpretation of Neolithic mortuary practices. In R. Bradley and J. Gardiner (eds.), *Neolithic Studies: a Review of Some Current Research* (BAR British Series 133): 189–218. Oxford: British Archaeological Reports.
Skeates, R.
 1991   Caves, cults and children in Neolithic Abruzzo, Central Italy. In P. Garwood, D. Jennings, R. Skeates and J. Toms (eds.), *Sacred and Profane. Proceedings of a Conference on Archaeology, Ritual and Religion, Oxford 1989*: 122–34. Oxford: Oxford University Committee for Archaeology.
 1999   Unveiling inequality. Social life and social change in the Mesolithic and Early Neolithic of East-Central Italy. In R. H. Tykot, J. Morter and J. E. Robb (eds.), *Social Dynamics of the Prehistoric Central Mediterranean*: 15–45. London: Accordia Research Institute.
Stravopodi, E.
 1993   An anthropological assessment of the human findings from the cave and the cemetery. In A. Sampson (ed.) *Skoteini Tharrounion: to Spilaio, o Oikismos kai to Nekrotafeio*: 378–91. Athens: Konstantopoulos Press.
Talalay, L. E.
 2002   Heady business: skulls, heads, and decapitation in Neolithic Anatolia and Greece. *JMA* 17: 139–63.
Tomkins, P.
 2004   Filling in the 'Neolithic background': social life and social transformation in the Aegean before the Bronze Age. In J. C. Barrett and P. Halstead (eds.), *The Emergence of Civilisation Revisited* (SSAA 6): 38–63. Oxford: Oxbow Books.
 2007   Communality and competition. The social life of food and containers at Aceramic and Early Neolithic Knossos, Crete. In C. Mee and J. Renard (eds.), *Cooking Up the Past: Food and Culinary Practices in the Neolithic and Bronze Age Aegean*: 174–99. Oxford: Oxbow Books.
Toufexis, G. and S. Manolis
 in press Tafes tis Neolithikis epochis apo to Neolithiko oikismo sti thesi Profitis Ilias Mandras, N. Larissas. *Archaeologiko Ergo Thessalias kai Stereas Elladas 2*. Volos.
Triantaphyllou, S.
 1999   Prehistoric Makriyalos: a story from fragments. In P. Halstead (ed.), *Neolithic Society in Greece* (SSAA 2): 128–35. Sheffield: Sheffield Academic Press.
 2001   *A Bioarchaeological Approach to Prehistoric Populations from Western and Central Greek Macedonia* (BAR International Series S976). Oxford: British Archaeological Reports.
 2002   Prota apotelesmata tis osteologikis exetasis tou skeletikou ilikou tis Neolithikis thesis Stavroupolis Thessalonikis. In D. Grammenos and S. Kotsos (eds.), *Sostikes Anaskafes sto Neolithiko Oikismo Stavroupolis Thessalonikis. Meros I*: 829–46. Thessaloniki: Dimosievmata tou Archaeologikou Institoutou Voreias Elladas.
 2004   Apotelesmata tis osteologikis exetasis tou skeletikou ilikou tis Neolithikis thesis Stavroupolis Thessalonikis kata tin anaskafiki chronia 2002–2003. In D. Grammenos and S. Kotsos (eds.), *Sostikes Anaskafes sto Neolithiko Oikismo Stavroupolis Thessalonikis. Meros II*: 613–24. Thessaloniki: Dimosievmata tou Archaeologikou Institoutou Voreias Elladas.
Urem-Kotsou, D. and K. Kotsakis
 2007   Pottery, cuisine and community in the Neolithic of north Greece. In C. Mee and J. Renard (eds.), *Cooking Up the Past: Food and Culinary Practices in the Neolithic and Bronze Age Aegean*: 225–46. Oxford: Oxbow Books.

Xirotiris, N.
   1982   Apotelesmata tis anthropologikis exetaseos ton kamenon oston apo ti Soufli Magoula
          kai tin Platia Magoula Zarkou. In K. Gallis (ed.), *Kafseis Nekron apo ti Neolithiki Epochi
          sti Thessalia*: 188–215. Athens: TAPA.
Wace, A. J. B. and M. S. Thompson
   1912   *Prehistoric Thessaly*. Cambridge: Cambridge University Press.
Weiss, K. M.
   1972   On the systematic bias in skeletal sexing. *American Journal of Physical Anthropology* 37:
          239–50.
Whittle, A. and M. Wysocki
   1998   Parc le Breos Cwm transepted long cairn, Gower, West Glamorgan: date, contents and
          context. *PPS* 64: 139–82.
Wysocki, M. and A. Whittle
   2000   Diversity, lifestyles and rites: new biological and archaeological evidence from British
          Earlier Neolithic mortuary assemblages. *Antiquity* 74: 591–601.
Yiannouli, E.
   1994   *Aspects of Animal Use in Prehistoric Macedonia, Northern Greece: examples from the Neolithic
          and Early Bronze Age*. PhD dissertation, University of Cambridge.
   2002   Imeri kai agria panida apo to Neolithiko oikismo sti Stavroupoli Thessalonikis. In D.
          Grammenos and S. Kotsos (eds.), *Sostikes Anaskafes sto Neolithiko Oikismo Stavroupolis
          Thessalonikis. Meros I*: 683–744. Thessaloniki: Dimosievmata tou Archaeologikou
          Institoutou Voreias Elladas.
   2004   Stavroupoli Thessalonikis: neotera dedomena apo tin archaeopanida tou Neolithikou
          oikismou. In D. Grammenos and S. Kotsos (eds.), *Sostikes Anaskafes sto Neolithiko Oikismo
          Stavroupolis Thessalonikis. Meros II*: 489–526. Thessaloniki: Dimosievmata tou Archaeo-
          logikou Institoutou Voreias Elladas.

9

Stones of Contention: Regional Axe Production and Hidden Landscapes on Neolithic Crete

Thomas F. Strasser

Over thirty years ago, John Evans described islands as laboratories of culture change (Evans 1973), an observation pertinent to an examination of the neolithisation of the Aegean. In the light of burgeoning evidence for pre-Neolithic activity on the Aegean islands (Sampson 1998; Chelidonio 2001; Sampson *et al.* 2002; Strasser 2003), models positing an absence of hunter-gatherer occupation of the Aegean archipelago (*i.e.*, Cherry 1981; 1990) can no longer be considered valid. Despite this, scholars still accept an exogenous introduction of farming practices to the Greek islands (Perlès 2001: 52–63; Runnels and Murray 2001: 45–52). Experimental research into early sea faring, based on actual remains of ancient craft, has demonstrated how such a transfer of domesticated animals and plants might have been achieved (Tichý 2001). In the case of Crete, where evidence for an indigenous pre-Neolithic presence is lacking, it seems most likely that an early farming community of exogenous origin colonised a previously undomesticated landscape (Broodbank and Strasser 1991) and was thereby presented with a plethora of choices in their adaptation to it.

From the perspective of neolithisation, the analysis of Neolithic stone axes from insular environments is potentially more rewarding than those from continental locations. Once the lithology of the axes and the geology of the island are understood, mechanisms of production and exchange can often be more easily traced because of the way insularity influences local and regional patterns of production and distribution. Among mainland cultures, an axe of regionally exotic lithology may potentially originate from a wide variety of geological sources due to the down-the-line trade (Renfrew 1972: 465–66). Since appropriate lithic resources are unevenly distributed throughout Crete, it is likely that the petrology of the axes would indicate local manufacturing and regional exchange. Analysis of close to 550 axes from Knossos and other Cretan Neolithic sites has confirmed the validity of this hypothesis (Strasser 2004; Strasser and Fassoulas 2003–4). Two axe groups and their implications for our present understanding of Neolithic settlement patterns are presented below.

Chronological Terminology: Out of the Frying Pan and into the Fire?

The chronological terminology for the Cretan Neolithic is currently in a state of flux. Nowicki (2002: 7–16) has summarised the issues surrounding the terms 'Late Neolithic', 'Final Neolithic' and 'Sub-Neolithic'. Tomkins is in the process of suggesting a complete restructuring of the dating system for the Cretan Neolithic that correlates it to the larger Aegean region (Tomkins this volume). It is well beyond the scope of this paper to resolve this complex issue, but the dates for the axes are obviously germane to the point presented here. Since the new chronology is only in the process of being introduced and has yet to be subjected to critical post-publication scrutiny, this paper follows the traditional chronology (Evans 1964; Vagnetti and Belli 1978; Tomkins this volume, table 3.1 for the relationship between traditional and new chronologies). Although the distinction between Late and Final Neolithic has long been murky (Branigan 1999: 59–60; 2000: 162), it is hoped that the Middle and Late Neolithic phases remain sufficiently distinct as to be relevant to the issues addressed below. In addition, if the Middle and Late Neolithic phases are transformed into sub-phases of the Final Neolithic, it should be kept in mind that the ceramics of the former are stylistically distinctive from those of the latter.

Regionality in Cretan Neolithic Stone Axe Production

The Neolithic represents a significant change in how humans exploited lithic resources. The transition to agriculture required new tools to clear land for farming, and to process domesticated plants. Consequently, a series of stone tools were developed to chop-down trees as well as mill or pound seeds. Ground-and-polished tools require stones with far different mineralogical qualities than their knapped counterparts (Strasser and Fassoulas 2003–4: 10). It is obvious that the conchoidal fracturing, desirable for flaked tools, would not function to fell trees or grind seeds. Instead, durable and abrasive qualities would be preferable in order to prevent the tools from breaking during chopping and milling, and to allow them to be rejuvenated (Perlès 2001: 232–37; Strasser 2004: 61). Since Crete, as an island, is composed of a restricted but complex range of geological facies, the Neolithic colonizers had to exploit stone sources in specific areas for many of their ground-and-polished tools. In the Knossos assemblage a variety of stones are used to manufacture axes. After analysis of smaller ground stone tool collections from other sites, regional types imported to Knossos have been recognized. Some of these imports originate not only from relatively distant areas, but also from locations where no contemporary Neolithic remains have been discovered.

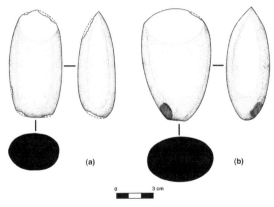

Figure 9.2. (above) Two east Cretan metamorphosed volcanic axes (a: Karydi; b: Magasa).

Figure 9.1. (left) Granodiorite axes from the Mirabello Bay region found at Knossos.

Mirabello Bay Granodiorite Axes (Figure 9.1)

During his 1969–70 excavations at Knossos, John Evans found two granodiorite axes (Evans 1971; Strasser and Fassoulas 2003–4). The first, a miniature ovate celt (KN 70/425) dates to Early Neolithic II, the other (KN 69/512), a miniature trapezoid (Wright 1992), from a transitional Middle-Late Neolithic deposit. Knossian axes are generally very small, made of soft stone and have a lustrous polish, features suggestive of a symbolic function. The granodiorite axes bear rough hafting ghosts and have unpolished surfaces on the shaft below the bevels and cutting edge. The hafting-ghost reveals how the tool was joined to the handle and thereby indicates a utilitarian function. Macroscopic observation recognized three main minerals that constitute 90% of the mass: white feldspars, grey quartz and black hornblende. All are well crystallized, randomly arranged within the rock and form regular crystals. Feldspars are present in a larger proportion than quartz, while biotite occasionally occurs in some examples. Granodiorites occur only in two small localities in Crete (Creutzburg *et al.* 1977). In the Kaloi Limenes area, in the southeast region of the Asteroussia mountain range, the granodiorites are coarse-grained (crystal size 5–15 mm) and contain the same amount of quartz, feldspar and biotite, but less hornblende. The granodiorite tools from Knossos could not derive from the Kaloi Limenes source because of differences in the mineral assemblage, grain size and overall texture. In the Mirabello Bay area of east Crete there are, however, granodiorite outcrops with exactly the same macroscopic characteristics as the axes from Knossos and these must have originated here. This confirms similar observations by Tomkins and Day (2001),

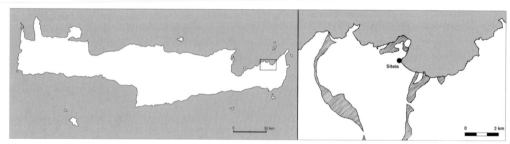

Figure 9.3. Map of outcrops of the Achladia and Skopi formations (cross-hatched areas) near Siteia (after Day 1995: fig. 110). Additional formations occur to the east and south of this area (see Gradstein 1973).

who conducted petrographic study of Early Neolithic ceramics from Knossos and noted a Mirabello Bay granodiorite fabric.

East Crete Metamorphosed Volcanic Axes (Figure 9.2)

Several different green-coloured axe groups can be identified within the group of Neolithic Cretan celts studied, each with different lithologies. A suite of greenish-grey axes regularly occur at sites in east Crete (*i.e.*, east of the Ierapetra isthmus). Several can be seen on display in the Siteia Museum, including five from the Magasa assemblage (Dawkins 1904–5: 260–68) two from Karydi and one from Kalamafka. A third Karydi axe of the same lithology is in Case 1 of the Herakleion Archaeological Museum. There are at least thirteen others in trays labelled 'Palaikastro' presently stored in the same museum, which include the finds from Magasa and material from other sites in the vicinity of Palaikastro collected early in the twentieth century. One is also on display in the Ayios Nikolaos Museum. The colour of the matrix of these axes most commonly approximates Munsell Grey 1 5/1 or 6/1 10Y and has distinctive white and black phenocrysts (for more specific petrographic descriptions see Gradstein 1973: 549; Day 1995: 152–53).

These axes have been independently identified by two separate geologists as comprising a metamorphosed volcanic conglomerate of a type found associated with the Achladia and Skopi formations (Figure 9.3; Fassoulas pers. comm.; Siddall pers. comm.; Gradstein 1973: 545–50). Previous analysis of this meta-morphosed igneous rock indicates that it is a 'strongly altered volcanic rock, which seems to be intermediate between a lava and a tuff...' (Gradstein 1973: 549). It was formed into cobbles in a marine environment and presently outcrops in the Achladia and Skopi formations at an average size of less than 10 cm, although some cobbles can be over three times larger (Gradstein 1973: 545). Consequently, they were pre-shaped in a manner advantageous for reduction into an axe. The cobbles release quite easily from their marl context and are sufficiently soft to be ground and polished into shape. This scenario of resource exploitation seems more likely than an actual quarrying of the stone (Perlès 2001: 233). These stones are found only on Crete east of the Ierapetra isthmus because

Figure 9.4. East Cretan metamorph-osed volcanic axes from Knossos. Clockwise from top left: (i) KN 70/782; (ii) KN 69/1067; (iii) KN 70/123; (iv) KN 70/542; (v) KN 70/275; (vi) KN 69/209.

they were formed during the Hercynian Orogeny that occurs only in this region of Crete, producing the oldest rocks now present on the island (Fassoulas 2000: 87–88; Siddall pers. comm.).

Both the geological and archaeological evidence support a working hypothesis that axes of this type are imports when found west of the isthmus of Ierapetra. At Knossos, there are six axes of this type from secure contexts that date to Early Neolithic II, Middle, Late and Final Neolithic (Figure 9.4). Several more have been identified in boxes labelled 'Stone axes *etc.* No provenance' stored in the Stratigraphical Museum. The descriptive terms used follow Wright (1992), while information regarding context was based on John Evans' unpublished notes and supplied by P. Tomkins.

KN 70/782 (Figure 9.4i)

This small trapezoid was found amongst collapsed wall debris overlying a house in Area RST (Level 12). The same context produced quite a large group of ground stone tools (hammers, querns, axes). It is probable that these were originally built into the walls of the house. The construction of the house, and probably thus the deposition of the axe, took place in Middle Neolithic, although the latest material from the final floors in the house (*i.e.*, those uppermost below the wall tumble) dates to the Middle-Late Neolithic transition.

KN 69/1067 (Figure 9.4ii)

This miniature ovate was discovered during cleaning of the inner face of the west wall of House G in Area KLMN (KL, Room 1, Level 6). House G has two main occupation phases, each ending with a kouskouras collapse. In the later phase, which dates to the Late Neolithic, the walls were rebuilt and buttressed.

Since the axe comes from high up in the preserved wall, it was probably deposited during this later phase, although the possibility that it belongs to the earlier phase (Middle-Late Neolithic transition) cannot be excluded.

KN 70/123 (Figure 9.4iii)

A second miniature ovate was found in a layer of wall collapse (thick pale grey kouskouras) overlying a large multi-roomed house in Area AABB (Level 129). Below this layer was a dark occupation layer with pottery dating to the Middle Neolithic. As with KN 70/782, this axe was most probably deposited within the wall of this house.

KN 70/542 (Figure 9.4iv)

A miniature trapezoid blank was also found in a grey kouskouras level overlying a large multi-roomed house in Area AABB (Level 216). The house had three phases, all of which fall within Early Neolithic II (Evans 1994: 11, figs. 5 [earliest phase] and 6 [latest phase]). Level 216 corresponds to the wall collapse of the middle phase of the house (Evans' phase B).

KN 70/275 (Figure 9.4v)

This miniature trapezoid comes from a mixed Final Neolithic-Early Minoan I (?) fill layer in Trench X (Level 2). The axe was found in the lowermost part of Level 2 during the excavation of an exterior surface with a spread of darker, possibly burned soil that had been roughly outlined by stones. The pottery from Level 2 is highly abraded and shows signs of sustained exposure to water.

KN 69/209 (Figure 9.4vi)

This fragment is from the cutting edge and margin of an axe and was found in an occupation level just to the west of House G in Area KLMN (Trench K, Level 9). Deposition of this level corresponds to the second phase of use of House G (see above KN 69/1067) and its pottery is Late Neolithic in date.

Discussion

These east Cretan metamorphosed volcanic axes not only reveal the exploitation of stone resources in east Crete that are distant from Knossos, but also, more significantly, suggest a Middle-Late Neolithic presence in areas where pre-Final Neolithic open-air settlements have yet to be discovered. It should be kept in mind that though Magasa has at times been considered an early site (Dawkins 1904–5: 268; Furness 1953: 108), modern scholars have generally dated the pottery to the Final Neolithic (*e.g.*, Nowicki 2002: 21; but see Tomkins this volume for an earlier date). The same holds true for Branigan's discovery of 'Late Neolithic' pottery in the Lamnoni basin (1999: 59–60; 2000: 162). Archaeological excavations and surveys have found little evidence for significant habitation in the Siteia region of east Crete in these earlier phases (Branigan 2000; Vokotopoulos 2000; Nowicki 2002), giving the impression that Knossos was, for the most part, an isolated settlement at this time.

The Knossian stone axe assemblage, however, reveals the exploitation of certain regions during the Neolithic where archaeological reconnaissance has heretofore failed to discern contemporaneous remains. The two granodiorite axes from pre-Final Neolithic levels at Knossos derive from the Mirabello Bay region (Strasser and Fassoulas 2003–4), where several intensive archaeological surveys have failed to discover any settlements of Early, Middle or Late Neolithic date (Watrous *et al.* 2000: 474; Hayden 2003; Betancourt 2005: 285; Haggis 2005: 59–62). Despite this lacuna of evidence for occupation, the axe data suggest the existence of an exchange network in polished stone axes rather than direct Knossian procurement (Strasser and Fassoulas 2003–4: 12). Neither the metamorphosed igneous examples from the Siteia region nor the granodiorite axes from the Mirabello Bay area have mineralogical qualities that make them preferable to cobbles found closer to Knossos.

Lost but not Forgotten

Why is there so little evidence for early settlements in east Crete? It is unlikely that archaeologists have failed to recognise Early, Middle or Late Neolithic pottery during their reconnaissances over the past century. Neolithic pottery is usually well fired, quite durable and with conspicuous styles of surface treatment. Moreover, it seems extraordinarily unlikely, given the length of the Neolithic, that our present understanding of the archaeological landscape reflects *actual* settlement and land-use patterns on Crete during this period. A possible explanation is that much of the Neolithic landscape in east Crete has either eroded away or been covered by colluvia (see Davis 2004 for a discussion of this problem on the Greek mainland). Haggis (2005: 61) reports Final Neolithic sherds in the Kavousi region in deep deposits, observed only in bulldozer furrows. More astonishing is Moody's observation (2000: 54–56) that Medieval flash floods and debris flows have altered the landscape considerably. Such extreme soil erosion may have led to masking of lowland sites of pre-Final Neolithic date and may be responsible for the sparse Cretan settlement reported by surface surveys, which is surprising when compared to the Early, Middle and Late Neolithic of the Greek mainland or Cyprus.

Recognising potential regional production centres through the study of raw material provenance of ceramic (*e.g.*, Tomkins and Day 2001) and ground-stone artefacts (*e.g.*, Strasser and Fassoulas 2003–4) recovered at Knossos is proving a more fruitful approach to understanding settlement history in pre-FN Crete. Thus, analyses of Knossian material provide crucial insights into the archaeology ot the rest ot the island, further underlining the importance of the work undertaken by John Evans at the site. It is perhaps through further excavation of targeted areas that more light can be shed on the Neolithic of Crete, beyond Knossos.

Acknowledgements

I would like to thank the organizers of the Round Table, Drs. Valasia Isaakidou and Peter Tomkins for inviting me to the conference. Gratitude is also due to Drs. S. Apostolakou, T. Cunningham, P. Day, J. Evans, D. Evely, C. Fassoulas, E. Hatzaki, A. MacGillivray, H. Sackett, and R. Siddall. N. Dolia, D. Faulmann, C. Havelaar. J. Morrison produced the illustrations. This research was conducted under the auspices of the British School at Athens, the American School of Classical Studies at Athens, and with the permission of the Greek Ministry of Culture and the Greek Archaeological Service. Financial support was generously provided by The Institute for Aegean Prehistory, California State University (Sacramento) and the Mediterranean Archaeological Trust.

Bibliography

Betancourt, P.
  2005   Discussion and conclusions. In P. Betancourt, C. Davaras and R. Hope Simpson (eds.), *Pseira IX. The Archaeological Survey of Pseira Island Part 2: The Intensive Surface Survey*: 275–306. Philadelphia: INSTAP Academic Press.
Branigan, K.
  1999   Late Neolithic colonization of the uplands of eastern Crete. In P. Halstead (ed.), *Neolithic Society in Greece* (SSAA 2): 57–65. Sheffield: Sheffield Academic Press.
  2000   Lamnoni – A Late Neolithic landscape in eastern Crete. *Pepragmena H'Diethnous Kritologikou Synedriou*: 161–67. Herakleion: Etaireia Kritikon Istorikon Meleton.
Broodbank, C. and T. F. Strasser
  1991   Migrant farmers and the Neolithic colonization of Crete. *Antiquity* 65: 233–45.
Chelidonio, G.
  2001   Manufatti litici su ciottolo da Milos (isole Cicladi). *Pegaso* 1: 117–44.
Cherry, J. F.
  1981   Pattern and process in the earliest colonization of the Mediterranean islands. *PPS* 47: 41–68.
  1990   The first colonization of the Mediterranean islands: a review of recent research. *JMA* 3: 145–221.
Creutzburg, N., C. W. Drooger, J. E. Meulenkamp, J. Papastamatiou, W. Sannemann, E. Seidel and A. Tataris
  1977   *General Geological Map of Greece: Crete Island (1:200.000)*. Athens: Geological Mapping of the Institute of Geological and Mining Research.

Davis, J.
 2004 Are the landscapes of Greek prehistory hidden? A comparative approach. In S. Alcock and J. Cherry (eds.), *Side-by-Side Survey: Comparative Regional Studies in the Mediterranean World*: 22–35. Oxford: Oxbow Books.
Dawkins, R. M.
 1904–5 Excavations at Palaikastro IV. 2. Neolithic settlement at Magasa. *BSA* 11: 260–8.
Day, P. M.
 1995 Pottery production and consumption in the Sitia bay area during the new palace period. In M. Tsipopoulou and L. Vagnetti (eds.), *Achladia: Scavi e Ricerche della Missione Greco-Italiana in Creta Orientale (1991–1993)*: 149–218. Rome: Gruppo Editoriale Internazionale.
Evans, J. D.
 1964 Excavations in the Neolithic settlement at Knossos. 1957–60. Part I. *BSA* 59: 132–240.
 1971 Neolithic Knossos: the growth of a settlement. *PPS* 37: 95–117.
 1973 Island archaeology in the Mediterranean: problems and opportunities. *World Archaeology* 9: 12–26.
 1994 The early millennia: continuity and change in a farming settlement. In D. Evely, H. Hughes-Brock and N. Momigliano (eds.), *Knossos: A Labyrinth of History. Papers Presented in Honour of Sinclair Hood*: 1–22. Oxford: Oxbow Books.
Fassoulas, C.
 2000 *Field Guide to the Geology of Crete*. Herakleion: Natural History Museum of Crete.
Furness, A.
 1953 The Neolithic pottery of Knossos. *BSA* 48: 94–134.
Gradstein, F. M.
 1973 The Neogene and Quaternary deposits in the Sitia District of eastern Crete. *Annales Géologiques des Pays Helléniques* 25: 527–72.
Haggis, D.
 2005 *Kavousi I. The Archaeological Survey of the Kavousi Region*. Philadelphia: INSTAP Academic Press.
Hayden, B.
 2003 Final Neolithic – Early Minoan I/IIA settlement in the Vrokastro area, eastern Crete. *AJA* 107: 363–412.
Moody, J.
 2000 Holocene climate change in Crete: an archaeologist's view. In P. Halstead and C. Frederick (eds.), *Landscape and Land Use in Postglacial Greece* (SSAA 3): 52–61. Sheffield: Sheffield Academic Press.
Nowicki, K.
 2002 The end of the Neolithic in Crete. *Aegean Archaeology* 6: 7–72.
Perlès, C.
 2001 *The Early Neolithic in Greece: The First Farming Communities in Europe*. Cambridge: Cambridge University Press.
Renfrew, C.
 1972 *The Emergence of Civilisation*. London: Methuen.
Runnels, C. and P. Murray
 2001 *Greece before History: An Archaeological Companion and Guide*. Stanford: Stanford University Press.
Sampson, A.
 1998 The Neolithic and Mesolithic occupation of the Cave of Cyclope, Youra, Alonnessos, Greece. *BSA* 93: 1–22.

Sampson, A., J. Kozlowski, M. Kaszanowski and B. Giannouli
    2002   The Mesolithic settlement at Maroulas, Kythnos. *Mediterranean Archaeology and Archaeometry* 2: 45–67.
Strasser, T. F.
    2003   The subtleties of the seas: thoughts on Mediterranean island biogeography. *Mediterranean Archaeology and Archaeometry* 3: 5–15.
    2004   Three axe groups from Neolithic Knossos. In G. Cadogan, E. Hatzaki and A. Vasilakis (eds.), *Knossos: Palace, City, State*: 61–65. London: British School at Athens.
Strasser, T. F. and C. Fassoulas
    2003–4   Granodiorite axes from Knossos and their implications for Neolithic trade on Crete. *Aegean Archaeology* 7: 9–12.
Tichý, R.
    2001   *Monoxylon Expeditions: Our Journey from the Neolithic*. Hradec Kralové: J. B. Productions (in Czech with English summaries).
Tomkins, P. and P. Day
    2001   Production and exchange of the earliest ceramic vessels in the Aegean: a view from early Neolithic Knossos, Crete. *Antiquity* 75: 259–60.
Vagnetti, L. and P. Belli
    1978   Characters and problems of the Final Neolithic in Crete. *SMEA* 19: 125–63.
Vokotopoulos, L.
    2000   Ochires protominoikes theseis stin periochi Zakrou. *Pepragmena H' Diethnous Kritilogikou Synedriou* : 129–46. Herakleion: Etaireia Kritikon Istorikon Meleton.
Watrous, L. V., H. Blitzer, D. Haggis and E. Zangger
    2000   Economy and society in the Gournia region of Crete. A preliminary report on the 1992–1994 field seasons of the Gournia project. *Pepragmena H' Diethnous Kritilogikou Synedriou*: 471–83. Herakleion: Etaireia Kritikon Istorikon Meleton.
Wright, K.
    1992   A classification system for ground stone tools from the prehistoric Levant. *Paléorient* 18: 53–81.

10

Neolithic Katsambas Revisited:
the Evidence from the House

Nena Galanidou and Katya Manteli

Between 1951 and 1963 Professor Stylianos Alexiou undertook extensive excavations on the west bank of the ancient Kairatos River, in the vicinity of Katsambas, the harbour-town of Knossos in Minoan times. This work was funded by the Archaeologiki Etaireia and was principally focused on the Late Minoan tombs in the area. However, the abundance of Neolithic finds on the surface adjacent to the necropolis attracted the attention of the excavator and prompted further investigations. In 1953, excavations in the Milathianakis field unveiled a rock-shelter containing highly fragmented pieces of human bones and skulls, animal bone, lithics and pottery, the greater part of which spanned the period from Neolithic to Late Minoan. In November 1953, upon completion of the rock-shelter excavation, Professor Alexiou and his team continued excavations a few meters to the northwest. Excavations there lasted for two successive seasons until 1954 and revealed the remains of a building named 'the Neolithic House by the Kairatos River'. Preliminary findings from these excavations testified to the special significance of the site in terms of the Cretan Neolithic and its cultural interaction with the Aegean (Alexiou 1956; 1957). Katsambas remains one of the earliest and most important Neolithic coastal sites on Crete, representing one of the pioneering Neolithic excavations on the island.

In the late 1980s, Professor Alexiou kindly granted N.G. permission to work on the finds from the rock-shelter and the house, along with full access to his excavation archive (daybooks, photographs, artefact drawings, site plan and the unpublished manuscript of an article), with a view to completing the final publication. His generosity extended to continuous advice, practical support and guidance in every aspect of this research. Although the archive material in itself offered undeniable documentation of the existence of a significant Neolithic site, it was only in the summer and autumn of 2005 that it became possible to re-examine the finds themselves. Following excavation the material was divided into different groups and, although some was exhibited, the greater part was stored separately in the storerooms and Scientific Collection of the Herakleion Archaeological Museum. It was only in 2002, during computerisation of the museum collections, that it became possible to locate all the different groups of the Katsambas assemblage at the various premises of the Ephoreia and the Museum. Today the material from the house and the rock-shelter has been unified and is currently stored for the purpose of study at the Stratigraphical Museum at Knossos. The new study program has brought together a group of different specialists. In addition to the authors, studies are being conducted by Nelly Phoca-Cosmetatou (animal bones), Argyro Nafplioti (human bones), Peter Tomkins and Peter Day (ceramic provenance and technology). This paper will focus explicitly on the architecture and finds (pottery, lithics) from the Neolithic house and is based on unpublished archival information and the results of the 2005 and 2006 study seasons.

Topography and Stratigraphy

The building lies on a rocky limestone hill, on the upper terrace of the left bank of the river Kairatos. The location commands views to the north across the Herakleion Bay to the island of Dia, to the east the banks of the Kairatos, and to the southeast along the two valleys that lead inland to Knossos. The closest point of reference remains the Skyllianakis villa, located on a terrace to the northeast, immediately below the one occupied by the Neolithic site. Excavation of the Neolithic building began with the investigation of a series of regularly placed rocks in its southern part and then continued northwards.

Early in the excavations, the building plan was unclear and note was made of the partial displacement of several wall stones caused by agricultural activity during historical times. This picture was clarified during the second year of fieldwork, as excavations went deeper and the remains of the building were fully revealed. The walls were without elaborate foundations, the stones simply being placed on the soil surface. Internal floors were fairly close to the surface at a maximum depth of 50 cm. The amount of deposit above and between the walls was notably small and was removed as a single stratigraphic unit. In certain areas, further distinction was made between smaller units defined by colour, such as the floor of Room II. Possible habitation features or individual finds were recorded by means of photographs or sketches in the excavation daybook. Although the majority (80.2%) of the deposit consisted of Neolithic finds, the presence of a significant number of Minoan sherds (19.8%) calls for reconciliation. If not an outcome of post-excavation mixing with finds from the rock-shelter, whose Minoan component is considerable, these must in all probability be intrusive, since the building lay very close to the surface in an area that was used repeatedly, especially in Late Minoan times. Moreover, study of the Minoan sherds recovered from the Neolithic house suggests that they have the character of surface material (see below). Fortunately, however, the excavator clearly kept a very detailed record of any irregularities observed during excavation. For instance, reference is made in the daybook to a number of intrusive finds (a coin and two iron horseshoes) at a depth of one metre.

Architectural Remains

Excavations were completed during 1954, revealing a rectangular building covering an area of approximately 70 square metres. Enrica Fiandra, the architect at the Italian Archaeological School in Athens, was commissioned to draw a detailed final plan, which was kindly made available to us for publication (Figure 10.1). The final plan offers a much more detailed picture of the building than the preliminary one drawn by Palamianakis (Alexiou 1957: 370, fig. 2). It thus forms the basis for all future discussion of the architectural remains.

According to the excavator (Alexiou 1957; *n.d.*), the main house consisted of a small 'but-and-ben' type room complex, bearing similarities to the Neolithic building at Magasa and the later Neolithic houses at Knossos. He indicates that Rooms I and II almost certainly had a roof made of wood and reeds, harvested from the adjacent Kairatos River, as probably also did Room III. The walls have an average width of 60–70 cm and are made of large, unworked stones with smaller stones, clay and bones inserted between them. Occasionally, when the stones were flat, they were placed on end. The floor in Room II was made of trampled white clay. External access to the building was via the bedrock from the south (Figure 10.1) and movement between the various internal spaces was achieved by means of clearly defined openings.

Around the core of the house the excavator identifies a simple, open-air enclosure, delimited to the south by a series of rocks that were hollow at their base and covered by deposits and on the remaining three sides by an insubstantial wall of large irregular stones. This hypothesis is based on the narrow width of the wall and the large distance at which its stones are placed. Within this enclosure were found the discarded bones of domesticated animals (identified by the Italian archaeozoologist Ginetta Chapello Cordero), suggesting that it was a disposal area for domestic refuse.

These observations and hypotheses are of great value because they are based on first-hand observation of the archaeological remains during excavation. They thus provide a solid point of departure for a consideration of the various constituents of the building. Present-day study of the Fiandra plan and the excavation photographs offers another perspective, perforce distanced from the original disposition of the material remains. Both can enter into a dialogue that at this stage is best represented as a series of questions, not all of which can yet be answered. Does the outer wall indeed represent an open-air enclosure or yard stretching along three sides of the building or can it be traced only on the east, west and perhaps also partly to the northwest? To the northeast, this wall is wider and better constructed, resembling walls from inside the building. Where was the entrance (or entrances) to this building and how was circulation within it achieved? Was there another entrance/opening in the northwest corner or was the wall simply not preserved there? Did the rock to the southeast really serve as an entrance or was it simply natural bedrock that lay at a higher level because of differences in the topography of the site? Was the superstructure of the walls made of mud brick? In view of the contemporaneity of the main bulk of the Katsambas house material to Knossos stratum V (see below) where clay pisé is well established (Evans 1964; 1971), the possibility that it was used at Katsambas should also be considered. Is there any evidence for functional differentiation of space within the building? In Neolithic households, the presence of hearths typically structures the use of domestic space. In the Katsambas house a possible hearth is noted in the daybook in the southwest corner close to a round flat stone that lay beyond the walls of the building. If there was indeed a hearth, its presence in what now appears to be a marginal area of the building plan, close to a trench dug during the Second World War, raises the issue of whether anthropogenic deposits in this part of the building have been eroded or destroyed by post-depositional processes.

Ultimately answers to such questions will provide a clearer picture of the main function of the building. Was it indeed a building used for permanent habitation by an agricultural community, a 'Neolithic house' as envisioned by the excavator, or was it used for some sort of rural economic activity, perhaps related to husbandry, horticulture or agriculture, that required only a temporary

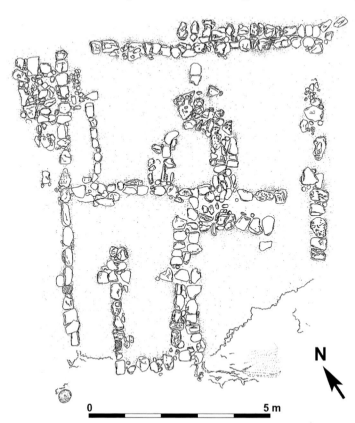

N

0   5 m

Figure 10.1. Katsambas house plan (final version).

human presence? Furthermore, was the human presence at Katsambas restricted to this single building or did this form part of a small, rural settlement? We shall return to these questions after examining the finds from the site.

Pottery

The pottery assemblage from the house comprises 1696 sherds dated to the Neolithic period (of which 1400 are medium to large in size) and 420 Minoan sherds (of which 150 are medium to large in size). Differences between the Neolithic and Minoan pottery are striking. The Neolithic assemblage is typologically homogeneous, with a reasonable number of fittings between sherds allowing the restoration of several vases. In contrast, the Minoan pottery is highly fragmented and typologically diverse. The small size and wide diversity of the Minoan assemblage could indicate that this derives from a surface scatter that subsequently became mixed in with the Neolithic deposit. Considering the later use of this area as an LM necropolis, we consider this scenario the most likely explanation.

According to the traditional Neolithic ceramic chronology the great majority of the Neolithic pottery is dated to the EN I (87%) and EN II (13%) periods (for the relationship between the traditional and new chronologies see Tomkins 2007; this volume, table 3.1). Comparative study of the EN pottery against that from Knossos (Evans 1964) indicates that the ceramics from the Katsambas house belongs to the Knossian tradition of ceramic production, but with certain local typological features. Moreover, macroscopic observation suggests that the Katsambas EN coarse pottery was to a large extent locally made and it is hoped that the forthcoming ceramic analysis will further clarify the issue of provenance.

Coarse ware (0.8–1.2 cm thick) accounts for more than 75% of the EN assemblage (Figure 10.2). The fabric is not very hard and breaks with relatively little effort. It is often rich in impurities and inclusions, which can reach 1.2 cm in length. Firing seems to have been performed at rather low temperatures and is always uneven with a tendency to over-firing. The internal surface is often darker than the outside and the core is yellowish buff or light brown/red to dark grey or black in cases of over-firing. The surface is often porous, although porosity in this case may be due to post-depositional conditions. In quite a number of specimens, details of forming and finishing techniques can be observed, including traces of finger-prints, mainly on interior surfaces and the thickening of vase walls through the application of successive layers of clay. The overall impression is that the coarse vases were products of relatively low expertise. It is possible, however, that the unsystematic mode of production organisation and means is more to blame for that effect than lack of expertise. The producers of the pottery from Katsambas chose a number of strategies in treating the outer surface to counteract irregularities in colour and evenness. These include red/brown burnishing of varying quality, application of a matt white coating, sometimes with thin striations (Figure 10.3, upper row), application of a thick red/brown slip that occasionally flakes off and slip burnishing. Coatings and slips are by far the most popular types of surface treatment. It seems that as a result of experimentation with slips, they produced a rarely encountered, watery, thin red slip, appearing in the main on coarse and medium coarse ware. This is a crude form of painting, with isolated bands of irregular width or red patches on the pot surface and more interestingly with a red band on bowl rims (Figure 10.3, bottom row). Though not producing any clear decorative motif, it represents an early attempt at painted decoration that was not sustained into later phases.

Coarse ware shapes are mostly deep open bowls and less often high-rimmed

Figure 10.2. (left) Sorting out the EN pottery: an overview.

0   5 cm

Figure 10.3. (left) EN sherds with white coating.

jars, with simple rim typology and usually vertical strap handles. Bases are, as a rule, flat and plastic decoration (Figure 10.4) is in the form of a series of plastic knobs under the rim, a form of decoration which finds exact parallels at EN I Knossos (Stratum V). Finally, there is one example of a deep bowl with a semicircular ear on the rim, beneath which is a plastic rib. The general typological appearance of the coarse ware compares closely with EN I Knossos (Evans 1964: 171, fig. 26: 14, 17, 19, 22). As a matter of fact, Furness' observation about the frequency of occurrence of darker inside surfaces on coarse ware at EN I Knossos (Furness 1953: 103) is also valid for Katsambas. A marked difference with Knossos may be found in the overall predominance of coarse ware at Katsambas (75% as opposed to ca 50% at Knossos). Another major difference is that a variety of surface treatments, not popular at Knossos (mainly white coated and red to brown slipped wares), appear at Katsambas. Furness' identification of white or yellow-white slip on MN unburnished coarse ware at Knossos is not an exact parallel (Furness 1953: 121), since red or brown slipped, burnished or un-burnished wares are quite popular at Katsambas, but only sporadic at Knossos.

On the contrary, fine ware is typologically and technologically similar to Knossian fine pottery, and it seems certain that at least some of it was imported from there. Bowls predominate and are mainly rounded or straight-walled, less often with a simple carinated profile. High-rimmed jars are rare. Fine ware is, as a rule, dark burnished and polished. Holes are sometimes to be found under bowl rims. Vertical tubular and flanged lugs are quite common on bowls as are wishbone and flap handles, while there is an example of a horn-lug. Decoration is common on fine ware bowls, with pointillé most popular, followed by incised motifs. Execution is careful and neat, and pointillé patterns are always well-defined by incisions. Decoration usually extends to the whole vase surface and patterns are often filled with white paste. Pointillé motifs include zig-zags, step patterns, bands and single lines, while incised patterns include zig-zags and

Figure 10.4. (above) EN sherds with plastic decoration.

Figure 10.5. (right) EN sherds with incised decoration.

chequered cross-hatched patterns, all of which are typical of the late EN I and EN II Knossian repertoire (Figure 10.5). Finally, the few occurrences of plastic knobbed decoration on fine ware are similar to late EN I Knossian examples.

An interesting picture emerges from preliminary macroscopic study of the Neolithic pottery. The amount of EN pottery and the energy invested in pottery manufacture show that we are not dealing with an isolated house production, but with a small production unit suitable for a small settlement. It seems probable that the task of this unit was the manufacture of coarse ware for local people. Its production was of lower quality and less standardized than that of Knossos in terms of firing and surface treatment. It does not seem probable that it represents a different tradition, since it closely follows the Knossian styles. The quantitative predominance of coarse ware indicates the rather simple needs of a small, rural community. Katsambas does not seem able to share or match the 'urban' spirit of Knossos, where fine ware of good quality was in greater demand. Fine ware at Katsambas is in small quantity but of good quality and probably imported from Knossos. Finally, further comparative study of the coarse and fine wares from Katsambas is likely to reveal more about the role and function of fine ware at the site.

Chipped and Ground Stone Tools

The chipped stone industry consists of only three retouched artefacts, two manufactured on red flint and one on obsidian. The latter is a flake with direct retouch on one lateral edge. The former are a blade with bifacial retouch along the lateral edges that converges on its distal front (typologically classifiable as a perforator) (Figure 10.6a) and a laminar flake with partial linear retouch on one lateral edge and truncation at the proximal end (Figure 10.6b). It is notable that no debitage, cores or primary stages of an operational sequence have been recovered. If this is not an effect of a sampling procedure, then the specimens recovered were preformed and retouched elsewhere and arrived on-site as ready-made tools. The sample of chipped stone artefacts from the building, though too small to permit any reliable comparisons with other Neolithic assemblages, falls within the same technical tradition as the EN I tools of Knossos studied by James Conolly (this volume; *n.d.*).

The polished stone tool assemblage

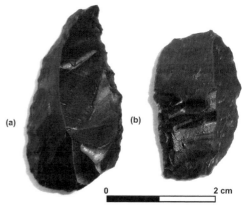

Figure 10.6. Two retouched chipped stone artefacts from Katsambas house.

Figure 10.7. Stone axes belonging to the group of large size.

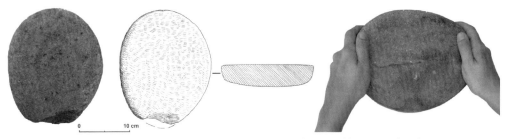

Figure 10.8. Ground stone tool and demonstration of its possible use as a handstone.

is larger, comprising a dozen polished stone axes manufactured from metamorphic rocks of medium or soft hardness, with a distinct morphology and technology of manufacture (Figure 10.7). With the exception of two or three largely polished bodies, the majority were produced by hammering or pecking the proximal part and polishing their active distal part only. In terms of size, two groups may be distinguished: larger ones approximately 8–8.4 cm in length, and smaller ones measuring 4.5–6 cm. Their outline is oval, with the occasional trapezoidal example. Cross-sections are in the vast majority round or oval and mostly symmetrical. Our macroscopic study has shown that at least half of the specimens must have been manufactured from raw material of the same origin, this being a dark grey-greenish soft stone with white or brown nerves. It is expected that petrographic study of this assemblage and comparative analysis with the axe groups from Neolithic Knossos (Strasser 2004; this volume) and elsewhere on Crete will shed further light on possible correlations between axe petrology and morphology.

The house has also yielded a number of ground stone tools used in food preparation. Amongst them are grinding slabs with a flat or slightly concave surface, handstones with round or square sections, pestles and a mortar, all of which were manufactured from river pebbles or rocks from the limestone marls that are found locally in the Kairatos catchment (Figure 10.8). Other finds include a mace-head and two or three whetstones with a square cross-section, two of which are small stones with traces of use as polishers. The mace-head was manufactured from a soft green stone, finished by means of polishing and used extensively prior to being discarded.

Chronology and Function: Some Early Thoughts

Katsambas was a satellite-site of Knossos in terms of distance and geography. Studies of lithic and ceramic typology and technology from the house suggest other links with Knossos in terms of economy and society. Our study thus far suggests that the vast majority of the pottery dates to the late EN I period, with perhaps some EN II. We anticipate that future systematic study of the Katsambas assemblage will further clarify issues of relative chronology, especially regarding EN I and EN II types. It is expected that full petrographic study of the ceramic assemblage will clarify its technology, provenance and relationship to Knossian and other contemporary assemblages as well as how post-depositional processes, such as prolonged exposure to water, may have affected its current state of preservation. Our study of the rockshelter material and publication of the recent discoveries by Ms Ioanna Serpetsidaki in a field adjacent to the house and rockshelter will offer complementary views on Neolithic settlement in the northern catchment of the river Kairatos. In the meantime, we can put together a few working hypotheses.

The study of the excavated lithic artefacts hints at the relative permanence of occupation at Katsambas. Plant-food processing activities were taking place on-site, and these would have required a period of occupation more compatible with longer stays than daily expeditions from, for example, Knossos. It thus follows that the Katsambas building may have indeed been a house, as Professor Alexiou originally envisioned it. This house could have accommodated a small social unit, which was most probably linked by kinship to the community at Knossos, but could alternatively have been relatively independent from them, sharing only a common technological and social universe. The possibility of a local production of coarse-ware thus needs to be understood in this context.

Old and new excavations at Knossos leave us in no doubt that the Katsambas house coincides with a phase of settlement expansion with plentiful evidence for year-round residential continuity (Evans 1971; Efstratiou *et al.* 2004: 47, fig. 1.3). Why the Katsambas community chose at that time to reside in this location and not, for example, at Knossos remains to be clarified. The position of Katsambas close to the Herakleion Bay and the good access to the sea that this ensures may have played a major role in its selection, but viewing Katsambas solely in terms of its location would be a rather limiting approach. We suspect that the decision to reside at Katsambas has more to do with the social dynamics of Cretan Neolithic communities at this time. Katsambas appears to be a site on a smaller scale than Knossos and thus augments the sample of smaller Cretan sites

(Magasa, Sphoungaras, Gerani, Kavousi, Gavdos), whose appearance is now dated to the late sixth/early fifth millennium BC (see Tomkins this volume). Katsambas therefore adds an interesting dimension to our picture of settlement in north-central Crete during this period. Detailed comparative study should in the future enable us to shift the discussion from the sphere of theoretical expectations to one firmly based in the archaeological record of the region.

Habitation at Katsambas was in all probability not restricted to a single house, but took the form of a small, rural settlement. This hypothesis was originally suggested by the excavator based on the abundance of Neolithic finds spread over an extensive area by the Kairatos northwest bank, and the presence nearby of a burial rockshelter. This hypothesis is further strengthened by our examination of the pottery and lithics from the house. It is not yet clear how many episodes of occupation in the history of human presence in the broader Kairatos catchment are represented at Katsambas. Further light may be shed on the time frame of human occupation by a forthcoming program of radiocarbon dating using organic remains that were, thanks to the excavator's foresight, collected and stored as part of the original excavation.

Acknowledgements

N.G. is grateful to Professor Stylianos Alexiou for entrusting her with the Katsambas publication. This research was made possible by financial support from INSTAP. Don Evely offered hospitality of a 'Cretan sort' to the Katsambas team at the Stratigraphic Museum at Knossos, saving the study of the material from the threat of another long delay caused by the closure of the Herakleion Archaeological Museum for restoration. Last, but not least, the editors of this volume should be thanked for their invitation to the Round Table meeting and for their valuable editorial assistance.

Bibliography

Alexiou, S.
   n.d.   Neolithikos synoikismos para ton Kairaton. Unpublished manuscript.
   1956   Anaskafai en Katsamba. *PAE* (1953): 299–308.
   1957   Anaskafai en Katsamba. *PAE* (1954): 369–74.
Conolly, J.
   n.d.   The knapped-stone industry of initial and early Neolithic Knossos. Unpublished report.
Efstratiou, N., A. Karetsou, E. S. Banou and D. Margomenou
   2004   The Neolithic settlement of Knossos: new light on an old picture. In G. Cadogan, E. Hatzaki and A. Vasilakis (eds.), *Knossos: Palace, City, State*: 39–49. London: British School at Athens.

Evans, J. D.
    1964   Excavations in the Neolithic settlement of Knossos, 1957–60, Part I. *BSA* 59: 132–240.
    1971   Neolithic Knossos: the growth of a settlement. *PPS* 37: 95–117.
Furness, A.
    1953   The Neolithic pottery of Knossos. *BSA* 48: 94–134.
Manteli, K. and D. Evely
    1995   The Neolithic levels from the Throne Room System, Knossos. *BSA* 90: 1–16.
Strasser, T. F.
    2004   Three axe groups from Neolithic Knossos. In G. Cadogan, E. Hatzaki and A. Vasilakis (eds.), *Knossos: Palace, City, State*: 61–65. London: British School at Athens.
Tomkins, P.
    2007   Neolithic: Strata IX–VIII, VII–VIB, VIA–V, IV, IIIB, IIIA, IIB, IIA and IC Groups. In N. Momigliano (ed.), *Knossos Pottery Handbook: Neolithic and Bronze Age (Minoan)*: 9–48. London: British School at Athens.

11

The Neolithic Settlement of Phaistos Revisited: Evidence for Ceremonial Activity on the Eve of the Bronze Age

Simona Todaro (S. T.) and Serena Di Tonto (S. D.)

In the course of several campaigns conducted at Phaistos over more than a hundred years, a large body of Neolithic material has been uncovered, representing one of the most substantial assemblages of that period in Crete. Since their discovery these deposits, which comprise ceramics and food remains as well as stone and bone implements, were interpreted as occupation refuse testifying to the existence of an open-air settlement that was roughly contemporary with the latest stages of the Neolithic settlement at Knossos (Pernier 1935: 107–9). It was only after L. Vagnetti's thorough study of the materials retrieved by D. Levi that the chronological time-span of the evidence and its relation with other Cretan Neolithic sites was better defined. The two occupation phases, identified on the basis of stratigraphy, were both attributed to the Final Neolithic period and were considered to be slightly later than Stratum I at Knossos, and contemporary with the latest stages of the Anatolian Chalcolithic period (Vagnetti 1973a: 118–28; Vagnetti and Belli 1978). However, Levi's excavations added very little information about the size and internal articulation of the settlement and apart from the rather problematic circular hut and a few rectilinear walls, the permanent character of the human presence on the hill at Phaistos continued to be attested only by floors of beaten earth or (more rarely) small stones and some fixed hearths.

Subsequent studies have tried to reconstruct the extent of human activity on the hill on the basis of the distribution of the pottery, which, in pure or mixed levels, was found almost everywhere beneath the palatial structures (Branigan 1988: 11–12; Watrous and Hadzi-Vallianou 2004: 221). However, before using this data to evaluate the size of the settlement or related matters such as population size and level of social complexity, it is necessary to bear in mind that, although differences in material culture are minor, indicating minimal internal development, the existence of two habitation phases cannot be doubted. This should warn us against the reliability of distribution maps created by plotting together all Neolithic remains as if they were simultaneously in use. Furthermore, not all of the Neolithic deposits could be characterised as primary deposition contexts, and amongst those unaffected by later disturbance it is necessary to distinguish between floor deposits and occupational refuse, in order to determine the extent of the settlement and understand the nature of the activities performed on the hill.

The stimulus for an overall re-evaluation of the Neolithic evidence from Phaistos, in terms of its nature and chronology, was given recent impetus by the discovery of several superimposed Neolithic and EM levels in two sectors of the hill: the area to the south of the ramp, which connected the lower and upper courts of the Palace (La Rosa 2004), and the area of Room XIX, located between the proto- and neo-palatial western facades (Figure 11.1; La Rosa 2006). This fortunate circumstance allowed the distinction stratigraphically, stylistically and typologically of two FN phases, broadly corresponding to FN III and FN IV of Tomkins' classification (2007; this volume), and two EM I phases roughly equivalent to the two stages detected by Warren at Lebena (Warren 2004: 115–18). Moreover, the new discoveries indicated that, while the first substantial buildings at Phaistos date to EM I (Todaro 2005: 33–34), the FN occupation was characterised by ephemeral architecture and by the performance of ceremonial activities that involved an emphasis on pouring and/or serving. In this paper we will

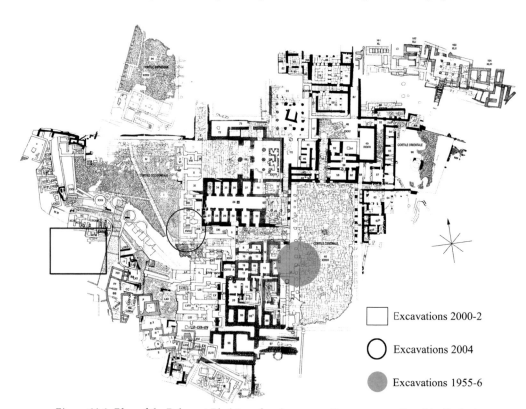

Figure 11.1. Plan of the Palace at Phaistos, showing excavation areas mentioned in the text.

focus on the Neolithic picture of the site, as revealed by the new data and a broader consideration of the depositional processes of the previously excavated deposits, and will address questions related to the nature of the activities that took place on the hill during the Neolithic, reconsidering also issues of habitation and function.

[*S. T. and S. D.*]

The Chronological Background: Towards a Better Definition of the Final Neolithic Period at Phaistos

The relative chronology of the Neolithic material from Phaistos, which Pernier classified as later than the Neolithic remains from Knossos (Pernier 1935: 107) and Levi as Chalcolithic (Levi 1964: 5), became better understood after the 1969–70 excavations at Knossos. In a trial trench opened beneath the West Court at Knossos, J. Evans uncovered a small group of ceramics that presented Phaistian characteristics and were believed at the time to be later than Stratum I at Knossos (Evans 1971: pls. III–IV). In 1964 Renfrew introduced the term Latest Neolithic to replace the label Sub-Neolithic, and then in 1972 introduced the term Final Neolithic to refer to the Neolithic deposits from Phaistos, Sub-Neolithic deposits, such as Partira as well as the later Neolithic deposits of Knossos as represented by Strata I–II. In this way, the chronological differentiation between Late and Final Neolithic in Crete started to disappear, and different scholars started to use one or the other label according to their personal preference (Nowicki 2002: 11–13).

In her study of the Phaistian Neolithic pottery L. Vagnetti accepted the use of the term Final Neolithic in place of the earlier labels used by the Italian excavators, but considered this phase to post-date the original 'Late Neolithic' phase at Knossos (Vagnetti 1973a: 125). In fact, in her comprehensive study she defined the Cretan FN period as a phase bridging 'LN' and EM I, which while anticipating EM features, retained much of the long preceding Neolithic tradition (Vagnetti and Belli 1978: 158–61). Moreover, although not formally dividing the period into sub-phases, Vagnetti stated that the 'Phaistos culture may represent an earlier stage, while the Partira-Ayios Nikolaos a later one' (Vagnetti and Belli 1978: 161). The two phases detected at Phaistos on a stratigraphic basis were instead considered to be part of the same chronological horizon, as they showed very little internal development. Later on, she again took up the problem of the chronological phasing of FN after the discovery of the Neolithic pottery assemblage from Nerokourou (Chania) that 'could be put in an advanced stage of the FN' (Vagnetti 1996: 37–38) when compared to Phaistos and Knossos.

Following and developing Vagnetti's statements, Nowicki proposed that the two stages attested at Phaistos and the finds from Katalimata be defined as FN I, and the finds from Nerokourou and from other sites, mostly located on rocky promontories and supposed to be settled by newcomers, as FN II (Nowicki 2002).

More recently, and on the basis of a detailed re-examination of the Neolithic pottery retrieved from Knossos, Tomkins has abandoned the traditional chronological terminology used for the Cretan Neolithic in favour of a system compatible with that used elsewhere in Greece and the Aegean (Tomkins 2007; this volume). Under the new system five FN phases, contemporary with the Aegean FN phase, are distinguished and these match the five-fold division of Late Chalcolithic in Syria and the four-fold division of Late Chalcolithic in Anatolia, with which these sub-phases are broadly contemporary. According to this new chronological scheme, the first occupation phase identified at Phaistos corresponds to FN III, the second to FN IV. In addition, a few incised specimens retrieved from the sounding beneath the Central Court could be attributed to FN II. This seems to be confirmed by the data gained from the newly investigated sectors of the site.

The first phase is represented by the strata that lay immediately on the bedrock, which contain mainly black burnished pottery, sometimes enriched by red encrusted decoration or by incised, jabbed or grooved decoration, organised in simple patterns. The second phase, documented in the upper strata, contains mainly brown and reddish burnished ware, with some pieces in black burnished ware. Red encrusted decoration disappears, although a few specimens present a wash of red ochre on their internal walls. Apart from rare cases of grooved decoration, most of the pots have a plain burnished surface. Red slipped and burnished ware, sometimes mottled, is very common, together with granulate ware and pottery characterised by a pinkish fabric and scribble-burnished decoration (Di Tonto 2006). The predominance of light coloured pottery, although probably related to a change of taste, was achieved thanks to a technological improvement in the firing process (Todaro 2005).

As far as the vessel typology of both phases is concerned, aside from many open shapes such as various types of bowl and dish of small or medium size, certain closed shapes such as high-necked jars (*vasi a bottiglia*) and jugs become common. The presence of horned vessels, wide spouted bowls, jugs and large bowls (up to 40 cm in diameter) suggests a determination to vary the formal repertoire. Such vessels were probably intended for use on special occasions or, particularly in the case of the large bowls, in collective rituals practised by a group rather than single individuals. A typical ceramic assemblage is composed of vessels that are connected to the storage, serving and consumption of food and drink, but some pots for cooking were also identified amongst the materials retrieved from the new excavations.

The study of these newly discovered stratigraphic sequences and the thorough examination of the ceramic material is still ongoing. The aim is to define the Neolithic pottery from Phaistos not only in terms of style (shape/decoration), but also according to fabric, quality and quantity of inclusions, surface treatment and typology, in order to create ware categories that will allow the Phaistian pottery to be more easily situated within the broader context of the

Greek Neolithic (Di Tonto 2006). Moreover, a programme of analyses, with the intention of determining the provenance of the clay and distinguishing locally made and imported pottery, is currently ongoing under the supervision of Dr. P. Day. From this study we expect to gain data and information that will allow Phaistos to be compared with other sites, both to improve the definition of its relative chronology and to address important issues such as craft specialization, the improvement of forming and firing techniques, regionalism and ceramic exchange within Crete.

[S. D.]

The Archaeological Data: Towards a Contextual Reassessment of the Activities Performed on the Phaistos Hill

Any contextual study of the FN remains from Phaistos must face the difficulty caused by the intrinsic nature of the excavations, which, due to the presence of later structures, could only ever explore areas of restricted dimensions. The already difficult task of cross-correlating the various stratigraphies is further complicated, in the case of Phaistos, by the existence of at least two habitation phases with only minor differences in material culture; by variations in the depth of the bedrock that obscure whether strata detected in adjacent trenches were part of the same context; and by the nature of the evidence, which mainly consists of debris from food preparation and consumption, discarded in the vicinity of various types of hearths. The newly discovered deposits, together with a more finely resolved ceramic chronology, have provided new data on the formation of the Phaistian stratigraphy that has allowed a full re-evaluation of the nature and character of FN occupation on the hill to be made.

In the area to the south of the Minoan ramp (excavated 2000–2002; Figure 11.1) two successive FN open-air cooking installations were detected between a large EM I red-plastered building, whose foundations had been set into the underlying FN stratum, and two successive rubbish dumps discarded directly on the bedrock when pottery of FN IV type was in use (Todaro 2005: 31, fig. 5). Each of the cooking installations comprised patches of burnt earth and animal bones, which, like the ceramic vessels, had each time been discarded *in situ*. These installations seem to be connected with the preparation and consumption of meat-based meals. Several burnt slabs and a flimsy wall, detected on the limit of the excavation trench, suggest that at least the latest cooking installation included a fixed hearth and might have belonged to the enclosed yard of a house.

A similar situation was recorded in the other recently investigated sector (Room XIX, excavated in 2004), where a FN IV open-air cooking installation, comprising a fixed hearth bounded on one side by a line of stones, two circular pits and a pillar-shaped stone, was identified beneath an EM I building whose foundations had been set into the underlying FN stratum (Figure 11.2). The hearth (1.20 × 1.80 m), which represented the re-occupation of the area after a temporary abandonment, was arranged within a clayey sterile layer and had a paved base encircled by smaller stones. Numerous sherds and fully preserved or largely restorable vessels were found above and around the paved area in association with pestles and animal bones. This ceramic material comprised a large quantity of sherds from high-necked jars in granulate ware, large black burnished serving vessels, large coarse ware jars and a unique specimen of a jug with white encrusted decoration. In addition there was an interesting set of vessels in red slipped and burnished ware (often mottled due to firing), comprising jugs, straight-sided bowls, carinated bowls with offset rim and a peculiar type of bowl with a horizontal beak that represents the first fully preserved specimen of a shape that hitherto was only attested at Phaistos by its V-shaped spout (Figure 11.3a; Vagnetti 1973a: 76, fig. 69, 25–31; 100, fig. 93, 3; table I, 2). Such a form type, if in fragmentary condition, would not be easily distinguished from the simple carinated bowl with offset rim.

Although only a small portion of the deposit was retrieved, and thus accurate quantification of the minimum number of participants is not possible, the scale and nature of the ceramic and faunal assemblages seem to testify to the

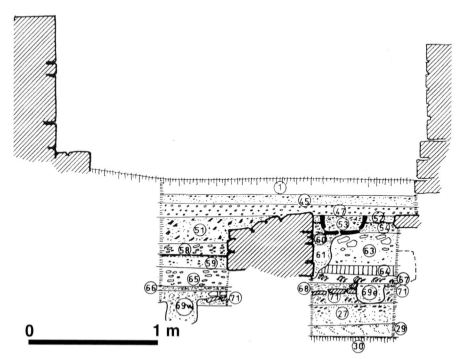

Figure 11.2. E–W section through Room XIX, with EM I wall and FN IV cooking installation, hearth (strata 71 and 68), two pits (69 w and 69 e) and a pillar shaped stone (outlined with a dashed line between strata 67 and 63).

preparation and consumption of food on a scale beyond the domestic/household level. The range of ceramic forms represented documents an emphasis on pouring and/or serving, which could have been related to specific acts of hospitality or communal ceremonial activity. Moreover, it is striking that, although only 38% of the animal bones have been identified, this represents the consumption and *in situ* deposition of at least 4 cattle, 4 sheep, 4 pigs, 2 rams and 1 agrimi (Masala in prep.). It also needs to be considered that, prior to the abandonment episode that preceded the placement of the hearth, this area had been used for a similar episode of consumption performed with a near identical set of vases that were subsequently also left *in situ* (Figure 11.3c–f). In this earlier event, also dating to FN IV, the hearth was arranged above the ruins of a wall, which had been purposely levelled, and the ceramic assemblage, amongst which a horned jar, was associated with 55 sea-shells and a fragment of what may be copper ore.

These two successive ceramic assemblages are characterised not only by similar form types (Figure 11.3), but also by identical patterns of deposition, with periods of intense activity followed by periods of abandonment. This impression, suggested by the stratigraphy of Room XIX, is confirmed by the data recorded by previous excavations in the vicinity (Rooms 28 and 29), which seem to belong to the same context as Room XIX. Cross-correlation of the stratigraphy in each of these three rooms – facilitated in the case of Rooms XIX and 29 by the existence of detailed graphic documentation (Figure 11.4) – shows such a surprising correspondence in hearths, abandonment levels and ceramic material that it prompts the conclusion that the entire area between the West Façade of the Palace and Room 28 was unroofed and had been periodically used during FN IV for episodes of food and drink consumption.

Figure 11.3. A selection of the most common pouring and drinking vessels associated with the two FN IV hearths.

The finds from Room 28, in particular the high percentage of miniature vessels, the piece of magnetic iron and a female figurine (Mosso 1908: figs. 4, 6; Pernier 1935: figs. 38–40), suggest that some supernatural beliefs might have inspired these large gatherings of people. However, before trying to determine the nature of the activities performed in this area, it is important to stress that similar episodes of preparation and consumption were also performed in other locations on the hill in FN IV, with almost identical sets of vessels thereafter left *in situ*. One such context was identified by Levi in 1955–6 in Trench II, located to the south of Corridor 7 (Figures 11.1 and 11.5). Here, two circular hearths

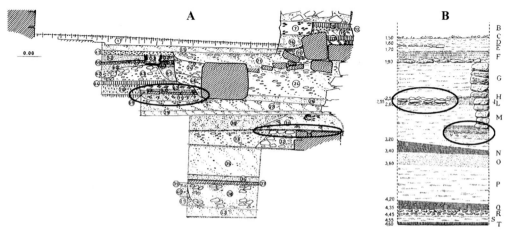

Figure 11.4. Section through rooms XIX (A) and 29 (B) with FN IV hearths highlighted.

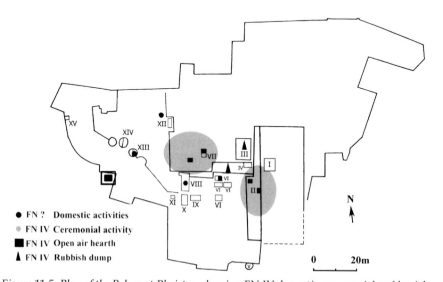

Figure 11.5. Plan of the Palace at Phaistos, showing FN IV domestic, ceremonial and burial areas.

composed of rectangular slabs were found just a few metres apart (Levi 1958: 337–39, figs. 189, 191). The better preserved of the two was surrounded by fully preserved vases, comprising a jug, a bowl and two jars (Vagnetti 1973a: 38–40, figs. 34, 36), which closely resemble those from the area facing the West Court. Similar vessels, but in a more fragmentary condition, were found near the other hearth (Vagnetti 1973a: 42, figs. 28–29), where a piece of copper was also collected (Vagnetti 1973a: 117, fig. 133 (4)), thereby further increasing the force of the analogy between this context and the one from the area that faces the West Court. Furthermore, 1121 animal bones and 59 sea shells were retrieved from Room 25, in a stratum that was detected at exactly the same level as the two hearths, and which was followed by an abandonment level (Strata f' and e' respectively in Vagnetti 1973a: 24). From this assemblage, parts of at least 21 sheep/goats, 10 pigs, 8 agrimi and 8 cattle were identified (Wilkens 1996), testifying to consumption on a very large scale.

The composition of the assemblages and the nature of deposition suggest that the circular hearths were also located in an open area and were used for the same sorts of activity as the rectangular ones detected in the area near the West Court. It is currently impossible, however, to ascertain whether the two contexts – apparently similar but associated with different types of hearths – testify to similar acts of consumption that involved distinct groups, for example competing households, or represent the debris of ceremonies performed for different purposes by the same group of people, such as the entire community.

Both hypotheses raise the question of where these people may have lived. The apparent lack of any domestic architecture, and indeed any evidence for domestic activities other than food preparation and consumption in the vicinity

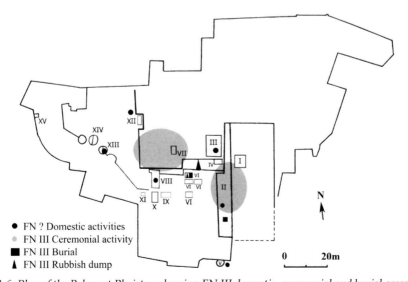

Figure 11.6. Plan of the Palace at Phaistos, showing FN III domestic, ceremonial and burial areas.

of the hearths, together with the regular *in situ* disposal of the debris from feasting activities (which would have made the yards of private houses inaccessible after a short time) suggests that the area of permanent habitation was located elsewhere. The assemblages retrieved from Trenches VIII, XII and XIII (Figure 11.5), which lack spouted vessels but contain spindle whorls, bones and stone tools, present themselves as potential locations of habitation, although their chronological position within the newly established FN–EM I sequence still needs to be ascertained.

A rather different pattern emerges for earlier FN activity (FN III) on the hill. This was concentrated in two sectors of the hill, namely the area beneath the Central Court and the Neo-palatial rooms that lay along its western side and the area between the West Façade and Room 29 (Figure 11.6). Possible domestic units are concentrated in the first sector, represented by the pseudo-rectangular building detected beneath Room 25 (Trench III), by a series of pits excavated on the bedrock in front of Room 23 (Trench II), and by the so-called circular hut uncovered to the south of the Central Court (Trench V). However, the pits, especially the one containing a large burnished bowl, could be related to the burial detected in front of Room 22, where the mandible had been replaced by a stone and the body had been covered by stones that were especially abundant between the legs and arms (Levi 1958: 341, fig. 193).

While very little can be said about the activities that took place within these domestic units, more evidence is available regarding the activities conducted on the bedrock in an area about 15 m to the south of the unit identified within Room 25 and 30 m to the north of the circular hut. Here, in proximity to a large artificial, plastered cavity that could have been used as a water cistern (Vagnetti 1973a: 14–15, figs. 3–5; Vagnetti and Belli 1978: 128) and in the same area as the later (FN IV) circular hearths, Levi found a very interesting assemblage composed of three unusual items that had been left on the bedrock (Levi 1958: 340, fig. 192), for which a cultic function has been cautiously proposed (Vagnetti and Belli 1978: 131). The assemblage included a triton shell broken at one end, a small jar and a pot with a strainer at the mouth, items which, apart from their red ochre decoration, seem to have in common a suitability for the preparation of some kind of beverage or infusion (Figure 11.7). Although the triton shell has generally been interpreted as a trumpet (Vagnetti and Belli 1978: 131), a use as a rhyton or libation vessel is suggested by

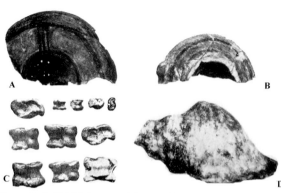

Figure 11.7. FN III Ceremonial assemblage: sieving pot (A); jar (B); astragaloi (C); triton shell (D) (not to scale).

its contextual associations, particularly the emphasis on pouring/drinking expressed by the high concentration of spouted-vessels, jugs, jars and bowls found in the vicinity. Many animal bones and a group of twelve astragaloi were also found, the latter in proximity to nine small holes that had been purposely cut into the soft bedrock and which, in Levi's opinion, had functioned as some sort of game (Levi 1958: 340).

Regardless of the specific function of each individual item, it is undeniable that these pouring/drinking vessels in black burnished ware with red ochre encrustation constitute a set for serving and consuming a particular kind of beverage that was prepared in the pot with the strainer. This particular practice seems to have formed part of an episode of open-air ceremonial activity located near a water cistern and which also involved preparation and consumption of meat-based food. After this the area was temporarily abandoned, only to be re-used later in FN IV for the large episode of consumption that took place in proximity to the two circular hearths mentioned above.

An analogous situation can be proposed for the area near the West Court. Here a very similar assemblage with pouring/drinking vessels in red encrusted ware, triton shells and astragaloi was brought to light in the lower levels of Rooms 28, 29 and XIX (Mosso 1908: 149–50, fig. 5), where the new excavations also uncovered a wall (Figure 11.4) that could have been contemporaneous with the building detected in Room 25 in the sector near the Central Court. As in the sector near the Central Court, this phase of activity near the West Court is characterised by several superimposed floors, testifying to a certain degree of continuity in occupation, and was followed by an abandonment (Vagnetti 1973a: 24). It would seem, therefore, that in FN III several structures were built on the hill in association with two relatively large, open areas where people gathered to participate in ceremonies that involved the consumption of food and primarily drink prepared and/or served in a sieving vessel.

[S. T.]

Evidence for Ceremonial Activity on the Eve of Bronze Age

This brief overview of the FN evidence from Phaistos has led to the identification of slightly different patterns of development in FN III and FN IV. In FN III several structures seem to have been organised around two communal open areas, where people gathered to participate in ceremonies that involved the preparation and consumption of drink served with a specialised set of drinking and pouring vessels decorated with red ochre encrustation. In FN IV the evidence for domestic architecture in the vicinity of the open areas decreases considerably and in fact the only area that currently suggests domestic activity is located on the west slope of the hill, in the area to the south of the Minoan ramp, which was apparently unoccupied in FN III. This apparent scarcity of built habitation during FN IV may simply be an artefact of the archaeological data. It is possible that other structures were originally present during FN IV, but are no longer preserved either because they were constructed from perishable materials or because they were swept away by the construction in EM I of large buildings with foundations set within the previous strata. Furthermore, if the assemblages from Trenches VIII, XII and XIII prove, through further study, to belong to FN IV, it would be possible to say that the entire western edge of the top of the hill was occupied by domestic units.

Although it is not yet possible to ascertain the extent of the FN IV inhabited area, it can be seen to have reached previously unoccupied areas, and was organised, like its FN III predecessor, around two communal open areas where local households might have gathered on specific occasions to perform ceremonies where food and drink were consumed. Such ceremonies may have served either an integrative function, preventing a tendency towards domestic isolation, or a competitive one, according to the models proposed by Halstead (1999: 89). Although the use of separate locations and different hearths seems to favour a hypothesis where competing local households engaged in episodes of formal hospitality with households from further afield in order to mobilize obligations of mutual help or obtain food and raw materials not locally available, the data is not yet sufficient to exclude the possibility that the two areas were used for different purposes, and on different occasions, by the community as a whole. If, however, the faunal material from the area near the Central Court (Wilkens 1996: 241) could be attributed to a single episode of consumption, this would be a powerful argument in favour of a further interpretation, namely Relaki's recent hypothesis that the Phaistos hill was periodically used by the communities in the wider area as a regional focus for the performance of activities that might have contributed to the construction of a sense of locality (Relaki 2004: 177).

At this stage of the research it can be simply stated that the two open areas of the hill, in both phases of the Neolithic period, were used for a particular type of communal activity that seems to have been specifically associated with Phaistos. The ceramic assemblages associated with this activity, principally the pouring vessels, are not in fact paralleled elsewhere, and even a site such as Gortyn which presents several similarities with Phaistos, seems not to have used spouted shapes (Vagnetti 1973b; Santaniello and Todaro in prep.). Future finds may obviously change this picture, but it is tempting to suggest that the memory of the ritual activity that occurred at Phaistos in the Final Neolithic period endowed the hill with a special status that contributed as much to its selection as the site of the First Palace as the fact that the hill overlooks the large plain of the Mesara with its substantial agricultural potential (Todaro in press).

[S. T.]

Discussion and Further Thoughts

Reconsideration of the old excavations and the supplementary information available from the new excavations at Phaistos has allowed the identification of two slightly different patterns of development for FN III and FN IV. During FN III several structures seem to have been organised around two open areas, while during FN IV two similar foci were periodically used for ceremonies where food and drink was consumed by several groups, whose nature and composition is unclear. Judging by the available data three scenarios could most plausibly explain these episodes of consumption: (1) they could represent episodes of intra-community commensality (2) they could represent episodes of inter-community formal hospitality, organised by Phaistian households with successful households from further afield (3) they could represent episodes of ceremonial consumption at a regional level, involving the communities of the surrounding territory. Choosing between these interpretations offered clearly depends on the spatial and social organization of the community settled at Phaistos, an issue that is the subject of doctoral research by both authors. Much work still remains to be done, but we hope to have given a glimpse of the potential information that can be gained from an integrated study of pottery typology, stratigraphy and spatial context. As this work develops, we hope to provide a firmer basis for understanding activity at the site at the end of the Neolithic and to bring greater precision to the chronology of this important period.

[S. T. and S. D.]

Acknowledgements

We would like to thank the organisers of the Round Table, P. Tomkins and V. Isaakidou, for their invitation to participate, and the Sheffield Centre for Aegean Archaeology for having financially supported Di Tonto's travel. We are also greatly indebted to P. Day, for his contribution to the first draft of the paper, to P. Halstead for his technical and moral support, and M. Metcalfe for having checked the English. We have also benefited greatly from comments that P. Tomkins made to the penultimate version. This paper is based on the authors' ongoing doctoral researches at Udine University (Di Tonto) and the University of Sheffield (Todaro). The jointly authored introduction is followed by separate discussions whose authorship is indicated by initials at the end of each section.

Bibliography

Branigan, K.
  1988 *Prepalatial. The Foundations of Palatial Crete. A Survey of Crete in the Early Bronze Age* (Second revised edition). Amsterdam: A. Hakkert.
Evans, J. D.
  1971 Neolithic Knossos: the growth of a settlement. *PPS* 37: 95–117.
Di Tonto, S.
  2006 Considerazioni preliminari sulla ceramica neolitica dei nuovi scavi di Festòs. *ASA* 83: 413–17.

Halstead, P.
    1999   Neighbours from hell? The household in Neolithic Greece. In P. Halstead (ed.), *Neolithic Society in Greece* (SSAA 2): 77–95. Sheffield: Sheffield Academic Press.
La Rosa, V.
    2004   Le campagne di scavo 2000–2002 a Festòs. *ASA* 80: 635–883.
    2006   I saggi della campagna 2004 a Festòs. *ASA* 83: 611–70.
Levi, D.
    1958   Gli scavi a Festòs nel 1956–7. *ASA* 19–20: 193–361.
    1964   *The Recent Excavation at Phaistos* (SIMA 11). Lund, Jonsered: Carl Bloms.
Mosso, A.
    1908   Ceramica neolitica di Phaistòs e vasi dell'epoca minoica primitiva. *Monumenti Antichi* 19: 141–218.
Nowicki, K.
    2002   The end of the Neolithic in Crete. *Aegean Archaeology* 6: 7–72.
Pernier, L.
    1935   *Il Palazzo Minoico di Festòs* (Volume I). Roma: La Libreria Dello Stato.
Relaki, M.
    2004   Constructing a region: the contested landscapes of prepalatial Mesara. In J. Barrett and P. Halstead (eds.), *The Emergence of Civilisation Revisited* (SSAA 6): 170–88. Oxford: Oxbow Books.
Todaro, S.
    2005   EM I–MM IA ceramic groups at Phaistos: towards the definition of a Prepalatial ceramic sequence in south central Crete. *Creta Antica* 6: 11–46.
    in press   The western Mesara before the rise of the Phaistian palace: prepalatial evidence from Phaistos, Aghia Triada and Patrikies. *Pepragmena I' Diethnous Kretologikou Synedriou*. Khania: Philologikos Syllogos o Chrysostomos.
Tomkins, P.
    2007   Neolithic: Strata IX–VIII, VII–VIB, VIA–V, IV, IIIB, IIIA, IIB, IIA and IC Groups. In N. Momigliano (ed.), *Knossos Pottery Handbook: Neolithic and Bronze Age (Minoan)*: 9–48. London: British School at Athens.
Vagnetti, L.
    1973a   L'insediamento neolitico di Festòs. *ASA* 34–35: 7–138.
    1973b   Tracce di due insediamenti neolitici nel territorio dell'antica Gortina. *Antichita Cretesi. Studi in Onore di Doro Levi. I*: 1–9. Catania: Università di Catania, Istituto di Archeologia.
    1996   The Final Neolithic: Crete enters the wider world. *Cretan Studies* 5: 29–39.
Vagnetti, L. and P. Belli
    1978   Characters and problems of the Final Neolithic in Crete. *SMEA* 68: 125–65.
Warren, P. M.
    2004   Part II. The contents of the tombs. In S. Alexiou and P. Warren, *The Early Minoan Tombs of Lebena, Southern Crete* (SIMA 30): 23–218. Sävedalen: Paul Åström.
Watrous, L. V. and D. Hadzi-Vallianou
    2004   Initial growth in social complexity (Late Neolithic-Early Minoan I). In L. V. Watrous, D. Hadzi-Vallianou and H. Blitzer (eds.), *The Plain of Phaistos. Cycles of Social Complexity in the Mesara Region of Crete*: 221–31. Los Angeles: Cotsen Institute of Archaeology, UCLA.
Wilkens, B.
    1996   Faunal Remains from Italian excavations on Crete. In D. S. Reese (ed.), *Pleistocene and Holocene Fauna of Crete and its First Settlers*: 241–61. Madison: Prehistory Press.

12

Obsidian in Transition: the Technological Reorganization of the Obsidian Industry from Petras Kephala (Siteia) between Final Neolithic IV and Early Minoan I

Cesare D'Annibale

Introduction

In the Aegean and Mediterranean in general, obsidian is often an integral component of Neolithic culture. In Crete, obsidian is present from the earliest Initial Neolithic levels at Knossos and continues to occur in varying proportions throughout the Neolithic and into the Late Bronze Age (Evans 1964: 231, 233; Carter 2004a; Conolly this volume). During this long period of usage, significant changes in production and consumption can be detected (*e.g.*, Carter 2003; 2004a), among the most significant of which is the appearance of a pressure flaked blade industry at some point during the FN–EM I period. Prior to FN, pressure-flaked blades are as good as absent from Cretan obsidian assemblages, principally the IN–LN assemblage from Knossos (Conolly this volume) and by EM II morphologically similar prismatic blades are a feature of most sites around the island. The precise nature and timing of this change have long been unclear. The recent excavation of an uninterrupted FN IV–EM I stratified sequence at the site of Petras Kephala in east Crete (Papadatos this volume; Tomkins this volume: table 3.1) has thus presented a rare opportunity to isolate and study this revolutionary change in obsidian industry in greater detail. Although Petras Kephala is unlikely to have been the ultimate place of origin of this change, it provides substantial evidence for observing processes of innovation and change in procurement, technology, production and consumption in a single location.

Provenance

The main sources of obsidian exploited throughout the Neolithic and Bronze Age in the Aegean are located on the island of Melos, at the sites of *Dhemenegaki* and *Sta Nychia*. The distinctive varieties encountered at these two sites usually allow macroscopic identification through use of variables such as colour, banding and translucency. Both varieties exhibit comparable quality and flaking properties, but different chronologies of exploitation, with the Dhemenegaki source being more popular during the Neolithic (Carter 2003: 78; Pappalardo *et al.* 2003). Although few analytical results have been published to date, all analysed samples from FN Phaistos proved to be Dhemenegaki obsidian, while the majority of EM I and all EM II samples from Phaistos and Ayia Triada were from Sta Nychia (Pappalardo *et al.* 2003). In general, a preference for Sta Nychia obsidian is a Bronze Age phenomenon on Crete (Carter 2003).

Preliminary macroscopic study of the FN IV–EM I obsidian assemblage from Petras Kephala indicates that Sta Nychia obsidian was the preferred variety during both the FN IV and EM I phases of occupation. The Dhemenegaki source plays a secondary role accounting for roughly 15% of the assemblage. Four groups of non-Melian obsidian were also identified in FN and EM I contexts, each comprising only a few pieces. Amongst these were a few possible pieces of Yali obsidian. While the well-known speckled obsidian from Yali lacks the flaking properties that might render it workable to the same degree as Melian obsidian, a new Yali source of markedly better quality has recently been identified in association with a FN site (Bassiakos *et al.* 2005: 18). For a definitive picture of which obsidian sources were used, we must await the results of further analytical work. On present evidence, however, east Aegean (Yali) and Anatolian obsidian sources are less common in east Crete than geographical proximity might had led one to expect.

Technology, Production and Consumption

The Petras Kephala obsidian assemblage consists of 1376 pieces, of which 1235 may be assigned to deposits laid down during FN IV and EM I. Although the EM I assemblage is larger, the relative proportions of the various artefact types remain constant between the two periods. Blades and flakes respectively constitute 30% and 8% of the FN IV assemblage and 29% and 9% of the EM I assemblage and splintered fragments are equally represented at 62% in both periods. The recovery of flakes from the initial shaping of cores is a clear indication that much of the obsidian was arriving in the form of raw nodules and not in prepared cores from some other processing or distribution sites. Flakes from initial blade core preparation are typically the rarest form of debitage produced. Included amongst the splintered fragments in the FN IV assemblage are 34 fragments of exhausted cores. The actual number of cores is likely to be smaller, as many of these fragments could derive from the same original core. Twice as many core fragments were recovered from EM I contexts.

Although obsidian is frequently present in Neolithic and Early Bronze Age lithic assemblages, it is important to try to quantify the volume of obsidian in circulation during any given period, before making statements about high or low frequencies. Replication experiments have shown that a single core weighing 500 g can produce over 300 pieces of debitage (D'Annibale and Long 2003). Since the FN IV–EM I obsidian assemblage from Petras Kephala can be traced back to a very low number of cores, the entire assemblage could be accounted for by a series of interspersed and sporadic arrival episodes over the course of the life of the settlement. This would suggest relatively limited access to the source of the raw material, something also indicated by the use of a particular technique, known as the bipolar or anvil technique. This technique maximizes the amount of usable material by reducing the remnants of exhausted cores and is thus regarded as secondary and sequential to that of the blade industry. Bipolar technology is common throughout the Neolithic and the Bronze Age. At Petras Kephala it is represented by an impressive 795 splintered pieces from the total of 926 pieces of waste from the FN IV and EM I assemblages and is commonly used to reduce blades and blade segments. The above evidence implies an exceedingly high level of 'obsidian stress' at the site and the most economic explanation for this is limited access to the raw material. Although the obsidian industry was geared towards blade production, some flakes were used as expedient tools. Flake utilization is primarily a Neolithic tradition at Petras Kephala. The FN IV component comprised 40 flakes, of which 30 had been utilized. This aspect of the industry, whereby use was made of waste products from the shaping of blade cores, is virtually absent (n=1) from the EM I obsidian assemblage. What makes this all the more notable is the extensive recycling of obsidian blades and core fragments during EM I. Despite the need to maximize the amount of obsidian available, perhaps to overcome the lack of incoming supply, the inhabitants chose not to utilize flakes. This radical neglect of a potential source of tool blanks must be related to a focus on selected activities necessitating the use of standardized blades.

Blade production at Petras Kephala is evenly represented in both FN IV and EM I assemblages. There are major differences, however, in blade morphology between the two periods. Neolithic blades (Figure 12.1) are typically large and many can be classified as flake/blades (here the term 'blade' is used rather loosely). Although they roughly correspond to classic forms, such as trapezoidal, triangular and multifaceted types, most exhibit individual attribute variables. Typical attributes include ragged or irregular incurving or outcurving lateral edges, inconsistent dorsal ridge spacing from previous blade removals and inconsistent length, width and thickness. Overall, very few blades are mirror images of each other, although limited quantities of carefully executed blades do exist (Figure 12.2 top row).

A novel aspect of the FN IV Petras Kephala blade industry is the presence of blades and bladelets that conform to a stricter sense of proportion (Figure 12.3 top row). Bladelets are also present alongside blades in the FN IV obsidian assemblage from Nerokourou in west Crete (Christopoulou 1989; Tomkins 2007:

Figure 12.1. (right) Final Neolithic blades from Petras Kephala.

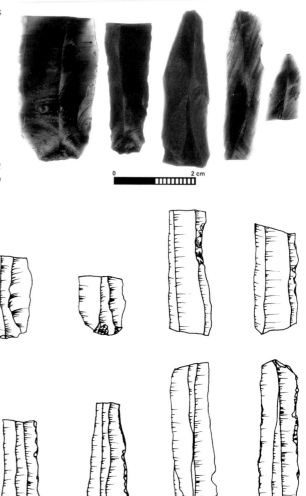

Figure 12.2. (below) Large blades from Petras Kephala: Final Neolithic IV (top row) and Early Minoan I (bottom row).

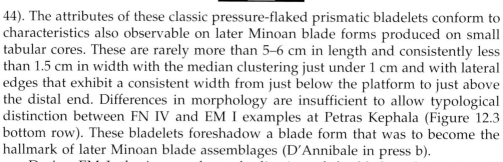

44). The attributes of these classic pressure-flaked prismatic bladelets conform to characteristics also observable on later Minoan blade forms produced on small tabular cores. These are rarely more than 5–6 cm in length and consistently less than 1.5 cm in width with the median clustering just under 1 cm and with lateral edges that exhibit a consistent width from just below the platform to just above the distal end. Differences in morphology are insufficient to allow typological distinction between FN IV and EM I examples at Petras Kephala (Figure 12.3 bottom row). These bladelets foreshadow a blade form that was to become the hallmark of later Minoan blade assemblages (D'Annibale in press b).

During EM I, the increased standardization of the blade industry is well

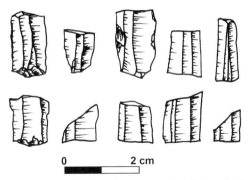

Figure 12.3. Bladelets from Petras Kephala: Final Neolithic IV (top row) and Early Minoan I (bottom row).

Figure 12.4. Microlith from bladelet from Petras Kephala.

illustrated by the fact that all tool types were now formed using blade blanks. Blades were retouched in order to create scraping edges, notches, and borer ends. Aside from their obvious use in a complete state, blades were also intentionally snapped to create segments or subjected to burin blows to create beaks or graving points to be used in composite tools. The most refined formal tools to be produced in this way are geometric microliths. Medial fragments of blades were segmented to sections less than 1 cm in size and then retouched to create working edges. Microlithic tools are exquisitely made and specifically intended for detailed work, possibly as drill bits, in association with other lapidary industries. A single example of such a tool, a trapeze, was recovered from a mixed FN/EM I context at Petras Kephala (Figure 12.4). Although no examples of this particular tool type have been reported from contemporary sites, 30 examples of microliths, dating from the EM II to LM periods, are known from the nearby settlements of Petras and Ayia Photia (D'Annibale in press a). These items appear to have a wide distribution in Crete, with examples known from EM sites such as Myrtos, Archanes, Platanos and Mochlos (Jarman 1972; Carter 2004b).

Although comparison with other FN–EB I obsidian assemblages around the Aegean is still in process, some general comments can be made. Blade production, subsequent burin technology and utilization of flakes are the main elements linking the Petras Kephala obsidian industry with that of the broader Aegean. Perhaps the closest parallels for the FN IV assemblage are to be found at FN IV Nerokourou, which presents almost identical blade forms and consumption patterns (Christopoulou 1989). A small number of blades and flakes are also present in FN III and FN IV contexts from Trench FF at Knossos (Evans 1971: pl. V; Tomkins 2007: 38, 41–42), although their technology of production remains to be clarified.

Some of the EM I blades from Petras Kephala (Figure 12.2 bottom row) bear a close resemblance to those from the EM I cemetery at Ayia Photia (Davaras 1971). Large prismatic blades, such as these, are characteristically long and wide and are produced using a macro-blade core. Thereafter, EM I macro-blade cores are restricted to mortuary contexts on Crete. They are generally regarded as a Cycladic element in the EM I assemblage from Ayia Photia, where they occur alongside other Cycladic or Cycladicising material culture of Kampos Group type (Day *et al.* 1998). Their presence at Petras Kephala, whose EM I assemblage lacks material of Kampos Group type and may thus partly or wholly pre-date Ayia Photia (Papadatos this volume), suggests access to a similar production technology and raises the possibility that Cycladic influence in the Siteia Bay area began at slightly earlier in EM I (pre-Kampos Group) than is currently envisaged. So far, however, none of the other studies of material from the site have produced corroborative evidence of Cycladic links. An alternative interpretation, based on the longer history of obsidian production now available from Petras Kephala, is that these large prismatic blades developed out of what is essentially a FN tradition of blade production. Large EM I blades from Petras Kephala are generally distinguishable from their FN IV counterparts by their more consistent dorsal scar spacing. As with some of the small bladelets, however, some EM I and FN IV large blades are typologically so close as to render them indistinguishable were it not for the independent dating evidence available. Such similarities suggest an industry in transition.

Obsidian Distribution Within the Site

At Petras Kephala the FN IV rectilinear structure and its associated extramural areas display the greatest concentration of obsidian with frequencies far in excess of those observed in rooms of the EM I complex (Papadatos this volume, fig. 15.3). There is also good evidence for blade production and consumption within the same space during FN and it would also appear that there was as much utilization of obsidian in adjoining *open* areas as there was in intramural contexts. Blade concentrations are, however, highest within the FN IV *structure* (n=80). On the other hand, the evidence from the EM I complex of rooms suggests a more restricted use of obsidian. Although obsidian was recovered from every room, only four of the rooms produced more than 50 pieces each and only one room produced more than 10 blades (n=14). These contrasts in distribution between FN IV and EM I may indicate changes in the use of space, with perhaps greater functional specialization emerging in EM I. The confinement of obsidian consumption to certain rooms in the EM I complex and the limited quantity of obsidian from outdoor areas may be indicative of restrictions in production and/ or consumption to which obsidian was becoming subject. Although there is little indication of specialized activity within the EM rooms, the internalization of obsidian production and consumption is a noteworthy forerunner to what was to be the norm in the later Bronze Age.

Technological Developments

The reorientation of the obsidian industry in Crete has been attributed to the transition from the use of a conical core in the Neolithic to a tabular core in the Bronze Age, a change that is generally evident in the rest of the Aegean as well (Van Horn 1980). The adoption of tabular cores may have gone a long way towards formalizing blade production. However, a mere change in shape alone would not result in such marked blade standardization and other factors must have been in play. Evidence from Petras Kephala suggests that changes in the technique of obsidian tool manufacture may be directly linked to the introduction of metal tools.

The likely practice of metallurgy at FN IV Petras Kephala (Papadatos 2007; this volume) and the scarcity or absence of direct evidence elsewhere in Crete at this time imply some sort of restricted, specialized production of metal objects and tools. In obsidian production, the replacement of a billet made of stone, wood, bone or antler by a copper equivalent is a natural one and privileged access to such copper billets may have facilitated certain technical developments in the FN IV obsidian industry at Petras Kephala. Although no such tool has been recovered, copper punches have been associated with the obsidian industry in later Minoan contexts, including MM II Petras (Evely 1993: 86–96; D'Annibale in press c). Moreover, microscopic examination of a number of core fragments, primary flakes and blades in the FN IV obsidian assemblage from Petras Kephala has revealed impact marks that are characteristic of a metal punch. These appear in the form of tiny circular impact marks or Hertzian cracks on the platform of blades and flakes. Such marks are typically produced by the application of force by a sharp indenter. Of more interest is a number of flakes and blades that exhibit trails consisting of semicircular or partial Hertzian cracks (Figure 12.5). The trails are evidence for a pointed tool slipping along the surface with pressure being exerted at a consistent level, but without enough force to produce a successful detachment (Lawn and Marshall 1979: 70–72). A degree of caution should be maintained here as the difference between experimentation and accident can be somewhat ambiguous. Experimental percussion on obsidian with a metal punch leaves single impact marks that may not be readily differentiated from trampling impact marks caused by stone grains and gravels. However, the trail of partial Hertzian cracks, such as that reproduced by Lawn and Marshall, is much harder to produce accidentally because concentrated and consistent pressure is needed.

For the most part the obsidian specimens that display these marks derive from FN IV contexts. Another interesting aspect is the near exclusive use of Dhemenegaki obsidian for this experimentation. These impact marks are perhaps an indication of initial experimentation with metal punches during FN IV. It is important to note that the use of a metal punch on its own does not eliminate variation introduced by the vagaries of the individual knapper. The application

Figure 12.5. Partial Hertzian cracks on a Neolithic blade from Petras Kephala.

of consistent force is not guaranteed with each strike and knapping with a metal punch is still prone to slippage and mis-hits that may disrupt a successful blade detachment. Rather, blade technology could not become fully standardized until some sort of core holding device was employed in conjunction with a simple lever mechanism to apply consistent pressure. As such, classic parallel-sided prismatic blades struck from a small tabular core do not become the norm until after the EM I period.

Conclusion

Precisely when a local obsidian pressure-flaked blade industry first manifests itself on Crete remains unclear. What is clearer, thanks to the evidence from Petras Kephala, is that the technology and production of obsidian goes through a period of transition between FN IV and EM I. What distinguishes the obsidian assemblage from Petras Kephala is the co-existence of blade types produced by different mechanisms in both FN IV and EM I contexts.

By EM I blade production becomes standardized to such a degree that blades are near mirror images of each other. The switch to a standardized blade manufacturing process seems to be aided by the use of metal flaking tools, the earliest evidence for which occurs in the FN IV obsidian assemblage. It is suggested here that a key enabling factor in the development of greater standardization is the introduction of metallurgy, specifically, privileged access to metal tools. That said, however, the hand-held pressure method, even assisted by metal tools, cannot on its own entirely eliminate individual variation and replicate proportions on a consistent basis. This can be overcome with a core holding device that incorporates a metal punch or pressure-flaking lever device. In this way, the reduction of obsidian inevitably becomes restricted to those with access to such specialised tools, thus removing access to obsidian technology and tools from general distribution among the community. This process of exclusion by technology seems to begin in FN IV with the arrival of metallurgy.

The restriction of obsidian consumption to specialized and formal tasks is likely to derive from socio-economic factors. In the later Bronze Age, obsidian becomes not only restricted to major sites, but also directly tied to specific authorities within these sites and its role in the realm of socio-political ideology is demonstrated through a conspicuous association with ritual and power (*e.g.*, Carter 2004a). It seems that the beginnings of this trend away from the fulfilment of household tasks can be detected during the crucial transition between FN IV and EM I at Petras Kephala.

Acknowledgements

I would like to thank Yiannis Papadatos, for providing me with the opportunity to analyse the obsidian from Petras Kephala, and Metaxia Tsipopoulou for granting me permission to study obsidian from a number of sites in east Crete. I am also grateful to Valasia Isaakidou and Peter Tomkins for their invitation to participate in the Round Table and this volume and for their encouragement.

Bibliography

Bassiakos, Y., V. Kilikoglou and A. Sampson
  2005   Yali Island: geological and analytical evidence for a new source of workable obsidian. *International Association of Obsidian Studies Bulletin* 33: 18.
Carter, T.
  2003   Problematizing the analysis of obsidian in the Aegean and surrounding worlds. In K. Polinger and R. Laffineur (eds.), *METRON. Measuring the Aegean Bronze Age* (Aegeum 23): 75–82. Liège: University of Liège and University of Texas at Austin.
  2004a Transformative processes in liminal spaces. In G. Cadogan, E. Hatzaki and A. Vasilakis (eds.), *Knossos: Palace, City, State*: 273–82. London: British School at Athens.
  2004b Mochlos and Melos: a special relationship? Creating identity and status in Minoan Crete. In L. P. Day, M. Mook and J. Muhly (eds.), *Crete Beyond the Palaces: Proceedings of the Crete 2000 Conference*: 291–307. Philadelphia: INSTAP Academic Press.
Christopoulou, A.
  1989   The stone tools. In I. Tzedakis and A. Sacconi (eds.), *Scavi a Nerokourou, Kydonias*. Roma: Recherche Greco-Italiane in Creta Occidentale I.

D'Annibale, C.
in press a
    Production and consumption of obsidian in the Siteia Bay Area: Final Neolithic through Late Minoan. In A. Kalokairinos (ed.), *Proceedings of the 9th Cretological Conference.* Herakleion: Society of Cretan Historical Studies.
in press b
    The Minoan obsidian and chipped stone industry connected with the Early Minoan remains and the Middle Minoan I rectangular building at Aghia Photia, Siteia. In M. Tsipopoulou (ed.), *Aghia Photia, Siteia.* Philadelphia: INSTAP Academic Press.
in press c
    The obsidian. In M. Tsipopoulou and E. Hallager (eds.), *The Hieroglyphic Archive of Petras, Siteia.* Danish Institute at Athens.
D'Annibale, C. and D. Long
  2003 Replicating Bronze Age obsidian blade manufacture: towards an assessment of the scale of production during the Minoan period. In K. Polinger and R. Laffineur (eds.), *METRON. Measuring the Aegean Bronze Age* (Aegaeum 23): 425–29. Liège: University of Liège and University of Texas at Austin.
Davaras, C.
  1971 An Early Minoan cemetery at Aghia Photia. *AAA* 4: 392–97.
Day, P. M., D. E. Wilson and E. Kiriatzi
  1998 Pots, labels and people: burying ethnicity in the cemetery at Aghia Photia, Siteias. In K. Branigan (ed.), *Cemetery and Society in the Aegean Bronze Age* (SSAA 1): 133–49. Sheffield: Sheffield Academic Press.
Evans, J. D.
  1964 Excavations in the Neolithic settlement at Knossos, 1957–60. *BSA* 59: 132–240.
  1971 Neolithic Knossos: the growth of a settlement, *PPS* 37: 95–117.
Evely, R. D. G.
  1993 *Minoan Crafts: Tools and Techniques* (SIMA 92). Göteborg: Paul Åström.
Jarman, M. R.
  1972 The obsidian. In P. M. Warren (ed.), *Myrtos. An Early Bronze Age Settlement in Crete*: 326–28. London: Thames and Hudson.
Lawn, B. R. and D. B. Marshall
  1979 Mechanisms of microcontact fracture in brittle solids. In B. Hayden (ed.), *Lithic Use-Wear Analysis*: 63–82. New York: Academic Press.
Papadatos, Y.
  2007 The beginning of metallurgy in Crete: new evidence from the FN–EM I settlement at Kephala Petras, Siteia. In P. M. Day and R. C. P. Doonan (eds.), *Metallurgy in the Early Bronze Age Aegean* (SSAA 7): 154–67. Oxford: Oxbow Books.
Pappalardo, G., A. Karydas, V. La Rossa, P. Militello, L. Pappalardo, F. Rizzo and F. P. Romano
  2003 Provenance of obsidian artefacts from different archaeological layers of Phaistos and Haghia Triada. *Creta Antica* 4: 287–300.
Tomkins, P.
  2007 Neolithic: Strata IX–VIII, VII–VIB, VIA–V, IV, IIIB, IIIA, IIB, IIA and IC Groups. In N. Momigliano (ed.), *Knossos Pottery Handbook: Neolithic and Bronze Age (Minoan)*: 9–48. London: British School at Athens.
Van Horn, D. M.
  1980 Observations relating to Bronze Age blade core production in the Argolid of Greece. *JFA* 7: 487–92.

13

The Final Neolithic (Late Chalcolithic) to Early Bronze Age Transition in Crete and the Southeast Aegean Islands: Changes in Settlement Patterns and Pottery

Krzysztof Nowicki

Knossos and Phaistos have long been regarded as the most important sites for the reconstruction of Neolithic settlement patterns in Crete (Tomkins 2000: 76). Knossos has yielded a long continuous sequence from the first Neolithic settlers to the beginning of the fourth millennium BC (Evans 1964), but the crucial transition between the Neolithic and the beginning of the Bronze Age (*i.e.*, the second half of the fourth millennium BC) is unfortunately poorly recorded at this site (Evans 1994: 19). Phaistos represents a different part of the story. The settlement on the later palatial hill seems to have been abruptly founded in the latter part of the FN (Vagnetti 1972–3), as was a similar site on the summit of the Gortyn acropolis (Vagnetti 1973). The defensible location and scale of Phaistos indicate that its inhabitants either moved from a low lying large settlement (still unknown) with a history similar to Knossos, or that it was settled by a number of families coming from hamlets and individual farms scattered over this part of the Mesara. But what was the reason for such a change in the local settlement pattern, and was it really a local change?

The phenomenon of moving settlements to high hills, during roughly the same period, has been observed elsewhere by Sinclair Hood who explained it with reference to possible security problems (Hood *et al.* 1964: 51; Hood and Warren 1966: 185). Lucia Vagnetti, however, wanted to see the process as connected with climatic changes (Vagnetti 1972–3: 132), but such a hypothesis does not explain the general changes in settlement pattern seen throughout the entire island. In this paper I will show that the transition between the Neolithic and Early Bronze Age in Crete was not smooth and gradual (Vagnetti 1996: 40) and was not restricted to changes in pottery manufacturing and metalworking as has been often argued. Changes in the second half of the fourth millennium BC are most strongly seen in settlement patterns and social structures (Nowicki 1999). A stricter attitude to territorial rights and a greater definition of identity also probably occurred at this time. It will be argued here that this was not an internal process that took place within isolated Cretan communities, but was stimulated by outside influence. It was probably directly attributable to physical intrusion by outsiders and most probably by immigrants arriving in a large number from the east.

The links between the changes in settlement organization in Crete and the situation in the region east of it in the fourth millennium BC are supported by fieldwork undertaken during the last few decades by A. Sampson in the islands of the Dodecanese (Sampson 1987; 1988) and by the author in Crete and its offshore islets (Nowicki 2002). These surveys have shown that a short-lasting population peak in the Dodecanese in the latest Chalcolithic period, contemporary with the late FN in Crete and the Cyclades – the phenomenon, first recorded by Simpson and Lazenby (1973), was followed by an abandonment of sites and depopulation. Quite the opposite pattern is found in Crete, where settlement numbers increased substantially during the last few centuries of the fourth millennium, particularly in the coastal zones. Many of these newly founded sites were located on defensible ridges. In Crete this sudden increase in the quantity of sites marked the beginning of the long-lasting development of Bronze Age communities. Such 'complementary' changes in two neighbouring areas prompt the conclusion that the processes were related to each other and a plausible scenario is that at least some of the Dodecanesian population may have been responsible for the foundation of the latest FN sites in Crete. This hypothetical migration was probably only one element of a much broader movement of west Anatolian people towards the west. The process probably started earlier, but entered a decisive stage during the second half of the fourth millennium. The most important result of the dynamic interaction that took place at that time, between the technologically more advanced and socially more stratified western Anatolian immigrants and the somewhat conservative south and central Aegean islanders, was the foundation of a completely new form of settlement organization and new communication networks. Both elements were essential for the later emergence of Bronze Age societies in Crete and the Cyclades.

The geography of FN and early EM I settlement can only be fully appreciated in the field and the phenomenon will be better understood only when more new evidence is published. The Neolithic settlements at Knossos and Phaistos, however important, cannot answer all the problems related to the transition between the Neolithic and the beginning of the Bronze Age (*e.g.*, Papadatos this volume). Some processes, especially hypothetical migration(s), are better illustrated by the great number of sites that until recently were either unknown or almost completely ignored in general discussions of the period.

Archaeological evidence for this process is now much more substantial than it was a few decades ago, when in 1978 Vagnetti and Belli were able to mention only six open air settlements and five 'undetermined' open air sites (Vagnetti and Belli 1978). However, this evidence is underestimated and often confused, partly because of the lack of a clearly defined chronology and partly because of the unjustified reservations of some scholars about the value of data from

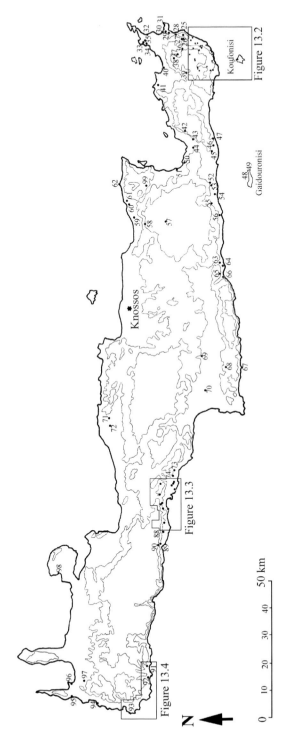

Figure 13.1. Map of Crete showing location of FN sites (defensible settlements only apart from Gaidouronisi and Koufonisi). (1–24: see Figure 13.2); 25. Traostalos; 26. Azokeramos Pentalitro; 27. Azokeramos; 28. Karounes Kastellas; 29. Plakalona; 30. Palaikastro Kastri; 31. Palaikastro Petsofas; 32. Itanos; 33. Cape Mavros; 34. Itanos Alatopatela Site 12; 35. Itanos Site 17; 36. Adravasti Endichti; 37. Magasa Vigli; 38. Palaio Mitato; 39. Kalamafki Kypia; 40. Petras Kefala; 41. Papadiokampos Agios Ioannis; 42. Kavousi Azoria; 43. Monastiraki Katalimata; 44. Vasiliki Kefala; 45. Vainia Stavromenos; 46. Panagia Paplinou Rousso Charakas; 47. Koutsounari Karfi; 48. Gaidouronisi Belegrina Bay; 49. Kataprosopo Bay; 50. Vrokastro; 51. Vathi; 52. Anatoli Pandotinou Korifi; 53. Anatoli Schistra; 54. Myrtos 'Charakas'; 55. Mythoi Kastello; 56. Faflagos; 57. Tzermiado Kastellos; 58. Krasi Armi; 59. Malia Profitis Elias; 60. Milatos Kastello; 61. Milatos; 62. Drepanon; 63. Dermatos Gorge; 64. Dermatos Kastrokefala; 65. Tsoutsouros; 66. Tsoutsouros Mandalos; 67. Lenda Leontari; 68. Apesokari Vigla; 69. Gortyn; 70. Phaistos; 71. Melidoni; 72. Viran Episkopi; 73. Kerannes Tseroni; 74. Drimiskos Agios Georgios; (75–87: see Figure 13.3); 88. Patsianos Kefala; 89. Vraskas Lakoudi; 90. Imbros Gorge; 91. Anydroi Profitis Elias; 92. Palaiochora Nerovolakoi; 93. Chrisoskalitissa; 94. Sfinari Korakas; 95. Phalasarna 'Acropolis'; 96. Kastelli (Trachilos) Selli; 97. Tsikalaria; 98. Stavros Leras; 99. Limnes Kefali.

Figure 13.2. Map of southeast Crete with FN defensible sites.
1. Zakros Kalyvomouri; 2. Zakros Gorge Kato Kastellas; 3. Kefali Agias Paraskevis; 4. Koufotos; 5. Kokkino Froudi; 6. Voukoliades; 7. Schinokefalo; 8. Kastellas Xerokampias; 9. Trachillas; 10. Xerokampos North; 11. Xerokampos Kastri; 12. Xerokampos Amatou (Paranoma, Kastellakia); 13. Agia Irini Kastri; 14. Livari Katharades; 15. Goudouras Kastri; 16. Goudouras Kastello; 17. Goudouras North-West; 18. Agia Triada Petrokopio; 19. Mesa Apidia; 20. Ziros Rizoviglo; 21. Ziros Patela; 22. Lamnoni 'Spilia'; 23. Lamnoni (Branigan's Site 23); 24. Koufonisi.

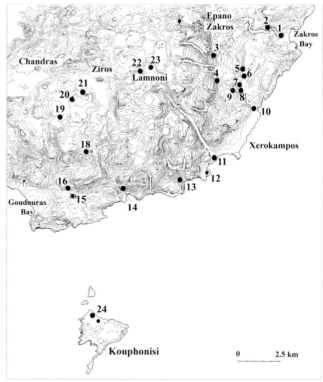

unexcavated sites. Now it is possible to talk of more than 100 well defined open air late FN settlements from just the group of sites with defensible characteristics alone (Figure 13.1; Nowicki 2002; 2004). A great number of these sites are located on the coast and two regions are worthy of special attention for their unusually high concentrations of settlements. The first is the eastern part of the Siteia peninsula (Figure 13.2) and the second is the south coast of the Rethymnon isthmus (Figure 13.3); several smaller clusters extend as far as the western coast between Palaiochora (Figure 13.4) and Phalasarna.

A Final Neolithic Refuge Site at Katalimata

New evidence relevant to the interpretation of changes in settlement pattern in Crete during the FN was revealed by excavations at Katalimata, located on the isthmus of Ierapetra (Nowicki 2002: 16–20; 2008). There can be no doubt that this inaccessible location must have been chosen for security reasons (Figure 13.5). Katalimata is located on rocky ledges, high on the northern cliff of the Cha gorge (ca. 290 m.a.s.l.), a location that is extremely difficult to access, but with excellent visibility over the Ierapetra plain.

Neolithic deposits were recorded at two places on Terrace C. One consisted

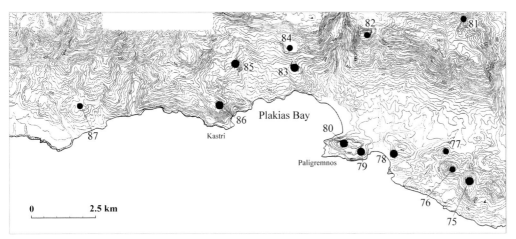

Figure 13.3. Map of the Plakias area with FN defensible sites.
75. Gianniou Plati; 76. Lefkogia Timios Stavros; 77. Lefkogia Modi; 78. Ammoudi Skinias; 79. Damnoni; 80. Plakias Korifi (Paligremnos); 81. Atsipades Korakias; 82. Mirthios Kirimianou; 83. Sellia Kastellos; 84. Sellia Kabana; 85. Sellia Kefala; 86. Sellia Kastri; 87. Argoules Chalepa.

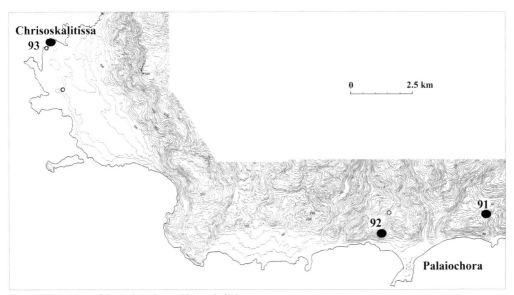

Figure 13.4. Map of the Palaiochora-Chrisoskalitissa area.
91. Anydroi Profitis Elias; 92. Palaiochora Nerovolakoi; 93. Chrisoskalitissa.

of an undisturbed stratum, 0.10–0.25 m in thickness, lying immediately on the bedrock. The soil was mixed with ash, sherds and animal bones. Chipped stone, ground stone and bone tools were also found. The second deposit was recorded in the eastern part of the terrace. Here, only a few tiny particles of charcoal were

Figure 13.5. Monastiraki Katalimata from southwest (C: Terrace C with FN deposits).

noted, pottery was occasional and neither animal bones nor ground stone tools were found (Nowicki 2008).

The pottery from Katalimata represents the native Cretan tradition of the FN, with features dating the site towards the end of that period (Figure 13.6). It is often burnished or polished on the surface, although not so well as the best examples from Knossos and Phaistos, being rather dull and ranging in colour from yellowish brown, through reddish brown, dark red, brown and black. Two sherds are decorated with incised 'seam pattern'. The core is most often dark olive grey to black. Inclusions consist of fine to medium grits of phyllite, sand and very fine white chalk. The shapes are mainly bowls (open, globular, carinated), cups and larger hole-mouthed jars; a few handles are of the strap type. The closest parallels for the Neo-

lithic pottery from Katalimata regarding surface treatment and form come from Knossos Stratum II, the lower stratum at Phaistos and from the surface of several unexcavated sites in the Ierapetra region, such as the rocky knoll of Pandotinou Korifi, south of Anatoli, and Vainia Stavromenos (the earliest material) (Figure 13.7; Todaro and Di Tonto this volume; Tomkins this volume). Although the Neolithic pottery from Katalimata lacks several distinctive elements of the earlier Phaistos FN assemblage, such as incised decoration, encrustation with red ochre, scoring and pattern burnishing it seems that we should place the Katalimata pottery in the period contemporary with the Phaistos and Gortyn material, close to but prob-

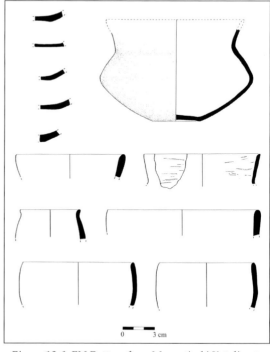

Figure 13.6. FN Pottery from Monastiraki Katalimata.

but probably after the end of the old Knossian 'Late Neolithic' phase (*i.e.*, post-Stratum IIB) and earlier than Nerokourou. It would thus belong to the period labelled by Vagnetti as the 'early stage' of the traditional Cretan FN period. I have suggested elsewhere that this be labelled as FN I (Nowicki 2002) and according to the revised Cretan Neolithic chronology by P. Tomkins this should be labelled FN III (Tomkins this volume; 2007).

The location of Katalimata raises the question of what the reasons were for occupation of such a defensible place in the Neolithic period. Considering the similarities between the Katalimata material and that from Phaistos and Gortyn, we should look for the answer perhaps not in the local situation in the Ierapetra isthmus, but in the circumstances that led to a shift of population to high hills throughout Crete.

The Topography of Late Final Neolithic Settlement

During FN III, Phaistos and Gortyn in the Mesara, like Katalimata and Pando-tinou Korifi in the Ierapetra region, were settlements which continued the Cretan Neolithic tradition. Changes in pottery, however, take place in the next (and final) phase of FN and a non-Cretan origin for some of them must be considered. Among such non-Cretan elements is the so-called 'cheese-pot' – a characteristic type of vessel with holes pierced before firing under the rim – that is diagnostic of Late Chalcolithic 3 and 4 and the transition to the Early Bronze Age all over the Aegean (Atkinson *et al.* 1904: 84; Caskey 1972: 359; Renfrew 1972: 141; Sampson 1984; 1987; Broodbank 2000: 83). The appearance of these vessels in Crete indicates external influence. The type is common at many Cretan coastal sites founded shortly before the beginning of the Bronze Age, that is during the latest FN (Figure 13.8), elsewhere termed FN II (Nowicki 2002) and FN IV according to Tomkins' revised Cretan Neolithic chronology (see Tomkins this volume).

The most characteristic features of these newly founded latest FN (FN IV) settlements in Crete are: (1) their defensibility, (2) their preference for coastal locations and (3) their specific concentration in certain areas, including regions which were marginal for later Bronze Age communities. These may indicate: (1) a serious tension between different groups within the population, (2) a strong orientation towards marine activity, and (3) temporary colonization of the coastal areas without considering their environmental potential to support long-lasting occupation. The latter two factors alone may indicate that the 'colonization' took place from the sea. All these arguments, among other factors, suggest a causal relationship between the establishment of the FN III settlements of Phaistos and Katalimata type and the historical circumstances which preceded and led to the foundation of new sites during FN IV, a selection of which will be presented below.

The appearance of these new settlements can be traced all over Crete, but is

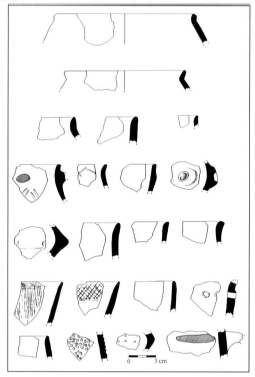

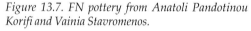

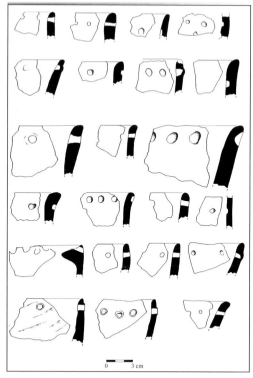

Figure 13.7. FN pottery from Anatoli Pandotinou Korifi and Vainia Stavromenos.

Figure 13.8. 'Cheese-pot' fragments from Cretan FN sites.

most characteristic along the coast with the same or similar patterns of site location occurring between the Palaikastro plain in the far east and the Phalasarna plain in the far west. Study of surface material has allowed the recognition of several new pottery groups. The difference between the old Cretan pottery Neolithic tradition and these new groups can be seen when we compare the pottery from Pelekita, Katalimata, and Pandotinou Korifi, on the one hand, with the Red Ware that dominated along the south coast between Zakros and Phalasarna, on the other. Other types of pottery are more common along the northern coast among which two groups are the most distinctive. The first group, more brown than red, with sandy inclusions and organic temper, is harder than the Red Ware and thus similar to the Late Chalcolithic pottery from the northern and central Dodecanese. The second group, with a large amount of calcareous and marble inclusions, seems to be linked to Cycladic FN–EB I pottery. The latter conclusion is further supported by the occasional (but very rare) appearance of the bowl with rolled rim on the northern coast. This shape, however, is absent or extremely rare along the south coast.

The largest concentration of latest FN sites (FN IV) has been recorded in the East Siteia region. Here all the available bays and other convenient natural

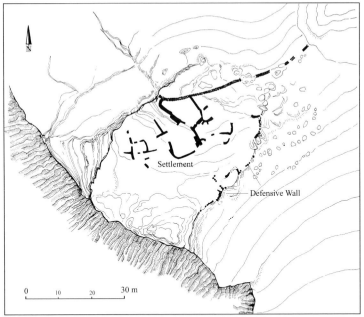

Figure 13.9. Plan of Livari Katharades.

harbours were taken over by new settlements situated in elevated places. The population of the settlements ranged from two or three households to over twenty households. Vokotopoulos has suggested that an average settlement in the Zakros basin was about 0.2 ha but some sites extend over an area of about 0.9 to 1.0 ha (Vokotopoulos 2000: 130). Among the largest are Zakros Gorge Kato Kastellas (ca. 0.8–1.0 ha), Xerokampos Kastri (ca. 0.6–0.8 ha) and Agia Irini Kastri (0.8–1.0 ha). The distribution of pottery, stone tools and in some cases architectural remains indicates that the full extent of the estimated area of these sites was occupied by domestic houses and their dependencies. However, precise numbers of households and forms of spatial organization are difficult to reconstruct because of a lack of comparanda from excavated sites. Many of these settlements were short lasting and much of their architecture was constructed of perishable material without any stone walls visible on the surface. On the other hand substantial stone architecture is preserved at several sites, such as Livari Katharades (see Schlager 1997: 15; 2001: 160), indicating a rather compact and defensive structure for these sites, with houses attached to each other and only small open areas left between individual units (Figure 13.9).

Earlier FN settlement in the coastal region of eastern Crete is characterized by very small sites, representing one or at most a few families, living in more or less temporary houses, as a rule on low hills, coastal terraces and in caves, such as Pelekita (Figure 13.10) on the coast, and Voivoda in an inland valley. The newly founded FN IV sites were larger and as a rule located on defensible ridges on rocky promontories or hills dominating a coastal plain. The natural defensibility of these sites was often complemented with fortification walls (*e.g.*,

Figure 13.10. Pelekita from south (the cave located where path ends).

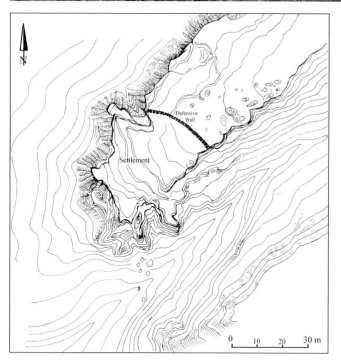

Figure 13.11. Plan of Kokkino Froudi.

Goudouras Kastello, Kokkino Froudi, Xerokampias Kastellas and Alatopatela – Site 12) (Nowicki 1999; Vokotopoulos 2000; Greco *et al.* 2002). The walls (usually 1.0 to 1.3 m thick) were constructed of large boulders, along one or two sides of a settlement, where the access was the easiest. Other sides were either entirely or partly defended by cliffs and very steep slopes (Figure 13.11).

Moving from the north to the south, the following coastal settlements were founded at this time: Palaikastro Kastri, Karoumes Kastellas, Kato Zakros

Figure 13.12. FN settlement in North Xerokampos.

Figure 13.13. Agia Irini Kastri from northwest.

Kalyvomouri, Xerokampos North (Figure 13.12), Xerokampos Kastri, Agia Irini Kastri (Figure 13.13) and Livari Katharades. Immediately behind this coastal zone, FN IV settlements were situated in the gorges which offered convenient communication routes to the inland uplands. In the Zakros Gorge a large FN IV settlement was located on the summit of Kato Kastellas and in the Xerokampias Gorge a small settlement occupied the northern part of the Kastellas ridge, which controlled the northern entrance to the gorge. The easiest point of access to Xerokampias Kastellas from the north was defended by a fortification wall. Close similarities in the topographical characteristics of these and other sites in the East Siteian region indicate that they were founded by groups of people representing the same wave of settlers, arriving at the same time and responding to the same historical circumstances. Karoumes Kastellas and Zakros Kalyvomouri occupied almost identical hills at the entry to the gorges on the edge of small coastal plains with sheltered bays and sandy beaches; Xerokampos North and Xerokampos Kastri lie at the extreme opposite ends of the Xerokampos plain (northeast and southwest), on similar rocky terraces above the gorges; Agia Irini Kastri and Livari Katharades were located on high and steep ridges, above small bays formed by the mouths of gorges.

The changes between the latest FN and early EM I period in the East Siteia peninsula were very dynamic and they are not easy to reconstruct solely on the basis of surveys (Branigan 1998). It seems that the coastal settlements expanded quickly to the interior. The next step in this inland expansion was the Epano Zakros basin where a number of FN IV–EM I sites were identified by Vokoto-poulos (2000). A great number of sites here were founded around the edges of the basin on defensible ridges, protruding from the neighbouring plateaus, and had fortification walls defending their accessible sides. The similar phenomenon of location of sites on defensible rocky ridges and defending them by walls can be also observed in higher inland plateaus. The largest density of sites has been recorded in the Ziros plateau with the FN IV–EM I settlements on Rizoviglo and Patela, on the hills above Mesa Apidi and near Agia Triada (Schlager 2001: 180; Nowicki 2002: 25). The second cluster has been identified in the Lamnoni plateau (Branigan 1998: 57–58; Nowicki 2002: 25–26) and another between Palaio Mitato and Magasa (Nowicki 2002: 21).

The late FN settlement pattern consisted not only of well defined defensive villages, but also of numerous smaller sites representing probably isolated houses and hamlets. Good examples of such sites have been identified by Branigan in the Lamnoni valley (Branigan 1998), and other similar sites were recorded on the road between Ziros and Katelionas, in the valley north of Livari, in the Mesa Apidi plateau, above Mavros Kampos (west of Epano Zakros) and in the Xerolimni-Magasa plateau. The pottery from these latter sites shows more advanced technology (better firing and more careful surface finishing), which points perhaps to an early EM I date. If such a tentative dating is supported by further research, these small dispersed sites might represent the slightly later third phase of settlement expansion (already in early EM I), following upon Phase 1 (initial FN IV coastal 'colonization') and Phase 2 (foundation of hilltop inland settlements). In this model Phase 2, with a large number of extensive sites on the hills dominating the East Siteian plateau, may reflect a short-lasting expansion and concentration of FN population under unstable historical conditions. The density of population between the end of FN and early EM I seems to have exceeded the natural resources of the occupied land and this phenomenon (of large settlements in the East Siteia plateaus) was not repeated again during later prehistoric periods. One may wonder, however, why such limitations were not realized by the FN IV settlers? The later, namely EM I–II and MM patterns, show in the plateaus a larger dispersion of people in small hamlets and individual farmsteads which allowed the land to be exploited in a more efficient way, while on the coast the population was concentrated in a few settlements. The latter phenomenon was probably related to the increasing role of sea-trade. The main EM I–II centres developed at or around the FN IV settlements of Palaikastro Kastri, Karoumes Kastellas and Kato Zakros Kalyvomouri. Smaller settlements continued below the FN IV hilltop sites of Xerokampos Kastri and Livari, but most of the FN IV defensible settlements, such as Zakros Gorge Kato Kastellas, Xerokampias Kastellas, Xerokampos North, and perhaps Agia Irini Kastri disappeared at the end of the FN IV or in the early EM I period. The same phenomenon is recorded in other regions of Crete, as for example in the Ierapetra Isthmus and in western Crete.

Almost nothing is known about FN settlements west of Goudouras; poor evidence of FN presence was recorded around Kalo Nero, but no proper settlement has been yet found in that area. The pattern becomes better visible again in the vicinity of Koutsounari and Ierapetra with two small sites on Karphi above Koutsounari and Rousso Charakas (west of Panagia Paplinou) located according to the same topographical 'rules' as those discussed for the East Siteia region. The main FN–EM I settlement in the Ierapetra district, however, was Vainia Stavromenos (Figure 13.14), which covered an area between 1.0 and 1.2 ha. This site may have played a similar role in shaping the FN–EM I settlement system on the south coast, as Petras Kephala and Mochlos did on the northern coast. Vainia Stavromenos was already inhabited in FN III (contemporary with Monastiraki Katalimata and Anatoli Pandotinou Korifi), but this phase was probably spatially restricted to the rocky knoll where the chapel now stands, whereas by the FN IV and early EM I periods the settlement spread down to extensive terraces to the west and southwest. Similar evidence for continuity in occupation through the FN III and FN IV periods at the same site or on other hills in the close vicinity was noticed in the hilly country between Kendri, Anatoli and Myrtos.

Farther to the west, FN IV defensible settlement continues along the south coast; Dermatos Kastrokefala and Lenda Leontari being among the most important sites. In general, however, the pattern between Ierapetra and Kali Limenes, along the coastal zone of the south Lasithi and Asterousia mountains, is not very clear yet; the number of sites is much lower than in the East Siteia peninsula and no large defensible settlements (such as Zakros Gorge Kato Kastellas and Xerokampos Kastri) have been identified. Instead, numerous small open air sites were recorded on the hills in the valleys which run across the Asterousia mountains between the coast and the Mesara plain (Vasilakis 1989–90).

The coast between Agia Galini and Preveli is mostly steep without large open plains. The landscape changes, however, in the bay of Plakias. Archaeological reconnaissance here has identified a large number of FN sites and indicates that FN IV settlements followed almost exactly the topographical 'rules' as described for the East Siteia peninsula (Figure 13.3): all rocky promontories and imposing hills in the Plakias Bay and the Lefkogia valley were occupied by FN IV sites. The strategic promontories of Paligremnos and Kastri, respectively on the eastern and western side of Plakias Bay, were settled (and probably fortified) at the same time as Zakros Gorge Kato Kastellas, Xerokampos Kastri, Agia Irini Kastri, Livari and Goudouras Kastello. The largest settlements in this area – Gianniou Plati (Figure 13.15) and Sellia Kastello – covered between 0.6 and 0.8 ha), but these were complemented by medium-sized settlements and hamlets

Figure 13.14. Vainia Stav-romenos from north.

Figure 13.15. Gianniou Plati from west.

Figure 13.16. Palaiochora Nerovolakoi from east.

(Ammoudi Skinias). FN IV material, identified by Peatfield and Morris on the peak of Atsipades Korakias (Morris and Batten 2000), may represent a specialized site, located on the edge of the initial 'colonization' area, beyond the massifs north of the Plakias-Lefkogia valley and looking down on the Agios Vasilios valley. A similar site may have been located on the summit of Kirimianou, above Mirthios, which dominates the western part of the same valley. The site was identified only on the basis of chipped chert stone, similar to those at Korakias, but no pottery has been recorded yet (but a similar situation was observed at Atsipades Korakias before the site was excavated).

The westernmost part of Crete is characterized by a few, rather narrow and not very fertile coastal plains. Yet, also here most of the plains and bays were settled by large communities in the same late phase of FN. The largest and probably most important in this part of Crete was Palaiochora Nerovolakoi (ca. 1.0–1.2 ha) (Figures 13.4 and 13.16). The pottery belongs to the Red Ware group, characteristic of the eastern and south coast, but flattened profile wishbone handles, including those of FN III type, seem to be more common here than in eastern Crete (Figure 13.17). The existence of such a large settlement in this area makes little sense considering that arable land is very restricted and poor. The only explanation for the curious foundation of Nerovola-koi might be that the location was chosen by newcomers landing here without much knowledge of the environmental factors. The ridge is the most characteristic landmark when Palaiochora is viewed from the sea. Nerovolakoi, well defended by cliffs on all sides and dominating the coastal strip, would be an ideal place for the first bridgehead after settlers had arrived on the coast, but before they had the chance to learn about the landscape and its resources. Soon after its foundation Nerovolakoi was abandoned and by early EM I its population had become dispersed along the coast to the west and east and into the interior. Never again would a settlement of a similar size as Nerovolakoi be built on the Pal-aiochora coast during the prehistoric periods. During EM I–II the narrow plain west of Palaiochora and the sheltered valley of Anydroi appeared

Figure 13.17. FN Pottery from Palaiochora Nerovolakoi.

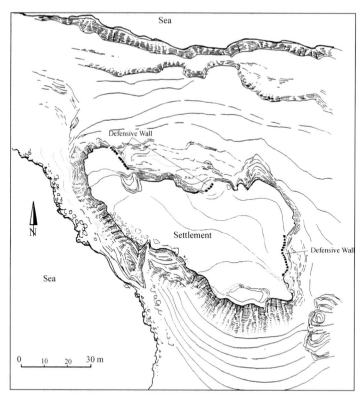

Figure 13.18. Plan of Sfinari Korakas.

to have been more conducive to a stable settlement system based on agriculture and herding.

Three FN IV citadels, similar to the type known from the Siteia region, were identified on the extreme western coast of Crete. The first, located on the summit of the Chrisoskalitissa ridge, is now almost completely destroyed, but sherds and chipped stone leave no room for doubt about its character and date. The general topography of the place and the later development of the settlement call to mind the location and earliest history of Palakaistro Kastri. The rocky ridge of Chrisoskalitissa, like Palaikastro Kastri, may have been only a small defensible 'citadel' that served a larger group of people who had settled on the coastal terrace immediately to the south, on the other side of a little bay. The lower settlement at Chrisoskalitissa developed during the EM I period, probably thanks to its key position in relation to land and sea routes, and went on to become the largest EM and MM site on the western coast (Hood 1965: 101–2).

Further to the north a FN IV site was recorded on the south edge of Sfinari Bay, on the rocky promontory of Korakas (ca. 100 m a. s. l.) (Figure 13.18). The summit of the ridge (ca. 100 m by 20–60 m in size) is covered with pottery of the Palaiochora Nerovolakoi type, basically the same Red Ware group (with 'cheese-pot' fragments) that appears at many similar settlements along the south coast of Crete. The settlement was defended by natural cliffs and a fortification wall, the

Figure 13.19. Phalasarna East Acropolis from southwest.

remains of which can be seen along the northeast and northern edges of the ridge. A similar wall defended the south side of the Phalasarna ridge, where another defensible FN IV settlement was located (Figure 13.19). The Phalasarna East Acropolis exemplifies the topographical characteristics of a FN IV coastal settlement. The ridge is entirely encircled by high cliffs and the site can only be accessed with difficulty from the south. The FN IV pottery, which is of the same type as that recorded at Palaiochora Nerovolakoi and Sfinari Korakas (and similar to the Zakros-Xerokampos group), is still visible along the southern edge of the ridge, despite the fact that the site was intensively used during the Hellenistic period. The same type of pottery as identified at Sfinari Korakas and Phalasarna, perhaps representing the same group of people, was recently identified on a steep slope immediately below the Leras Cave at Stavros (Akrotiri) on the north coast near Chania. This site is at least 60 by 80 m in size and provides evidence for links between the western coast and the area of the north coast in the vicinity of Nerokourou.

First Bridgeheads – Offshore Islands

The evidence presented above suggests the existence of two main groups of defensible sites with different pottery traditions, Phaistos and Katalimata, on one hand, and Zakros Gorge Kato Kastellas and Palaiochora Nerovolakoi, on the other. The first group probably represents the old Neolithic Cretan population,

Figure 13.20. Map of Gaidouronisi showing location of the FN II sites.

Figure 13.21. FN II site on Gaidouronisi from west.

while the second may correspond to immigrants that arrived from beyond Crete and took over all the bays and coastal plains. Unexpected evidence supporting such a reconstruction was found recently on the small islands of Koufonisi and Gaidouronisi (Chrisi) located at a distance of ca. 6 km and 14 km respectively from the south coast of Crete.

On Gaidouronisi a FN IV settlement, much eroded by the sea, was identified on a small promontory that bounds Belegrina Bay on the west (Figures 13.20 and 13.21). Erosion has destroyed most of the original surface, but the exposed bedrock is densely covered with sherds (Figure 13.22). Pottery is concentrated in several clusters which may indicate the position of completely eroded houses. In places the number of sherds exceeds 50 per square metre. Despite the erosion stone constructions are visible at the highest point of the promontory and on the western slope. The site extends over an area of ca. 0.6–7 ha (ca. 100–130 m east-west by 60–80 m north-south). On both sides of the promontory there are sandy beaches that would have allowed boats to land. The southern coast of Crete between Arvi and Koutsounari (with all main landmarks) can clearly be seen from the site; visible also is the coast of the Asterousia to the west and Koufonisi to the east. The pottery is badly eroded by sea water and the original surface has completely worn away. The fabric seems to indicate some sort of relationship with the Red Ware group, but there are even closer similarities with the Dodecanesian group. A small piece of Giali obsidian in one of the sherds is the best indicator of direct links between the site on Gaidouronisi and the area of the central Dodecanese, namely Nisiros, Giali and perhaps southern Kos. The presence of large numbers of 'cheese-pots' further supports the Dodecanesian connection. The second site on Gaidouronisi is located on the eastern coast, on the northern side of the Bay of Kataprosopo. This was a hamlet or a very small settlement, consisting probably of a few houses, which unlike the Belegrina site survived into the early EM I period.

FN IV evidence on Koufonisi is of a different character (Figure 13.2). Several closely-spaced clusters of pottery occur along the northern coast and the site is either of an enormous size (ca. 500 m by 50–80 m) or alternatively there are two sites with several

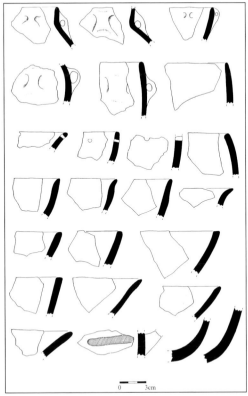

Figure 13.22. Pottery from the FN II (IV) site on Gaidouronisi.

small clusters of pottery between them. The first large concentration of pottery (mixed with MM and LM sherds) is located on high ground on the northern promontory and spreads out to the southeast for a distance of about 200 m. The second main concentration of sherds is situated about 100 m northwest of the chapel and covers an area of at least 0.5 ha. In the southern part of the site (or cluster of sites) the pottery is almost exclusively of the Red Ware type, whereas in the northern part a substantial amount of the sherds belong to the harder Dodecanesian group. The occupation of this part of Koufonisi can be more easily explained if we reconstruct the original shape of the island as it was in the second half of the fourth millennium BC. Most probably, the two little islets that at present extend a few hundred metres to the north were at that time a crescent shaped peninsula, forming a large bay sheltered from northwestern winds. The large size of the site and the quantity of pottery indicate a very substantial number of people living or temporarily residing here in the FN IV period, at the same time as defensible ridges were being suddenly settled on the opposite side of the narrow strip of sea, separating the island from the Cretan coast. Because

Koufonisi is an island too small to support such a large community for a longer period we have to assume that the FN IV settlement was only a temporary phenomenon during a time of dramatic change in the East Aegean.

On both islands (Gaidouronisi and Koufonisi) FN IV sites were located on low coastal terraces without any natural or artificial defences. This prompts the question of why, in the same period, people should have chosen such different locations for their settlements, namely undefended extensive sites on Gaidouronisi and Koufonisi and defensive settlements on the Cretan coast? The most plausible answer must take into consideration the likely geo-political situation in Crete at the time. Crete was a large island with the substantial native population concentrated in a few large centres such as Knossos and Phaistos and dispersed in smaller groups through all geographical zones. It is hard to see how the arrival of new people, arriving probably in substantial numbers, could have occurred without resistance and tension regarding the exploitation and ownership of land. Both sides of any potential conflict had good reasons to feel insecure. The situation on little islets, such as Koufonisi and Gaidouronisi, situated a few miles off the Cretan shore, would have been different. They could not be defended against an enemy coming from the sea, even if they had been temporarily or seasonally occupied before FN IV, a hypothesis that is not yet proven. On the other hand these islets were perfect bridgeheads which could have been used by newcomers as the first temporary sites before a further expansion onto the Cretan coast. A similar role may have been played by other 'habitable' islands around Crete, such as Dionisades, Pseira, Dia and Gavdos.

The Dodecanesian Connection?

These latest FN coastal settlements in Crete must be seen as representing a phenomenon contemporary with the foundation of many latest FN settlements throughout the Cyclades, of which Agia Irini Period I and Paoura on Keos are among the best known (Figure 13.23). Many of these new Cycladic settlements had topographical characteristics similar to the sites in Crete, as exemplified by a small settlement on a rocky ridge at Kampos Komikias on the western coast of Naxos (Figure 13.24) and Agios Ioannis Kastri on Astypalaia. It is less clear, however, if the hilltop sites such as Minoa on Amorgos and Chora on Ios belonged to the same group of possible immigrants or represented, like Katalimata in Crete, the earlier population of those islands.

When analyzing the phenomenon of latest FN settlement in Crete, special attention has to be paid to the islands of the Dodecanese, where a great number of Late Chalcolithic 3 and 4 sites have been identified by Simpson and Lazenby (Simpson and Lazenby 1973) and more recently by Sampson (Sampson 1987) (Figure 13.25). However, the problem of Late Chalcolithic 3–4 (late FN) defensible sites in the Dodecanese requires more field research. The site of Kastri on Astypalea

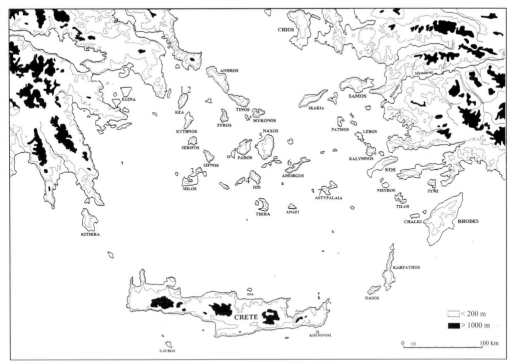

Figure 13.23. (above) Map of the South Aegean. 1. Ag. Irini on Kea, 2. Paoura on Kea, 3. Phylakopi on Milos, 4. Chora Kastri on Ios, 5. Kampos Komikianos on Naxos, 6. Minoa on Amorgos, 7. Ag. Ioannis Kastri on Astypalaia.

Figure 13.24. (left) Kampos Komikias on Naxos.

has topographical characteristics very similar to Cretan coastal sites. The same can be said about three sites on Symi: Pedi Gria (Figure 13.26), Chora Kastro and the site south of and above Panormitis, which is different from that on the northern promontory of the same bay (Sampson 1987: fig. 60). The easiest points of access to Pedi Gria and Panormitis were defended by walls which call to mind the defensive constructions identified at FN IV settlements on Crete. On Tilos a defensible site at Livadia Faneromeni (Figure 13.27), defended by cliffs and

Figure 13.25. The Dodecanese with the FN sites mentioned in the text. KASOS: 1. The site south of the Airport, 2. Chelatros; KARPATHOS: 1. Finiki, 2. Moulas, 3. Leftoporos, 4. Ag. Theodoros, 5. Gigla, 6. Vouno; TILOS: 1. Livadia Faneromeni, 2. Chora Kastri; SYMI: 1. Panormitis, 2. Pedi Gria, 3. Chora; KOS: 1. The site near Ag. Stefanos; KALYMNOS: 1. Chrysocheroi, 2. Vathy; LEROS: 1. Partheni.

probably also partly by a wall, dominated the southern part of the coastal plain. Some sites were located at a slightly greater distance from the sea, but also on hills or rocks dominating their immediate vicinity (*e.g.*, Chrysocheroi on Kalymnos), others were founded on small islands that offered scarcely any agricultural hinterland, such as Kastri on Alimnia and a series of sites on Giali (Sampson 1987). Settlements were also located on more gently-sloping hills (*e.g.*, Astypalaia Vai), low promontories and coastal plains (*e.g.*, Partheni on Leros).

This period is also well represented on the two Dodecanesian islands nearest to Crete: Karpathos and Kasos (Melas 1985; pers. comm.). The site on the rocky promontory of Moulas on Kasos (Figure 13.28) (Nowicki 2004: 97) must have been founded at that time, but it is unusual in that occupation continued into the EB I and II periods. Its location calls to mind the topography of Palaikastro Kastri. Some of the FN defensible sites on Karpathos were defended by walls, as is indicated by poor remains of such constructions at Afiartis Gigla and Afiartis Vouno (Melas 1985; pers. comm.). Sites along the western coast of Kasos appear to have a slightly different character. Here the wide coastal strip, stretching for at least 3 km (between the airport and the southern edge of the coastal plain), is densely scattered with Red Ware of a type identical to that characteristic of eastern and southern Crete. The sites must represent extensive but rather short-lasting occupation (individual

Figure 13.26. Pedi Gria on Symi from northwest.

Figure 13.27. Livadia Faneromeni on Tilos from southwest.

Figure 13.28. Moulas on Karpathos from northwest.

houses, hamlets, small settlements) located close to the sea without any concern about security. The topographical situation is identical with that recorded on the northern coast of Koufonisi (see above). The most plausible interpretation of this choice of site location is, like Koufonisi, that the entire area was temporarily occupied by a large number of people that were on their way somewhere else, most probably to Crete. The site of Trapeza on the Chelatros Bay in the southern part of Kasos (Melas 1985: 46) must have been founded in the Late Chalcolithic (FN) period, but has occupation continuing into EB I. A few sherds from this site exhibit similarities with the material from Vainia Stavromenos.

An interesting difference between Crete and the Dodecanese, however, is the fact that, whereas in Crete (and the Cyclades) the appearance of a large number

Figure 13.29. Pottery from the Dodecanese (D) and Crete (C). D 1: Partheni on Leros (after Sampson 1987, Figure 128); D 2: the site near Ag. Stefanos on Kos; D 3: Panormitis on Symi; D 4 and D 5: Pedi Gria on Symi; D 6 and D 7: the site near Ag. Stefanos on Kos; D 8: Kalythies on Rhodes (after Sampson 1987: fig. 25); C 1: Ag. Paraskevi (Zakros); C 2: Xerokampos Kastri; C 3: Livari Katharades; C 4: Dermatos Kastrokefala; C 5: Xerokampos Kastri; C 6: Ag. Irini.

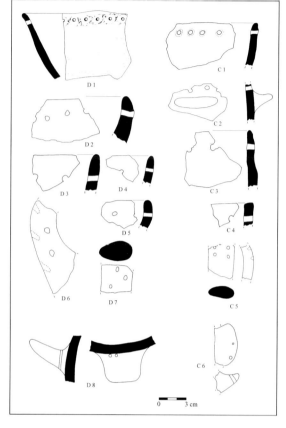

of new FN IV sites marked the beginning of substantial population growth that continued through EB I–II, the Late Chalcolithic 3–4 population peak in the Dodecanese is followed by a sudden drop in the number of settlements, probably indicating considerable depopulation. The situation on Karpathos may have been somewhat different, but here EB I–II sites still have defensible characteristics. This may by another important argument in favour of migration from western Anatolia and the Dodecanese towards Crete. The similarities between the pottery of the Cretan and Dodecanesian sites must be seen as very meaningful in this context (Figures 13.29 and 13.30).

Summary

I have argued elsewhere that the widespread shift of settlement to higher and more defensible hills throughout Crete and the foundation of new sites along the Cretan coast are linked processes (Nowicki 2002). Settlements of the Phaistos and Katalimata types may have anticipated (in FN III) the coastal sites of Xerokampos Kastri and Palaiochora Nerovolakoi type (in FN IV). FN III and FN IV pottery might be seen as partly overlapping and the differences between FN III and FN IV pottery may reflect not only a chronological sequence, but also the different origins of the pottery producers. Sites of the Phaistos and Katalimata type were probably founded by Cretans looking for security at a time when interaction with the outside world, rather than internal problems, forced them to

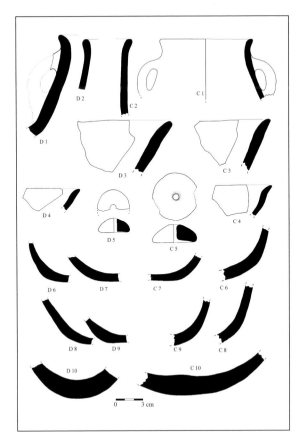

Figure 13.30. Pottery from the Dodecanese (D) and Crete (C). D 1 and D 2: Kastro on Alimnia (after Sampson 1987: fig. 105); D 3: Panormitis on Symi; D 4 and D 5: Pedi Gria on Symi; D 6: Partheni on Leros (after Sampson 1987: fig. 120); D 7: Koumelo on Rhodes (after Sampson 1987: fig. 88); D 8 and D 9: Partheni on Leros (after Sampson 1987: fig.120); D 10 Koumelo on Rhodes (after Sampson 1987: fig. 87). C 1 and C 2: Dermatos Kastrokefala; C 3: Ag. Irini; C 4: Gaidouronisi; C 5: Palaiochora Nerovolakoi; C 6: Ag. Irini; C 7: Livari; C 8 and C 9: Gaidouronisi; C 10: Palaiochora Nerovolakoi.

move to better-defended locations. The newcomers that settled in the coastal areas, in particular along the eastern and southern coasts, did not feel safe either and looked for defensible promontories or rocky 'acropoleis' above coastal plains and bays. The two types of site represent two stages of a historical process of conflict between the local Cretan Neolithic population and their Chalcolithic neighbours coming from the east. Unstable settlement and signs of conflicts, as recorded on the Dodecanesian islands, are indications that the problems were coming probably from the Anatolian coast. This new population element must have consisted of several different groups, a situation that can be reconstructed from different types of pottery. Southern Crete was dominated by the Red Ware group, the development of which shows direct links with later painted EM I pottery. Similar pottery was recorded in the south Dodecanese, in particular Karpathos and Kasos, but also Rhodes and Symi. However, Red Ware in the south Dodecanese is commonly found together with pottery showing a north Dodecanesian influence (as represented for example by fabrics with glassy quartz). The northern coast of Crete yields more evidence for ceramic links with the north and central Dodecanese and Cyclades. Early Minoan cultural differentiation in Crete may have been due to the complexity of the population structure that emerged during the crucial period of the latest FN (Betancourt 1999; Hayden 2003). Analysis of settlement patterns and how they change together with evidence for pottery differentiation allow four main elements of population to be proposed: (1) a native Neolithic Cretans, (2) a Red Ware group which seems to be particularly strong in eastern and southern Crete, (3) a northern and central Dodecanesian group, well represented now at Kephala Petras and several other coastal regions in northeast Crete. At Petras, however, this latter group may have been eventually replaced by a group close to or identical with the later phase of the Red Ware group (see Papadatos this volume), and (4) a group related to the earliest phase of the Pelos culture in the Cyclades, identifiable in some pockets along the northern coast with occasional links traceable as far as Chrisoskalitissa in the far west. All the groups share some similar characteristics in their material culture and had probably been in contact long before the process of dramatic settlement change started in the Aegean. The most enigmatic seems to be the Red Ware group and particularly its interaction with the very strong native element in the Mesara. The number and size of sites suggest that their inhabitants could not just come from the Dodecanese, but had to derive also from the Anatolian mainland. The archaeological evidence presented above, supports Peter Warren's earlier hypothesis of 'some movement of people into Crete from the west Anatolian region to join the Late Neolithic population at the end of the fourth millennium and beginning of the third' (Warren 1973: 43), and Sinclair Hood's idea that 'Early Minoan IA reflected the coming of immigrants' (Hood 1990a; 1990b: 368).

In a chronological sense the Cretan Neolithic could be said to end with the FN III period, while FN IV could be seen as the beginning of a new era in a social and economic development that more or less smoothly continued through the EM I period. Although analysis of settlement patterns does not provide a complete picture, it is certainly more relevant to the problem than the hitherto more usual analyses of tombs and their contents. The locations of many of these sites are strongly orientated towards the sea and defensibility was clearly a serious concern. These two facts tell us something about the character of the inhabitants of these settlements. After colonization in FN IV the settlement pattern underwent substantial changes during the early EM I period. This led to a better exploitation of natural resources and better control of the hinterland. Tensions between different groups in Crete and beyond the island continued at least for a time into EM I, but the development of a new form of social organization and a new political system was already under way. This created the conditions for more stable settlement, at least in some areas and particularly along the northern coast.

Acknowledgements

I would like to thank the organizers of the conference for the invitation to speak and other members of the Department, in particular Umberto Albarella, for their excellent hospitality in Sheffield. I am much obliged to the directors of the Chalasmenos Project, Metaxia Tsipopoulou and the late Wiliam Coulson, for their invitation to participate, which allowed me to excavate at Katalimata. Yiannis Papadatos, Simona Todaro, Peter Tomkins and Manolis Melas kindly shared with me their knowledge of the material from Petras, Phaistos, Knossos and Karpathos; Saro Wallace and Peter Tomkins helped with editing the English.

Bibliography

Atkinson, T., R. Bosanquet, C. Edgar, A. J. Evans, D. Hogarth, D. Mackenzie, C. Smith and F. Welch
  1904 *Excavations at Melos.* London: Macmillan.
Betancourt, P.
  1999 What is Minoan? FN/EM I in the Gulf of Mirabello region. In P. Betancourt, V. Karageorghis, R. Laffineur and W.-D. Niemeier (eds.), *MELETEMATA. Studies in Aegean Archaeology Presented to Malcolm H. Wiener as he Enters his 65th Year* (*Aegaeum* 20): 33–41 Liège: University of Liège.
Branigan, K.
  1998 Prehistoric and early historic settlement in the Ziros region, eastern Crete. *BSA* 93: 23–90.
Broodbank, C.
  2000 *An Island Archaeology of the Early Cyclades.* Cambridge: Cambridge University Press.
Caskey, J.
  1972 Investigations in Keos. Part II: A conspectus of the pottery. *Hesperia* 41: 357–401.
Evans, J. D.
  1964 Excavations in the Neolithic settlement of Knossos 1957–60: Part I. *BSA* 59: 132–240.
  1994 The early millennia: continuity and change in a farming settlement. In D. Evely, H. Hughes-Brock and N. Momigliano (eds.), *Knossos, a Labyrinth of History. Papers Presented in Honour of Sinclair Hood*: 1–20. London: British School at Athens.
Greco, E., Th. Kalpaxis, N. Papadakis, A. Schnapp and D. Viviers
  2002 Travaux menés en collaboration avec l'École Française en 2001. Itanos (Crète orientale). *BCH* 126: 577–82.
Hayden, B.
  2003 Final Neolithic–Early Minoan I/IIA settlement in the Vrokastro area, Eastern Crete. *AJA* 107: 363–412.
Hood, M. S. F.
  1965 Minoan sites in the far west of Crete. *BSA* 60: 99–114.
  1990a Settlers in Crete *c.* 3000 B.C. *Cretan Studies* 2: 151–58.
  1990b Autochthons or Settlers ? Evidence for immigration at the beginning of the Early Bronze Age in Crete. *Pepragmena tou ST' Diethnous Kritologikou Synedriou* A1: 367–75. Chania: Philologikos Syllogos o Chrysostomos.
Hood, M. S. F., P. M. Warren and G. Cadogan
  1964 Travels in Crete. *BSA* 59: 50–99.
Hood, M. S. F. and P. M. Warren
  1966 Ancient sites in the province of Ayios Vasilios, Crete. *BSA* 61: 163–91.
Melas, E.
  1985 *The Islands of Karpathos, Saros and Kasos in the Neolithic and Bronze Age* (SIMA 68). Göteborg: Paul Äström.
Morris, C. and V. Batten
  2000 Final Neolithic pottery from the Atsipades peak sanctuary. *Pepragmena H' Diethnous Kritilogikou Synedriou*: 373–82. Herakleion: Etaireia Kritikon Istorikon Meleton.
Nowicki, K.
  1999 The Final Neolithic refugees or the Early Bronze Age newcomers? The problem of defensible sites in Crete in the late fourth millennium BC. In P. Betancourt, V.

Karageorghis, R. Laffineur and W.-D. Niemeier (eds.), *MELETEMATA. Studies in Aegean Archaeology Presented to Malcolm H. Wiener as he Enters his 65th Year (Aegaeum 20)*: 575–81. Liège: University of Liège.

2002   The end of the Neolithic in Crete. *Aegean Archaeology* 6: 7–72.

2004   Report on investigations in Greece. XI. Studies in 1995–2003. *Archeologia Warsaw* 55: 75–100.

2008   *Monastiraki Katalimata: Excavation of a Cretan Refuge Site, 1993–2000.* Philadelphia: INSTAP Academic Press.

Renfrew, C.

1972   *The Emergence of Civilisation.* London: Methuen.

1996   Who were the Minoans? Towards the population history of Crete. *Cretan Studies* 5: 10–27.

Sampson, A.

1984   The Neolithic of the Dodecanese and the Aegean Neolithic culture. *BSA* 79: 239–49.

1987   *H Neolithiki Periodos sta Dodekanisa.* Athens: Tameio Archaiologikon Poron kai Apallotrioseon.

1988   *H Neolithiki Katoikisi sto Yiali tis Nisyrou.* Athens: Evoiki Archaiophilos Etaireia.

Schlager, N.

1997   Minoische bis rezente Ruinen im fermen Osten Kretas. *Jahresheften des Österreichischen Archäologischen Institutes* 66: 2–83.

2001   Plaistozäne, neolitische, bronzezeitliche und rezente Befunde und Ruinen im fernen osten Kretas. *Jahresheften des Österreichischen Archäologischen Institutes in Wien* 70: 157–220.

Simpson, R. H. and J. F. Lazenby

1973   Notes from the Dodecanese III. *BSA* 68: 127–70.

Tomkins, P.

2000   The Neolithic period. In D. Huxley (ed.), *Cretan Quests. British Explorers, Excavators and Historians*: 76–85. London: British School at Athens.

2007   Neolithic: Strata IX–VIII, VII–VIB, VIA–V, IV, IIIB, IIIA, IIB, IIA and IC Groups. In N. Momigliano (ed.), *Knossos Pottery Handbook: Neolithic and Bronze Age (Minoan)*: 9–48. London: British School at Athens.

Vagnetti, L.

1973   Tracce di due insediamenti neolitici nel territorio dell'antica Gortina. *Anticita cretesi. Studi in Onore di Doro Levi*:1–9. Catania: Università di Catania, Istituto di Archeologia.

1972–3   L'insediamento neolitico di Festòs. *ASA* 50–51: 7–138.

1996   The Final Neolithic: Crete enters the wider world. *Cretan Studies* 5: 29–40.

Vagnetti, L. and P. Belli

1978   Characters and problems of the Final Neolithic in Crete. *SMEA* 19: 125–63.

Vasilakis, A.

1989–90 Proistorikes theseis sti Moni Odhigitrias, Kaloi Limenes. *Kritiki Estia* 3: 11–80.

Vokotopoulos, L.

2000   Ochires protominoikes theseis stin periochi Zakrou. *Pepragmena H' Diethnous Kritilogikou Synedriou*: 129–46. Herakleion: Etaireia Kritikon Istorikon Meleton.

Warren, P. M.

1973   Crete 3000–1400 B.C.: immigration and the archaeological evidence. In R. A. Crossland and A. Birchall (eds.), *Bronze Age Migrations in the Aegean. Archaeological and Linguistic Problems in Greek Prehistory* (Proceedings of the First International Colloquium on Aegean Prehistory, Sheffield): 41–50. London: Duckworth.

14

Between a Rock and a Hard Place: Coping with Marginal Colonisation in the Later Neolithic and Early Bronze Age of Crete and the Aegean

Paul Halstead

In a highly influential series of early papers, Andrew Sherratt emphasised that the spread of farming in Europe entailed not only the initial expansion to west and north of the 'agricultural frontier', but also the subsequent, long-term infilling of the landscape. While early farming sites tended to concentrate in lowland areas with rich and tractable soils, later infilling took farming to higher altitudes with a shorter growing season and to poorer or less tractable soils (Sherratt 1972; 1980; 1981). The latter process of 'marginal colonisation', he argued, both stimulated and was enabled by a range of innovations in residential patterns (Sherratt 1990), in farming methods and strategies (Sherratt 1981), in the scale and significance of regional and inter-regional exchange (Sherratt 1976; 1982) and, more indirectly, in craft production and cultures of consumption (Sherratt 1987; 1997; 1999). Of these suggested innovations, Andrew's name is perhaps most strongly associated with his model of a 4–3 millennium BC 'secondary products revolution' (hereafter 'SPR'), in which the ox-drawn ard facilitated extensive cultivation of infertile soils, progressive forest clearance enabled the maintenance of larger herds, milking and wool-gathering provided farmers in marginal locations with exchangeable products, and the (later) acquisition of pack-horses and donkeys facilitated long-distance trade. Arguably as significant as these various models, however, was the underlying heuristic ploy of exploring the problems posed by occupation of agriculturally marginal areas and the responses to these problems adopted by prehistoric communities.

The following paper explores approaches to understanding marginal colonisation in the later Neolithic and Early Bronze Age of Crete and the Aegean. Despite the distinctive nature of the Neolithic of the 'big island' or *megalonisos*, Crete has much in common with the wider Aegean – especially southern Aegean – in terms both of the evidence for marginal colonisation and of the models adopted for its interpretation. To facilitate comparison on a regional scale, this paper uses Tomkins' 'mainland-friendly' chronological labels for the Cretan Neolithic (Tomkins this volume).

The debt to Andrew Sherratt's work will be evident below both in the argument developed and in the writings of other scholars that are reviewed. An oral version of this paper was delivered in January 2006, at the first Sheffield Aegean Round Table attended by Andrew as a member of staff of the host department. I imagined that I was embarking on a dialogue that would be long and fruitful – not least because Andrew was so excited about results of his collaborative research into milk residues in Neolithic ceramics from Greece (*e.g.*, Kotsakis *et al.* in press) and elsewhere. After brief exchanges, we postponed more serious discussion to a later meeting that sadly never took place.

Marginal Colonisation in Crete and the Aegean?

As elsewhere in Europe, known earlier Neolithic settlements in Greece and the Aegean are distributed very unevenly, with a strong bias towards the traditional 'bread-basket' plains and rolling hills of the north and east-central mainland – especially Thessaly (Theocharis 1973; Wijnen 1982; Andreou *et al.* 1996; Perlès 2001: 113–20). Known sites of this date are rare in the northwest and southern mainland, and in the islands of the Aegean where they are largely restricted to the bigger landmasses such as Crete. Apparent examples of subsequent marginal colonisation include LN infilling of the southern Larisa plain in Thessaly (Halstead 1984), LN–EB occupation of progressively smaller Aegean islands (Cherry 1981; 1990; Broodbank 1999), (LN/)FN and/or EB proliferation of sites in the southern mainland (Phelps 1975; Douzougli 1996a; Whitelaw 2000) and on Crete (Watrous 1994; Nowicki 2002; Tomkins this volume) and other islands (*e.g.*, Broodbank 1989; Broodbank and Kiriatzi 2007), and LB–EIA evidence for widespread occupation of the mountainous northwest of Greece (Kilian 1973; Halstead 1991; Douzougli 1996b; Douzougli and Zachos 2002).

Again mirroring a pattern that has attracted attention in other parts of Europe (*e.g.*, Shennan 1986), marginal colonisation in Greece and the Aegean was apparently accompanied by shifts in the size, longevity and form of occupation sites. In the central and northern mainland, many earlier Neolithic settlements, such as Sesklo and Argissa in Thessaly and Nea Nikomedia in central Macedonia, formed or developed into compact (0.5–2 ha) and long-lived village communities that left behind very visible *magoules* or *tells* with stratigraphic sequences spanning much of the Neolithic (*e.g.*, Theocharis 1973). At Knossos on Crete (Evans 1971; Whitelaw 2004; Tomkins this volume) and at Kouphovouno and a few other sites in the southern mainland (Johnson 1996; Mee 2001), apparently more isolated early villages were also long-lived but may have grown to a larger size (>2 ha). The more recently recognized 'flat-extended' sites, such as EN Revenia-Korinou (Besios and Adaktylou 2006) and EN Giannitsa B (Chrysostomou 1994) in central Macedonia, perhaps represent less compact settlements than the *tell* sites and are certainly less prominent in the landscape, but may likewise have housed some form of local 'village' community.

By contrast with these relatively large and often long-lasting early farming villages, marginal colonisation tends to be represented by smaller and shorter-lived sites. In Thessaly, several LN foundations in the southern Larisa plain take the form of smaller 'hamlets' (≤0.5 ha), more closely spaced than the earlier villages (Halstead 1984). In the central Aegean Cyclades, a few LN settlements matched in size the early farming villages of the central and northern mainland (Broodbank 1999), but most of the far more numerous FN and EB sites seem to have been much smaller, perhaps sheltering no more than a few families, and again were often short-lived. In different parts of the southeast mainland, settlement expanded beyond the early villages, perhaps in LN and especially in FN or EB (Johnson 1996; Cavanagh 1999; Whitelaw 2000), and is best known from small and ephemeral surface scatters encountered in intensive field survey. On central Crete, a handful of LN sites is known beyond Knossos, but widespread occupation of the west, centre and east of the island is first evident in the numerous late FN sites, often small and short-lived, that have been located by a combination of intensive survey and extensive reconnaissance (Watrous 1994; Branigan 1999; Nowicki 2002; this volume; Tomkins this volume). The contrast between EN–MN and LN–EB settlement patterns is reinforced when evidence for use of caves, as well as open-air sites, is considered. While EN–MN activity is documented at very few caves (*e.g.*, Theopetra in Thessaly – Kyparissi-Apostolika 1999; Franchthi in the southeastern mainland – Jacobsen 1981), evidence for LN–EB use of caves is abundant – especially in the southern mainland and islands (*e.g.*, Diamant 1974; Watrous 1994) – and so broadly replicates, temporally and spatially, the evidence from open-air sites for belated 'marginal' expansion. While some caves have yielded assemblages not obviously different from those at open-air habitation sites (*e.g.*, Zachos 1999), others seem to have been used for mortuary or ritual purposes (*e.g.*, Demoule and Perlès 1993:404; Papathanasiou 2001; Tomkins in press). Both categories (or both interpretations), however, suggest belated colonisation of the more rugged parts of the southern Aegean.

Before attempting to interpret these apparently related patterns of marginal colonisation and of more dispersed and less stable settlement, the possibility must be considered that they are artefacts of the demonstrably uneven survival and investigation of the archaeological record. To begin with problems of uneven survival, rising sea level has doubtless drowned many EN–MN and perhaps LN *coastal* sites (Lambeck 1996 – the rate of rise slows dramatically from the fifth millennium BC) and so might account for the apparent paucity of early farming settlement on small islands (Theocharis 1973: 57). In the case of a large island such as Crete, however, the rising sea level invaded a relatively small proportion of the total land surface during the 7–5 millennia BC and so does not account for the present rarity of pre-FN sites. A problem of more general relevance is the burial of low-lying sites by alluvium and destruction of others upslope by erosion, but why should these processes have *selectively* affected long-lived early villages in southern Greece and/or smaller and more ephemeral LN–EB sites in the east-central and northern mainland? The argument that Neolithic farmers triggered intensive erosion and alluviation in Thessaly earlier than in the southern mainland (van Andel *et al.* 1990) might conceivably lead to such regional differences in the age of lost sites, but as a side-effect of belated 'marginal' colonisation of the southern Aegean. Anyway, the dating evidence for these geoarchaeological generalisations is as yet slender (Endfield 1997) and more detailed studies in central Macedonia suggest considerable local variability in the chronology of erosion and alluviation (Krahtopoulou 2000; pers. comm.) that would be expected to blur, rather than create the illusion of, regional contrasts in settlement pattern.

Turning to problems of uneven investigation, most intensive survey projects have been carried out in southern Greece (*e.g.,* Rutter 1993) and many of the known long-lived *tell* villages of east-central and northern Greece were located by extensive reconnaissance. Intensive pedestrian survey in the Langadas basin of Central Macedonia (Andreou *et al.* 1996), however, did not identify the numerous small later Neolithic or EB sites so typical of the southern Aegean and nor do differences in field methodology account for the scarcity of prominent *tell* villages in the latter region. Conversely, in different parts of the southern Aegean, intensive survey (*e.g.,* Cavanagh 1999; Broodbank and Kiriatzi 2007) and extensive reconnaissance (*e.g.,* Howell 1970; Blackman and Branigan 1977; Broodbank 1999) have each suggested a broadly similar picture of dispersed LN–EB settlement. Different periods of occupation are also more or less amenable to archaeological detection, depending on the durability and distinctiveness of their artefacts – especially the most abundant ceramics. For example, early EN occupation is probably under-reported from surface surveys, because the repertoire of ceramic shapes is narrow and simple and decoration is rare (Halstead 1984). MN ceramics are highly distinctive throughout the eastern mainland, however, and their rarity in the southern mainland is thus unlikely to be due to failures of identification. On the other hand, FN ceramics are rarely decorated and so should be vulnerable to non-recognition (cf. Rutter 1983), but have been very widely reported in southern Aegean survey and reconnaissance projects.

In practice, of course, the extant record of settlement distributions has been shaped by a synergy of uneven survival and uneven investigation. For example, on the basis of intensive survey in the Boiotia region of east-central Greece, it has been argued that early sites have been so attenuated by taphonomic processes that scarce surviving artefacts are only recovered in the context of the hyper-intensive collection of surface material from richer and thus more visible sites of later date (Bintliff *et al.* 1999; Bintliff 2005). The Neolithic landscape of Boiotia, it is further suggested, included large numbers of hitherto unrecognised early sites of small dimensions and short duration (Bintliff *et al.* 2006). Likewise, at Knossos, stone axes and mineral inclusions in ceramics provide indirect evidence of human activity in the Mirabello area of east Crete (Tomkins and Day 2001; Strasser this volume) pre-dating that registered in the present site record. These finds may indicate the existence in east Crete of permanent early settlements that are buried or eroded or simply undiscovered. Alternatively, they may reflect ephemeral Knossian exploration of other parts of the island. The extant settlement record is plainly incomplete and it is inherently likely that small early sites have been lost in Boiotia and elsewhere, perhaps including east Crete. The point at issue here, however, is whether earlier Neolithic settlement was *relatively* dense in the east-central and northern mainland and *relatively* sparse elsewhere and whether the initially 'unpopular' southern Aegean was widely occupied by a rash of LN–EB sites that tended to be *relatively* small and short-lived. There is as yet no compelling reason to attribute this apparent contrast in settlement patterns to uneven site survival and/or archaeological investigation (also Davis 2004). On the contrary, the evidence from caves – which are easier to locate than small open-air sites and also provide very different taphonomic contexts – strongly supports the picture of a massive LN–EB expansion of human activity in the southern Aegean. Indeed, even in Boiotia, the emerging evidence of 'hidden' sites is interpreted as evidence for later Neolithic-EB expansion of settlement onto drier interfluves from the well-watered valleys favoured in the earlier Neolithic (Bintliff *et al.* 2006).

Marginality

To what extent were regions such as the southern Aegean and northwest mainland Greece 'marginal' for early farmers, other than in the circular sense of having sparse or no trace of human occupation in the earlier Neolithic? Marginality, in the sense of a region being relatively unsuitable for human occupation, must be assessed contextually (an issue also discussed by Stellatou 2006) – relative to particular forms of land use, levels of intra- and inter-regional integration, and so on. Available Neolithic and Bronze Age assemblages of animal bones (*e.g.*, Payne 1985; Halstead 1996) and seeds (Hansen 1988; Halstead 1994: 204–5, table 1; Valamoti 2007: 92–93, table 6.1) are overwhelmingly dominated by the remains of domesticates and the scarcity of evidence for hunting or gathering of wild resources is particularly marked at EN and MN villages. The balance of reliance on livestock and crops is less easy to assess directly, but taxonomic, biometric, dental microwear and palynological evidence suggests that domestic animals were reared in modest numbers, while mortality data suggest that they were not managed to enhance milk production and so to maximise their potential contribution to human diet (Halstead 1996; 2000). For basic ecological reasons, livestock are anyway – other things being equal – less productive than grain crops per unit land area (*e.g.*, Legge 1981) and so dietary dependence primarily on staple grain crops is particularly likely for earlier Neolithic village settlements. It has been suggested that these early farmers took advantage of naturally irrigated and fertilised flood plains to grow crops (Sherratt 1980; van Andel and Runnels 1995; Bintliff *et al.* 2006), but many early sites are located in very different environmental settings (Wilkie and Savina 1997) and anyway the timing of floods is often too late to be compatible with Old World grain crops. A few early villages are located close to perennial springs (Johnson 1996), which provide more manageable sources for artificial irrigation, and opportunistic watering of grain plots in dry years may have been locally important to survival, but it seems inevitable that early farmers in the Aegean were overwhelmingly dependent on *rain-fed* cultivation.

Early farming villages, concentrated in the traditional wheat-growing lowlands of the east-central and northern mainland (Renfrew 1972: 272, fig. 15.2), seem to have occupied a favourable environment for grain-based subsistence. Recent land use is a product of historical contingency (notably patterns of land tenure and dependence on markets) as well as of climate and soils (*e.g.,* Vergopoulos 1975; Psikhogios 1987), however, and so does not suffice to demonstrate that other parts of Greece and the Aegean would have been marginal for Neolithic grain producers. Nonetheless, much of the southeast mainland, eastern Crete and the Cyclades must always have been relatively marginal for farmers dependent on staple grain crops, because rainfall is both low (close to the minimum for most Old World cereals and pulses) and variable. Of course climate has not remained unchanged over the millennia under discussion here, but the nature of the inevitable changes is unclear: there is no reason to imagine that global shifts in temperature or precipitation will have affected all marginal regions of the Aegean in the same way and, as noted already, local proxy records (palynological and geoarchaeological) presently pose acute problems of chronology and interpretation. Anyway, over large parts of the semi-arid southern Aegean, steep slopes and thin soils with poor water retention exacerbate the problems of low rainfall; indeed, even in the wet highlands of northwest mainland Greece, steep terrain and thin soils conspire to make drought as big an impediment to grain crops as is the short growing season at high altitude. It may reasonably be assumed, therefore, that frequent harvest failure was inevitable in those parts of the southern Aegean that are today rendered agriculturally marginal by a combination of climate and topography. Moreover, anecdotal reports from elderly farmers on Cycladic Naxos and on northern Crete suggest that winds pose a significant hazard to crop growth on exposed coasts, implying that small islands were probably particularly risky locations for dependence on grain growing.

By contrast, the scarcity or absence of known early farming villages in central and western Crete and the southwest mainland are not so easily attributable to climatic, topographic or edaphic obstacles to farming. The two latter regions enjoy slightly higher rainfall (Furlan 1977) than eastern Thessaly, where known early villages are densest. They also include areas of fertile lowland that, while less amenable than the plains of Thessaly and Macedonia to large-scale cereal-growing on ox-based estates or mechanised farms, were surely large enough to support a number of long-lived Neolithic villages. Central Crete is slightly more arid and the longevity of Neolithic Knossos might partly be due to its perennial water supply (and potential for irrigation in drought years) and to its location in a valley sheltered from coastal winds. For simple geological reasons, however, more or less perennial springs are quite widespread in southern (and northwest) Greece, so it is unlikely that water supply prevented the early development of several long-lived rivals to Knossos.

The relative isolation of Knossos in central Crete and of Kouphovouno in the southern mainland, even if not attributable to environmental constraints, may nonetheless be related to the relatively large size that these sites seem to have attained during the Neolithic. The density of EN villages in east-central and northern Greece presumably reflects the rapid budding off of new communities from initial farming settlements that, whether populated with acculturated indigenous foragers or immigrant farmers or a mixture of both, were few in number. In Crete and Laconia and perhaps other parts of the southern mainland, population growth seems instead to have been accommodated for much longer in a single expanding settlement. Knossos and Kouphovouno may have proved powerful magnets for their growing numbers of inhabitants because alternative sources of mates or neighbourly assistance were distant. In the east-central or northern mainland, any splinter group contemplating establishment of a new settlement would be taking this decision in a much richer social landscape, with several nearby sources of mates or assistance to choose from. The initial isolation of Knossos may be attributable to its probable origin in a long-distance, sea-borne colonising venture (Broodbank and Strasser 1991). The origins of the contrasting earlier Neolithic settlement patterns of Laconia and Thessaly or Central Macedonia might plausibly be attributed to the adoption of farming by a single foraging band in Laconia and by several neighbouring bands in the latter two areas. This suggestion is ecologically plausible, but not as yet amenable to empirical testing. The question also lies beyond the remit of this paper. For now, it is enough to note that the 'marginality' of the southern Aegean may have been social as much as ecological or economic.

'Economic' Responses to Marginal Colonisation: Pastoralism and the 'Secondary Products Revolution'

Given that the semi-arid south*eastern* Aegean was ecologically marginal for grain production, several scholars have linked the belated expansion of settlement in this area to proposed innovations in subsistence practices. These innovations, variously regarded as pre-adaptations to or consequences of marginal colonisation, include:

(1) application of ox-drawn ard-ploughs to ease cultivation of poor soils or dry interfluves (van Andel and Runnels 1988; Johnson 1996; Bintliff *et al.* 2006);
(2) a switch from wheat to barley as the staple cereal in the Cyclades (Renfrew 1973: 163–64; Johnson 1996);
(3) domestication of the vine and olive and development of diversified 'Mediterranean polyculture' (Renfrew 1972);

(4) greater use of wild resources (Renfrew 1973: 163; Halstead 1987);
(5) and increased reliance on herding and such secondary products as milk and
      wool (*e.g.*, Halstead 1981: 326–27; Sampson 1992; Watrous 1994; Johnson
      1996; Cavanagh 1999).

Given the critical tone of what follows, it should be acknowledged that the
present author has previously endorsed several of these proposals.

In Andrew Sherratt's SPR model, use of the ox-drawn scratch-plough or
'ard' enabled poor soils to be cultivated on a larger scale than was possible by
hand, thus off-setting low area-yields. In an Aegean context, such use of the ard
has been proposed for the third millennium BC in the southeast mainland (van
Andel and Runnels 1988) and Crete (Watrous 1994) and from a little earlier in
Boiotia (Bintliff *et al.* 2006), essentially on the grounds of changes in site location
and of synchrony with the proposed 4–3m BC SPR. Clay figurines of yoked cattle
from EB Nemea-Tsoungiza (Pullen 1992) clearly indicate knowledge of the
potential of animal traction in the 3m BC southern mainland, but the most direct
evidence for *actual use* of draught animals is frequent pathological traces on
cows at Knossos from at least the sixth millennium BC onwards (Isaakidou
2006). Draught cattle may have facilitated the long-term expansion of the
community at Knossos (Isaakidou this volume) and so delayed rather than
enabled FN marginal colonisation on Crete. Consideration of recent pre-
mechanised farming suggests that the proposed value of the ard in tilling *poor*
soils is also questionable. First, draught cattle require large quantities of pasture
and/or fodder and these may be scarcer in the semi-arid lowlands of, say, east
Crete or at upland sites with cold winters and steep slopes than in the relatively
sheltered and well-watered landscape around Knossos. Secondly, many poor
soils are also light-textured, so that low yields per unit of land need not
necessarily represent unacceptably low yields per unit of human labour.
Moreover, in marginal locations where cultivable land is steep or interrupted by
boulders and gullies, the benefits of using draught animals rather than human
labour are much reduced. For these reasons, manual cultivation was widespread
in difficult terrain in the recent past and it seems unlikely that draught animals
played a crucial role in enabling LN–EB marginal colonisation.

Turning from methods of tillage to crops grown, reliance on barley by
Neolithic farmers in the Cyclades was proposed, in the infancy of Aegean
archaeobotany, on empirical grounds too slender to be taken seriously today.
Anyway, it is far from clear that barley would have been more tolerant of poor
growing conditions than the glume wheats that dominate Neolithic cereal
assemblages in mainland Greece (Halstead 1994: 204–5, table 1; Valamoti 2007:
92–93, table 6.1).

The remaining three suggested innovations all involve diversification of the
earlier Neolithic farming economy and so would, at least to some degree, have
reduced the risks associated with growing grain crops in regions of low rainfall
or poor soils. Olives and vines, being deep-rooted perennials, are vulnerable to

unfavourable weather at different times of year from annual grain crops and, from this perspective, their combination in Mediterranean polyculture is an effective risk-buffering tactic (Forbes 1976). Archaeobotanical and palynological evidence is slender, however, for LN–EB cultivation of either perennial in the southern Aegean (Runnels and Hansen 1986; Hamilakis 1996a) and indeed systematic exploitation of (morphologically wild) grapes is first documented at a LN village in *northern* Greece (Valamoti *et al.* 2007). Moreover, the olive takes several years to recover from the damage inflicted periodically by severe late frosts and so is a very unreliable *staple* food source. On present evidence, it seems unlikely that either perennial made a major direct contribution to the dietary problems of LN–EB marginal colonists.

Wild plants and animals, rare on EN–MN village sites in Greece, are better represented in some LN–EB archaeobotanical and faunal assemblages (*e.g.*, von den Driesch 1987; Halstead 1994: 204–5, table 1), but still only as minor components. Wild resources were evidently valued, as several non-domesticate animal species (especially fallow deer) were apparently introduced to islands lacking an indigenous large mammalian fauna (Halstead 1987; Yannouli and Trantalidou 1999). Introduced deer may have been a significant crop pest, however, and on small islands may have been very vulnerable to over-hunting. Moreover, on the largest island – Crete, the clearest non-domesticate introductions during the Neolithic seem to have been small fur-animals (*e.g.*, badger, marten – Jarman 1996; Isaakidou 2004) that offered limited potential as dietary staples. While gathering and hunting doubtless offset shortages of staple grain crops to varying degrees, available evidence suggests that the dietary contribution of wild plants and animals ranged from minimal to modest.

The source of dietary diversification that perhaps offered greatest potential, and has certainly received greatest attention in the literature, is greater reliance on domestic animals or, more grandly, the development of pastoralism. Probably the most important factor favouring pastoral models is the location of many 'marginal' LN–EB sites in the southern Aegean (and likewise their LB–EIA counterparts in the uplands of northwest Greece) in landscapes now over-whelmingly given over to grazing rather than cultivation. It is questionable, however, whether any of these sites occupy landscapes where grain production is impossible (as opposed to difficult) and cultivation in the recent past is usually (in my experience, invariably) recalled by elderly local residents or evident from remnant terrace walls, clearance cairns, threshing floors and the like. For example, on the basis of this author's very limited travel around Crete, tillage is either still practised or documented by material traces and oral accounts on the rugged summit of the Asterousia range and around the upland basins of Katharo, Lasithi and Limnarkaro, and Nidha. Likewise, there are signs of present or past cultivation in the immediate vicinity of FN sites (despite apparently 'defensive' hilltop locations) in east, west and south Crete (see plates in Nowicki 2002). The degree of dependence on livestock in areas marginal for grain production is thus historically contingent and site location alone is insufficient evidence for greater reliance on herding in the past.

Another recurrent line of argument has linked apparent impermanence of residence at marginal sites with the mobile lifestyle that is more characteristic of large-scale herders than of arable farmers. For example, at FN Doliana in the Pindos foothills of northwest Greece, hearths and floors were not accompanied by traces of any superstructure, inviting comparison with the flimsy shepherds' huts seen in the area today (Douzougli and Zachos 2002: 126), but the level of investment in house building is influenced by cultural considerations other than length of residence (*e.g.*, Whittle 1996; Halstead 1999; Kotsakis 1999). Similarly, interpretation of LN–EB use of caves in the southern Aegean is easily coloured by widespread recent use of such natural shelters by herders and their sheep or goats, but caves served a variety of purposes in both the recent and distant past and their use to house animals (*e.g.*, Payne 1985: 219) is not necessarily linked to large-scale herding. Mobility in the context of seasonally transhumant or nomadic herding has also been suggested on the basis of stylistic similarities of artefacts over long distances – for the MN southern mainland (Jacobsen 1984) and LB–EIA northwest mainland (Kilian 1972; 1973), but prehistorians happily attribute similar empirical phenomena to different forms of social interaction (*e.g.*, long-term migration, exchange between sedentary groups) in geographical contexts apparently less conducive to pastoralism.

In principle, the seasonality or otherwise of habitation can be explored more directly by examining the ages – and thus times of year – at which the animals deposited on sites were killed. Assuming late winter/early spring births for sheep, goats, cattle and (more problematically) pigs, domestic animals seem to have been slaughtered (implying that at least some human residents were present) more or less year-round at a series of early village sites and, among 'marginal' sites, at LN–FN Zas cave on the Cycladic island of Naxos and at the small FN open-air site of Doliana in northwest Greece (Halstead 2005). On Crete, the same has been argued for Knossos throughout its 6000 years of EN–LB occupation (Isaakidou 2004). This exercise is by no means unassailable (see cautionary notes in Halstead 2005 and more pessimistic comments in Milner 2005) and anyway results from a handful of sites can only be extrapolated to the whole of Greece with considerable caution, but it offers no grounds for assuming marginal LN–EB sites to have been used on a more seasonal basis than village sites in 'core' areas of Neolithic settlement. On the other hand, year-round occupation of all marginal sites would not preclude the seasonal absence of a few inhabitants to take some or even most livestock to distant but richer pastures. Such seasonal movement of livestock (for which, it must be stressed, there is as yet no evidence) could potentially have enabled a 'marginal' LN–EB settlement to maintain more animals on a higher plane of nutrition than would otherwise have been possible.

Most faunal assemblages have been so filtered by partial identification, retrieval, survival and deposition that published minimum numbers of individuals offer meaninglessly low underestimates of the absolute numbers of animals originally slaughtered – let alone of the numbers of *live*stock once kept. Nonetheless, the *relative* frequencies of different species may offer some hints as to absolute numbers of livestock. Sheep overwhelmingly dominate the faunal assemblages of earlier Neolithic village sites (*e.g.*, Halstead 1996; for Knossos – Isaakidou this volume), even though much of the surrounding landscape (whether made up of mature woodland or of more open scrub or parkland) was probably more suitable for cattle, goats and pigs. One interpretation of this apparent contradiction is that livestock were few enough to be largely confined to cleared arable land (stubble, fallow, sprouting cereals), which sheep are ideally suited to exploit. Faunal assemblages from LN–EB 'core' village sites, including Knossos (Isaakidou this volume) and FN Phaistos and EB Agia Triada (Wilkens 1996) on Crete, tend towards a more balanced mix of sheep(/goat), cattle and pigs. Conversely, several 'marginal' sites exhibit high proportions of both sheep and goats with few pigs or cattle (Halstead 1996, 31: fig. 2); on Crete, most assemblages from the marginal sites of LN Gerani Cave (Jarman 1996), FN–EB Petras Kephala (Isaakidou in prep.; Papadatos this volume) and EB Myrtos-Fournou Korifi (Jarman 1972), Sentoni Cave (Hamilakis 1996b) and Debla (Warren and Tzedhakis 1974) are too small for reliable estimation of taxonomic proportions, but most include all four principal domestic animals. The contrasting taxonomic composition of 'core' and 'marginal' LN–EB assemblages may reflect the keeping of livestock in larger numbers, exceeding the carrying capacity of local fields and so sensitive to differences in the surrounding uncultivated landscape. The suggestion that livestock numbers increased through the Neolithic, as the landscape was progressively opened up, has been made many times for temperate Europe (*e.g.*, Clark 1947; Legge 1981; Sherratt 1981; Schibler and Jacomet 1999). A similar trend is inherently plausible for the Mediterranean and is consistent with the osteological evidence for taxonomic composition, but it would be rash to claim more. Independent support might, in principle, be sought in the geoarchaeological and palynological records of landscape change, but such changes tend to be dated rather coarsely and it is difficult to discriminate between climatic and anthropogenic causes – let alone between the impact of arable farming and herding (Endfield 1997; Halstead 2000; Krahtopoulou 2000).

Finally, because of its chronological correspondence with Andrew Sherratt's 4–3m BC SPR, some scholars have linked later Neolithic-EB marginal colonisation in the southern Aegean not only to a greater emphasis on herding, but also more specifically to the exploitation of the secondary products milk and wool. While the latter can only contribute to diet indirectly, as the raw material for exchangeable textiles (Sherratt 1981; van Andel and Runnels 1988), milk is a rich direct source of nutrition as animals managed for milk production can produce far more calories than the same number of animals exploited just for their meat (*e.g.*, Legge 1981). As the economic mainstay of recent pastoralists both in Greece (*e.g.*, Campbell 1964) and elsewhere (*e.g.*, Dahl and Hjort 1976), milking has been attractive to prehistorians as a subsistence innovation that might have facilitated marginal colonisation. The project on which Andrew Sherratt was working at the time of the 2006 Round Table had established that milk was already being processed in ceramic vessels by the late sixth millennium BC at LN Stavroupoli in northern Greece (Kotsakis *et al.* in press). Although this project analysed Neolithic vessels from only the north of Greece, it clearly does not favour a link between the inception of milking and marginal colonisation in the southern Aegean. It might be argued that marginal colonisation was instead associated with more *intensive* management of domestic ruminants for milk products. Faunal evidence for kill-off patterns suggests a non-specialised 'meat' strategy, however, for both sheep and goats at LN–EB Zas cave on Naxos in the Cyclades (Halstead in prep.), for undifferentiated sheep/goat at LN–FN Skotini cave on Evvia (Kotjabopoulou and Trantalidou 1993) and LN–FN Kalythies cave on Rhodes (Halstead and Jones 1987), and also for sheep and cattle at the 'marginal' FN open-air site of Doliana in northwest Greece (Halstead *et al.* in prep.). At Knossos on Crete, deaths of sheep, goats and cattle likewise match a 'meat' strategy throughout the Neolithic, while possible EB emphasis on sheep wool, goat hair and cattle traction occurs too late to have any bearing on marginal colonisation (Isaakidou 2004; 2006). The 'meat' strategy, involving slaughter of many animals as juveniles or subadults, is compatible with non-specialised exploitation of milk or other secondary products (Payne 1973), but available evidence offers no grounds for linking marginal colonisation in the Aegean to either the beginning or the intensification of milking.

It is not denied that domestic animals may have played a significant role in enhancing the viability of marginal LN–EB settlements. For villages in 'core' areas of Neolithic settlement, livestock probably served a variety of uses including the clearance and manuring of stubble and perhaps fallow fields, the grazing of early cereal growth on fertile plots to prevent lodging of crops, and the conversion of failed crops or surplus grain into an edible resource (*e.g.*, Halstead 1990; 2006a; Mainland and Halstead 2005). As a food source, domestic animals doubtless brought welcome diversity into a grain-based diet. Perhaps more importantly, both practical considerations and empirical data suggest that carcasses were shared widely or consumed in large-scale commensality (*e.g.*, Halstead 2006b; Pappa *et al.* 2004; Urem-Kotsou and Kotsakis 2007; Isaakidou 2007). Livestock would thus have provided a means of converting crop residues and surplus grain into social alliances and debts. In the event of failure of staple grain crops, domestic animals probably offered both an alternative source of food and a key means of securing assistance from kin, neighbours and friends. In marginal settlements, subject to more frequent and more severe crop failures, domestic animals presumably played a similar buffering role – indeed this role may have been enhanced if larger herds were kept. In the absence of evidence for intensive dairying, however, livestock arguably had limited potential as a staple food source for LN–EB marginal colonists. Consistent with this argument, palaeopathological and isotopic analysis of human skeletons suggests a broadly similar (and probably grain-based) diet at LN and EB Makriyalos in northern Greece (Triantaphyllou 2001) and at Alepotrypa and other marginal LN–FN sites in southern Greece (Papathanasiou 2003; 2005). Nonetheless, because direct evidence for both animal management and human diet is restricted to very few sites, it is worth exploring in more detail the practical implications of reliance on animal husbandry in the southern Aegean.

Living Off Livestock in the LN–EB Southern Aegean: Modelling Benefits and Costs

Modelling the possible contribution of livestock to subsistence at marginal LN–EB sites faces many unknowns, but may still be instructive. As a point of departure, it will be assumed that small marginal sites represent farmsteads of single nuclear families rather than hamlets of several families (the latter requiring considerably more food). A family of five persons may have needed to consume something on the order of 10, 000 kcal/day. Using figures for African and Middle Eastern livestock, such a family might have been sustained by the carcasses of between 45 large and 90 small sheep per year, culled from a flock of some 140–280 head; the required flock size might fall to 84–109 head if milk was consumed as well as meat (Dahl and Hjort 1976: 140–1, 209, table 9.2, 219, table 9.4).

Aegean LN–EB domestic animals were small and slightly built, so the higher estimates for flock size are most relevant for present purposes. The preceding estimates also assume an average of 4000 kcal/kg of mutton, whereas Middle Eastern food composition data (Sabry and Rizck 1982) suggest that even a substantially lower average of 2500 kcal/kg may err on the side of generosity. On this basis, a family of five could have been sustained by 4 kg of moderately fatty lamb or mutton (off the bone) per day. This could in turn have been achieved by killing, say, a 2–3 month old suckling lamb every day, an older lamb every two days or a yearling/adult ewe every three days. Available mortality data (from both core village and marginal cave sites) suggest that many sheep and goats were culled as older lambs, sub-adults and young adults (say between 3 months and 3 years of age). With reasonably optimistic assumptions as to lambing rate and natural mortality, a breeding flock of 200 adult ewes might sustain an annual cull of 60 older lambs in May–August (when high temperatures make it difficult for a family to consume larger carcasses) and 60 sub-adults/young adults/mature adults during the cooler months of September–April. Including female lambs and yearlings kept as future breeding stock, a few rams and juveniles (mostly males) intended for consumption in their second or third year, the flock needed to sustain a wholly carnivorous family might fluctuate between ca 350 and 500 head from one lambing season to the next (amounting to a similar culling rate to that assumed by Dahl and Hjort).

The costs of feeding and herding such a flock must be considered. Allowing something like one hectare of rough pasture per animal (le Houerou 1977), the flock would need in the course of a year to graze over ca 4 km² – the equivalent of a circular catchment of radius slightly in excess of 1 km. Flocks of sheep and goats today routinely graze over much greater distances on a daily basis and, in the absence of milking or of the need to avoid cultivated plots, a flock of 350–500 could be herded without difficulty by a single family. On the other hand, although the original spacing between small marginal sites is uncertain (not least because of the difficulty of demonstrating contemporaneous occupation of neighbouring short-lived sites), even early villages in Thessaly seem to have been as close as 2–3 km to their nearest neighbour (Halstead 1984; Perlès 1999). A flock large enough to sustain carnivory, therefore, may well have required movement beyond the 'territory' of an individual marginal settlement.

In practice, this assessment of the viability of carnivorous pastoralism is excessively optimistic on several counts. First, sheep and goats tend to be fairly evenly represented at marginal sites (Halstead 1996: 31, fig. 2) and goat meat is leaner than lamb or mutton, so estimation of required flock size for sheep alone is likely to be a serious underestimate. Secondly, while management of a flock of 500 sheep may be quite feasible for a single family (*e.g.*, Dahl and Hjort 1976: 254–56), herding of large numbers of both sheep and goats and of smaller numbers of cattle and pigs (as per the faunal record) might well be very challenging, given the contrasting feeding requirements and habits of the four species. Thirdly, the condition (and hence carcass fat content) of all four species of livestock fluctuates through the year in response to seasonal changes in quality of diet. In addition, breeding adults lose condition during rutting (males) or pregnancy and lactation (females), while lambs and kids may lose weight for a few months after weaning. It is thus questionable whether a year-round supply of fat-rich fresh meat was achievable. One solution would be to preserve fat meat for storage, but this is neither easy nor very reliable in the hot climate of the southern Mediterranean (*e.g.*, Halstead 2007) and available mortality data suggest that livestock were slaughtered piecemeal through the year (Halstead 2005). Alternatively, a carnivorous family might attempt to minimise the effects of seasonal variation in grazing quality by subdividing herds, so that the best pasture was reserved for animals to be fattened for consumption (perhaps at the expense of breeding animals and reproductive rates), and/or by seasonal displacement to distant pasture at higher or lower altitude. Subdivision of herds or removal of *some* animals to distant pastures (removal of *all* livestock is contradicted by available mortality data – Halstead 2005), however, may have overstretched the herding labour of individual households. Of course, this last problem could be solved if a few households joined forces, but a hamlet of say five households would require more than 20 km² of pasture, representing probably over-generous spacing between contemporary marginal sites of more than 5 km. Finally, the preceding calculations make no provision for bad years – whether due to poor pasture or animal diseases. The suggested herd of 500 head would have to be expanded considerably to allow for periodic heavy losses – with obvious detrimental effects on the balance between livestock numbers and the availability of both pasture and herding labour. And this precaution would do nothing to solve the short-term problem that humans lose weight on a diet of lean meat (Speth 1983: 143–59). In sum, in the face of labour constraints on flock size and of seasonal and inter-annual variation in carcass quality, it seems highly improbable that a continuous and reliable food supply could have been won from carnivorous pastoralism in the prehistoric Aegean.

Consumption of milk as well as meat offers several advantages. First, oral accounts of mid-20c (*i.e.*, extensive) sheep and goat herding suggest that a ewe or nanny might comfortably produce as many calories in milk in one season as her carcass would yield at the end of her life. With intensive dairying rather than pure carnivory, a family might theoretically live off a smaller flock, the size of which also fluctuated more in tune with the seasonal rhythm of pasture quality (say between 150 and 250 head), though this is *not* the husbandry strategy indicated by available mortality data. Secondly, cheese is more easily preserved than meat and so stored cheese might be eaten at times of year when only lean meat was available. On the other hand, pregnant and lactating females are particularly vulnerable to disease or poor nutrition, milking and cheese making (especially of hard, storable cheeses) are very labour-intensive (cf. Nitsiakos 1985; Kapetanios 2003), early weaning (to maximise milk yields for human consumption) tends to result in smaller and less vigorous lambs or kids, and breeding females may compete for the best pasture with sub-adults to be fattened for consumption. By comparison with pure carnivory, therefore, a mixed meat/dairy strategy may require a smaller herd and less pasture and may provide a less seasonal food supply, but places greater (probably intolerable) strain on the labour of single families. Again, problems of labour supply could be mitigated by collaboration between families – albeit perhaps at the cost of increased competition for pasture. Milking and cheese making are sufficiently labour-intensive, however, that the potential for surplus production of storable cheeses as a cushion against bad years would probably have been very limited. Large-scale storage would also make seasonal mobility more difficult – especially before equid pack-animals became widely available.

The practical difficulties of pastoral production were solved by recent specialist herders in a variety of ways: seasonal mobility between lowland (winter) and upland (summer) pasture; collaboration of several households to allow separate herding of productive females and non-productive males/yearlings; and especially by exchanging relatively expensive animal products for cheaper staple grains (*e.g.*, Campbell 1964: 363–64). Available faunal evidence lacks any indication of seasonal mobility, of rearing a single taxon (easing the labour problems of herding large numbers of animals) or of specialisation in exchangeable secondary products. Reliance on exchange will also, surely, have been a very risky strategy. Elderly Cretans recall how the price of grain staples rose steeply during World War II to the point that a kilogram of cheese was exchanged for a similar quantity of flour (compared with perhaps 10 kg of flour pre-war). In the absence of an urban market, failure to exchange animal products at a favourable rate would inevitably have been frequent, making specialised pastoralists vulnerable to starvation not only in years when their animals under-produced, but also when their exchange partners suffered poor grain harvests.

It may be objected that the preceding discussion is predicated on the unreasonable assumption of marginal sites being occupied by specialised pastoralists, rather than by herders that also grew a few crops. The difficulty of living off animal produce, however, suggests that any herders who also grew crops would rapidly become mixed farmers primarily dependent *on their own grain crops*. Consideration of bad years reinforces this conclusion: after a failed harvest, retention or borrowing of a modest amount of seed corn may enable crop growing on a sufficient scale in the following year, whereas a herd decimated by epidemic or severe weather takes a few years to rebuild. Moreover, after the rare disaster of loss of a whole flock, recovery may depend on the loan or gift of a few animals from several other herders and so the long-term viability of animal-based subsistence arguably requires that a pastoral lifestyle is pursued by numerous households – and this, of course, increases competition for pasture and for favourable exchanges with grain producers in less marginal locations.

Mixed farming has many practical advantages: livestock provide manure for crops, while stubble and fallow fields tend to offer richer pasture than uncultivated land; and the combination of crops and livestock offers a more secure subsistence base than reliance on either in isolation. On the other hand, crops and livestock compete for labour and the herding of animals becomes far more labour-intensive if areas of pasture are interspersed with growing crops that must not be grazed (Koster 1977). For this reason, recent mixed farming households in Greece often built up a flock of perhaps 50–100 sheep, but only at the point in the domestic cycle when teenage sons provided the necessary surplus of human labour for herding and milking, and they later sold off the flock to finance marriage settlements or the purchase of land. Wealthier arable farmers were more likely to run such flocks throughout the domestic cycle, but with the assistance of hired shepherds. While livestock probably did play an important role in making Neolithic subsistence more reliable, therefore, both in 'core' villages and marginal hamlets/farmsteads, their potential to provide the *dietary mainstay* of marginal LN–EB communities has arguably been grossly overestimated by many scholars.

'Social' Responses to Marginal Colonisation: Residence, Identity and Exchange

If the previous section has offered few grounds for attributing delayed marginal colonisation to changes in subsistence practices, the frequently small size of LN–

EB settlements in the southern Aegean, each representing perhaps just a few households or even one household, marks a clear change in residential patterns and social strategies.

The potential relevance of such dispersed settlement to land use and subsistence must be acknowledged. Just as it has been argued that the large size of early Neolithic villages effectively enforced reliance on high-yielding, staple grain crops, so small LN–EB sites offered greater opportunities for reliance on food procurement strategies, such as herding or foraging, that are less productive per unit of land area. On-site archaeobotanical and zooarchaeological remains, however, argue against greater reliance on foraging and offer little support for an increased role for herding. Moreover, small FN–EB sites are often more closely spaced than earlier village settlements and so, depending on the relative longevity and archaeological visibility of early villages and small FN–EB sites, population density may even have increased and the range of viable subsistence options narrowed.

Unambiguously, however, the small size of many FN–EB sites implies significant shifts in the degree and form of interdependence between 'households'. In earlier villages, there is debate as to the extent to which the inhabitants of individual 'houses' represented independent household units of production, consumption and agricultural decision-making (*e.g.*, Halstead 1995; 2006b; Tomkins 2004; Kotsakis 2006), but close proximity will have facilitated and legitimised claims on neighbours for mutual assistance. The inhabitants of small FN–EB sites had few close neighbours and so will have needed strategies other than daily face-to-face encounter to secure necessary assistance from other members of the scattered local population. In practice, the need for mutual exchanges or loans of human labour, tools, breeding and perhaps working animals, seed corn and the like could probably be met from immediate neighbours or from residents of nearby hamlets, encountered regularly outdoors (*e.g.*, while grazing livestock) or easily visited in their homes. Periodic assistance after crop failure, however, was more likely to be available from farmers located far enough away to be subject to good and bad harvests in different years. Although the broken terrain and localised weather patterns of the southern Aegean may have allowed some scope for such mutual risk-buffering between nearby hamlets, more severe failures will have required assistance from partners further afield (*e.g.*, on the other side of a mountain ridge), encountered more infrequently.

The exchange of craft goods doubtless played a significant role in establishing and maintaining such distant social relationships (*e.g.*, Mauss 1970; Sherratt 1976; Wiessner 1982) and perhaps in reciprocating 'gifts' of grain (O' Shea 1981). Consistent with such expectations, many marginal hamlets in the southern Aegean engaged in impressive levels of regional exchange of craft goods – obvious examples are the movement of fine pottery in EBII eastern Crete (Whitelaw *et al.* 1997) and of a wide range of items in the EBII Cyclades (Renfrew 1972; Broodbank 2000). FN and EBI phases of marginal colonisation are less obviously associated with such regional networks, but exchange may have taken a less archaeologically visible form – for example, wives, livestock, fine textiles, or recycled metals. On the other hand, regional and even inter-regional exchange is well attested in the millennia preceding marginal colonisation – for example, cores or blades of Melian obsidian and of flint from northwest Greece and perhaps the Balkans at EN Argissa in Thessaly (Perlès 1990), and marine shell ornaments at inland LN sites in Thessaly (Tsuneki 1987). Moreover, where direct evidence is lacking (and systematic provenance studies are rare), regional ceramic styles amply document social interaction on a scale intermediate between that required for inter-marriage and that documented by the movement of obsidian and high-quality flint (*e.g.*, Washburn 1983; Cullen 1984). Comparison of the volume of exchange in different periods or regions is arguably meaningless, given the scarcity of data and the problem of variable archaeological visibility. Even if the apparently intensive exchange of EBII is taken as typical of the phase of marginal colonisation as a whole, however, the evidence for regional interaction from EN onwards makes it difficult to argue that marginal colonisation was delayed until FN–EB because of the absence of exchange networks.

It is possible, however, that dispersed marginal settlement facilitated regional exchange, as well as making it more essential. Earlier village communities in 'core' areas of farming settlement invested heavily in communal cohesion and identity, through collective labour projects (digging massive circuit ditches – *e.g.*, Kotsakis 1999; Pappa and Besios 1999), through the mixing and dispersal of adult human skeletons (Triantaphyllou 1999; this volume) and through use of standardised, but carefully made serving vessels (Pappa *et al.* 2004; Tomkins 2007; Urem-Kotsou and Kotsakis 2007). That commensality played a major role in promoting solidarity within the local village community is suggested by the apparently wide sharing of large animal carcasses (Isaakidou 2004; Halstead 2006b; 2007), the frequent location of cooking facilities *outdoors* and so open to the scrutiny of neighbours (Halstead 1995) and the care invested in making fine 'tableware' (*e.g.*, Kotsakis 1983; Sherratt 1991). Such emphasis on local commensality may have discouraged the production and accumulation of surplus by individual households within village communities (Flannery 1972) and so impeded the maintenance of a range of reliable *distant* social relationships. Conversely, one advantage of dispersed settlement will have been reduced obligations to dissipate resources among immediate neighbours and so greater freedom to target surplus on gifts or hospitality to distant exchange partners whose help may be needed in bad years. The strong association of Aegean marginal colonisation with dispersed settlement may thus be due to the central role of the latter in making the former viable.

One attraction of this model is that it may offer a rationale for the timing of marginal colonisation in the Aegean. Over the course of the Neolithic, village sites in core agricultural areas witness erosion of communal cohesion: the investment of labour shifted from collective projects to individual houses (Kotsakis 1999); cooking facilities were progressively located indoors or within yard walls that enclosed first small groups of LN houses and then individual FN–EB households (Halstead 1995); elaborate ceramic tableware largely disappeared in the FN; and dispersal of human remains gave way from the EBA to individual burial (Nakou 1995; Triantaphyllou this volume). Marginal colonisation, beginning on a small scale in LN Thessaly and then proliferating rapidly in the FN–EB southern Aegean, thus took place when the collective ties of the early villages had already dissolved in favour of smaller social groups, comparable in size with later hamlets and farmsteads.

As well as facilitating regional exchange, the growing architectural and social isolation through the Neolithic of the household or household cluster may have fundamentally altered the size of social group capable of social reproduction. The dispersal of adult human remains on early village sites, together with the contrasting treatment of juveniles (Triantaphyllou this volume), suggests that some major rites of passage were under communal control, and the same may well have been true for marriage. Land too was probably at least partly under communal control. For example, the ditches encircling flat-extended sites arguably represent collective enclosure of cultivated land (the sparsely inhabited 28 ha enclosure at LN Makriyalos I was surely too large for an animal pen and too small for pasture). On the more compact tell villages, houses repeatedly rebuilt on the same spot may indicate domestic rights to particular residential plots and perhaps, by extension, to cultivated plots (Kotsakis 1999; 2006; Halstead 2006b). On the other hand, the longevity of many tell villages (perhaps continuously occupied for millennia) suggests that some communal mechanism existed for redistributing plots without living owners among residents without land (see also Isaakidou this volume). Moreover, as in modern Greece, any household rights to cultivated plots were probably embedded within communal rights to forage and pasture animals on uncultivated land and perhaps also to graze crop stubble and fallow plots. In the recent past, those who infringed such collective agreements on where and when they could graze or sow were often sanctioned by imprisonment of offending livestock or treatment of growing crops as pasture (*e.g.*, Nitsiakos 1985; Halstead field notes). In sum, dispersed settlement may have been unviable, for a combination of social, economic and ideological reasons, in the context of strongly cohesive early village communities.

Some Conclusions

There are obvious difficulties and potential dangers in comparing and interpreting the results of largely extensive reconnaissance in northern Greece and of intensive surveys concentrated in the southern Aegean. Nonetheless, it seems clear that EN–MN (seventh–sixth millennia BC) farming settlements were concentrated in particular regions and generally took the form of relatively large 'villages', while several regions with little or no known early farming population were extensively colonised from the LN (sixth–fifth millennia BC) and especially FN–EBA (fourth–third millennia BC) by small 'hamlets' or 'farmsteads'. Some of the regions apparently colonised belatedly (*e.g.*, eastern Crete, the Cyclades) are marginal for grain growing, by virtue of low and uncertain rainfall and/or of steep terrain supporting thin soils of modest fertility and low moisture retention. Other regions colonised belatedly (*e.g.*, the southwest mainland, western Crete), however, are not self-evidently unsuitable for grain crops and, it is tentatively suggested, may have been under-populated because mobile foraging was a viable alternative way of life, albeit one of low archaeological visibility.

Although belated colonisation of regions marginal for growing grain crops perhaps invites explanation in terms of some form of subsistence innovation, there is as yet little or no evidence to support such adaptation. Conversely, dispersed settlement may have played a critical role in facilitating regional exchange and so enabling marginal colonisation. Whereas the inhabitants of early farming villages were apparently subject to strong obligations to share food with close neighbours, their counterparts in later hamlets or farmsteads may have been more free to invest surplus from good years in maintaining a portfolio of distant exchange relationships. Furthermore, the delay in colonisation of marginal regions may perhaps be understood in terms of long-term social change in village communities over the four millennia of the Neolithic: the gradual loosening of communal ties in favour of individual households arguably created the conditions in which hamlets and farmsteads were capable of economic survival and social reproduction.

The gradual isolation of the household from the early village community has been accounted for in terms of an indigenous Aegean response to inherent contradictions between collective sharing and storage (Halstead 1995; Kotsakis 1999; 2006; for a similar trajectory in the Near East, see Flannery 1972; 2002; Wright 2000). Empirically, this model seems preferable to suggestions that village settlement and an elaborate material culture, placing emphasis on the household, were implanted in Europe at the beginning of the Neolithic from a Near Eastern source (*contra* Childe 1957; Perlès 2001; and, to some extent, Hodder 1990). In practice, such a stark choice between indigenous and diffusionist interpretations may be unnecessary and the convergent material cultures (*e.g.*, female figurines, painted tableware) of the Neolithic of the Levant, Anatolia and southeast Europe might reflect the transmission of social norms and moral precepts as well as parallel responses to similar practical problems. Marginal colonisation in the Aegean, however, may have taken place over a long period of time – three millennia if LN expansion in the southern Larisa plain is included (although perhaps very rapidly on Crete – Tomkins this volume). Moreover, despite the common phenomenon of dispersed residence, the extent to which the loosening of communal solidarity was projected in the burial record varies greatly between regions: a more or less clear preference for individual inhumations in the Early Bronze Age of northern Greece (*e.g.*, Triantaphyllou 2001), the southern mainland

(Cavanagh and Mee 1998) and the Cyclades (Nakou 1995) contrasts with collective tombs in EB southern Crete (Watrous 1994). Marginal colonisation surely promoted closer integration of populations around (and ultimately beyond) the Aegean (Renfrew 1972; Broodbank 2000), but it seems to have been driven overwhelmingly by local processes of social change that had been set in train at an early stage of the Neolithic in Greece.

This chapter largely rejects not only a close link between LN–EB marginal colonisation in the Aegean and a 'secondary products revolution', but also the growing emphasis in Andrew Sherratt's later work on the seminal role of the Near East in driving cultural change in 4–3m BC Europe. On the other hand, Andrew's writings also explored extensively the interplay, *within* different regions of Europe, between changing patterns of settlement, land use, exchange, consumption and identity. The intellectual debt of the preceding discussion to this latter strand within Andrew's work is self-evident.

Acknowledgements

I thank Valasia Isaakidou and Peter Tomkins both for access to unpublished work, referred to above, and for critical observations on an earlier draft of this paper. I apologise, especially to the latter, for my failure to fall into line on some issues!

Bibliography

van Andel, T. and C. Runnels
    1988   An essay on the 'emergence of civilization' in the Aegean world. *Antiquity* 62: 234–47.
    1995   The earliest farmers in Europe. *Antiquity* 69: 481–500.
van Andel, T., E. Zangger and A. Demitrack
    1990   Land use and soil erosion in prehistoric and historical Greece. *Journal of Field Archaeology* 17: 379–96.
Andreou, S., M. Fotiadis and K. Kotsakis
    1996   Review of Aegean prehistory 5: the Neolithic and Bronze Age of northern Greece. *AJA* 100: 537–97.
Besios, M. and F. Adaktylou
    2006   Neolithikos oikismos sta 'Revenia' Korinou. *AEMTh* 18: 357–66.
Bintliff, J.
    2005   Human impact, land-use history, and the surface archaeological record: a case study from Greece. *Geoarchaeology* 20: 135–47.
Bintliff, J., P. Howard and A. Snodgrass
    1999   The hidden landscape of prehistoric Greece. *JMA* 12: 139–68.
Bintliff, J., E. Farinetti, K. Sarri and R. Sebastiani
    2006   Landscape and early farming settlement dynamics in central Greece. *Geoarchaeology* 21: 665–74.
Blackman, D. and K. Branigan
    1977   An archaeological survey of the lower catchment of the Ayiofarango valley. *BSA* 72: 13–84.

Branigan, K.
   1999   Late Neolithic colonization of the uplands of eastern Crete. In P. Halstead (ed.), *Neolithic Society in Greece* (SSAA 2): 57–65. Sheffield: Sheffield Academic Press.
Broodbank, C.
   1989   The longboat and society in the Cyclades in the Keros-Syros culture. *AJA* 93: 319–37.
   1999   Colonization and configuration in the insular Neolithic of the Aegean. In P. Halstead (ed.), *Neolithic Society in Greece* (SSAA 2): 15–41. Sheffield: Sheffield Academic Press.
   2000   *An Island Archaeology of the Early Cyclades.* Cambridge: Cambridge University Press.
Broodbank, C. and T. F. Strasser
   1991   Migrant farmers and the Neolithic colonization of Crete. *Antiquity* 65: 233–45.
Broodbank, C. and V. Kiriatzi
   2007   The first 'Minoans' of Kythera revisited: technology, demography, and landscape in the Prepalatial Aegean. *AJA* 111: 241–74.
Campbell, J. K.
   1964   *Honour, Family and Patronage.* Oxford: Oxford University Press.
Cavanagh, W.
   1999   Revenons à nos moutons: surface survey and the Peloponnese in the Late and Final Neolithic. In J. Renard (ed.), *Le Péloponnèse: archéologie et histoire*: 31–65. Rennes: Presses Universitaires Rennes.
Cavanagh, W. and C. Mee
   1998   *A Private Place: Death in Prehistoric Greece.* Jonsered: Paul Åström.
Cherry, J. F.
   1981   Pattern and process in the earliest colonization of the Mediterranean islands. *PPS* 47: 41–68.
   1990   The first colonization of the Mediterranean islands: a review of recent research. *JMA* 3: 145–221.
Childe, V. G.
   1957   *The Dawn of European Civilisation.* London: Routledge and Kegan Paul.
Chrysostomou, P.
   1994   Oi neolithikes erevnes stin poli kai tin eparkhia Giannitson kata to 1991. *AEMTh* 5: 111–25.
Clark, G.
   1947   Sheep and swine in the husbandry of prehistoric Europe. *Antiquity* 21: 122–36.
Cullen, T.
   1984   Social implications of ceramic style in the Neolithic Peloponnese. In W. D. Kingery (ed.), *Ancient Technology to Modern Science, volume 1*: 77–100. Columbus: American Ceramic Society.
Dahl, G. and A. Hjort
   1976   *Having Herds: Pastoral Herd Growth and Household Economy.* Stockholm: University of Stockholm.
Davis, J. L.
   2004   Are the landscapes of Greek prehistory hidden? A comparative approach. In S. E. Alcock and J. F. Cherry (eds.). *Side-by-Side Survey: Comparative Regional Studies in the Mediterranean World*: 22–35. Oxford: Oxbow Books.
Demoule, J.-P. and C. Perlès
   1993   The Greek Neolithic: a new review. *Journal of World Prehistory* 7: 355–416.
Diamant, S. R.
   1974   *The Later Village Farming Stage in Southern Greece.* PhD dissertation, University of Pennsylvania.

Douzougli, A.
   1996a   The Peloponnese. In G. A. Papathanassopoulos (ed.), *Neolithic Culture in Greece*: 126–28. Athens: Goulandris Foundation.
   1996b   Epirus – the Ionian Islands. In G. A. Papathanassopoulos (ed.), *Neolithic Culture in Greece*: 46–48. Athens: Goulandris Foundation.
Douzougli, A. and K. Zachos
   2002   L'archéologie des zones montagneuses: modèles et interconnexions dans le Néolithique de l'Épire et de l'Albanie méridionale. In G. Touchais (ed.), *L'Albanie dans l'Europe préhistorique*: 111–43. Paris: École Française d' Athènes.
von den Driesch, A.
   1987   Haus- und Jagdtiere im vorgeschichtlichen Thessalien. *Prähistorische Zeitschrift* 62: 1–21.
Endfield, G. H.
   1997   Myth, manipulation and myopia in the study of Mediterranean soil erosion. In A. Sinclair, E. Slater and J. Gowlett (eds.), *Archaeological Sciences 1995*: 241–48. Oxford: Oxbow Books.
Evans, J. D.
   1971   Neolithic Knossos: the growth of a settlement. *PPS* 37: 95–117.
Flannery, K.
   1972   The origins of the village as a settlement type in Mesoamerica and the Near East: a comparative study. In P. J. Ucko, R. Tringham and G. W. Dimbleby (eds.), *Man, Settlement and Urbanism*: 23–53. London: Duckworth.
   2002   The origins of the village revisited: from nuclear to extended households. *American Antiquity* 67: 417–33.
Forbes, H.
   1976   'We have a little of everything': the ecological basis of some agricultural practices in Methana, Trizinia. *Annals of the New York Academy of Sciences* 268: 236–50.
Furlan, D.
   1977   The climate of southeast Europe. In C. C. Wallen (ed.), *World Survey of Climatology 6, Climates of Central and Southern Europe*: 185–235. Amsterdam: Elsevier.
Halstead, P.
   1981   Counting sheep in Neolithic and Bronze Age Greece. In I. Hodder, G. Isaac and N. Hammond (eds.), *Pattern of the Past: Studies in Honour of David Clarke*: 307–39. Cambridge: Cambridge University Press.
   1984   *Strategies for Survival: an Ecological Approach to Social and Economic Change in the Early Farming Communities of Thessaly, N. Greece*. PhD Dissertation, University of Cambridge.
   1987   Man and other animals in later Greek prehistory. *BSA* 82: 71–83.
   1990   Waste not, want not: traditional responses to crop failure in Greece. *Rural History* 1: 147–64.
   1991   Present to past in the Pindhos: specialisation and diversification in mountain economies. *Rivista di Studi Liguri* 56: 61–80.
   1994   The North-South divide: regional paths to complexity in prehistoric Greece. In C. Mathers and S. Stoddart (eds.), *Development and Decline in the Mediterranean Bronze Age*: 195–219. Sheffield: J.R. Collis.
   1995   From sharing to hoarding: the Neolithic foundations of Aegean Bronze Age society? In R. Laffineur and W.-D. Niemeier (eds.), *POLITEIA. Society and State in the Aegean Bronze Age* (Aegaeum 12): 11–20. Liège: University of Liège.
   1996   Pastoralism or household herding? Problems of scale and specialisation in early Greek animal husbandry. *World Archaeology* 28: 20–42.

1999   Neighbours from hell: the household in Neolithic Greece. In P. Halstead (ed.), *Neolithic Society in Greece* (SSAA 2): 77–95. Sheffield: Sheffield Academic Press.

2000   Land use in postglacial Greece: cultural causes and environmental effects. In P. Halstead and C. Frederick (eds.), *Landscape and Land Use in Postglacial Greece* (SSAA 3): 110–28. Sheffield: Sheffield Academic Press.

2005   Resettling the Neolithic: faunal evidence for seasons of consumption and residence at Neolithic sites in Greece. In D. Bailey, A. Whittle and V. Cummings (eds.), *(un)settling the Neolithic*: 38–50. Oxford: Oxbow Books.

2006a   Sheep in the garden: the integration of crop and livestock husbandry in early farming regimes of Greece and southern Europe. In D. Serjeantson and D. Field (eds.), *Animals in the Neolithic of Britain and Europe*: 42–55. Oxford: Oxbow Books.

2006b   *What's Ours is Mine? Village and Household in Early Farming Society in Greece*. Amsterdam: University of Amsterdam.

2007   Carcasses and commensality: investigating the social context of meat consumption in Neolithic and Early Bronze Age Greece. In C. Mee and J. Renard (eds.), *Cooking Up the Past: Food and Culinary Practices in the Neolithic and Bronze Age Aegean*: 25–48. Oxford: Oxbow Books.

Halstead, P. and G. Jones
1987   Bioarchaeological remains from Kalythies cave, Rhodes. In A. Sampson (ed.), *I Neolithiki Periodos sta Dodekanisa*: 135–52. Athens: Ministry of Culture.

Hamilakis, Y.
1996a   Wine, oil and the dialectics of power in Bronze Age Crete: a review of the evidence. *OJA* 15: 1–32.

1996b   Cretan Pleistocene fauna and archaeological remains: the evidence from Sentoni Cave (Zoniana, Rethymnon). In D. S. Reese (ed.), *Pleistocene and Holocene Fauna of Crete and its First Settlers*: 231–39. Madison: Prehistory Press.

Hansen, J. M.
1988   Agriculture in the prehistoric Aegean: data versus speculation. *AJA* 92: 39–52.

Hodder, I.
1990   *The Domestication of Europe*. Oxford: Blackwell.

le Houerou, H. N.
1977   Plant sociology and ecology applied to grazing lands research, survey and management in the Mediterranean basin. In W. Krause (ed.), *Handbook of Vegetation Science 13: Application of Vegetation Science to Grassland Husbandry*: 211–74. The Hague: Junk.

Howell, R. J.
1970   A survey of eastern Arcadia in prehistory. *BSA* 65: 79–127.

Isaakidou, V.
2004   *Bones from the Labyrinth: Faunal Evidence for the Management and Consumption of Animals at Neolithic and Bronze Age Knossos, Crete*. PhD dissertation, University College London.

2006   Ploughing with cows: Knossos and the 'secondary products revolution'. In D. Serjeantson and D. Field (eds.), *Animals in the Neolithic of Britain and Europe*: 95–112. Oxford: Oxbow Books.

2007   Cooking in the labyrinth: exploring 'cuisine' at Bronze Age Knossos. In C. Mee and J. Renard (eds.), *Cooking Up the Past: Food and Culinary Practices in the Neolithic and Bronze Age Aegean*: 5–24. Oxford: Oxbow Books.

Jacobsen, T. W.
1981   Franchthi cave and the beginning of settled village life in Greece. *Hesperia* 50: 303–19.

1984   Seasonal pastoralism in southern Greece: a consideration of the ecology of Neolithic urfirnis pottery. In P. M. Rice (ed.), *Pots and Potters: Current Approaches in Ceramic Archaeology*: 27–43. Los Angeles: UCLA Institute of Archaeology.

Jarman, M. R.

1972   Appendix 6: the fauna. In P. M. Warren (ed.), *Myrtos: an Early Bronze Age Settlement in Crete*: 318–20. London: Thames and Hudson.

1996   Human influence in the development of the Cretan fauna. In D. S. Reese (ed.), *The Pleistocene and Holocene Fauna of Crete and its First Settlers*: 211–29. Madison: Prehistory Press.

Johnson, M.

1996   Water, animals and animal technology: a study of settlement patterns and economic change in Neolithic southern Greece. *OJA* 15: 267–95.

Kapetanios, A.

2003   The 'socialisation' of animals in Epirus, Ikaria and Crete: the material and symbolic role of man-animal relations of production in the process of social formation. In E. Kotjabopoulou, Y. Hamilakis, P. Halstead, C. Gamble and P. Elefanti (eds.), *Zooarchaeology in Greece: Recent Advances*: 283–90. London: British School at Athens.

Kilian, K.

1972   Zur mattbemalten Keramik der ausgehenden Bronzezeit und der Früheisenzeit aus Albanien. *Archäologisches Korrespondenzblatt* 2: 115–23.

1973   Zur eisenzeitlichen Transhumanz in Nordgriechenland. *Archäologisches Korrespondenzblatt* 3: 431–35.

Koster, H. A.

1977   *The Ecology of Pastoralism in Relation to Changing Patterns of Land Use in the Northeast Peloponnese.* PhD dissertation, University of Pennsylvania.

Kotjabopoulou, E. and K. Trantalidou

1993   Faunal analysis of the Skoteini cave. In A. Sampson (ed.), *Skotini Tharrounion*: 392–434. Athens: A. Sampson.

Kotsakis, K.

1983   *Keramiki Tekhnologia kai Keramiki Diaforopoiisi: Provlimata tis Graptis Keramikis tis Mesis Neolithikis Epokhis tou Sesklou.* PhD dissertation, University of Thessaloniki.

1999   What tells can tell: social space and settlement in the Greek Neolithic. In P. Halstead (ed.), *Neolithic Society in Greece* (SSAA 2): 66–76. Sheffield: Sheffield Academic Press.

2006   Settlement of discord: Sesklo and the emerging household. In N. Tasić and C. Grozdanov (eds.), *Homage to Milutin Garašanin*: 207–20. Belgrade: Serbian Academy of Sciences and Arts, Macedonian Academy of Sciences and Arts.

Kotsakis, K., D. Urem-Kotsou, R. Evershed, A. Sherratt and M. Copley

in press Epinan oi neolithikoi georgo-ktinotrofoi gala? I marturia gia tin arkhaioteri katanalosi galaktos stin Ellada. *Praktika Sunedriou 'I Istoria tou Ellinikou Galaktos kai ton Proionton tou'.* Xanthi.

Krahtopoulou, A.

2000   Holocene alluvial history of northern Pieria, Macedonia, Greece. In P. Halstead and C. Frederick (eds.), *Landscape and Land Use in Postglacial Greece* (SSAA 3): 15–27. Sheffield: Sheffield Academic Press.

Kyparissi-Apostolika, N.

1999   The Neolithic use of Theopetra cave in Thessaly. In P. Halstead (ed.), *Neolithic Society in Greece* (SSAA 2): 142–52. Sheffield: Sheffield Academic Press.

Lambeck, K.

1996   Sea-level change and shore-line evolution in Aegean Greece since Upper Palaeolithic time. *Antiquity* 70: 588–611.

Legge, A. J.
   1981   The agricultural economy. In R. J. Mercer (ed.), *Grimes Graves Excavations 1971–72*: 79–103. London: Her Majesty's Stationery Office.
Mainland, I. L. and P. Halstead
   2005   The diet and management of domestic sheep and goats at Neolithic Makriyalos. In J. Davies, M. Fabis, I. Mainland, M. Richards and R. Thomas (eds.), *Diet and Health in Past Animal Populations: Current Research and Future Directions*: 104–12. Oxford: Oxbow Books.
Mauss, M.
   1970   *The Gift*. London: Routledge and Kegan Paul.
Mee, C.
   2001   Nucleation and dispersal in Neolithic and Early Helladic Laconia. In K. Branigan (ed.), *Urbanism in the Aegean Bronze Age* (SSAA 4): 1–14. London: Sheffield Academic Press.
Milner, N.
   2005   Can seasonality studies be used to identify sedentism in the past? In D. Bailey, A. Whittle and V. Cummings (eds.), *(un)settling the Neolithic*: 32–37. Oxford: Oxbow Books.
Nakou, G.
   1995   The cutting edge: a new look at early Aegean metallurgy. *JMA* 8: 1–32.
Nitsiakos, V.
   1985   *A Vlach Pastoral Community in Greece: the Effects of its Incorporation into the National Economy and Society*. PhD dissertation, University of Cambridge.
Nowicki, K.
   2002   The end of the Neolithic in Crete. *Aegean Archaeology* 6: 7–72.
O'Shea, J.
   1981   Coping with scarcity: exchange and social storage. In A. Sheridan and G. Bailey (eds.), *Economic Archaeology* (BAR International Series 96): 167–83. Oxford: British Archaeological Reports.
Papathanasiou, A.
   2001   *A Bioarchaeological Analysis of Neolithic Alepotrypa Cave, Greece*. Oxford: J. and E. Hedges.
   2003   Stable isotope analysis in Neolithic Greece and possible implications on human health. *International Journal of Osteoarchaeology* 13: 314–24.
   2005   Health status of the Neolithic population of Alepotrypa, Greece. *American Journal of Physical Anthropology* 126: 377–90.
Pappa, M. and M. Besios
   1999   The Makriyalos project: rescue excavations at the Neolithic site of Makriyalos, Pieria, northern Greece. In P. Halstead (ed.), *Neolithic Society in Greece* (SSAA 2): 108–20. Sheffield: Sheffield Academic Press.
Pappa, M., P. Halstead, K. Kotsakis and D. Urem-Kotsou
   2004   Evidence for large-scale feasting at Late Neolithic Makriyalos, N Greece. In P. Halstead and J. Barrett (eds.), *Food, Cuisine and Society in Prehistoric Greece* (SSAA 5): 16–44. Oxford: Oxbow Books.
Payne, S.
   1973   Kill-off patterns in sheep and goats: the mandibles from Asvan Kale. *Anatolian Studies* 23: 281–303.
   1985   Zoo-archaeology in Greece: a reader's guide. In N. C. Wilkie and W. D. E. Coulson (eds.), *Studies in Honor of William A. McDonald*: 211–44. Minneapolis: University of Minnesota Press.
Perlès, C.
   1990   L' outillage de pierre taillée néolithique en Grèce: approvisionnement et exploitation des matières premières. *BCH* 114: 1–42.

1999   The distribution of magoules in eastern Thessaly. In P. Halstead (ed.), *Neolithic Society in Greece* (SSAA 2): 42–56. Sheffield: Sheffield Academic Press.

2001   *The Early Neolithic in Greece*. Cambridge: Cambridge University Press.

Phelps, W. W.
1975   *The Neolithic Pottery Sequence in Southern Greece*. PhD dissertation, University of London.

Psikhogios, D. K.
1987   *Proikes, Foroi, Stafida kai Psomi: Oikonomia kai Oikogenia stin Agrotiki Ellada tou 19ou Aiona*. Athens: Ethniko Kentro Koinonikon Erevnon.

Pullen, D. J.
1992   Ox and plough in the Early Bronze Age Aegean. *AJA* 96: 45–54.

Renfrew, C.
1972   *The Emergence of Civilisation*. London: Methuen.

Renfrew, J.
1973   Agriculture. In D. R. Theocharis (ed.), *Neolithic Greece*: 147–64. Athens: National Bank of Greece.

Runnels, C. and J. Hansen
1986   The olive in the prehistoric Aegean: the evidence for domestication in the Early Bronze Age. *OJA* 5: 299–308.

Rutter, J. B.
1983   Some thoughts on the analysis of ceramic data generated by site surveys. In D. R. Keller and D. W. Rupp (eds.), *Archaeological Survey in the Mediterranean Area* (BAR International Series 155): 137–42. Oxford: British Archaeological Reports.

1993   Review of Aegean Prehistory 2: The prepalatial Bronze Age of the southern and central Greek mainland. *AJA* 97: 745–97.

Sabry, Z. I. and R. L. Rizek
1982   *Food Composition Tables for the Near East*. Rome, Washington: FAO, USDA.

Sampson, A.
1992   Late Neolithic remains at Tharounia, Euboea: a model for the seasonal use of settlements and caves. *BSA* 87: 61–101.

Schibler, J. and S. Jacomet
1999   Archaeozoological and archaeobotanical evidence of human impact on Neolithic environments in Switzerland. In N. Benecke (ed.), *The Holocene History of the European Vertebrate Fauna*: 339–54. Leidorf: Rahden.

Shennan, S.
1986   Central Europe in the third millennium BC: an evolutionary trajectory for the beginning of the European Bronze Age. *Journal of Anthropological Archaeology* 5: 115–46.

Sherratt, A.
1972   Socio-economic and demographic models for later European prehistory. In D. L. Clarke (ed.), *Models in Archaeology*: 477–542. London: Methuen.

1976   Resources, trade and technology. In G. Sieveking, I. Longworth and K. Wilson (eds.), *Problems in Economic and Social Archaeology*: 557–81. London: Duckworth.

1980   Water, soil and seasonality in early cereal cultivation. *World Archaeology* 11: 313–30.

1981   Plough and pastoralism: aspects of the secondary products revolution. In I. Hodder, G. Isaac and N. Hammond (eds.), *Pattern of the Past: Studies in Honour of David Clarke*: 261–305. Cambridge: Cambridge University Press.

1982   Mobile resources: settlement and exchange in early agricultural Europe. In C. Renfrew and S. Shennan (eds.), *Ranking, Resource and Exchange*: 13–26. Cambridge: Cambridge University Press.

1987   Cups that cheered: the introduction of alcohol to prehistoric Europe. In W. Waldren and

R. Kennard (eds.), *Bell Beakers of the Western Mediterranean: the Oxford International Conference 1986* (BAR International Series 331): 81–106. Oxford: British Archaeological Reports.

1990   The genesis of megaliths: monumentality, ethnicity and social complexity in Neolithic north-west Europe. *World Archaeology* 22: 147–67.

1991   Palaeoethnobotany: from crops to cuisine. In F. Queiroga and A. P. Dinis (eds.), *Paleoecologia e Arqueologia 2*: 221–36. Vila Nova de Famalicao.

1997   *Economy and Society in Prehistoric Europe: Changing Perspectives*. Edinburgh: Edinburgh University Press.

1999   Crops before cash: hunting, farming, manufacture and trade in earlier Eurasia. In C. Gosden and J. G. Hather (eds.), *The Prehistory of Food*: 13–34. London: Routledge.

Speth, J.
1983   *Bison Kills and Bone Counts*. Chicago: Chicago University Press.

Stellatou, A.
2006   *Final Neolithic and Early Bronze Age Settlement in the Southern Aegean: a Comparative Spatial Analysis of Three Regional Surveys*. PhD dissertation, University College London.

Theocharis, D. R.
1973   *Neolithic Greece*. Athens: National Bank of Greece.

Tomkins, P.
2004   Filling in the 'Neolithic background': social life and social transformation in the Aegean before the Bronze Age. In J. Barrett and P. Halstead (eds.), *The Emergence of Civilisation Revisited* (SSAA 6): 38–63. Oxford: Oxbow Books.

2007   Communality and competition. The social life of food and containers at Aceramic and Early Neolithic Knossos, Crete. In C. Mee and J. Renard (eds.), *Cooking Up the Past: Food and Culinary Practices in the Neolithic and Bronze Age Aegean*: 174–99. Oxford: Oxbow Books.

in press Domesticity by default: rethinking Neolithic cave-use in Greece and the Aegean. In H. Moyes (ed.), *Journeys into the Dark Zone: a Cross-Cultural Perspective on Caves as Sacred Spaces*. Boulder: University Press of Colorado.

Tomkins, P. and P. Day
2001   Production and exchange of the earliest ceramic vessels in the Aegean: a view from Early Neolithic Knossos, Crete. *Antiquity* 75: 259–60.

Triantaphyllou, S.
1999   Prehistoric Makriyalos: a story from the fragments. In P. Halstead (ed.), *Neolithic Society in Greece* (SSAA 2): 128–35. Sheffield: Sheffield Academic Press.

2001   *A Bioarchaeological Approach to Prehistoric Cemetery Populations from Central and Western Greek Macedonia* (BAR International Series 976). Oxford: British Archaeological Reports.

Tsuneki, A.
1987   A reconsideration of Spondylus shell rings from Agia Sofia magoula, Greece, *Bulletin of the Ancient Orient Museum* 9: 1–15.

Urem-Kotsou, D. and K. Kotsakis
2007   Pottery, cuisine and community in the Neolithic of north Greece. In C. Mee and J. Renard (eds.), *Cooking Up the Past: Food and Culinary Practices in the Neolithic and Bronze Age Aegean*: 225–46. Oxford: Oxbow Books.

Valamoti, S. M.
2007   Traditional foods and culinary novelties in Neolithic and Bronze Age northern Greece: an overview of the archaeobotanical evidence. In C. Mee and J. Renard (eds.), *Cooking Up the Past: Food and Culinary Practices in the Neolithic and Bronze Age Aegean*: 89–108. Oxford: Oxbow Books.

Valamoti, S. M., M. Mangafa, H. Koukouli-Chrysanthaki and D. Malamidou

2007   Grape-pressings from northern Greece: the earliest wine in the Aegean? *Antiquity* 81: 54–61.
Vergopoulos, K.
1975   *To Agrotiko Zitima stin Ellada, i Koinoniki Ensomatosi tis Georgias.* Athens: Exandas.
Warren, P. M. and Y. Tzedhakis
1974   Debla. An Early Minoan settlement in western Crete. *BSA* 69: 299–342.
Washburn, D. K.
1983   Symmetry analysis of ceramic design: two tests of the method on neolithic material from Greece and the Aegean. In D. K. Washburn (ed.), *Structure and Cognition in Art*: 138–64. Cambridge: Cambridge University Press.
Watrous, V.
1994   Review of Aegean Prehistory 3: Crete from earliest prehistory through the Protopalatial period. *AJA* 98: 695–753.
Whitelaw, T. M.
2000   Settlement instability and landscape degradation in the southern Aegean in the third millennium BC. In P. Halstead and C. Frederick (eds.), *Landscape and Land Use in Postglacial Greece* (SSAA 3): 135–61. Sheffield: Sheffield Academic Press.
2004   Estimating the population of Neopalatial Knossos. In G. Cadogan, E. Hatzaki and A. Vasilakis (eds.), *Knossos: City, Palace, State*: 147–58. London: British School at Athens.
Whitelaw, T. M., P. M. Day, E. Kiriatzi, V. Kilikoglou and D. E. Wilson
1997   Ceramic traditions at EMIIB Myrtos Fournou Korifi. In R. Laffineur and P. P. Betancourt (eds.), *TECHNE. Craftsmen, Craftswomen and Craftsmanship in the Aegean Bronze Age* (Aegaeum 16): 265–74. Liège: Université de Liège.
Whittle, A.
1996   Houses in context: buildings as process. In T. Darvill and J. Thomas (eds.), *Neolithic Houses in Northwest Europe and Beyond*: 13–26. Oxford: Oxbow Books.
Wiessner, P.
1982   Risk, reciprocity and social influences on !Kung San economics. In E. Leacock and R. Lee (eds.), *Politics and History in Band Societies*: 61–84. Cambridge: Cambridge University Press.
Wijnen, M.
1982   *The Early Neolithic I Settlement at Sesklo: an Early Farming Community in Thessaly, Greece.* Leiden: Leiden University Press.
Wilkens, B.
1996   Faunal remains from Italian excavations on Crete. In D. S. Reese (ed.), *Pleistocene and Holocene Fauna of Crete and its First Settlers*: 241–61. Madison: Prehistory Press.
Wilkie, N. C. and M. E. Savina
1997   The earliest farmers in Macedonia. *Antiquity* 71: 201–7.
Wright, K.
2000   The social origins of cooking and dining in early villages of western Asia. *PPS* 66: 89–121.
Yannouli, E. and K. Trantalidou
1999   The fallow deer (*Dama dama* Linnaeus, 1758): archaeological presence and representation in Greece. In N. Benecke (ed.), *The Holocene History of the European Vertebrate Fauna*: 247–81. Leidorf: Rahden.
Zachos, K. L.
1999   Zas Cave on Naxos and the role of caves in the Aegean Late Neolithic. In P. Halstead (ed.), *Neolithic Society in Greece* (SSAA 2): 153–63. Sheffield: Sheffield Academic Press.

15

The Neolithic-Early Bronze Age Transition in Crete: New Evidence from the Settlement at Petras Kephala, Siteia

Yiannis Papadatos

Although widely regarded as a dynamic and significant phase in Minoan prehistory (Vagnetti and Belli 1978; Hood 1990a; Vagnetti 1996; Nowicki 2002; Hayden 2003), the Neolithic-Early Bronze Age (EBA) transition in Crete poses problems of two sorts. First, there are problems of definition and relative chronology. This is not surprising since no published site has produced a complete stratigraphic sequence from FN to EM I (see Figure 15.1 for sites mentioned in the text). At the long-lived, multi-period sites of Knossos and Phaistos, material of this date has long been known to exist, but often in mixed, secondary deposits that lack clear stratigraphic evidence of succession and it is only now that that the first stratified FN–EM I deposits are beginning to be located (Tomkins 2007; this volume; Todaro and Di Tonto this volume). This has led to serious misunderstandings and problems of definition. The existing literature is also unclear on the chronological relationship between the Neolithic sequences at Knossos and Phaistos (Manteli and Evely 1995: 11; Vagnetti 1996: 37–38), although resolution of this issue seems to be imminent (Todaro and Di Tonto this volume; Tomkins 2007; this volume). Furthermore it has recently been

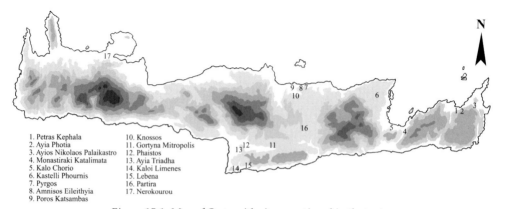

1. Petras Kephala
2. Ayia Photia
3. Ayios Nikolaos Palaikastro
4. Monastiraki Katalimata
5. Kalo Chorio
6. Kastelli Phournis
7. Pyrgos
8. Amnisos Eileithyia
9. Poros Katsambas
10. Knossos
11. Gortyna Mitropolis
12. Phaistos
13. Ayia Triadha
14. Kaloi Limenes
15. Lebena
16. Partira
17. Nerokourou

Figure 15.1. Map of Crete with sites mentioned in the text.

shown that the EM I assemblage hitherto considered to be earliest at Knossos, the Palace Well deposit, should actually be dated towards the end of this period and cannot represent the beginning of EBA in Crete (Wilson and Day 2000: 51–56). Although reconsideration of old assemblages at both Knossos (Tomkins 2007) and Phaistos (Todaro 2005) has brought us closer to a solution, the problem cannot be fully resolved until either a new, complete and undisturbed FN–EM I sequence is found at these sites or an external point of reference, that is a new stratigraphic sequence from another site, is located. In the rest of Crete, however, the available evidence is based either on single-phased domestic assemblages, such as Monastiraki Katalimata (Nowicki 2002: 16–20), Gortyna Mitropolis (Vagnetti 1973), Kaloi Limenes (Vasilakis 1987), Nerokourou (Vagnetti *et al.* 1989), Kastelli Phournis (Manteli 1992), or on unstratified – and often disturbed – funerary and cave assemblages, such as Partira (Mortzos 1972), Ayios Nikolaos-Palaikastro (Tod 1903), Amnisos-Eileithyia (Betancourt and Marinatos 2001), Trapeza (Pendlebury *et al.* 1935–6) and Lebena (Alexiou and Warren 2004: 118). Although the above sites could be placed in the Neolithic-EBA transition, none of them has stratified material from *both* the FN and EM I periods that might allow the character and features of the transition to be clarified. The confusion is increased when the same assemblages are often considered FN, sub-Neolithic or early EM I (for a detailed discussion see Nowicki 2002: 11–15; Tomkins 2007). Moreover, in several cases, especially in surface surveys, when typology cannot provide a precise date, the general and obscure term 'FN/EM I' is often used (Haggis 2005: 47). Therefore, consensus has been lacking not only regarding the definition of the FN and EM I periods, but also concerning the precise dating of the assemblages that represent these transitional phases. These are fundamental problems that go beyond simple terminology and have had significant implications for the way we define, understand and interpret the Neolithic-EBA transition.

Beyond relative chronology, the second major issue concerns the historical conditions that caused the emergence of the cultural features that characterize the EBA and differentiate it from what was happening during the Neolithic. Late FN and EM I are characterized by new settlement patterns, population mobility and expansion (Watrous 1994: 701; Branigan 1998: 80–84; Vokotopoulos 2000; Nowicki 2002; Hayden 2003), changes in pottery styles (Hood 1990b; Betancourt 1999; Nowicki 2002), the development of metallurgy (Muhly 2004; Papadatos 2007) and the emergence of formal burial customs (Vagnetti and Belli 1978: 150–51; Betancourt 1999: 36–37). The interpretation of these changes, however, is a matter of ongoing debate. Several scholars have explained them as the result of population movements from other areas into Crete (Warren 1974: 41–43; Hood 1990a; 1990b; Nowicki 1999; 2002; Hayden 2003: 395). There is disagreement, however, as to the precise chronology of these movements, variously dated to FN or EM I, and as to the place of origin of the newcomers, which is also variously located in the Dodecanese and southwest Anatolia, the Troad and northeast Aegean, Cilicia or the coast of Syro-Palestine. At the same time, other scholars have argued that the emergence of the EBA in Crete was a long and gradual process, often with external influences, but without any significant migration (Branigan 1970: 201; Evans 1974: 19–21; Vagnetti 1996: 39).

The excavation of an FN–EM I settlement at the site of Petras Kephala in east Crete thus provides a rare opportunity to study the Neolithic-EBA transition in greater detail. The aim of this paper is to summarize the evidence from the site and outline its implications for the issues discussed above. Study of the Petras Kephala material is at a preliminary stage, and the following discussion should be treated as a re-examination of the old problems in the light of the new evidence rather than as a definitive resolution of the issues involved.

The Site

Test excavations carried out during 2002–2004 at Petras, near Siteia, by the 24th Ephorate of Prehistoric and Classical Antiquities, have revealed remains of habitation dated to FN IV and EM I. The site lies on the north slope of the Kephala hill (Figure 15.2), 200 m east of the lower hill, where the Minoan town and the palace of Petras have been unearthed (Tsipopoulou 1999; 2002). The excavation covered an area of about 360 m² but surface survey has shown wide distribution of FN and EM I pottery on the north and east slopes (Tsipopoulou 1990: 321; Nowicki 2002: 28), suggesting a relatively large area of habitation. Although this distribution seems partly to reflect erosion and bulldozing activities (especially on the east slopes), there is evidence for *in situ* material as well, especially on the southeast slopes of the hill. It is impossible to give a precise estimate of the size of the settlement, but it seems clear that the excavation revealed a relatively small proportion of the total area of FN–EM I habitation on the Kephala hill.

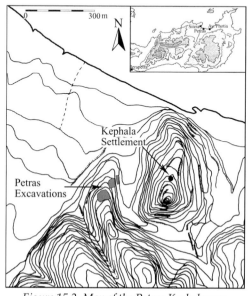

The architectural evidence is rather complex and suggests several successive phases of occupation, during which some older walls went out of use and were covered by new structures, whilst others were reused as part of new building complexes (Figure 15.3). The earliest architectural remains, dated to the very end of the Neolithic (FN IV), consist of

Figure 15.2. Map of the Petras Kephala area.

several straight walls on the west edge of the excavated area, defining two rectilinear rooms parallel to each other. The latest architectural remains are dated to EM I and consist of several straight walls forming a large building complex with at least eight rooms. Several curvilinear walls belong, on the basis of orientation and structure, to an earlier architectural phase of this building complex. Some of these were reused in the EM I building complex, whilst the rest went out of use. The precise dating of these curvilinear walls remains unclear, but they certainly belong to an intermediate architectural phase between the FN IV rooms and the EM I building complex. There is no evidence for any dramatic event separating the various phases and the reuse of some of the older curvilinear walls indicates that the gap between the intermediate and EM I phases was not long. The end of the settlement, at some time during EM I, was also not marked by any major event. The site was probably simply abandoned – there are no indications for fire destruction. The earliest remains found underneath the Petras palace are dated to EM IIA (pottery) and EM IIB (architecture and pottery) (Tsipopoulou 2002: 136), suggesting a shift of habitation from the steep Kephala hill to the lower and more accessible palace hill. It is difficult at present, however, to determine whether or not there was a hiatus between the abandonment of the Kephala hill and the occupation of the palace hill.

The pottery of the site (currently under study by the author and P. Tomkins) clearly indicates two main phases of occupation (FN IV and EM I). Most of the FN pottery comes from the west edge of the site, where deep, undisturbed deposits were found inside and around the two rooms. This pottery belongs to a single stylistic phase, dated by parallels to FN IV, and in its majority is coarse to semi-coarse with dark grey to black core. The surface is burnished with a dull red to brown colour. The same is also true for the finer vases, though their surface is occasionally highly polished. Shapes are restricted to open and semi-

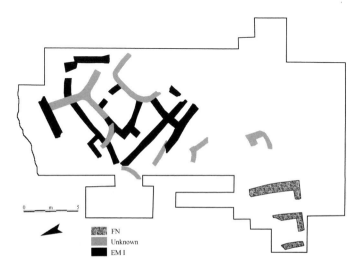

0   m   5

FN
Unknown
EM I

Figure 15.3. Petras Kephala: Plan of the excavated architectural remains.

closed vases, mainly cups (Figure 15.4a–b), open bowls (Figure 15.4c) and collared jars (Figure 15.4d). The bases are usually rounded, although some large jars have a pointed base. The rims are simple, often slightly everted. Strap handles prevail and vertical handles of circular section are rare. There is also a large number of 'cheese-pots' (Figure 15.4f). Close parallels for the assemblage can be found both within and outside Crete. There are many forms, such as the round-based curved or carinated bowls with everted or flared rim (Figure 15.4e), that are typical of Cretan FN IV assemblages at Phaistos and Knossos (Vagnetti 1972–3: 55 fig. 57(14); 64, fig. 63(17–23); 66, fig. 64; Tomkins 2007: fig. 15(11)). On the other hand, the frequency with which 'cheese-pots' occur contrasts sharply with the FN IV deposits at Knossos and Phaistos, and brings Kephala closer to Nerokourou in west Crete (Vagnetti *et al.* 1989) as well as to sites beyond Crete, such as Partheni on Leros, Alimnia on Rhodes and Gyali near Nissyros (Sampson 1984; 1987; 1988). A high frequency of 'cheese-pots' has also been noted in surface material from Kasos, Karpathos and sites in east, south and west Crete (Nowicki 2002: 28; this volume).

In addition to FN IV pottery, the site has also produced limited quantities of earlier material, dated to FN I–III. This ceramic material is fragmentary and was found not *in situ*, but mixed with FN IV and EM I pottery in open areas and beneath the floors of the EM I building complex. Nevertheless, it is very important as it indicates some sort of activity in the area prior to FN IV.

The pottery of the later phase probably dates to the earlier part of EM I. It was found inside and outside the rooms of the EM I building complex, on the

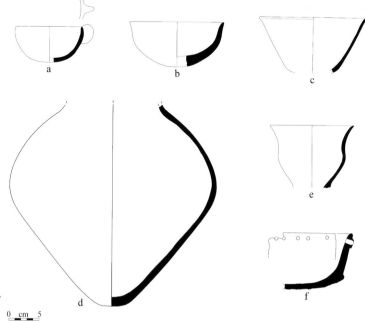

Figure 15.4. Petras Kephala: Final Neolithic pottery.

0 cm 5

floors and in the layers of building collapse. The EM I ceramic assemblage consists of two major components. The first comprises the burnished wares, mainly Dark Grey Burnished and smaller quantities of Red/Brown Burnished and Orange/Buff Burnished. The vessels in these wares are primarily serving vessels. Most common is the high-pedestalled bowl (Figure 15.5a), with holes or fenestrations on the foot, vertical handles of circular or elliptical section and occasionally small 'rivets' or knobs on the rim. Less frequent is the carinated convex cup (Figure 15.5b) with curved base, and with a vertical tubular or elliptical handle or a vertically pierced triangular lug. Other shapes in burnished wares are the miniature suspension pyxis (Figure 15.5c), the collared jar and the shallow bowl or deep plate (Figure 15.5d). Jugs are extremely rare, with only two small specimens with pinched-out spout from 20 crates of pottery. It should be also noted that pattern burnished decoration is quite rare, restricted to pedestalled bowls and cups, and consists of reserved panels with simple, thin, vertical or diagonal lines.

The second major component of the EM I assemblage is the Washed and Wiped Ware, with red to brown surface. In general, the fabric is coarser and more friable than that of the burnished pottery, and the vases produced were used mainly for food preparation and medium-scale storage. The most common shape is the hole-mouthed spherical jar (Figure 15.6a), with curved, heavily wiped or even scored base, square incurving rim and two handles below the rim. These handles are something between a strap handle and a tubular handle in section. The jars are made in various sizes and were used for both cooking and storage. Another very common vessel is the baking plate (Figure 15.6c), the base of which is rough due to its probable manufacture in a hollowed-out cavity in the earth.

An interesting feature of the EM I assemblage is the limited quantity of Dark-on-Light painted ware, represented by a few sherds and a single example of a two-handled collared jar. More common (but still no more than 5% of the total) is Red Slipped ware, in which the entire vase is covered with a red to brown slip, always different from the colour of the clay. It is represented by various medium-sized shapes, the commonest being the two handled collared jar or tankard (Figure 15.6b). Finally, there are several thick-walled sherds from very large open vessels or pithoi. These are occasionally painted inside and/or

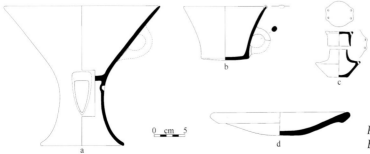

0 cm 5

Figure 15.5. Petras Kephala: Early Minoan I pottery.

outside with red slip, which in one case creates a dripping pattern (Figure 15.6d). These vases also have complex relief decoration on the exterior, consisting of highly pronounced ribs and knobs that form linear or curvilinear motifs. Unfortunately, it was impossible to restore a full profile, but these sherds may be derived from no more than five to seven pithoid vases.

In contrast to the FN ceramic assemblage, the EM I pottery does not indicate any significant influence or affinity with areas outside Crete. Instead, its parallels lie entirely with EM I assemblages from across the island. Numerous features favouring an early EM I date include the fenestrations on the pedestalled bowls, the limited presence of pattern burnished decoration, the absence of high biconical chalices of Pyrgos type, the projections or horns on the rims of the burnished bowls and cups, the miniature suspension pyxides, the curved bases of the carinated convex cups, the strap-like handles on the hole-mouthed jars, the limited presence of painted decoration, and the virtual absence of jugs. Close parallels can be found at Partira (Mortzos 1972) and Ayios Nikolaos-Palaikastro (Tod 1903), and amongst the earliest EM I material from Lebena (Alexiou and Warren 2004: 118) and Phaistos (Todaro 2005). The dating is reinforced by the fact that the pottery shows little affinity with EM I assemblages contemporary with the 'Kampos group' horizon. This is true not only for assemblages with Cycladic affinities, such as Ayia Photia (Davaras and Betancourt 2004), Pyrgos (Xanthoudides 1918) and Poros Katsambas (Wilson *et al.* 2004), but also with other non

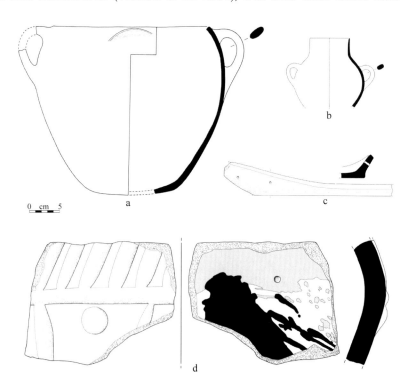

Figure 15.6. Petras Kephala: Early Minoan I pottery.

Cycladic-related assemblages, such as Kalo Chorio (Haggis 1996) and Ayia Triadha (Todaro 2003). Considering that all these sites should be dated towards the end of the EM I period (Warren 1984; Wilson and Day 2000), it seems safe to conclude that Petras Kephala is earlier.

Chronology

Petras Kephala, with its clear and undisturbed stratified sequence running from the end of FN into EM I, brings much needed clarification to the chronological problems of the Neolithic-EBA transition. Regarding the end of the Neolithic, the Petras Kephala material sheds new light on the sub-phasing of this period and its relationship with EM I. It has been suggested that the old 'FN' period could be divided into two sub-phases (Vagnetti 1996: 38; Nowicki 2002: 15): 'FN I', an earlier phase represented by Phaistos and Katalimata; and 'FN II', a later phase represented by Nerokourou and other sites with 'cheese-pots'. Indeed, it seems that sites of the 'cheese-pot' horizon (such as Petras Kephala and Nerokourou) belong to a later stage, that is FN IV, while assemblages like Katalimata find parallels in the preceding FN III period, as represented at Knossos and Phaistos (Tomkins 2007; Todaro and Di Tonto this volume). On the other hand, it should be noted that Petras Kephala has parallels not only with sites of the 'cheese-pot' horizon, but also with latest Neolithic (FN IV) assemblages at Knossos and Phaistos. This would seem to indicate that the difference between these sites is cultural rather than chronological, a possibility not excluded by Nowicki (2002: 65) or Vagnetti (1996: 38; Vagnetti and Belli 1978: 161). Since 'cheese-pots' are traditionally considered an off-island feature, their presence may indicate outside influence. The evidence from Petras Kephala thus suggests that 'cheese-pot' sites are contemporary with other latest FN assemblages, in which 'cheese-pots' are rare or absent. The presence of 'cheese-pots' at some sites may indeed signal a *late* date within FN, but their absence does not necessarily indicate an *early* one.

A second significant conclusion is that all assemblages that have been considered as 'sub-neolithic' or Final Neolithic in the literature, such as Partira and Ayios Nikolaos (Vagnetti and Belli 1978: 161), are contemporary with the EM I material from Petras Kephala, and therefore should be placed early in EM I, a view reinforced by the similar dating of the earliest material at Lebena (Alexiou and Warren 2004: 118). These assemblages are quite distinct from the FN IV material from Petras Kephala and instead exhibit features that characterize the EM I pottery from the site, such as dark grey burnished surfaces, pattern burnished decoration, miniature suspension pyxides, one-handled cups with convex base, and the virtual absence of dark-on-light painted pottery and jugs.

Finally, the Petras Kephala assemblage demonstrates clearly that it is indeed possible to divide EM I into two sub-phases. Stylistically, the latest pottery from the site bears little similarity to the ceramic assemblages from sites of the 'Kampos group', such as Ayia Photia, Poros Katsambas and Pyrgos. This difference is particularly striking between the Petras Kephala and Ayia Photia assemblages. Despite their proximity, there are no parallels between the two sites. Although we cannot exclude some chronological overlap, it seems clear that the EM I material from Petras Kephala represents a cultural horizon that is earlier than the 'Kampos group' horizon, which in this area is represented by Ayia Photia. Given that the 'Kampos group' is dated towards the end of EM I (Renfrew 1984; Warren 1984: 59–60; Wilson and Day 2000: 50–56), we should return to the old division of EM I into two sub-phases (EM IA and EM IB), a suggestion reinforced by recent work on the stratigraphic sequence at Phaistos (Todaro 2005).

The Advent of the Early Bronze Age

Petras Kephala also provides valuable new evidence for the broader context of the FN–EBA transition and the processes that lead to the emergence of features characteristic of the EBA on Crete. The two copper ores and six pieces of copper slag found at Petras Kephala constitute the earliest evidence to-date for metallurgical activities in Crete (Papadatos 2007). These were found beneath the EM I floors, in mixed deposits containing FN and EM I pottery and are thus certainly earlier than the EM I building complex. It is unclear whether they can be dated as early as FN IV, but there is indirect evidence to support this hypothesis. Several pieces of burnt clay found in undisturbed FN IV deposits seem to have been subjected to temperatures higher than normally occur in a pottery kiln (there is no evidence of a burnt destruction), and so may plausibly be associated with metallurgical activity (Papadatos 2007). Hitherto, metallurgy on Crete has been considered a later development (Day *et al.* 1998: 145; Betancourt 2003), associated with later EM I (*i.e.*, 'Kampos Group' horizon) sites, such as Ayia Photia and Poros Katsambas, which have strong Cycladic affinities (Dimopoulou 1997; Davaras and Betancourt 2004). The Kephala evidence alters this picture, as it shows that metallurgy in Crete probably developed earlier, in a different cultural and chronological horizon, before the Cycladic expansion of the 'Kampos group' phase (Papadatos 2007). Moreover, with this evidence in mind, Crete no longer appears a world apart, isolated from the metallurgical developments of the rest of the Aegean. Instead, it can be added to a growing number of FN Aegean sites that have produced similar evidence for early metallurgical activity, such as Sitagroi, Kephala on Keos and Gyali (Nakou 1995: 3–8; Muhly 2002: 77).

The introduction of metallurgy probably at the very end of the Neolithic marks a significant step towards the material culture characteristic of the EBA. In the case of pottery technology and typology, however, the evidence suggests that major changes occurred in the following period, at the beginning of EM I. The pottery from Petras Kephala, which during FN IV is relatively unvaried in terms of form, decoration and surface treatment, in EM I changes dramatically. For the first time wares are characterized by greater variation in surface treatment and functional specialisation (*e.g.,* burnished wares for serving/drinking purposes, washed and wiped ware for cooking and storing). Moreover, the wares that appear in this phase continue (though not without changes and additions) until at least EM IIB. Therefore, from the point of view of style (and relative chronology), it is the introduction of these wares that signals the advent of the EBA. The same can be suggested for the obsidian technology of Petras Kephala, which in EM I shows evidence for change and innovation, with the appearance of the first fine prismatic blades. These are very different from their earlier, FN, counterparts and similar to the standard form that predominates in the rest of the EBA all over the Aegean (D'Annibale this volume).

Population Movements and Cultural Change

The last issue to be addressed concerns the historical conditions that brought about the changes signalling the advent of the EBA in Crete. The evidence from Petras Kephala suggests that, if an external element is to be identified, it is in the FN IV period. The stylistic affinities with the Dodecanese, provided by the 'cheese-pots' could, on their own, be taken to indicate not just cultural influence, but also population movements from this area into Crete (see also Nowicki this volume). Similar observations concerning affinities with pottery from outside Crete have been made for the contemporary site of Nerokourou (Vagnetti 1996) and for other sites identified by surveys all over Crete (Nowicki 2002). On the other hand, the preliminary results of petrographic analysis show that the bulk of the FN IV pottery was made locally (Nodarou pers. comm.). Moreover, the presence of FN I–III material, albeit fragmentary and in secondary deposits, indicates that the site had a long history of habitation before FN IV.

The differences between the FN IV pottery of Petras Kephala and the typical Cretan material of Knossos and Phaistos, seen especially in the frequency of the 'cheese-pots', reinforces the idea that at the end of the Neolithic there existed in Crete two different cultural traditions, one continuing the long Neolithic tradition, and a new one also bearing affinities with areas outside Crete (Vagnetti 1996; Nowicki 2002). As suggested above, this difference is cultural rather than chronological. The distribution of these sites does not seem to be coincidental. In terms of excavated sites, the new tradition is best represented by Nerokourou in the far west and Petras Kephala in the far east of Crete. Surface surveys reinforce this picture, since sites of this 'new' tradition tend to concentrate at the two extremities of Crete, and are almost absent from the central part of the island (Nowicki 2002). It seems that, during this period, Crete communicated with the wider Aegean world mainly through these areas. Historically, the western and eastern parts of the island had frequent, bi-directional contacts with their adjacent areas. For this reason, it would be a mistake to assume the same origin for either the cultural links or any potential newcomers. In the case of Petras Kephala the affinities are with the Dodecanese, while for Nerokourou perhaps we should look towards the Peloponnese (Vagnetti 1996: 34).

Because of the preliminary stage of this study, it is not yet possible to give a definite answer to whether Kephala Petras and Nerokourou represent simple cultural influence or population movements. Whatever the case, it seems clear that through these sites the wider Aegean world 'intrudes' into Crete, creating new cultural and perhaps social/demographic conditions, and introducing an entirely new technology, that of metallurgy, which for the moment is only certainly attested at Petras Kephala and possibly at Chrysokamino (Betancourt *et al.* 1999; Muhly 2004).

If we associate this 'new' FN IV tradition with an external cultural or ethnic element, however, how should we interpret the changes observed at Petras Kephala in EM I, in domains such as architecture, pottery and obsidian technology? How important were these changes and to what degree do they represent a real break in the cultural sequence? Should they be interpreted in terms of external factors, internal processes, or maybe a combination of both? The changes that signal the advent of the EBA in Crete were first recognized at Knossos and interpreted in terms of population movements at the beginning of EM I (Warren 1974; Hood 1990a; 1990b). At first glance, Petras Kephala shows similar (if not sharper) changes and breaks in material culture at the beginning of the EM I period, but a more detailed study of the available evidence suggests that the picture is not that simple.

In the architecture, the change to a single, multi-roomed agglomerative building perhaps indicates transformations in the organisation of activities within the local society, or social structure, but transition from one period to the next was not a traumatic one, nor marked by any catastrophic event. In the pottery, the introduction of the first wares with functional specialization and diverse surface treatment contrasts sharply with the monotonous dark red burnished surface of FN IV, and indicates changes in aesthetic preferences, firing technology and the social meaning of pottery. The preliminary results of the archaeometric study, however, show the use of *similar local* clay pastes in both periods (Nodarou pers. comm.). In the chipped stone, the introduction of the first *fine* prismatic blades and the increased level of uniformity and standardization suggest transformations in knapping technology (D'Annibale this volume), but these can be interpreted not as groundbreaking innovations introduced from off-island, but the result of increased experience and gradual advancement.

It seems certain that, in contrast to FN, the changes at the beginning of EM I had little to do with the Dodecanese or with any other area outside Crete. Moreover, although the evidence from Petras Kephala may indeed indicate marked changes in material culture from FN IV to EM I, this is not necessarily the case for the entire island. At Knossos and Phaistos ceramic and other evidence now suggests continuity and gradual transformation rather than a sharp break (Todaro 2001; 2005; Tomkins 2007). Whatever happens at each site during the Neolithic-EBA transition, there is one clear similarity of great significance, namely that all the cultural features that appear in EM I, whether they represent a break (Petras Kephala) or continuity (Phaistos, Knossos) from FN, characterize almost the entire EBA all over Crete. Despite local variations and changes through time, agglomerative architecture, diversity in ceramic wares and fine prismatic blades continue throughout the EBA and across the island. For this reason, it is surely an oversimplification, at least, to attribute these changes to short-lived external influences on just parts of the island of Crete.

The significance of Petras Kephala is that it allows us to restate the problem and rephrase the question. Considering that the site provides evidence for a 'new' cultural tradition in FN, it is important to examine to what degree this tradition (a) survives into EM I, and (b) plays a role in the formation of the cultural elements that characterize the EBA of Crete. It is impossible to give definite answers at the moment, but full study and analysis of the Petras Kephala assemblages will provide valuable insights into these problems and possibilities.

Acknowledgements

I would like to thank the director of the Petras excavations, Metaxia Tsipopoulou for giving me permission to study and publish the material from Petras Kephala. For permissions to study, I would like to thank the Greek Archaeological Service, the 24th Ephoreia of Prehistoric and Classical Antiquities, and the director Vily Apostolakou. I am indebted to the INSTAP Study Centre for East Crete and its director Tom Brogan for providing facilities for the study of the material. For comments and discussions related to the paper I also thank Krzystof Nowicki, Cesare D'Annibale, Eleni Nodarou, Peter Tomkins and Metaxia Tsipopoulou. The conservation of the vases was carried out by Michel Roggenbucke and Kathy Hall, and the drawings by Doug Faulmann. The study related to this paper took place as part of the project 'Study and Publication of the FN–EM I settlement at Kephala Petras, Siteia' funded by INSTAP.

Bibliography

Alexiou, S. and P. M. Warren
    2004   *The Early Minoan Tombs of Lebena, Southern Crete* (SIMA 30). Sävedalen: Paul Åström.
Betancourt, P.
    1999   What is Minoan? FN/EM I in the Gulf of Mirabello region. In P. Betancourt, V. Karageorghis, R. Laffineur and W.-D. Niemeier (eds.), *MELETEMATA. Studies in Aegean Archaeology Presented to Malcolm H. Wiener as he Enters his 65th Year* (*Aegaeum* 20): 33–41. Liège: University of Liège.

2003   The impact of Cycladic settlers on Early Minoan Crete. *Mediterranean Archaeology and Archaeometry* 3: 3–12.

Betancourt, P., J. D. Muhly, W. Farrand, Co. Stearns, L. Onyshkevych, W. Hafford and D. Evely
1999   Research and excavation at Chrysokamino, Crete, 1995–1998. *Hesperia* 68: 343–70.

Betancourt, P. and N. Marinatos (eds.)
2001   To spilaio tis Amnisou: i ereuna tou 1992. *AE* (2000) 139: 179–236.

Branigan, K.
1970   *The Foundations of Palatial Crete*. London: Duckworth.
1998   Prehistoric and early history settlement in the Ziros region, eastern Crete. *BSA* 93: 23–90.

Davaras, C. and P. Betancourt
2004   *The Hagia Photia Cemetery I. The Tomb Groups and Architecture*. Philadelphia: INSTAP Academic Press.

Day, P., D. Wilson and E. Kiriatzi
1998   Pots, labels and people: burying ethnicity in the cemetery of Aghia Photia Siteias. In K. Branigan (ed.), *Cemetery and Society in the Aegean Bronze Age* (SSAA 1): 133–49. Sheffield: Sheffield Academic Press.

Dimopoulou, N.
1997   Workshops and craftsmen in the harbour town of Knossos at Poros-Katsambas. In R. Laffineur and P. Betancourt (eds.), *TECHNE. Craftsmen, Craftswomen and Craftsmanship in the Aegean Bronze Age* (Aegaeum 16): 433–38. Liège: University of Liège.

Evans, J. D.
1974   The archaeological evidence and its interpretation: some suggested approaches to the problem of the Aegean Bronze Age. In R. A. Crossland and A. Birchall (eds.), *Bronze Age Migrations in the Aegean*: 17–26. London: Duckworth.

Haggis, D.
1996   Excavations at Kalo Khorio, East Crete. *AJA* 100: 645–81.
2005   *Kavousi I: The Archaeological Survey of the Kavousi Region*. Philadelphia: INSTAP Academic Press.

Hayden, B.
2003   Final Neolithic – Early Minoan I/IIA settlement in the Vrokastro area, Eastern Crete. *AJA* 107: 363–412.

Hood, M. S. F.
1990a   Settlers in Crete c.3000 B.C. *Cretan Studies* 2: 150–58.
1990b   Autochthons or settlers ? Evidence for immigration at the beginning of the Early Bronze Age in Crete. *Pepragmena tou ST' Diethnous Kritologikou Synedriou* A1: 367–75. Chania: Philologikos Syllogos O Chrysostomos.

Manteli, K.
1992   The Neolithic well at Kastelli Phournis in eastern Crete. *BSA* 87: 103–20.

Manteli, K. and D. Evely
1995   The Neolithic levels from the Throne Room System, Knossos. *BSA* 90: 1–16.

Mortzos, C.
1972   Partira. Mia proimos Minoiki kerameiki omas. *Epetiris Epistimonikon Erevnon tou Panepistimiou Athinon* 3: 386–421.

Muhly, J. D.
2002   Early metallurgy in Greece and Cyprus. In Ü. Yalçin (ed.), *Anatolian Metal II* (Der Anschnitt, Beiheft 15): 77–82. Bochum: Deutsches Bergbau-Museum.
2004   Chrysokamino and the beginnings of metal technology on Crete and in the Aegean. In L. P. Day, M. S. Mook and J. D. Muhly (eds.), *Crete Beyond the Palaces: Proceedings of the Crete 2000 Conference*: 283–89. Philadelphia: INSTAP Academic Press.

Nakou, G.
  1995   The cutting edge: a new look at early Aegean metallurgy. *JMA* 8: 1–32.

Nowicki, K.
  1999   The Final Neolithic refugees or the Early Bronze Age newcomers? The problem of defensible sites in Crete in the late fourth millennium BC. In P. Betancourt, V. Karageorghis, R. Laffineur and W.-D. Niemeier (eds.), *MELETEMATA. Studies in Aegean Archaeology Presented to Malcolm H. Wiener as he Enters his 65th Year* (Aegaeum 20): 575–81. Liège: University of Liège.
  2002   The end of the Neolithic in Crete. *Aegean Archaeology* 6: 7–72.

Papadatos, Y.
  2007   The beginning of metallurgy in Crete: new evidence from the FN–EM I settlement at Kephala Petras, Siteia. In P. Day and R. Doonan (eds.), *Metallurgy in the Early Bronze Age Aegean* (SSAA 7): 154–67. Oxford: Oxbow Books.

Pendlebury, H. W., J. D. C. Pendlebury and M. B. Money-Coutts
  1935–6 Excavations in the plain of Lasithi, I, the cave of Trapeza. *BSA* 36: 5–131.

Renfrew, A. C.
  1984   From Melos to Syros: Kapros Grave D and the Kampos Group. In J. A. MacGillivray and R. L. N. Barber (eds.), *The Prehistoric Cyclades*: 41–54. Edinburgh: Department of Classical Archaeology.

Sampson, A.
  1984   The Neolithic of the Dodecanese and Aegean Neolithic culture. *BSA* 79: 239–49.
  1987   *H Neolithiki Periodos sta Dodekanisa*. Athens: Tameio Archaiologikon Poron kai Apallotrioseon.
  1988   *H Neolithiki Katoikisi sto Yiali tis Nisyrou*. Athens: Evoiki Archaiophilos Etaireia.

Tod, M. N.
  1903   Excavations at Palaikastro, II. Hagios Nikolaos. *BSA* 9: 336–43.

Todaro, S.
  2001   Nuove prospettive sulla produzione in stile Pyrgos nella Creta meridionale: il caso della pisside e della coppa su base ad anello. *Creta Antica* 2: 11–28.
  2003   Haghia Triada nel periodo Antico Minoico. *Creta Antica* 4: 69–95.
  2005   EM–MM IA ceramic groups at Phaistos: towards the definition of a prepalatial ceramic sequence in south central Crete. *Creta Antica* 6: 11–46.

Tomkins, P.
  2007   Neolithic: Strata IX–VIII, VII–VIB, VIA–V, IV, IIIB, IIIA, IIB, IIA and IC Groups. In N. Momigliano (ed.), *Knossos Pottery Handbook: Neolithic and Bronze Age (Minoan)*: 9–48. London: British School at Athens.

Tsipopoulou, M.
  1990   Minoiki katoikisi stin periochi tis polis tis Siteias. *Pepragmena tou ST' Diethnous Kritologikou Synedriou* (A2): 305–321. Chania: Philologikos Syllogos O Chrysostomos.
  1999   Before, during, after: The architectural phases of the palatial building at Petras, Siteia. In P. Betancourt, V. Karageorghis, R. Laffineur and W.-D. Niemeier (eds.), *MELETEMATA. Studies in Aegean Archaeology Presented to Malcolm H. Wiener as he Enters his 65th Year* (Aegaeum 20): 847–55. Liège: University of Liège.
  2002   Petras Siteia: the palace, the town, the hinterland and the Protopalatial background. In J. Driessen, I. Schoep and R. Laffineur (eds.), *Monuments of Minos, Rethinking the Minoan Palaces* (Aegaeum 23): 133–44. Liège: University of Liège.

Vagnetti, L.
   1972–3   L'insediamento neolitico di Festos. *ASA* 50–51: 7–138.
   1973   Tracce di due insediamenti neolitici nel territorio dell'antica Gortina. *Antichita Cretesi. Studi in Onore di Doro Levi I.* (Cronache di Archeologia 12): 1–9. Catania: Università di Catania, Istituto di Archeologia.
   1996   The Final Neolithic: Crete enters the wider world. *Cretan Studies* 5: 29–39.
Vagnetti, L. and P. Belli
   1978   Characters and problems of the Final Neolithic in Crete. *SMEA* 19: 125–63.
Vagnetti, L., A. Christopoulou and I. Tzedakis
   1989   Saggi ne gli stati Neolitici. In I. Tzedakis and A. Sacconi (eds.), *Scavi a Nerokourou Kydonias* (Recherche Greco-Italiane in Creta Occidentale I): 9–97. Roma: Edizioni Dell'Ateneo.
Vasilakis, A.
   1987   Anaskaphi neolithikou spitiou stous Kalous Limenes tis notias Kritis. *Eilapini: Studies in Honour of Professor N. Platon*: 45–53. Herakleion: Dimos Irakleiou.
Vokotopoulos, L.
   2000   Ochires protominoikes theseis stin periochi Zakrou. *Pepragmena tou H' Diethnous Kritilogikou Synedriou* : 129–46. Herakleion: Etaireia Kritikon Istorikon Meleton.
Warren, P. M.
   1974   Crete 3000–1400 B.C.: immigration and the archaeological evidence. In R. A. Crossland and A. Birchall (eds.), *Bronze Age Migrations in the Aegean. Archaeological and Linguistic Problems in Greek Prehistory* (Proceedings of the First International Colloquium on Aegean Prehistory, Sheffield): 41–50. London: Duckworth.
   1984   Early Minoan – Early Cycladic chronological correlations. In J. A. MacGillivray and R. L. N. Barber (eds.), *The Prehistoric Cyclades*: 55–63. Edinburgh: Department of Classical Archaeology.
Watrous, L. V.
   1994   Review of Aegean Prehistory 3: Crete from earliest prehistory through the Protopalatial period. *AJA* 98: 695–753.
Wilson, D. E. and P. M. Day
   2000   EM I chronology and social practice: pottery from the early palace tests at Knossos. *BSA* 95: 21–63.
Wilson, D., P. M. Day and N. Dimopoulou
   2004   The pottery from Early Minoan I–IIB Knossos and its relations with the harbour site of Poros-Katsambas. In G. Cadogan, E. Hatzaki and A. Vasilakis (eds.), *Knossos: Palace, City, State*: 67–74. London: British School at Athens.
Xanthoudides, S.
   1918   Megas Protominoikos taphos Pirgou. *ADelt* 4: 136–70.

16

Long After Hippos, Well Before Palaces: A Commentary on the Cultures and Contexts of Neolithic Crete

Cyprian Broodbank

The Kraken Wakes

For the past few decades Neolithic Knossos, and with it much of Neolithic Crete, has been lost in slumber, invisible and shielded from the trampling of millions of feet through the Minoan palace above it, barely stirred by archaeological pin-pricks into the Kephala tell or the occasional probing article, and lulled by the soporific repetition of interpretations dating back to the 1960s and 1970s. This volume therefore marks an exciting recent development, a re-awakening of interest over the last few years in what information we can derive from one of the Aegean's largest, tallest and longest-inhabited early settlement mounds, happily coupled with a growing recognition of the pan-Cretan extent of sites dating to the latest phases of the Neolithic, at least as this period is presently defined. Meanwhile the surrounding world has also moved on. This contribution offers some reflections on what we now know about Knossos and Crete during the Neolithic, and on how this knowledge fits into wider contemporary patterns. In the latter respect, it is complemented (and in scope far exceeded) by the Sherratts' reconstruction (this volume). Sitting beside Andrew Sherratt at this Round Table, for what I little knew was to be the last time, I was constantly aware of the swirling loops and arrows of large connections that his writing hand described as the papers were delivered. But equally salutary was the presence, on my left, of Yannis Papadatos, the exemplary excavator of another Kephala (this one at Petras), a small site in east Crete that will tell us important things about how it actually looks on the ground. The health and future of Cretan Neolithic studies relies, of course, on both these approaches, and it is in this spirit that the following remarks are made.

Before the Beginning

The inertia that has reigned for so long over the Neolithic of Crete is nowhere better exemplified than in the extraordinary fact that the date of the earliest verified presence on the island (Knossos Stratum X, attributed to an Aceramic or Initial Neolithic and beginning 7000–6700 BC, according to radiocarbon dates from a wooden stake, or 6500 BC, on one from charred grain [Perlès 2001: 85–88]) remains exactly the same, *and on the basis of much the same data*, as it did at the time of Cherry's last review of Mediterranean island colonisation (1990: 158–63), which treatment itself reported no substantial change from his initial analysis in 1981 (Cherry 1981: 43) and indeed, as he observed, previous discussions a decade before that. Here we have no choice but to resort to evidence drawn from beyond Cretan archaeology if we want to ascertain how likely this situation is to reflect ancient reality.

In this respect, the past fifteen years have fortified a pattern already emergent in 1990, namely that Crete is the only one of the 'big five' Mediterranean islands to have revealed no agreed evidence of an antecedent hunter-gatherer presence, seasonal or permanent (Broodbank 2006 for fuller discussion; see also below for one possible exception). Keeping only to secure identifications, in the central Mediterranean, barely insular Sicily was entered in the Aurignacian (30,000+ years ago; Chilardi *et al.* 1996) and permanently settled by at least 14,000 BC (Mussi 2001: 327–28). Corsica and Sardinia (conjoined at lower glacial sea-levels) were reached, maybe temporarily, some time close to the Last Glacial Maximum (22,000–18,500 BC; Klein Hofmeijer 1997: 18–20, table 1.1, fig. 1.3; Melis and Mussi 2002), and have so far produced nine sites used by foraging trappers and inshore fishers from the late ninth or eighth millennia BC (Costa 2004: 19–41). Most famously, Cyprus has Akrotiri-*Aetokremnos* (Simmons 1999), which marks a definite late eleventh to early tenth millennium BC presence, bolstered now by the discovery of further coastal sites almost certainly of comparable date (Ammerman *et al.* 2006), and regardless of ongoing disagreement as to whether the bird and mollusc eaters of *Aetokremnos* were also responsible for the deaths of the pigmy hippopotami whose bones dominate the rock shelter's lower stratum.

Long-range seafaring in the Mediterranean appears to have developed for the first time in the harsh climatic conditions of the Younger Dryas (10,800–9600 BC), to which period both the first Cypriot evidence and the earliest attested usage of Melian obsidian at Franchthi can be dated (Broodbank 2006: 208–11). By the early Holocene it was well established, at least in the eastern Mediterranean. Such ninth to eighth millennium BC Mesolithic island sites as the Cyclops cave on Youra and Maroulas on Kythnos attest to widespread mobile exploitation of parts of the maritime Aegean by probably patchily distributed populations living around its shores. Only in the case of Mallorca, which is unusually distant from the mainland, are the earliest dates for a fairly large Mediterranean island moving in the opposite direction, casting doubt on the proposed evidence of a hunter-gatherer presence and even subsequent early arrivals in favour of a relatively pristine colonisation horizon by farming groups in the later third millennium BC (Ramis and Alcover 2001; Ramis *et al.* 2002).

Given that Crete was accessible via inter-island crossings only slightly longer at contemporary sea-levels than those between the Cyclades, and considerably shorter than the single 70–100 km leap to Cyprus, we are effectively faced with the alternative of either accepting the likelihood of a so far undetected pre-Neolithic presence, maybe as far back as the Younger Dryas, or of producing good reasons as to why Crete might have bucked the trend. The merits of the former option cannot be assessed properly as long as we continue to assume that the traces of any putative hunter-gatherers should simply emerge serendipitously from the excavation of Bronze Age or later sites, or in the course of diachronic intensive field surveys. Neither of these methods, at least as practiced in the Aegean, is designed to maximise this likelihood (cf. Runnels *et al.* 2005). Instead, different kinds of targeted prospection strategies will be required, in particular the trial trenching of a large sample of caves and rock-shelters, including unprepossessing small coastal ones, to judge by *Aetokremnos* and the Corsican site of Monte Leone (Vigne and Desse-Berset 1995; Costa *et al.* 2003), coupled with the exploration of appropriate surface exposures, such as the coastal aeolian formations now examined to such good effect by Ammerman and his colleagues on Cyprus.

Concerning the degree to which Crete formed an attractive destination (or not) for seasonal visitation or longer stays, we equally need to clarify our picture of the island's ecology and resources before the 7th millennium BC. Here, at least, there has been some progress in the dating of several fossil horizons of endemic animals (Reese 1996), although with largely negative results from our perspective. In particular, with the rejection of a faulty radiocarbon date of 12,135 ± 485 bp on a bone from Katharo, the horizon dominated by pygmy hippopotami is now securely dated to far back in the Middle and probably Lower Pleistocene, in contrast to this species' proven survival on Cyprus until well after the Last Glacial Maximum. An ensuing horizon dominated by several deer species and large elephants developed early in the Upper Pleistocene, but cannot on present evidence be shown to continue later than some 21,000 years ago, on the most optimistic interpretation of the data, or at least twice as long ago if a more cautious approach is adopted (Reese *et al.* 1996; even this date applies only to the deer). What happened after that and up to the 'banalisation' of the island's fauna at the start of the Neolithic (Vigne 1999: 314), whether there remained any land fauna larger than a murid (though it might be noted that a slender diet of birds and molluscs may have sustained the users of *Aetokremnos*), and what might have happened to the island's vegetation with or without endemic grazers (Rackham and Moody 1996: 123–24), unfortunately remains anyone's guess (Lax and Strasser 1992 for one scenario). One uncertain yet tantalising clue is the late 19th century discovery in west Crete of a mineralised human cranium and other fragments cemented into a littoral breccia that also contained deer bones (Facchini and Giusberti 1992). The justified scepticism that has greeted attempts to date this deposit by the Protactinium/Uranium method coupled with pollen analysis to some 50,000 years ago has distracted from the observation that *any* association between human remains and those of endemic deer is significant in this context, regardless of its precise antiquity.

The Neolithic Colonisation of Crete as a Mainstream Process

When we turn to the mechanisms behind the inception of a farming community on the island shortly after 7000 BC, we encounter a quite different situation, with Crete now fitting better than ever into a wider Mediterranean context. Seventeen years ago, the transfer to Crete of a small nucleus of farmers, their domesticated plants and animals and the remainder of their cultural universe (as analysed by Broodbank and Strasser 1991) could be either taken as an unusually archaeologically visible example of a widespread maritime and terrestrial migratory process, or dismissed as an odd insular anomaly within a norm defined by indigenous hunter-gatherer adoption of Neolithic traits. Today, regardless as to whether details of the Broodbank and Strasser model for Crete need nuancing, there is no doubt that jump dispersal and enclave colonisation were indeed important elements of the process by which the Neolithic expanded throughout the Mediterranean. Indeed, Crete's thunder has in this respect been stolen by the recognition of a similar transfer of much of the Levantine PPNB package, plus fallow deer, to Cyprus in the late ninth millennium BC, more than a thousand years earlier (*e.g.*, Peltenburg *et al.* 2000). Maritime transfers by groups of farmers are now widely considered to have occurred not only in the eastern (van Andel and Runnels 1995; Perlès 2001) but also the central (Chapman and Müller 1990) and western Mediterranean (Zilhão 1993; 2000; Binder 2000). In this sense, and as has been pointed out earlier (Broodbank 1999: 21, 34–35), the Neolithic colonisation of Crete is, unlike the peopling of smaller islands later in the Neolithic, not so much a specifically insular event, as one manifestation of a growing proficiency in maritime transport during the early Holocene that brought into contact areas of land hitherto isolated from each other, either by the sea or long, circuitous land connections. That proficiency was itself a dual inheritance of hunter-gatherer seafaring skills developed in and after the Younger Dryas, and the demographic as well as ideological dynamics of the earliest Neolithic communities (Broodbank 2006: 216).

Two specific further points may be made about the arrival of the Neolithic on Crete. One is that the potential presence of earlier hunter-gatherers need cast little or no doubt on the intrusive nature of the process, so amply documented by the suite of non-local domesticates at Knossos and now supported, in addition, by Conolly's analysis of the lithics from Stratum X (this volume). Once again, Cyprus provides a parallel, for despite Watkins' exploration of an hypothetical continuity between the *Aetokremnos* and earliest Aceramic Neolithic phases (Watkins 2004), the latter is generally considered to reflect a new population influx bearing with it a cluster of early domesticates and wild species co-present at the junction point of Anatolia and the Levant, rather than acquisition of such novelties by pre-existent Cypriot hunter-gatherers. Interestingly, much the same is now argued for Corsica and, by implication, Sardinia (Costa 2004: 42–71), both once bastions of hunter-gatherer uptake models (*e.g.*, Lewthwaite 1988). Secondly, and whilst acknowledging the words of caution offered by Kostas Kotsakis (this volume) concerning the dangers of an excessive concentration on origins, as opposed to investigation of the constitution of a given region's Neolithic *in situ*, a better knowledge of the Cretan Neolithic antecedents might well prove useful in explaining why Crete's early material culture differs in important respects from that of the central Aegean. It could even conceivably shed light on the linguistic history of the island and the lack of parallels for the language(s) later recorded in the Linear A and Hieroglyphic scripts. Specifically, the suggestion (made on the grounds of crop types [Colledge and Conolly 2007; see also Conolly this volume] and maybe also slightly later ceramic parallels with Mersin) of a south Anatolian coastwise maritime expansion, building on the tradition evident on Cyprus, places Crete in a different phylogeny from the Thessalian Neolithic, which probably reflects an extension of expansion across the Anatolian plateau. There is liable to be a lot to learn about the nature and timing of the Neolithic advance in the current blind spot (or rather narrow ellipse) between the gulfs of Iskenderun and Mirabello.

Enlivening the Early to Late Neolithic

Once established, the Cretan Neolithic continues to exhibit a dappled appearance in terms of current knowledge, with patches of light alternating with others of shadow. Of the latter, the most profound concerns the enduring failure to detect the remains of substantial numbers of settlements on the island until the FN, save possibly for some MN at Gerani cave and LN at Katsambas and a handful of other small sites scattered across the island (Tomkins this volume; Galanidou and Manteli this volume; the revised chronology for the Cretan Neolithic proposed by Tomkins [2007; this volume] is adopted throughout this paper). Indeed, this point was underscored at the Round Table by the fact that all the new sites reported there date to the latest phases of the Neolithic. That our picture of earlier Cretan settlement is misleading and that Knossos was markedly less isolated than was once assumed (*e.g.*, Broodbank 1992: 47–50) is decisively demonstrated by Tomkins' identification of pottery fabrics at Knossos that derive from other parts of the island (this volume). Strasser (this volume) makes a similar argument on the basis of stone axes, where the counter-case for resource procurement from Knossos seems unlikely given the poor quality of some of the pieces, although his evidence relates to the FN, with one example of a stone axe found in a LN context (following Tomkins' revised chronology). An absence of other settlements also makes no demographic sense in that, according to Tomkins' chronology and spatial estimates (this volume), Knossos remained too small to be self-sustaining for a very long time indeed.

Why should the first 2500 years of farming settlement be so hard to detect on the ground, in one of the most thoroughly dug-over and surveyed regions of the

Mediterranean? Any contemporaries of effectively aceramic Stratum X, which lacks the abundant stone bowls of the Cypriot Aceramic Neolithic, might well be hard to find in the open, and indeed consist of no more than a modest scatter of lithics of low diagnosticity. But the virtually complete absence of evidence from excavated caves, and the continuing invisibility of open sites even long after pottery is amply attested at Knossos, argues for a more profound bias, even when factors such as sherd survival on the surface are taken into account (cf. Cherry *et al.* 1988 for a case study from the Nemea valley). The most plausible explanation is that until the LN, and especially FN, the inhabitants of Crete favoured some specific settlement niche in the landscape that has been disproportionately obliterated by subsequent natural and anthropogenic processes. One possibility is the coastal zone, which still remained vulnerable to post-glacial sea-level rise until the start of the 4th millennium BC, but there is no indication of such an orientation in the food remains at Knossos. Altogether more likely are locations beside good alluvial bottom land along perennial rivers, exemplified by the situation of Knossos itself, where the Neolithic site had the unusual good fortune to be later capped and preserved, and perhaps the river's course also stabilised, thanks to the growth of the later palatial city. If this last suggestion is correct, the most fruitful strategy for detecting other early sites, particularly during the EN–MN, would be to prospect the environs of Crete's limited number of potentially perennial waterways. Petrographic analysis has shown that many non-local sherds at Knossos nonetheless come from the wider catchment of the Herakleion basin, a further indication that early sites clustered in such well-watered, clement environments (Tomkins this volume).

One area that has been illuminated by recent work is the question of contacts with off-island groups before the FN, an issue that relates, of necessity, almost entirely to Knossos. The mere presence of obsidian, and also a far rarer exotic in the form of a piece of amethyst (Conolly this volume), does not, of course, demonstrate contact with other people, as the former could have been acquired by direct access to the sources (apparently with some difficulty, to judge by intensive use of the material) and the latter brought with the first settlers. Early contact is, however, now proven by small amounts of imported, and possibly also exported, pottery, mainly in the EN–MN phases (Tomkins this volume; Tomkins and Day 2001), and a few probably pressure-flaked obsidian blades for which there is no evidence of local manufacture (Conolly this volume). Here I would like to offer a few cautionary remarks, largely aimed at rescuing the baby from the fate of the bathwater. Clearly, such finds prove that Knossos was no more utterly isolated within the Aegean than it was on Crete itself, but we can still ask how closely integrated both the site and the island were with the remainder of the Aegean at different stages of the Neolithic.

Some of the new evidence is decidedly ambivalent in this respect, particularly with regard to technological learning and other forms of transmission. For example, according to Conolly (this volume) Knossos' overall lithic technology conspicuously did not converge with that of the EN mainland, whilst at a later date the trans-Aegean horizon of LN stone projectile points, which reaches as far as the southern Cyclades (Broodbank 2000: 120–23) and Antikythera (Bevan and Conolly pers. comm.), still appears to exclude Crete entirely. Conversely, Isaakidou's identification of the employment of cattle, primarily females, for some form of traction as early as the EN (2006), well before anything similar is attested on the Greek mainland, may reflect a local development, whether similar to or distinct from the classic later male ox-plough combination (Isaakidou this volume). A further idiosyncrasy is the fact that, as Mina (this volume) demonstrates, while the early Cretan Neolithic figurines share many generic features with those elsewhere in the Aegean, they do not follow the subsequent trend on the Neolithic mainland from an emphasis on body decoration towards one on clothing and jewellery. And lastly, what is implied by the fact that the pottery imports decline at Knossos in the LN, just as evidence for the introduction of exogenous ceramic styles and other practices takes off (Tomkins 2004)? Is this a reflection of a shift to other media of exchange, or a substitution of one form of contact for another, as the islands to Crete's north became more fully settled?

This last question raises broader issues that are relevant also to the explanation of the later changes seen during the FN, namely where and why we prioritise models of shared descent, as opposed to ones based on network contacts, or others grounded in independent functional convergence, when we try to make sense of the observed similarities between Cretan and external ways of doing things. In fact all the major Mediterranean islands exhibit diachronically fluctuating patterns of affiliation and distinction relative to neighbouring mainland regions during the Neolithic, and it is amongst the nuances of these that we must seek some of the keys to the constitution of their societies. To put it bluntly, Neolithic Crete may have been no Easter Island, but it was equally no Lipari (Robb and Farr 2005 for a recent summary of the latter).

One additional, very welcome advance that is magnificently manifested by the papers in this volume is a change in the manner of envisaging Neolithic Knossos, no longer simply as a bewildering succession of strata clogged with innumerable sherds, lithics and bones, but instead as the relics of a dynamic living community, a place full of people (this is not to belittle in any sense the importance of such data classes; for example, Isaakidou's comprehensive study of the animal bone assemblage effectively renders obsolete all previous interpretations based upon it). This development has taken place despite the restrictions on open-area exploration that are imposed by the overlying Minoan palace, and is therefore quite an achievement. As a result, Knossos can at last start to contribute to the kinds of discourses opened up by similar research on Levantine PPN communities (Kuijt 2000), spectacularly at Çatalhöyük (Hodder 2006), and on the Neolithic of Thessaly (Halstead 1999; Kotsakis 1999), the Balkans (Tringham and Krstić 1990; Bailey 2000), and the central Mediterranean (Robb 2007).

A good example of this approach is Isaakidou's exploration (this volume) of the changing social relations that are implied by shifts in the degree of control over (and proximity to) key agricultural resources, mainly arable land and an increasingly large number of cattle (integrated in a distinctive package of intensive horticultural, manuring and transport practices defined by her as 'gardening with cows'), as the community at Knossos grew larger. This traces a convincing route towards intra-communal differentiation between the established households that controlled such resources, and newer ones that did not. There are clear links here to Tomkins' analysis of the evolving, and sharpening, definition of the household over time (Tomkins 2004; also Halstead 1995). In this context it is worth recalling that, although previous investigations have used the size of Knossos as one means of gauging the likelihood of internal social differentiation (Broodbank 1992), the LN communities in Thessaly that reveal plausible indices of such distinctions in the form of elevated central megara are typically quite small. At 0.8 ha, Dimini is a fraction the size of Neolithic Knossos at its maximum extent, even with this now cautiously revised downwards by Tomkins (this volume) to 1.75–2.5 ha in LN II (although Whitelaw [pers. comm.] considers that data from recent intensive surface collection around the tell could imply a markedly greater extent, at least as large as the 4–5 ha of previous estimates). This observation might encourage a search for indices of potential complexity at MN and later Knossos regardless of its exact size and density of occupation, and encourage a broad spectrum of strategies for its detection through material remains. Indeed both Broodbank (1992) and Tomkins (2004) identify a wide range of behavioural changes at the site over the timespan that on the new chronology covers the later MN and LN phases.

A different but complementary perspective on Knossian Neolithic societies is promoted by Mina and Triantaphyllou (this volume), both of whose analyses shed light on the symbolic and ideological aspects of life (and death) on the tell, and bring us closer to the people who actually inhabited it. Mina takes a sophisticated approach to the manner in which figurines, most of which are female, were used to negotiate gender relations and assert the roles of women within the community. Despite a very limited amount of excavation relative to the mainland, Cretan figurines comprise over 10% of her corpus of Aegean Neolithic examples, a fact that perhaps underlines their importance in this respect on the island, and at Knossos in particular. Particularly interesting is her observation that the more polarised, competitive gender relations suggested by figurine forms in the later Neolithic of the Greek mainland find no echo on Crete, where figurines remain more conservative, and gender relations therefore arguably more integrated. Triantaphyllou also detects intriguing and, from a mainland perspective, sometimes anomalous patterns. At Knossos, in addition to the presence of child burials, scattered bones of adults are present within the settlement, the latter a phenomenon that in the central and northern mainland is perhaps associated with sprawling flat settlements more than tell sites. Does this mis-match point to another aspect of Knossian difference, or merely the failure to detect extramural Neolithic (and equally EBA) cemeteries in areas later swamped by the growth of the huge second millennium town?

The Many Surprises of the 'Final Neolithic'

This brings us to the period that, for the present, we will call the FN in obedience to the conventions of this Round Table and Aegean terminology. It is here, I think, that we encounter the greatest surprises. The first of these is the length of the period, from about 4500 BC up to a dovetailing with the EBA around 3200–3000 BC, according to the Aegean-wide chronology espoused by Tomkins (this volume). The resultant time-span occupies roughly a third of the entire duration of the Neolithic, a fact that begs for the sub-division that it is currently receiving, and that provides ample room for any number of social and cultural dynamics, not all of which need be synchronous.

The second surprise, if one foreshadowed by earlier tallies (Vagnetti and Belli 1978), is the explosion of evidence for sites elsewhere on the island, following a modest start in the LN. According to Nowicki (this volume), who must take the credit for the discovery and surface documentation of many of them, there are now over a hundred open-air FN sites known on Crete. Most of these new sites appear to date to the later FN (III–IV). But even within this shorter sub-period there is ample evidence for variation (Nowicki 2002; this volume; Tomkins this volume), whether in material culture (some local in derivation, some indicative of off-island connections), extent (from tiny sites to ones as much as two hectares in area), location (from rich lowland zones to small satellite islands, though note Tomkins' suggestion [this volume] of an earlier, LN, phase on Gavdos), and local topographic features (coastal promontories, caves, defensible, sometimes fortified, hill-tops and even such eyries as Katalimata). Although the extent of settlement at Knossos at this juncture is unclear (Tomkins this volume), the apparent survival of a reasonably large site, even if perhaps static now in terms of growth, is itself quite unusual in a southern Aegean context. It will be interesting to see to what extent Nowicki's grand alignment of these and other later FN developments into two sequent horizons, as well as his proposal of an historical narrative of aggressive infiltration of parts of the island from overseas, and the local response to it, survives the test of excavation at a sample of these sites. Investigations at one such site, Petras Kephala, already promise to refine greatly the late FN to EBA transition, and the processes contemporary with it (Papadatos this volume). The boom in site numbers during the later FN raises immediate questions. For one thing, in addition to local growth, does it also indicate a substantial degree of in-migration to the extremities of Crete from neighbouring islands (particularly those of the southeast Aegean but perhaps also Kythera [Broodbank and Kiriatzi 2007: 260, 264]), as Nowicki suggests and as predicted by modelling of inter-island colonisation in the southern Aegean at this time (Broodbank 1999: 31–32, fig. 1.8)? This seems quite possible, although the proof may remain elusive given the multiple factors that could explain broad ceramic parallels between Crete and other parts of the Aegean (Papadatos this volume, for a sober discussion). Furthermore, what do all these new dots on the map mean in terms of society and economy? Nowicki's surface data suggest that most are farmsteads and small hamlets, whilst Halstead (this volume) provides a roughly quantified criticism, and a trenchant one, of the problematic logic behind the common supposition, often applied to Crete and elsewhere in the Aegean and Mediterranean, that such small new sites, especially the many examples in upland areas, reflect emergent pastoral communities. Halstead's basic case seems irrefutable, but it is worth recalling his earlier observation that as the size of farming communities reduces, the viability of enlarging the stock-raising component – for meat, dairy products or most likely a bit of both – could potentially expand to a degree (Halstead 1996). Thus, an increase in herding within such a mixed regime might emerge as a *consequence* of colonisation of marginal land, itself initially triggered, in Halstead's view, by social changes such as greater household independence, a consequent greater tendency to community fission, and the improved efficacy of exchange networks at tying together scattered groups. Under such circumstances, as well as in the context of a shift in climate (see below), we might envisage experiments with the relative risks and advantages of various ratios of crop- to animal-oriented activity, in other words some testing of the elasticity of the basic envelope. This might explain the striking appearance of 'cheese-pots' on and beyond Crete in the later FN, sometimes in large numbers. These are certainly not an index of the first milking (which occurred far earlier, *e.g.*, Rowley-Conwy 2000) but could argue for an enhanced interest in the production of durable dairy goods. Similar small-scale experimentation might have resulted in olive domestication by the FN or EBA (cf. Asouti 2003), and once allied to palatial capital investment may help to explain the apparent ease with which Crete entered the wider eastern Mediterranean interaction sphere during the second millennium BC, a world in which secondary products and processed tree crops comprised a pre-defined element closely tied into core cultural values and behaviour.

Our third surprise should not be one at all (Nakou 1995; Zachos 1996; Muhly 2002), yet it is nonetheless good to see local production of copper suggested during the FN in almost certainly early contexts at Petras Kephala (Papadatos this volume), and elegantly confirmed there by the identification of scars from a metal punch used for obsidian production (D'Annibale this volume). Mina's observation (this volume) that new blue and green mineral pigments appear on Cretan FN figurines is also surely significant.

Perhaps most striking of all is the fourth surprise, namely the identification of open-air ritual areas at FN III–IV Phaistos, beneath the later palace, and from contexts encountered in old and recent excavations that have only now been brought together and interpreted by Todaro and Di Tonto (this volume). The finer stratigraphic details remain to be resolved, but these contexts variously reveal the residues of large-scale animal cooking and consumption, ritual apparatus such as triton shells and miniature vessels, concentrations of specialised pouring and serving vessels and, from other broadly contemporary contexts, human remains and a long-known, enigmatic round structure. Substantial remains of houses are, in contrast, rather elusive, and domestic occupation may have been restricted to parts of the site and separated by open ground used for feasts and other rituals, whether of a competitive or integrative nature, and of unknown intra- or inter-community scope, high on the ridge overlooking the Mesara plain. Interestingly, it is in a Knossian phase (FN IB) preceding the inception of this activity at Phaistos (FN III) that Tomkins (2007) identifies the appearance of a new suite of pouring and drinking shapes. Such finds from one or more of the later palatial centres must surely dangle the tremendous temptation of retrojection for any expert in Cretan Bronze Age ritual. But what is really demanded is exactly the opposite, the cumulative exploration, moving forwards through time, of how an early, loose cluster of phenomena (open courts, public consumption, ritual apparatus, human bones and round buildings) gradually became codified through the course of the EBA and into the palatial age into discrete practices variously associated with the gods and death. It will also raise anew the question as to precisely when, within or just after the closing stages of the FN, the first round tombs and other funerary structures began to be built, and how this development overlaps with the cave burials witnessed during the FN.

Standing back from the details, two more general points emerge. One is how many features of the Cretan EBA are already present during the FN. These include a widely settled landscape differentiated between large and small communities whose consumption behaviours may have differed (Tomkins this volume); the primacy in terms of size, of Knossos and perhaps Phaistos; ritual activity at larger foci and, on the basis of finds of FN IV cups, also at the later peak sanctuary of Atsipades (Morris and Batten 2000); drinking practices; funerary activity; metallurgy; and possibly increasing interest in secondary products and tree crops. If one wanted to induce real chaos in an already fraught chronological structure (see below), a case could be made for calling the later Cretan FN 'Early Minoan 0' (but see Papadatos this volume, on changes in ceramic and lithic technology that do align with the traditional division between the FN and EBA). The differences between these two periods are surely more to do with how such elements were combined and socially mobilised, than with the presence or absence of any one of them.

The second observation is that although similarities with many traits seen on FN Crete can be found across much of the contemporary Aegean and further afield, a particularly close parallel is with the Ozieri culture on Sardinia (*c.* 4000–3200 BC), which also witnessed an explosion of settlement, including in upland areas, alongside the growth of big lowland villages, the creation of at least one monumental ritual space (the Monte Accoddi platform), early use of metals and abundant off-island contacts (Webster 1996: 47–52). This is a useful reminder of the fact that the Cretan FN need not be interpreted only as a distant refraction of emergent large-scale developments in the Fertile Crescent, or as a local sub-region of the Aegean world, but as a creation of wider Mediterranean and perhaps insular conditions, conditioned by local antecedent history.

The Climates of the Times

Before concluding with a few practical observations, one further comment should be made about the frameworks within which we approach the Cretan, and indeed the entire Old World, Neolithic. This concerns climate change during the Holocene. Aegeanists have long tacitly ignored this, and understandably, given its historical association with lurid scenarios based on slender evidence. But over the last decade or so, prompted by current alarm over global warming, there have been major advances in the documentation of palaeoclimate and its environmental impact, through lake and sea cores and a mass of other proxy data, not least in the Mediterranean (*e.g.*, Roberts 1998; Rosen 2007). We continue to ignore such changes at our interpretative peril.

Put simply, the early settlers who followed the lush valley of the Kairatos river upstream to its confluence with a babbling brook, overlooked by a promising knoll, were not simply exploiting a different micro-environment from those who 3500 years later settled a wild limestone mesa-top in east Crete, but were also operating within a fundamentally different climatic regime. The period 7000–5500 BC lay largely within the early Holocene optimum, when the climate of the eastern Mediterranean was markedly wetter and less seasonal than it is in the present. Oscillations became more frequent after about 5500 BC (around the MN–LN boundary, as the first settlements beyond Knossos start to become archaeologically visible). The shift to the semi-arid, highly seasonal, unpredictable regime prevalent today, which underwrites our models of Mediterranean risk-spreading behaviour, developed around 4000–3500 BC, in the middle of the FN, in tandem with the emergence, as close to Crete as is Thessaly, of a hyper-arid Sahara in place of a cattle-grazed expanse of lakes, savannah and steppe. The rise of olive in Cretan pollen cores in the later Neolithic (Moody and Rackham 1996: 82, 125) could reflect an expansion of drought-tolerant, often evergreen species as well as early efforts at exploiting or domesticating tree-crops on the island. And one does not need to be some monster of environmental determinism to add that the increase in aridity and unpredictability are surely implicated in the dramatic shifts in settlement patterns on Crete in the fourth millennium BC, which exhibit all the classic contemporary pan-Mediterranean features: dispersal, marginal colonisation by small groups, increased mobility, flux among regional populations, often defensive sites suggestive of conflict and a growing different-iation between core communities occupying the best niches and smaller ones on their fringes. The fact that many later FN communities vanish before the start of the EBA may reflect the damage rapidly done to marginal arable land under increasingly arid conditions, and the inexperienced or opportunistic nature of some FN strategies (a point also made by Nowicki this volume). Rather than ignore such potential connections between climate and history, the way forward is to improve our understanding of the timing and ecological effects of climate change in the Aegean context, and simultaneously to develop better ways of shedding light on the kinds of decisions made by different social groups and individuals as such new challenges and opportunities arose across an in-creasingly uneven and unstable playing field.

Knossos Calling

I can think of no fitter closing tribute to this volume than to urge the importance of getting its message over loud and clear to the wider community of archaeologists in the Fertile Crescent, Anatolia and the Mediterranean and Balkan worlds. One crucial step in this respect must be the establishment of a universally agreed and transparent chronological scheme, both relative and absolute. The revised labelling of the Knossian phases to bring them in line with the remainder of the Aegean is a welcome advance that I hope, once its basis is fully published and verified, will be universally approved and adopted (Tomkins 2007; this volume). For instance, a former Knossian 'EN II' that aligned with the pan-Aegean LN was never a wise idea. Most other obstacles in the way of this goal concentrate in the FN. One issue is, of course, whether this period would be better labelled as a Chalcolithic. Overall, the answer is surely 'yes'; the Aegean 'Final Neolithic' originated simply as a filler-term for a time-gap that started to emerge in the 1960s (Renfrew 1972: 68–80). 'Chalcolithic' would improve alignment with the Levant, Anatolia and the Balkans, countering the time-warp effect of maintaining a Neolithic contemporary with the Uruk expansion, as Sherratt and Sherratt (this volume) point out, and is compatible (unlike the case of Temple-period Malta, 3600–2500 BC) with the first local appearance of copper. But this is a decision to be made on an Aegean-wide basis, for to label Crete 'Chalcolithic' while the remainder of the Aegean hid in its Final Neolithic would be a service to no-one (unless as a terminological Trojan horse). More readily achievable is a consensus concerning the calendrical duration of this name-challenged phase. In this respect it is a little worrying that, whilst Tomkins' scheme is pentapartite and begins at around 4500 BC, Nowicki's (2002) has just two phases, and starts a millennium later, such that his FN I and II roughly match Tomkins' FN III and IV. This is not good for an island attempting to get back into the scholarly mainstream. Happily, the community of scholars working on this period is currently so restricted that the group brought together at this Round

Table is in effect quorate and empowered to decide upon a final scheme with a legitimacy that is rare even in regional studies. I hope that they grasp this nettle firmly and with a decisive outcome.

The other necessary dimension is the continued momentum towards analysis and swift, full publication of the 1950s and 1960s excavations at Knossos, including not only each material class but also the crucial details of context, coupled, of course, with similar work at a range of other sites across the island. Our efforts to understand the dynamics of the wider Neolithic world stretching from Mesopotamia to western Europe are all too often crippled by the number of key excavations that remain unpublished or published only in a very preliminary form, often before the material-specific studies by relevant experts had been given time to take their course. In this quasi-Manichean situation, where darkness predominates and light is often illusory, Neolithic Knossos comprises one potentially brilliant source of illumination, thanks to the combination of a new generation of scholars with the commitment and enthusiasm to analyse high-resolution material excavated almost half a century ago (even if the absence of archaeobotany stands out sorely), and the exceptional generosity of the excavator, John Evans, in facilitating their unfettered access to material and records. It is profoundly to be hoped that the British School at Athens, the body with publication responsibility for this material, will continue to provide equally effective support for this endeavour, not least at the publication stage. If so, Neolithic Knossos, to date the only deeply stratified, seemingly continuously occupied Neolithic site on the island (and so even more interpretatively dominant than its Bronze Age successor), will be able to take its place as a reliable reference point on a much wider stage and, no less vitally, to act as a standard against which to assess variation within the island as new fieldwork and analysis begin to fill in and extend our picture of early Cretan society.

Acknowledgements

My thanks to the convenors of the Round Table for the invitation to participate and offer some closing remarks on the day and in this volume, as well as to Debi Harlan and John Bennet for their warm hospitality.

Bibliography

Ammerman, A. J., P. Flourentzos, C. McCartney, J. Noller and D. Sorabji
    2006   Two new early sites on Cyprus. *Report of the Department of Antiquities, Cyprus*: 1–21.
van Andel, T. H. and C. Runnels
    1995   The earliest farmers in Europe. *Antiquity* 69: 481–500.
Asouti, E.
    2003   Wood charcoal from Santorini (Thera): new evidence for climate, vegetation and timber exports in the Aegean Bronze Age. *Antiquity* 77: 471–84.

Bailey, D. W.
  2000 *Balkan Prehistory: Exclusion, Incorporation and Identity*. London: Routledge.
Binder, D.
  2000 Mesolithic and Neolithic interaction in southern France and northern Italy: new data and current hypotheses. In T. D. Price (ed.), *Europe's First Farmers*: 117–43. Cambridge: Cambridge University Press.
Broodbank, C.
  1992 The Neolithic labyrinth: social change at Knossos before the Bronze Age. *JMA* 5: 39–75.
  1999 Colonization and configuration in the insular Neolithic of the Aegean. In P. Halstead (ed.), *Neolithic Society in Greece* (SSAA 2): 15–41. Sheffield: Sheffield Academic Press.
  2000 *An Island Archaeology of the Early Cyclades*. Cambridge: Cambridge University Press.
  2006 The origins and early development of Mediterranean maritime activity. *JMA* 19: 199–230.
Broodbank, C. and T. F. Strasser
  1991 Migrant farmers and the Neolithic colonization of Crete. *Antiquity* 65: 233–45.
Broodbank, C. and E. Kiriatzi
  2007 The first 'Minoans' of Kythera revisited: technology, demography, and landscape in the Prepalatial Aegean. *AJA* 111: 241–74.
Chapman, J. and J. Müller
  1990 Early farmers in the Mediterranean basin: the Dalmatian evidence. *Antiquity* 64: 127–34.
Cherry, J. F.
  1981 Pattern and process in the earliest colonization of the Mediterranean islands. *PPS* 47: 41–68.
  1990 The first colonization of the Mediterranean islands: a review of recent research. *JMA* 3: 145–221.
Cherry, J. F., J. L. Davis, A. Demitrack, E. Mantzourani, T. F. Strasser and L. E. Talalay
  1988 Archaeological survey in an artifact-rich landscape: a Middle Neolithic example from Nemea, Greece. *AJA* 92: 159–76.
Chilardi, S., D. W. Frayer, P. Gioia, R. Macchiarelli and M. Mussi
  1996 Fontana Nuova di Ragusa (Sicily, Italy): southernmost Aurignacian site in Europe. *Antiquity* 70: 553–63.
Colledge, S. and J. Conolly
  2007 A review and synthesis of the evidence for the origins of farming on Cyprus and Crete. In S. Colledge and J. Conolly (eds.), *The Origins and Spread of Domestic Plants in Southwest Asia and Europe*: 53–74. Walnut Creek, CA: Left Coast Press.
Costa, L. J.
  2004 *Corse préhistorique: peuplement d'une île et modes de vie des sociétés insulaires (IXe – IIe millénaires av. J.-CA.)*. Paris: Errance.
Costa, L. J., J.-D. Vigne, H. Bocherens, N. Desse-Berset, C. Heinz, F. de Lanfranchi, J. Magdeleine, M.-P. Ruas, S. Thiébault and C. Tozzi
  2003 Early settlement on Tyrrhenian islands (8th millennium cal. BC): Mesolithic adaptation to local resources in Corsica and northern Sardinia. In L. Larsson, H. Krindgen, K. Knutsson, D. Loeffler and A. Akerlund (eds.), *Mesolithic on the Move*: 3–10. Oxford: Oxbow Books.
Facchini, F. and G. Giusberti
  1992 *Homo sapiens sapiens* remains from the island of Crete. In G. Brauer and F. H. Smith (eds.), *Continuity or Replacement: Controversies in* Homo sapiens *Evolution*: 189–208. Rotterdam and Brookfield: A. A. Balkema.

Halstead, P.

1995   From sharing to hoarding: the Neolithic foundations of Aegean Bronze Age society? In R. Laffineur and W.-D. Niemeier (eds.), *POLITEIA: Society and State in the Aegean Bronze Age* (Aegaeum 12): 11–20. Liège: University of Liège.

1996   Pastoralism or household herding? Problems of scale and specialization in early Greek animal husbandry. *World Archaeology* 28: 20–42.

1999   Neighbours from hell? The household in Neolithic Greece, in P. Halstead (ed.) *Neolithic Society in Greece* (SSAA 2): 77–95. Sheffield: Sheffield Academic Press.

Hodder, I.

2006   *Çatalhöyük: The Leopard's Tale.* London: Thames and Hudson.

Isaakidou, V.

2006   Ploughing with cows: Knossos and the 'secondary products revolution'. In D. Serjeantson and D. Field (eds.), *Animals in the Neolithic of Britain and Europe*: 95–112. Oxford: Oxbow Books.

Klein Hofmeijer, G. K.

1997   *Late Pleistocene Deer Fossils from Corbeddu Cave: Implications for Human Colonization of the Island of Sardinia* (BAR International Series 663). Oxford: Tempus Reparatum.

Kotsakis, K.

1999   What tells can tell: social space and settlement in the Greek Neolithic. In P. Halstead (ed.), *Neolithic Society in Greece* (SSAA 2): 66–76. Sheffield: Sheffield Academic Press.

Kuijt, I.

2000   *Life in Neolithic Farming Communities: Social Organization, Identity, and Differentiation.* New York: Kluwer Academic/Plenum.

Lax, E. and T. F. Strasser

1992   Early Holocene extinctions on Crete: the search for the cause. *JMA* 5: 203–24.

Lewthwaite, J.

1988   Isolating the residuals: the Mesolithic basis for man-animal relationships on the Mediterranean islands. In C. Bonsall (ed.), *The Mesolithic in Europe*, 541–55. Edinburgh: John Donald.

Melis, R. and M. Mussi

2002   S. Maria is Acquas, a new pre-Neolithic site: southwestern Sardinia. In W. H. Waldren and J. A. Ensenyat (eds.), *World Islands in Prehistory: International Insular Investigations.* (BAR International Series 1095): 454–61. Oxford: Archaeopress.

Morris, C. and V. Batten

2000   Final Neolithic pottery from the Atsipades peak sanctuary. In *Pepragmena H' Diethnous Kritilogikou Synedriou*: 373–382. Herakleion: Etaireia Kritikon Istorikon Meleton.

Muhly, J. D.

2002   Early metallurgy in Greece and Cyprus. In Ü. Yalçin (ed.), *Anatolian Metal II* (Der Anschnitt, Beiheft 15): 77–82. Bochum: Deutsches Bergbau-Museum.

Mussi, M.

2001   *Earliest Italy: An Overview of the Italian Paleolithic and Mesolithic.* New York and London: Kluwer Academic/Plenum.

Nakou, G.

1995   The cutting edge: a new look at early Aegean metallurgy. *JMA* 8: 1–32.

Nowicki, K.

2002   The end of the Neolithic in Crete. *Aegean Archaeology* 6: 7–72.

Peltenburg, E., S. Colledge, P. Croft, A. Jackson, C. McCartney and M. A. Murray

2000   Agro-pastoralist colonization of Cyprus in the 10th millennium BP: initial assessments. *Antiquity* 74: 844–53.

Perlès, C.
   2001   *The Early Neolithic in Greece: The First Farming Communities in Europe.* Cambridge: Cambridge University Press.
Rackham, O. and J. Moody
   1996   *The Making of the Cretan Landscape.* Manchester: Manchester University Press.
Ramis, D. and J. A. Alcover
   2001   Revisiting the earliest human presence in Mallorca, western Mediterranean. *PPS* 67: 261–69.
Ramis, D., J. A. Alcover, J. Coll and M. Trias
   2002   The chronology of the first settlement of the Balearic islands. *JMA* 15: 3–24.
Renfrew, C.
   1972   *The Emergence of Civilisation.* London: Methuen.
Reese, D. S.
   1996   *Pleistocene and Holocene Fauna of Crete and Its First Settlers.* Madison: Prehistory Press.
Reese, D. S., G. Belluomini and M. Ikeya
   1996   Absolute dates for the Pleistocene fauna of Crete. In D.S. Reese (ed.), *Pleistocene and Holocene Fauna of Crete and Its First Settlers*: 47–51. Madison: Prehistory Press.
Robb, J. E.
   2007   *The Early Mediterranean Village: Agency, Material Culture and Social Change in Neolithic Italy.* Cambridge: Cambridge University Press.
Robb, J. E. and R. H. Farr
   2005   Substances in motion: Neolithic Mediterranean 'trade'. In E. Blake and A. B. Knapp (eds.), *The Archaeology of Mediterranean Prehistory*: 24–45. Oxford: Blackwell.
Roberts, N.
   1998   *The Holocene: An Environmental History* (2nd edition). Oxford: Blackwell.
Rosen, A. M.
   2007   *Civilizing Climate: Social Responses to Climate Change in the Ancient Near East.* Lanham: Altamira Press.
Rowley-Conwy, P.
   2000   Milking caprines, hunting pigs: the Neolithic economy of Arene Candide in its West Mediterranean context. In P. Rowley-Conwy (ed.), *Animal Bones, Human Societies*: 124–32. Oxford: Oxbow Books.
Runnels, C., E. Panagopoulou, P. Murray, G. Tsartsidou, S. Allen, K. Mullen and E. Tourloukis
   2005   A Mesolithic landscape in Greece: testing a site-location model in the Argolid at Kandia. *JMA* 18: 259–85.
Simmons, A. H. and associates
   1999   *Faunal Extinction in an Island Society: Pigmy Hippopotamus Hunters of Cyprus.* New York: Kluwer Academic/Plenum.
Tomkins, P.
   2004   Filling in the 'Neolithic background': social life and social transformation in the Aegean before the Bronze Age. In J. C. Barrett and P. Halstead (eds.), *The Emergence of Civilisation Revisited* (SSAA 6): 38–63. Oxford: Oxbow Books.
   2007   Neolithic: Strata IX–VIII, VII–VIB, VIA–V, IV, IIIB, IIIA, IIB, IIA and IC Groups. In N. Momigliano (ed.), *Knossos Pottery Handbook: Neolithic and Bronze Age (Minoan)*: 9–48. London: British School at Athens.
Tomkins, P. and P. M. Day
   2001   Production and exchange of the earliest ceramic vessels in the Aegean: a view from early Neolithic Knossos, Crete. *Antiquity* 75: 259–60.

Tringham, R. and D. Krstić (eds.)
   1990   *Selevac: A Neolithic Village in Yugoslavia* (Monumenta Archaeologica 15). Los Angeles: Institute of Archaeology, UCLA.
Vagnetti, L. and P. Belli
   1978   Characters and problems of the Final Neolithic in Crete. *SMEA* 19: 125–63.
Vigne, J.-D.
   1999   The large 'true' Mediterranean islands as a model for the Holocene human impact on the European vertebrate fauna? Recent data and new reflections. In N. Benecke (ed.), *The Holocene History of the European Vertebrate Faunas: Modern Aspects of Research* (Archäologie in Eurasian 6): 295–322. Rahden: Marie Leidorf.
Vigne, J.-D. and N. Desse-Berset
   1995   The exploitation of animal resources in the Mediterranean during the Pre-Neolithic: the example of Corsica. In A. Fischer (ed.), *Man and Sea in the Mesolithic: Coastal Settlement Above and Below Present Sea Level*: 309–318. Oxford: Oxbow Books.
Webster, G. S.
   1996   *A Prehistory of Sardinia, 2300–500 BC* (Monographs in Mediterranean Archaeology 5). Sheffield: Sheffield Academic Press.
Watkins, T.
   2004   Putting the colonization of Cyprus into context. In E. Peltenburg and A. Wasse (eds.), *Neolithic Revolution: New Perspectives on Southwest Asia in Light of Recent Discoveries on Cyprus*: 23–34. Oxford: Oxbow Books.
Zachos, K. L.
   1996   Metallurgy. In G. A. Papathanasopoulos (ed.), *Neolithic Culture in Greece*: 140–43. Athens: Nicholas P. Goulandris Foundation – Museum of Cycladic Art.
Zilhão, J.
   1993   The spread of agro-pastoral economies across Mediterranean Europe: a view from the far west. *JMA* 6: 5–63.
   2000   From the Mesolithic to the Neolithic in the Iberian peninsula. In T. D. Price (ed.), *Europe's First Farmers*: 144–82. Cambridge: Cambridge University Press.

17

The Neolithic of Crete, as Seen from Outside

Andrew Sherratt and Sue Sherratt

Inspired by a stimulating weekend, the following commentary was written in the afternoon immediately after the Round Table closed. It is a typically Andrew Sherratt paper, covering with broad brushstrokes a canvas that stretches from Mesopotamia to the Carpathians – with Crete playing a very small part in the whole. As he wrote, we argued about details, but, also as usual, Andrew was reluctant to run the risk of obscuring the seamlessness of the big picture with unnecessarily fussy distractions. It normally took quite a lot of battling to get to the point where we were both entirely happy with a joint text – but in this case there was no time or opportunity for this. I have not attempted to rewrite the paper in the form it might have reached had we continued to discuss it, or in response to editorial comments, since this would inevitably turn it into something quite different which would no longer be so recognisably Andrew's. In any case, since he is no longer here to argue with, my heart would not be in it. I simply remind readers that, as the title (given by Andrew) implies, this is an attempt to place the Neolithic of Crete in a broader context. [SS]

The period which on Crete, as in Greece more generally, is called 'Neolithic' lasts on current estimates for some four millennia, roughly from 7000 to 3000 BC. While these bracketing dates are themselves – like the sequence which they enclose – greatly in need of chronological refinement, it will be some time before more precise estimates are possible. The advantages which abundant *tell* sites, with their high visibility in the landscape and often clearly stratified accumulations of mud-brick architecture, confer on adjacent areas of Anatolia, Thessaly/ Macedonia and the Balkans are simply not present in the undulating and stony terrain of Crete. Sites like Knossos, the most *tell*-like and with a convincingly continuous sequence (Tomkins 2007), are comparative rarities on the island; but Knossos is above all the site where the most prominent palatial structures emerged during the Bronze Age. This locational continuity from the beginning of the Cretan Neolithic right down to the developed urbanization of the later second millennium is one of the most striking features of Knossos – which makes the question of the earlier character of such a site yet more interesting, even while it effectively precludes its systematic interrogation.

Caught as we are in this methodological double-bind, it may be a useful exercise to elaborate a series of predictive expectations, based on our existing knowledge of neighbouring areas. While this knowledge is itself imperfect, and still very variable from region to region, it may serve to counter the otherwise understandable desire to try to reconstruct from fragments patterns which are more easily perceptible elsewhere. Of course, it runs the risk of imposing arbitrary patterns in a self-confirming way; but if approached in the right spirit it may at least raise hypotheses which the hard work of empirical investigation may evaluate and if necessary discard. It is with this in mind that the following remarks, composed with the benefit of hearing the latest reports from the front line of research, are offered.

The first observation to make in this context is one of terminology. It would be very valuable, in presenting a picture of east Mediterranean development over this period to students, if the very nomenclature did not give the impression that the whole of the south Aegean was an unchanging backwater, remaining 'Neolithic' when other areas had progressed well beyond the Stone Age. While it would be naïve to believe that archaeological labels simply mean what they say, and that 'Copper Age' or 'Bronze Age' accurately describe technological stages (in Childe's phrase), nevertheless congruence with neighbouring terminologies might suggest that the last millennium and a half of this long 'Neolithic' period might usefully be called by some other name (Copper Age, Chalcolithic, Eneolithic), if only to overcome the impression of millennial isolation. (Similar arguments, incidentally, apply to a term such as 'Epipalaeolithic', which again gives the equally misleading impression of a passive hangover from a previous period, quite at odds with its innovative character.) This is not to say that there is some single, canonical terminology into which Cretan and other south-Aegean developments could easily be slotted: indeed, the suggestion only serves to draws attention to the entirely arbitrary regional traditions which have grown up in adjacent countries in the usage of these terms, inconsistent even for the same culture across national boundaries, as is often the case in the Balkans! Nevertheless there is a case for separating off at least the final millennium or so of what is still called (Final) 'Neolithic' in Crete, and dignifying it with a separate label. After all, copper metallurgy did indeed exist in Crete during the later part – perhaps all – of this period, and copper objects even before. It would, at the very least, draw attention to the fact that not all of the Cretan experience was completely unique; and it might even prompt terminological reform (or at least the confrontation of contradictions in regional usage) in adjacent areas. Glyn Daniel, in writing *The Three Ages* as long ago as 1943, argued that such labels would eventually give way to periods based simply on absolute dating. We may agree with the sentiment, whilst recognizing that this millennial optimism may take another generation to achieve. It is still worthwhile using the terms we have in the light of our current understanding of the evidence.

The Beginning of the Cretan Neolithic

That said, let us turn to the beginning of the Neolithic. In this case, there is nothing belated or hung-over about Crete; quite the reverse, for the ballpark-estimate (one can say no more on the present radiocarbon evidence) of *circa* 7000 cal BC is arguably half a millennium before a rather more secure estimate for the onset of the Neolithic in Thessaly, especially now that the 'pre-ceramic' levels at Argissa have been subject to reassessment (Reingruber 2004; Reingruber and Thissen 2005). When more dates, with secure contexts, are at our disposal, we shall be able to evaluate this difference; but it already suggests the possibility that the different characters of the first Neolithic in the two regions may relate to different areas of origin within Anatolia. It is an old idea that the Thessalian Neolithic represents a 'plantation' (to use a sixteenth-century word) of population from the other side of the Aegean, and a transfer of patterns of culture which had grown up on the plateau and spread either down the Meander or by way of northwest Anatolia; and after a period of disfavour this idea is gradually gaining acceptance once again. (The Franchthi sequence, by contrast, would represent the more gradual transformation of a long-established indigenous population, under the impact of this intrusion.) Could one therefore imagine a separate area of origin for the Cretan Neolithic? The occupation of Thessaly forms part of a more general pattern of occupation of fertile inland basins by groups like those using painted pottery first in Macedonia and Bulgaria, and then in Serbia and southern Romania (at a time when human populations were experiencing the stresses of the 6200 climatic event, from which farming populations may have recovered more rapidly than foraging ones). It replicated to some extent the pattern which had developed in Cappadocia, the Konya Plain, and the Pisidian Lake district in the period from 8000 to 6500 BC, and broadly speaking formed an extension of this Plateau tradition. While the introduction of Neolithic culture to Crete would also have involved island-hopping, this may have been of a different kind from that presumably involved in the transfer of farming to Thessaly.

The date of 7000 BC for the appearance of the Neolithic in Crete – however broad and imprecise – suggests approximate contemporaneity with an earlier development than the occupation of Thessaly, namely the extensive incorporation into the Neolithic sphere of indigenous groups on the north Levantine littoral and along the Anatolian coasts south of the Taurus. This is the point at which the Mersin sequence begins, and is echoed in an extensive scatter of later Neolithic sites in Cilicia – at least a millennium after the appearance of Neolithic sites on the inner side of the Taurus in Cappadocia, and presumably reflecting the resistance of relatively dense indigenous populations in a fertile environment, who initially saw no reason to change their way of life (in the same way that Mesolithic populations around the Black sea similarly resisted the spread of farming). Note that Cyprus had already been settled for more than a millennium by this date, perhaps in a movement of population parallel to the first appearance of Neolithic populations on the Anatolian plateau, and that movement by sea was an established aspect of early Holocene littoral existence.[1] The distinctive feature of developments around 7000 BC was the incorporation of areas – especially coastlands – which would have been optimal habitats for foraging groups, rather than expansion into relatively empty areas in the interstices of existing populations, which had hitherto been the characteristic mode of Neolithic expansion. The appearance of the Neolithic on Crete could relate as much to this process of 'littoral conversion' as to the kind of deliberate plantation postulated later for Thessaly. In a way, it matters less whether there was any pre-existing permanent (Mesolithic or 'Epipalaeolithic') population on Crete or not: the island took its place in a chain of south-Anatolian coastal communities linked by sea and by a common adoption of key elements of the farming package. Obsidian from Melos could have circulated indirectly to arrive in Crete perhaps via the Dodecanese, or by a variety of indirect routes. This would explain both the different ceramic traditions in Crete and Thessaly, with its basket-inspired painted designs, and the rather different pattern of obsidian use in the two areas. (The first Cretan pottery might well have its background in a rather different set of organic containers, for instance leather, whose shapes were now ceramicised.)

There is no reason to suppose, however, that the cultivation-techniques of early Cretan farmers differed radically from those employed in Thessaly or further north; and, as in other areas, the first farming populations were highly selective in their choice of landscapes to settle. Thus small areas of well-watered bottomland provided an exceptional resource for techniques still best described as varieties of floodwater farming. The relatively small communities would have been supported by intensive cultivation of what were often quite restricted patches of suitable soil. The creation of fields in such environments was designed to manage and maximize the retention of spring floodwater, and the creation of banks or small dykes would have provided a continuing investment which – while not justifying the term 'irrigation' – might eventually have been describable as small-scale water harvesting. This productivity and continuing potential may help to explain the continuity of settlement at a site such as Knossos, which moreover lay on a river that made it reachable from the sea by dugout. Such a combination of local resources and accessibility for coastal traffic, combined perhaps with its suggestive visual relationship to the extraordinarily striking peak of Juktas, may have ensured its long-term attractiveness as a nodal settlement, which lasted from the first Neolithic down to Roman times. This persistence, through successive enlargements down to its achievement of urban status in the second millennium and growth to a size comparable with some of the larger Bronze Age towns of the east Mediterranean, implies continuing innovation in its subsistence base, perhaps initially through expansion of livestock-keeping and eventually by use of the plough and a larger scale terracing of the surrounding landscape. The dating of such developments will be discussed below, in the context of other developments.

Crete and a Wider World After its Initial Settlement

No area within the Neolithic oecumene was truly isolated, though integration is more notable in certain phases than others. One phase which, over an area from Mesopotamia to central Europe, saw the emergence of larger cultural entities was the mid-sixth millennium BC. Within the Fertile Crescent the 'Ubaid complex, previously a south-Mesopotamian phenomenon, extended north to take over the Halaf area of the Jazira, so creating a uniform block throughout Mesopotamia – the cultural unity behind its later civilization. At the same time in temperate Europe, the LBK complex spread from its formation area in Transdanubia both westward as far as the Low Countries and eastward to Moldavia. Although these two large entities, in the Near East and Europe respectively, came into existence for quite different reasons, their degree of uniformity over such vast distances is symptomatic of the operation of processes capable of affecting patterns of human behaviour on an unprecedented scale. In the area in between these two macro-phenomena, in Middle Chalcolithic Anatolia, a degree of reorientation took place which resulted in part from the appearance of farming groups in the forested north of the area, previously avoided. This in itself must be seen in the context of the conversion of the Black Sea from a freshwater lake to an extension of the Mediterranean, as rising seawaters spilled over the Bosphorus sill. One effect of this was to destabilize the Mesolithic coastal communities and hasten their integration into the network of adjacent farming groups, in another major episode of forager integration, and also to open up a major alternative corridor of contact between Anatolia and southeast Europe via the Black Sea and the Danube.

The period during which Crete moved to a Late Neolithic (late in its Early Neolithic I phase, according to the conventional terminology) was thus an eventful one across the entire continent and beyond, from which Crete is unlikely to have been isolated. One feature common to the ceramic development both of the Balkans and much of Anatolia was the increasing prominence of dark burnished wares, decorated by incision and white infill in geometric motifs. This took over from painted, basket-like patterns not only in southeast Europe (where it has long been associated with Vinča), but also affected large areas of Anatolia; indeed, Childe specifically compared Veselinovo and Büyük Güllücek, partly on account of their knob-handles – which, along with wishbone-handles, are another characteristic feature of this style. Southeast Anatolia was unaffected by these changes, continuing as a member of the painted-pottery cultures of the Fertile Crescent. Rather than the change being attributable to anything happening in this area, it looks more as if central and western Anatolia (in what is there called the Middle Chalcolithic) had shifted their orientation, to become members of a Balkan club rather than a cultural community centred in the Fertile Crescent. What may lie behind this metaphor? One element is the penetration of more forested parts of the landscape, rather than restriction to riverine and lake-edge locations in otherwise dry lowlands. Without implying any reductive explanation, this would imply a change in the material and visual environment, with wood perhaps becoming more prominent for organic containers than reed baskets, for instance. Such a widespread common experience might lie behind the common stylistic trend, including such specific features as incision and three-dimensional handle forms characteristic of woodwork. Circulation of such items, either as goods in themselves or more likely as small containers for relatively precious organic or inorganic materials, would have propagated features of this style into areas such as Crete. (This seems a more plausible medium than linen textiles, which are usually plain, and there is no evidence of wool until later).

A much more fundamental transition-point in the prehistory of European farmers took place from the middle of the fifth millennium BC; and it is in this context that the term 'Final Neolithic' runs the risk of underselling the increasing participation of the southern Aegean in what was happening elsewhere. Two themes characterise these developments: the extensive adoption of copper metallurgy (at least elsewhere in the southern Aegean, and arguably perhaps also on Crete), and a degree of settlement dispersion (cf. S. Sherratt 2000: 15). The two were not necessarily directly connected, and though one may have reinforced the other they were not simply different aspects of the same phenomenon. The term 'dispersion' applies, in different ways, to developments in different parts of Europe, and is indicative of a long-term trend. Whereas in the Near East the *tell* continued as the major unit of social existence, and developed into an expression of urban form (until these inconvenient mud acropoleis were increasingly abandoned in the later second and first millennia BC in favour of flatter locations nearby), in southeast Europe the climax of *tell*-building (and elaborately painted pottery) occurred around 5000 BC. Thereafter, although *tell*s were still occupied and new ones founded, they were in general smaller and less long-lasting than their 'classic' predecessors. One symptom of this is the increasing importance of funerary behaviour in the 'settlement' pattern, which in several areas might be more realistically described as a 'settlement and cemetery' pattern, since in areas as different as the Great Hungarian Plain and the North European and Atlantic coastlands the settlements themselves were complemented by – or in the latter cases, subsidiary to – a set of funerary or ceremonial sites which anchored the scattered domestic sites to a symbolic focus of the community. This shift from a set of primarily face to face daily on-site relationships to a more constructed belonging together of several residential units has been described as 'the splitting up of the primary horticultural community' (A. Sherratt 1997: 367), for this major unit – as much as the individual constituent house or *domus* (Hodder 1990) – formed the ideological basis of Neolithic solidarity right from the beginnings of cultivation. In the Mediterranean, (as, indeed in the north of England and notably the Peak District!), caves provided a naturally numinous alternative to megalithic monuments or Tiszapolgar cemeteries, and may well have been the foci of ceremonies and mortuary ritual which collectively connected the constructed community both with itself and other worlds – no doubt, as usual in the Neolithic, involving the consumption of mind-altering substances as a key part of the procedure.

The association with metallurgy arises in part from its role in symbolizing more explicitly these physically more distant relationships, in the way that Copper Age cemeteries like Tiszapolgar or Varna invest considerable mobile (artefactual) wealth in symbolizing individual roles and personae – in a manner which was increasingly to become a standard feature of prehistoric burial practices from this time onwards. It is notable in many areas that the elaborate coding of 'face to face' messages on tablewares gave way to plainer sorts of pottery (which only recovered their specificity of messaging in the often metallic shapes associated with drinking ceremonies at the dawn of the Bronze Age), and the focus of cultural elaboration shifted to more spectacular media of display of which copper and then silver were the most striking examples. These new, concentrated stores of value, as well as leading to a more focused pattern of procurement by maritime routes, would also have begun to potentiate differentiation and a (small) degree of capital concentration, permitting more complex arrangements between more independent and diverse households perhaps beginning to some degree to specialize in their balance of crops and livestock over a wider range of environments. While the analogies lie more with Pomo trade-beads than the degree of capital concentration and specialization which underlay the emergence of urban communities, the phenomena of later fifth and earlier fourth millennium Europe are a manifestation of similar principles.

Nevertheless it was in the Fertile Crescent that the breakthrough to urbanism occurred, and the intimate relationship between that process and the increase in the scale and distance of raw materials procurement means that it is likely at some stage to have had effects on the Aegean. For the later part of the 'Final Neolithic/Copper Age' period, therefore, some spinoff from these large-scale processes in neighbouring areas is likely to be detectable – even before the direct 'impact' which defines the formal beginning of the Bronze Age. There is, in any case, a wide range of comparisons in the earlier fourth millennium for types of pottery which reflect new social consumption practices, before the canonical appearance of the jug/cup complex which Renfrew perceptively associated with the formal serving of wine – classically expressed in Anatolian EBA cultures and EC grave assemblages (Renfrew 1972: plate 16), and echoed further north in the Baden culture and its neighbours in central and southeast Europe (A. Sherratt 2003). These standardized vessel combinations plausibly relate to an institution-alized drinking complex, probably using a variety of fermented sugars (and no doubt some traditional psychtropics too, now infused in liquid form). However, even before this EBA horizon, there is a series of standardized small drinking-vessels, some in consistent combination with other vessels, which in the case of the Funnel-beaker (*Trichterbecher*) complex has given their name to a cultural group. Other examples include the widely-distributed two-handed vessels which link Bulgarian/Romanian late Salcutsa and Hungarian late Bodrogkeresztur cultures, reaching up into southern Poland. An intercultural emphasis on specific modes of drinking is thus widely evident in early fourth-millennium Europe, from the borders of the Aegean to the western Baltic (A. Sherratt 1997: 378–80). So widespread a phenomenon is likely to be symptomatic of the spread of new social practices, in 'international' codes comparable to the role-signifying use of fine stone or metal objects, especially axes, by prominent individuals. The appearance of a 'drinking culture' in Final Neolithic assemblages on Crete (Tomkins 2004: 55) might plausibly be seen as an echo of the same phenomenon.

However, the potential Anatolian background or participation in such practices is unclear, partly because of the paucity of sites at this crucial time (with the exception of Beycesultan and Aphrodisias), and partly because of the terminological confusion surrounding use of the term 'Early Bronze Age'. When only the Troy sequence was effectively known from western Anatolia, with a notional date of 3000 BC for its inception, the beginning of Troy I became a baseline for defining what was 'EBA' in the eastern Aegean. An earlier date was admitted by Mellink at Tarsus and in the 'Amuq, while in southeast Anatolia the transition from 'Late Chalcolithic' to EBA has become associated with the expansion of Kuro-Arax peoples into the Malatya basin and beyond, replacing the advanced Uruk-influenced temple-centred polity at Arslantepe at some time around 3200 BC. In Mesopotamia itself, the term EBA is not traditionally used – although 'Late Chalcolithic' is generally employed to describe pre-urban cultures, followed by the urban cultures termed successively 'Protoliterate' and 'Early Dynastic'. In Egypt, too, 'Predynastic' precedes 'Protodynastic' and then Old Kingdom (early dynastic). In the Levant, however, it has become traditional to use EBA to denominate the changes associated with the appearance of complex societies in Egypt and Mesopotamia, with an EB IA beginning somewhere in the middle of the fourth millennium, associated with the initial Uruk impact, and EB IB corresponding to the changes which further north (the end of the Uruk colonies) have been taken to signal the beginning of the EBA.

It is clear that a mixture of historical and archaeological phenomena – none of which (with the possible exception of this period in the 'Amuq) directly corresponds with the inception of bronze metallurgy in the sense of tin-copper alloying! – have been elevated to diagnostic status in regional terminologies. Allied to the general confusion in Anatolia, with inherited problems like van den Osten's use at Alishar of 'Copper Age' to describe what elsewhere would be termed EBA, this is a recipe for total misunderstanding of what is a fast-moving historical episode with potentially wide-ranging effects on surrounding areas. While it may be too late to impose any consistent archaeological terminology on this diversity of local systems – and the prescription might well be to move as soon as possible to a neutral terminology based on absolute chronology – it is nevertheless important to know what is at stake in making inter-regional comparisons at this time, in order to move towards a historical understanding of what was going on. Fortunately, in terms of what is happening in Anatolia, a wide-ranging critical survey of the Anatolian Chalcolithic by Ulf Schoop (2005) allows a more systematic comparison of relevant fourth-millennium assemblages, and clarifies the options in interpreting Aegean developments during this time.

The Uruk expansion along the Euphrates, beginning in the Middle Uruk period *circa* 3600 BC, marked the first impact in the west of urbanization processes beginning earlier in the millennium in southern Mesopotamia, and whose distant contacts were perhaps already evident in the northern Caucasus at Maikop. Its association with the procurement of metals and other raw materials seems evident (though it has been disputed). Evidence of its effects on Egypt at the beginning of the Protodynastic period imply contacts to the Levantine coastlands, and the Amuq and Cilicia are likely to have been important intermediaries and experienced its effects (in the same way that the Malatya basin witnessed the growth of a local polity under strong Uruk influence). When the Euphrates colonies disappeared, around 3200 BC, local groups took over the northern networks and the Kuro-Arax culture expanded from its base in eastern Anatolia and Georgia into areas formerly connected to the Uruk complex. While the character of political authority changed (contrast the temples at Arslantepe with the succeeding princely grave [Frangipane 2001]), there is no reason to assume a slackening of economic activity; indeed, coming from metal-rich mountain areas the Kuro-Arax peoples had a particular expertise in metallurgy and especially the working of sheet-metal – of copper-based alloys as well as the more easily worked precious metals. Whereas the Uruk diaspora was associated with a specifically lowland diet and consumption-habits (reflected for instance in the spread of their most ubiquitous artefact, the bevel-rim bowl) and the production of beer, the Kuro-Arax populations came from the homeland of the grape – of which the seeds of a domesticated variety were recovered from Arslantepe – and made a highly burnished, dark-faced pottery which almost certainly reflects metal originals in its appearance and shapes. The stylistic features (and contents) of the ceramic assemblage which thereafter became diagnostic of 'Early Bronze Age' behaviour in other parts of Anatolia and the Aegean thus had their origins in the post-Uruk cultural expansion of this area – in parallel, incidentally, to an eastern 'post-Uruk' expansion around the Iranian plateau, associated with the proto-Elamite network. (The Late Uruk collapse, furthermore, was itself essentially a re-orientation of trading contacts, which in the succeeding Jemdat Nasr period were directed southwards, down the Persian Gulf, to alternative metal sources in Oman.) The fourth millennium as a whole, therefore, witnessed an astonishing expansion and proliferation of urban-centred trading networks, initially (like Britain after the Industrial Revolution) largely dominated by a single cultural bloc and its dependents, but eventually giving rise to a plurality of culturally contrasting interaction spheres, each with its characteristic cultural practices and style (one of which, of course, was the new civilization of Egypt). The importance of Uruk expansion was to disseminate around the Fertile Crescent a whole range of previously localized innovations, which thereafter were incorporated, reinterpreted or rejected by neighbouring beneficiaries, or creatively mixed in new ways.

The key to many of these innovations was the degree of capital concentration and economies of scale which were first possible in urban communities. These promoted what may have been small-scale local practices to the level of mass production, taking textile-making and the fermentation of grain and milk products to the level of small industries, and requiring more intensive forms of cultivation, livestock-rearing and container-production, as well as new modes of transport, to new levels. It was in this context that advanced forms of plant and animal management, and their associated mechanical technologies, were developed to a stage where they were capable of being transmitted as standardized practices to communities in the surrounding areas, even beyond the limits of the urbanization process itself. Thus while writing and sealing with cylinder-seals were only adopted in the context of secondary urbanization (in the case of Egypt), it is plausible to see such features as woollen textiles, tree-crops, the use of donkeys as transport animals, and the use of paired draught for ploughs and carts as being widely promoted by the Uruk expansion – to 'escape' thereafter into economically expanding regions, energized and motivated by the injection of new commodities, and coming to be adopted more widely over the whole area from southeast Europe to northwest India.

These features were integrated into new, culturally-specific configurations in key areas such as eastern Anatolia and the 'Amuq/Cilicia population node (and also places like Byblos), in the context of what may well have been secondary state formation with the extensive networks of trade and exchange which supported it. The trans-Anatolian appearance of specific items of drinking-equipment such as the *depas*, initially in Cilicia but extending to the eastern Aegean (probably via east-west land-routes across Anatolia), is symptomatic of a continuing process of transmission which subsequently brought further innovations such as wheelmade pottery into the western orbit. While the full impact of this transmission was only evident in the third millennium, these processes were evidently beginning in the closing centuries of the fourth millennium, and are thus relevant to the closing phase of what in south Aegean terms is still the 'Final Neolithic', when the cupellation of silver followed by the first signs (in EB I) of the exploitation of woolly sheep first make their appearance there. A full understanding of this episode will only be possible after a systematic comparison and dating of assemblages which at present are variously labelled 'Late Chalcolithic' or 'EBA' within Anatolia, and there is no space to undertake it here (though Schoop's monograph [2005] has considerably clarified the picture). In some areas the spinoff from urban economies may have penetrated piecemeal into existing local settings (as perhaps was the case with the use of silver), before the collective impact of tree-crops, woollen textiles, plough-based cultivation, and the formal consumption of grape-wine from sheet-metal vessels which collectively characterise the cultural pattern that the term 'EBA' effectively describes. Nevertheless the cultural development of the Aegean in the later fourth millennium will only make sense within the context of these wider developments – and by its final centuries even on Crete it seems perverse to continue to use the term 'Neolithic' for this fast-moving phase.

Coda

The term 'Neolithic', as used in the southern Aegean, thus encompasses up to four millennia, in which not just the Aegean but large areas of the western Old World were fundamentally transformed, first into farmers and then into members of a web of inter-connected communities which included a whole range of societies from fully urban ones to less complex ones whose lives were nevertheless profoundly altered by the existence of more advanced neighbours with whom they were – intermittently or sometimes dramatically – in contact. Throughout this period, Crete was a member of a wider community and participated in the slow evolutionary processes as well as the more intrusive episodes of contact which collectively altered the lives of its inhabitants. Through the slow buildup of such changes, the people of Knossos were prepared for the new role that was to be thrust upon them at the end of the third millennium, as the hub of contacts in a new and enlarged network of communication, and in which they took their place at the centre of a new pattern of culture and statehood.

Notes

1   While the earliest preserved examples come from northern rather than southern Europe, there is no reason to assume that logboats (dugout canoes) were not widely used in a not-yet deforested Mediterranean in which wood was plentiful. (These should not be confused with EBA longboats, which were probably based on the dugout canoe principle, but with the addition of washstrakes and a high stern.)

Bibliography

Daniel, G.
  1943   *The Three Ages: an Essay in Historical Method*. Cambridge: Cambridge University Press.
Frangipane, M.
  2001   Centralization processes in Greater Mesopotamia: Uruk 'expansion' as the climax of systemic interactions among areas of the Greater Mesopotamian region. In M. Rothman (ed.), *Uruk Mesopotamia and its Neighbours. Cross-cultural Interactions in the Era of State Formation*: 307–47. Santa Fe: School of American Research Press.
Hodder, I.
  1990   *The Domestication of Europe*. Oxford: Blackwell.
Reingruber, A.
  2004   Die Argissa Magula in Thessalien. Das frühe und das beginnende mittlere Neo-lithikum im Lichte transägäischer Beziehungen. *Archäologisches Nachrichtenblatt* 9: 209–14.

Reingruber, A. and L. Thissen
    2005   14C Database for the Aegean catchment (Eastern Greece, Southern Balkans and Western Turkey) 10,000–5500 cal BC. In C. Lichter (ed.), *How Did Farming Reach Europe? Anatolian-European Relations from the Second Half of the Seventh through the First Half of the Sixth Millennium cal BC:* 295–329. Istanbul: Ege Yayınları.
Renfrew, A. C.
    1972   *The Emergence of Civilisation.* London: Methuen.
Schoop, U.
    2005   *Das Anatolische Chalkolithikum. Eine Chronologische Untersuchung zur Vorbronzezeitlichen Kultursequenz im Nördlichen Zentralanatolien und den Angrenzenden Gebieten.* Remshalden: Bernhard Albert Greiner.
Sherratt, A.
    1997   *Economy and Society in Prehistoric Europe: Changing Perspectives.* Edinburgh: Edinburgh University Press.
    2003   The Baden (Pécel) culture and Anatolia: perspectives on a cultural transformation. In E. Jerem and P. Raczky (eds.), *Morgenrot der Kulturen. Frühe Etappen der Menschheitsgeschichte in Mittel- und Südosteuropa. Festschrift für Nándor Kalicz zum 75. Geburtstag:* 415–29. Budapest: Archaeolingua.
Sherratt, S.
    2000   *Catalogue of Cycladic Antiquities in the Ashmolean Museum: The Captive Spirit.* Oxford: Oxford University Press.
Tomkins, P.
    2004   Filling in the 'Neolithic background': social life and social transformation in the Aegean before the Bronze Age. In J. C. Barrett and P. Halstead (eds.), *The Emergence of Civilisation Revisited* (SSAA 6): 38–63. Oxford: Oxbow Books.
    2007   Neolithic: Strata IX–VIII, VII–VIB, VIA–V, IV, IIIB, IIIA, IIB, IIA and IC Groups. In N. Momigliano (ed.), *Knossos Pottery Handbook: Neolithic and Bronze Age (Minoan):* 9–48. London: British School at Athens.